Scott,

Finding words what we need to know.

Best,
Jessie McGyn

RETIRE
READY

RETIRE READY

A Plan Sponsor's Guide to Financial Wellness

Moral, Ethical, Prudent 401(k) Decision-Making *for* Employers *and* Plan Fiduciaries

TERRI McGRAY, CFP®, AIF®

www.retirerightseries.com

Copyright © 2019 Terri McGray, CFP®, AIF®.

All rights reserved. No part of this book may be used or reproduced by any means, graphic, electronic, or mechanical, including photocopying, recording, taping or by any information storage retrieval system without the written permission of the author except in the case of brief quotations embodied in critical articles and reviews.

This book is a work of non-fiction. Unless otherwise noted, the author and the publisher make no explicit guarantees as to the accuracy of the information contained in this book and in some cases, names of people and places have been altered to protect their privacy.

For more information, timely updates, and links to valuable reference materials, please visit www.retirerightseries.com.

Archway Publishing books may be ordered through booksellers or by contacting:

Archway Publishing
1663 Liberty Drive
Bloomington, IN 47403
www.archwaypublishing.com
1 (888) 242-5904

Because of the dynamic nature of the Internet, any web addresses or links contained in this book may have changed since publication and may no longer be valid. The views expressed in this work are solely those of the author and do not necessarily reflect the views of the publisher, and the publisher hereby disclaims any responsibility for them.

Any people depicted in stock imagery provided by Getty Images are models, and such images are being used for illustrative purposes only. Certain stock imagery © Getty Images.

ISBN: 978-1-4808-7372-8 (sc)
ISBN: 978-1-4808-7373-5 (hc)
ISBN: 978-1-4808-7371-1 (e)

Library of Congress Control Number: 2019901710

Printed in the United States of America

Archway Publishing rev. date: 5/3/2019

Retire Ready is for educational purposes only. The information provided herein is intended to help you understand the general issue and does not constitute any tax, investment, or legal advice nor assure that, by using the information provided, you will be in compliance with ERISA regulations. Consult your tax, financial, or legal adviser about your own unique situation and your company's benefits representative for rules specific to your plan.

No strategy assures success or protects against losses. Investing in securities, such as mutual funds, involves risk, including possible loss of principal.

All indices referenced are unmanaged and cannot be invested into directly. The principal value of a target date fund is not guaranteed at any time, including at the target date, which is the approximate date investors plan to start withdrawing their money.

Case studies are for illustrative purposes only. Your experiences may vary based on your specific situation.

Dedicated to my beautiful girls, Jaclyn, Madison, and Cody.
Cherish the past.
Enjoy the present.
Embrace the future.

The future belongs to those who believe
in the beauty of their dreams.
—Eleanor Roosevelt

My dream is for Americans to be able to enjoy their elderly years with dignity –free from financial dependency.
-Terri McGray

CONTENTS

Introduction — xv

CHAPTER 1 — 1
OUR NATIONAL RETIREMENT CRISIS

Retirement Is a Concern for Americans — 8
Background — 10
Why Employers Need to Care about Their Employees' Retirement Health — 18
The Future — 20
How Employers Can Lead Change — 21

CHAPTER 2 — 27
THE 401(K) PLAN

The Nonprofit 403(b) Plan — 29
The Team — 30
Plan Adoption Agreement — 35
Trustee Services — 37
Recordkeeping — 38
Third-Party Administrator (TPA) — 40
Nondiscrimination Testing and Top-Heavy Plans — 41
The Safe Harbor Plan — 44
Summary Plan Description — 48
Elective Deferrals and Contribution Limits — 49

Participant Notices 50
Distribution Rules. 52
Hardship Distributions 54
Filing Requirements 56
CPA Audit 57
Prohibited Transactions 60
In Summary 61

CHAPTER 3   63
FIDUCIARY

Who Is the Fiduciary? 66
Implication of Being a Fiduciary 70
Retirement Plan Committee 73
Meeting Your Fiduciary Responsibilities 80
Limiting Liability 81
Plan Benchmarking 82
Plan Fees 84
Investment Benchmarking 86
Investment Policy Statement 88
404(c) 92
Qualified Default Investment Alternative 96
In Summary 97

CHAPTER 4   101
PROVIDERS AND ADMINISTRATORS

Trust vs. Group Annuity Platform 102
Open Architecture Plans / Investment Options 104
Third-Party Administration—Bundled vs. Unbundled 111
Provider Evaluation 115
Changing Providers 117
Plan Conversion 127
Blackout Notices 131
In Summary 133

CHAPTER 5
PLAN DESIGN
135

Enrollment Eligibility	138
To Match or Not to Match, That Is the Question	141
Vesting Schedules	147
AutoMagic!	152
Automatic Enrollment	156
Auto-Increase	159
Default Investments	162
Auto Re-enrollment	164
"I Don't Want to Force My Employees!"	167
5 + 1 = 10™ System	169
The Roth 401(k)	172
Profit Sharing	176
401(k) Annuities—Qualified Longevity Annuity Contract (QLAC)	178
In Summary	181

CHAPTER 6
INVESTMENTS
183

Plan Sponsor Investment Choices	187
Fiduciary Monitoring	194
Asset Allocation Options	204
Modern Portfolio Theory	206
Asset Classes for 401(k) Plans	213
Target Date Funds: "To versus Through" Glidepath	218
Self-Directed Option	221
Exchange-Traded Funds	223
Collective Investment Trusts	224
In Summary	226

CHAPTER 7 — 229
PLAN FEES

Administration Fees	236
Investment Fees	237
Advisor Fees	239
12b-1 Fees	240
Fiduciary Fees	240
Trustee Fees	241
Transaction or Individual Service Fees	241
Revenue Sharing	241
Fee Benchmarking: Getting Out the Yardstick	244
In Summary	247

CHAPTER 8 — 251
EMPLOYEE EDUCATION: BUILDING RETIREMENT READINESS

Plan Health Measures: How Do You Spell Success?	251
Education Program	255
Basic Investment Strategies	259
Dollar Cost Averaging	259
Dividends	263
Capital Gain Distributions	268
The Power of Time	270
Stock Market Volatility	271
Investing for Retirement	278
Rate-of-Return Targets	286
In Summary	290

CHAPTER 9 — 293
BEHAVIORAL FINANCE: HOW EMOTION AND PSYCHOLOGY IMPACTS SUCCESS

The Psychology That Impacts Your Employees	293
Overconfidence Bias	296
Loss Aversion	300

Confirmation Bias	304
Control Bias	308
Recency Bias	310
Hindsight Bias	312
Inertia	314
Herd Mentality	316
In Summary	318

CHAPTER 10 — 321
THE 401(K) FINANCIAL ADVISOR

Investment Advisor vs. Broker	331
3(21) Fiduciary or 3(38) Fiduciary	333
The Search Process: To RFP or Not	337
The Finalist Presentation	341
The Onboarding Process	344
In Summary	351

CHAPTER 11 — 353
DEPARTMENT OF LABOR INVESTIGATIONS AND PLAN AUDITS

What to Do if You Get a DOL Audit Letter	372
Should You Hire an ERISA Attorney?	373
ERISA-Requested Documents	377
DOL Violations	378
Proactive Approach	378
If You Discover an Error through Internal Self-Audit	379
Fiduciary Insurance	382
Cyber Risk	384
Fidelity Bond Insurance	385
Employee Benefit Liability Insurance	385
Other Business Liability Insurance	386
Insurance Options—Conclusion	386
In Summary	387

CHAPTER 12 — 391
HUMAN CAPITAL MANAGEMENT: EXPANDING OPPORTUNITIES

Retirement for Women	395
Retirement Planning for Older Employees	399
Retirement Planning for Married Couples	403
Retirement Planning for Single Workers	406
Retirement for Widows or Widowers	409
Millennials and the Future of Retirement	411
Motivating Employees	418
In Summary	421
Resources	425
Acknowledgments	435

INTRODUCTION

One day while getting my wellness checkup, I started talking with my doctor about work. I asked him what the hardest part of his job was. Now I expected him to say it was diagnosing illnesses or treating patients, so I was quite surprised to hear him reply, "The hardest part of my job is getting patients to do what I ask of them." He further explained, "You tell a patient, 'I need you to get this lab done, see this specialist, pick up this medicine.' And when they come back a month later, they haven't done any of it. Either they couldn't afford it, or it was too intimidating, or they simply didn't make the time.

"There is a huge difference," he continued, "between being an expert in medicine and being an expert in health care." He said, "I went to school to become an expert in medicine. But you can diagnose illnesses with precision and be up to date on all the latest treatment and yet still have patients who remain sick or whose health deteriorates." He added, "That's largely because they don't take their drugs as prescribed or get the tests they need. They just don't do what they need to do. So, I learned practicing health care means I need to understand medicine from the patient's point of view. For patients, treatment is intimidating, confusing, expensive, and time-consuming." He admitted, "Nothing I diagnose or prescribe matters until I've addressed these realities with my patients. Even the perfect solution makes no difference to the patient who doesn't adopt it."

As I carefully considered this, I realized my business is no different. The capital markets don't fail us, but investors fail to use the markets properly, and thus they fail to enjoy financial security. Retirement plans don't fail us, but participants fail to use them properly and as a result end up with inadequate retirement income. Solving financial problems is not difficult. The difficulty lies in getting people to take the action required to fix their problems. Whether it's updating their wills or living trusts, increasing their 401(k) contributions, or buying more life insurance, people procrastinate. It's part of human nature to do so.

Americans are dragging their feet on saving and planning properly for their retirement. And we are running out of time as the largest segment of our population is turning sixty-five. Unfortunately, retirement planning is not something anyone can afford to delay, because time is the only real power anyone has when it comes to retirement savings. Once we lose time, we can't get it back. The reality is that most Americans face a disturbingly high risk of running out of money before they die. You've read the statistics. You don't have to be a rocket scientist to do the math. People are not saving enough for their retirement. If you are age sixty-five, research suggests it could require over $130,000 just to cover your share of medical expenses over your lifetime. Social Security retirement and Medicare are not enough to ensure a good quality of life. To make matters even worse, most employees today don't have a pension. Sadly, I believe we are well below our basic retirement income needs in this country. With most workers under the age of fifty having no access to a pension, and with the future projected insolvency of Social Security and Medicare, the situation looks rather bleak.

America is facing a retirement crisis. This predicament will impact all of us, even those of us who do save and prepare properly, *because this is an economic issue*, no different from the housing bubble and ensuing crisis, which was an economic issue that impacted *everyone*. You may have bought your home responsibly and paid your bills on time, yet you still felt the effects of the 2008 Great Recession. You saw your retirement account drop substantially in value. You saw your home value plunge. You may have lost your job or perhaps worked for a company that suspended 401(k) matching. You may have even had to close down a business. Many Americans had to file bankruptcy. Business owners had to restructure their companies, lay off workers, and reorganize their debt. The actions of others, especially when we're talking about a large enough number of people, impact all of us. The shortfall in America's retirement savings will most certainly have an impact on our quality of life, business profits, investment performance, and taxes, as well as on access to things like medical care, *even if one has sufficient financial means*. The National Conference on Public Employee Retirement Systems (NCPERS) estimates an impact of $1.3 trillion of consumption lost if government pensions are dismantled. This estimate doesn't account for $277.6 billion lost in state and local revenues. Like it or not, we are all in this together.

Americans over the age of fifty-five represent the largest and fastest-growing segment of our population. The Baby Boomers who led us into rock and roll, fast food, and SUVs are now leading us into retirement challenges never before seen in history. And this segment of our population represents massive consumer power. In fact, this market demographic currently represents more than half of our consumer demand. That's very commanding. Without their buying power, US businesses and the world at large is sure to feel the impact. The financial well-being of our aging Americans is critical to our total economic health.

Some believe the United States of America is becoming a socialist state, with increasing government control amid an aggressive redistribution-of-wealth strategy involving disproportionate taxes. The cost of repairing the 2008 financial crisis has left us with a burgeoning federal debt at a time when the largest segment of our population is heading into retirement. State pension deficits and fiscal imbalances, coupled with our growing need for adequate retirement and health care, may force expanded federal- government-run programs. It may be our only choice to help Americans in their elderly years. Time is running out, and consequently, our options are growing more limited.

As an employer (business owner, HR director, controller, CFO) you have a major influence on your company and the lives of your employees. You have the power to help your employees retire ready. While your firm alone may not be able to influence behavior in all the nearly thirty million US businesses today, if we all work together, we can slowly move the needle toward retirement readiness one firm at a time. If you have a 401(k) plan in place for your employees, you are well on your way. However, it's not enough. I've written this book to present what you can and should be doing to ensure success with your company 401(k).

How do *you* measure success? You might have thought about this differently, but if every employer were to measure the success of their 401(k) plan by *retirement readiness*, we may all be able to retire ready. The good news is that many providers and professionals in the industry have the tools to do this and are raising the awareness with plan sponsors (another term used interchangeably in this book that refers to employers who sponsor a 401[k] or qualified retirement plan). In fact, the term *retirement readiness* may even sound familiar to you. The groundwork is being laid across the nation. Awareness is the first step, but the next step and the greatest challenge today is implementation.

November 10, 2018, marked the thirty-two-year anniversary for 401(k)'s. Considering that these plans were initially challenged by legislative changes designed to curtail their use, it's impressive to see that 401(k) plans have arguably grown to be the most common retirement plan in the United States. But that does not mean they are on track to be the most successful. These plans have not been without growing pains, and we continue to face many obstacles. Rules and regulations have a powerful influence on the ability of these plans to ultimately help Americans prepare for retirement. But the real power lies in the hands and with the actions of employers and employees.

I'm going to give you the framework for how to establish and maintain a successful 401(k) as measured by ensuring your employees are retirement ready. Understand, this is no easy feat. Human nature is such that we tend to make many mistakes when it comes to saving, investing, and managing our retirement funds. Human nature is to procrastinate, so in order to enable your employees to be retirement ready, you must help them overcome one of the greatest natural human tendencies. However, you have the power to influence and motivate your employees to take action. I am confident *Retire Ready* will help you increase your plan participation, among other things.

Human nature is to be loss-averse. What this creates is employees who buy high and sell low. Poor investment performance is causing irrevocable damage to employees' retirement preparedness. I dedicate the whole of chapter 6 to investment education. We also are inclined, especially in today's tech age, to be extremely impatient. This short-sightedness adversely influences our retirement security, whether from starting our savings too late to being manic with our investments. Your employees may have "choice conflict," meaning too many selections, which leads to inaction. Inertia is also a human tendency that can limit our potential. We tend to stick with what we're doing even if it's not the best strategy, and this may be harmful to our retirement success, especially if we aren't doing the things we need to do to meet our needs. In chapter 9, I write about how to help your employees overcome the self-imposed limitations that impede results.

If your 401(k) has become overlooked as a key employee benefit, you are not alone. Many business owners, especially those who own smaller businesses, find that managing these plans can be a nuisance. Maybe too few of your employees are interested in your plan. Perhaps you have to go through expensive and laborious CPA audits every year, distribute confusing documents to your employees, or furnish your plan administrator with a barrage of documents that you can't follow or understand. If you find this process, filing the 5500 forms and sorting through all kinds of confusing documents and procedures, to be a headache, you are not alone. Perhaps *you* aren't even participating because of discrimination testing hurdles, which begs the question, why even have a plan at all?

The questions are endless: how to enroll, how to change investments, how to change beneficiaries, how to process loans, how to handle terminations, and how to understand confusing acronyms and codes like QDROs, QDIAs, 408(b)(2), and 404(c). If you find being a steward of your 401(k) frustrating, you probably need professional assistance to help you run your plan. There's plenty of qualified help available and ready to assist. But you must take the time to seek out the *right* team for the job, which is something that many employers neglect to do. Yet it makes sense to do so for many reasons.

Surveys show 401(k) plans are one of the most important benefits you can offer based on feedback from employees. If your employees aren't taking advantage of the plan, it's probably because they are not properly educated. According to numerous studies, the most talented and qualified employees have acknowledged that having access to a 401(k) is *very important* to them. Undeniably, employers who are champions of their 401(k) have an edge when it comes to retaining quality employees. A good 401(k) or company-sponsored retirement plan can boost morale and increase productivity. If you help employees move toward retirement readiness, you will more likely build employee loyalty. Considering that most of your employees are working for you because they need to earn a paycheck, being a champion of your retirement plan means taking this benefit seriously so you can help your employees become financially independent. Studies show that most employees are mindful of their retirement, even if they are underfunding their plan. And for those who aren't attentive, you can lead them toward retirement readiness. If you don't, you may find yourself stuck with aging employees who work because they can't afford to retire. Research shows that workers over the age of sixty are happy workers *if they don't financially need to work*. But if they must work because they have no other financial means, studies show they are not content and are likely to be detrimental to morale and productivity.

Let's face it, it's hard to maintain fervent output as we age. Who wants to work an entire lifetime and finally hit that stage in life when your body wants to slow down, only to discover you can't afford to retire? While today many are choosing to work beyond normal retirement age, there is a big difference in attitude between those who *have to* work and those who *want* to work.

An important key to a successful retirement plan is to focus on the employee. Everyone is caught up in compliance and audits and fees, but the central part of your retirement plan is your employees and their need for retirement security. Sure, you need to dot your *i*'s and cross your *t*'s, distribute documents in a timely manner, and be compliant. But what your employees really need is education, investment support, and personal retirement planning guidance. The benefit to you is that you will provide your employees with a way to retire with dignity while you transition your workforce to younger, less costly workers. This is the same reason pension plans were initially created.

Today, the hot topics of 401(k) plans seem to be more about regulation, so chapter 3 will review your fiduciary requirements and compliance. And while these details (fair and reasonable fees, suitable investments, disclosure, and transparency) are all very important, a great plan—a successful plan—goes well beyond ERISA compliance. A plan that will enable your employees to get to a successful retirement requires diligent work, attention, and creative effort. If your advisory team helps you accomplish this, you are well on your way to great success.

Granted, a great 401(k) team is likely going to charge more than average fees (and they should because they are performing services that are far above average), but the costs pale in comparison to the difference you can make for your employees' financial future. So, while employers seem to be hung up on low fees in today's regulatory world, the essence of ERISA compliance is to place your employees' best interest first. Which is in their best interest: getting to a successful retirement or paying the lowest fees? It is doubtful you will find a way to do both, because training your employees to build a successful retirement requires a lot of proactive leadership. Some might argue lower fees translate into better investment performance, making retirement success more probable. Sure, in the absence of a great financial wellness program, this may be true. But as you read on, you will learn that investment performance is only one of *many* hurdles we must overcome to help our employees achieve retirement success. Even more than that, employees need to learn how to overcome their own self-imposed restrictions. I emphatically declare that lower fees will not save America's retirement system. We need a comprehensive financial wellness program that focuses on employees' needs to help avert our national retirement crisis. Fair and reasonable fees are only one of many issues, and in the grand scheme, splitting hairs over 0.10 percent or 0.25 percent may be compromising the real need for American workers. Today, fees have been compressed to the point of forcing professionals to cut services, which is totally contrary to what we need. We need to increase services in order to help workers retire ready.

In our final phase of life, we don't want to get up by an alarm clock or lose sleep over money. We want to enjoy time with our family and friends and pursue hobbies and dreams. Most people in their eighties no longer identify themselves as an engineer, or HR manager, or quality control supervisor. They are proud grandparents, golfers, gardeners, bridge players, etc. If you are the employer who helps lead your employees to enjoy a comfortable retirement, you are showing a level of regard for your employees that transcends the job and surpasses company profits. *You* are the champion.

Retire Ready is about taking a different approach to your 401(k). It's written for the business owner or employer who wants to make a difference in his or her own business and to the most valuable asset you have—your employees. If you don't care about your employees' financial wellness, you should stop reading now, because you have very little to gain from this book. I've dedicated nearly thirty years of my life to helping employees work toward retirement success. I understand the frustrations you feel as an employer buried in the compliance and complexities of plan management. I *really* understand the confusion and ambiguity your employees face as they try to navigate through the maze of retirement planning. The sheer magnitude of financial decisions employees must make today, and the gravity of their actions, easily makes retirement a daunting task. Many of your employees were not schooled on such financial decisions. Our education system falls short in teaching many concepts that I believe to be essential, even if subjective, such as nutrition and health, finance, parenting, relationships, etiquette, and decorum. You may have a health and wellness program for your employees to promote healthier lifestyles. Having a financial wellness program is equally as critical. After all, the absence of money causes stress, depression, and family problems and affects health.

Consequently, in today's world, financial education is critical to happiness. While we know money doesn't buy happiness (just look at Hollywood and you can see that), lack of money does not create a joyful life. Indeed, poverty or perpetual deprivation can create downright unhappiness. Money certainly isn't *all* that matters, but it can't be completely unimportant without eventual consequences. If your employees are living hand-to-mouth when they have a paycheck, imagine what their lives will be like in retirement. If your employees are spending recklessly and taking on excessive debt, they have developed habits that are very difficult to break. Yet, facing poverty in old age is an even greater shock. Would you rather take a 10 percent cut in pay now or a 75 percent cut in pay later?

According to various studies, anywhere from 33–40 percent of Americans are living paycheck to paycheck, which means chances are that as many as four out of every ten of your employees are likely making unwise financial decisions. Once your employees understand that the little actions they take today can dramatically change their lives in their future, they will gain more confidence. People who live paycheck to paycheck are under tremendous stress. It's emotionally taxing to run out of money before the end of the month. But learning to gain control of finances is empowering and offers great reward. Once you help your employees start on the path toward retirement success, you can help them break bad habits and set the pace for a renewed approach to their futures. Of course, such a shift doesn't happen overnight, nor is it easy to accomplish, but the greatest rewards in life are rarely, if ever, easy.

You can begin the journey of leadership now and reap lasting rewards, as an advocate for your employees as well as for your business.

At this point, you may be wondering if it's your job or your business to attempt to steer your employees toward financial wellness. Candidly, many businesses initially resisted the idea of health wellness. After all, if your employees choose to smoke, drink, or overeat and suffers heath issues, like diabetes as a result, is it your business? Where do you draw the line in terms of your responsibility as an employer? Well, we have learned that such lifestyles often lead to higher medical insurance costs, disability expenses, and even litigation risks. So like health wellness plans that promote healthy lifestyle choices (instituting a walk program at work or providing nutritional educational seminars), financial wellness also focuses on education and awareness. Financial wellness is not about forcing a lifestyle or obligating your employees to be fiscally responsible. It's not about requiring your employees to write a budget or appointing someone to supervise their finances. Just as health wellness is not designed to shame your employees for smoking or eating junk food but instead focus on leading by setting good examples, financial wellness is about providing the tools and support to encourage financial competency and promote behavior and decisions that build good financial health.

For the purposes of this book, I want to define roles. An employer who establishes a 401(k) is called a "plan sponsor." I refer to the employer and the plan sponsor interchangeably. If you are a plan sponsor, you are a "fiduciary" under the law. Be sure to read chapter 3 because some of your employees may also be considered fiduciaries, even if unintended. This could put you and your firm at risk, so be sure you understand what this means. An employee who contributes to a 401(k) is called a "participant." A "plan provider" is generally an investment firm, bank, or insurance company that offers the recordkeeping platform for your 401(k). A "Third Party Administrator" (TPA) may be bundled into your plan, or you may have a separate arrangement with a firm responsible for drafting the documents needed to establish your plan (aka Plan Summary Documents) and maintain it. This includes the discrimination testing and IRS filing for your plan. The TPA handles the overall administration of your plan. Finally, a "financial advisor," also called the "broker of record," is typically a licensed consultant who helps connect all parties involved and works with you as you strive to accomplish your goals and run a successful plan.

As in any industry, there are varying degrees of competencies, skill sets, and qualifications for each of these roles. The key is to be sure your hired team (provider, TPA, and advisor) are qualified, competent, and capable to meet the needs of your plan based on the size of your company, demographics, and overall objectives. Most providers have a niche market where they are the most competitive based on a plan profile, such as number of participants or assets under management. For example, there are providers who have great platforms and models for start-up plans. However, such a provider may not be able to offer you what you need if you have a large plan. Carriers will be more competitive with pricing, investment flexibility, or support if they are aligned to your plan's size and scale. In other words, you can easily outgrow your team. You may have hired a financial advisor to help you when your plan was small, but now that your firm has merged or grown, perhaps you need a more robust team to help deliver the education and one-on-one support you desire. In chapter 4 you will learn how to shop wisely for a new provider or team and how to assess your current provider and administrator. If you don't have a great advisor, chapter 10 will address how to step up the services of your existing team to promote retirement wellness.

Retire Ready can be read front to back or you may find it most helpful to use as a reference tool. Each chapter focuses on a specific subject matter related to a 401(k) plan and/or driving retirement wellness. Because I've found plan sponsors to have varying levels of knowledge about this subject, I've written this book to serve as a resource to assist you with whatever is of most concern or interest. If you are just starting your first 401(k), you may want to read the book in entirety before you embark on this journey. On the other hand, if you have experience overseeing a 401(k) already, you may want to jump to chapters that are of most interest or relevant to your pressing needs. However, I do encourage you take the time if not now, at some point in the near future, to review the basics written throughout this book, as well. I have found those involved in running company-sponsored retirement plans may fall victim to making assumptions or decisions based on preconceptions, misunderstandings or partial information, and in today's world that may lead to trouble with compliance and regulations.

The focus of *Retire Ready* is on how to run a successful retirement plan. And to do that, you need to start with a great platform. First, though, you need to understand what is under the hood of your plan and how it all works. If you were buying a new car, you may not want to know how it was engineered, but you do want to know that what you are buying is of quality and a good value relative to the price, and you also need to know the rules of the road and how to drive the car safely before you get behind the wheel. Of course, a car is tangible, so you can more easily see, feel, and recognize the difference between a luxury car, a sports car, and a utility vehicle and you can also more readily see the dangers of the road. A 401(k), on the other hand, is intangible, so it is very difficult to readily identify the differences from one plan to the next, or even to recognize the important differences, aside from cost. As with most anything, purchase price is only one consideration and, in fact, is not the most important consideration. If that were the case, Tesla, BMW, and Mercedes would likely go out of business. Without understanding the mechanics of a 401(k), you probably won't be able to make sound decisions that are in the best interest of your employees. While you may not want to be an expert, as a fiduciary the law requires you to make decisions that are in the best interest of your participants *first and foremost*. Therefore, to do your job properly, you need to understand the differences between plans and the basic mechanics of your 401(k). In other words, you need to understand the rules of the road and how to operate (or drive) the plan safely for the benefit of your employees.

But don't worry, you will learn all of this is an easy-to-follow format in *Retire Ready*.

CHAPTER 1
OUR NATIONAL RETIREMENT CRISIS

Linda has been working for you as an office manager for over twenty-five years. She's sixty-seven years old and started working for you back when your company was young and small and had very limited resources. But over the years, your firm has grown, and Linda's dedication has helped you expand your staff. She has run your office with ease and confidence. Although not a highly paid employee, she has been instrumental to the success of your business. She has stuck with you through the good times and bad, even when you couldn't give her the raises she deserved.

Linda just informed you she is going to retire because her husband has had some health changes and she wants to be able to enjoy their time together in retirement. You want the best for Linda as she has become a dear, trusted employee. She showed you her 401(k) statement, which only had a balance of $160,000. You know she contributed as much as she could afford on her modest salary, and upon seeing her balance, you regret that you couldn't offer more than a small match. You realize it hasn't really amounted to much. She never complained, but she is asking how much income you think she could generate from her retirement savings to make it last the rest of her life. What do you tell Linda?

Is America really headed for a retirement crisis? I believe the answer is yes. American workers are not saving adequately for their retirement, and the facts show that millions are in danger of running out of money during their elderly years. Unfortunately, the problem appears to be only getting worse. The consequences of this could be severe for both American families and the US economy, as a large share of households may be forced to rely on their children, charities, or the government to help make ends meet. Rather than staying in control of their lives, millions of Americans could find themselves foraging through their elderly years partially or fully dependent on others for financial support. This means many elderly Americans may have to accept a standard of living significantly below what they had envisioned or have enjoyed during their working years.

If you are shocked to learn this, just look at the numbers. Common sense suggests that every working person should be saving for his or her future, but the facts show this is not happening. To the extent that Americans are saving and contributing to a 401(k) or other type of retirement account, statistics show that the average worker is significantly underfunding his or her retirement. Not only are we saving too little, but also we are starting too late and—perhaps even worse—not investing wisely. The average amount saved for retirement varies by age, but the National Institute of Retirement Security reports that nearly two-thirds of those nearing retirement age are at risk of falling short of their required retirement income.

How much money is needed for retirement? Do most workers even know how much they need to save? While surveys show that confidence in retirement success is high for those who save, the data indicates that many of these workers are overconfident and will probably fall short. The truth is, very few people have taken the time to calculate how much they really need. Most employees don't even know how to go about determining this, even though online tools are readily available. What is clear is that no matter how retirement income needs are projected or how assets are measured, an unacceptably large share of Americans appear to be at risk of being forced into a much lower standard of living in their elderly years. The most probable estimates report that approximately half of all Americans will have insufficient assets to sustain a secure retirement. Even more sobering is the fact that nearly one-fourth of retirees may have nothing but social security. How many people today rely on social security income alone? The numbers may disturb you. What percentage of Americans don't save *anything* for retirement? It is a far higher number than you would probably imagine. How many of your own employees are not saving anything for their retirement? Let's look at the realities.

More than 75 percent of workers don't believe they will have enough money in retirement. The average retirement age today is rising. You may remember the 1990s era when people were retiring as early as fifty-five years old. Today, the average age is still relatively young at sixty-three, but that number is rising, and even then, this question remains: how many are retiring by force versus by choice? Many employees will declare, perhaps half jokingly, that they will work forever or until they drop, but we know this is not a reasonable plan. The ability to work until death is largely dependent upon two factors that are completely out of one's control: health and the economy. Furthermore, there is a big difference in attitude and abilities between an employee who *wants* to work beyond normal retirement age and one who *has to work*. Which type of employee do you want? The absence of retirement readiness could inadvertently put you in a position where you have aging employees costing you more in wages, insurance, and benefits, and in return you may get a bad attitude and lower productivity. Retirement at age sixty-three today also raises the question of how many opted to just retire after they lost their jobs during the Great Recession. Many gave up looking for jobs and decided to go into retirement, assuming they would be able to sustain themselves, but they may have severely underestimated the impact of inflation, longevity, and health-care costs.

The average length a person spends in retirement is twice as long as it was in the 1960s. Today, people live an average of eighteen years in retirement. Of course, this is merely an average, which means that half of all retirees live beyond this. Do you want to take the chance that you will be among the 50 percent who live beyond this average? Do you want to risk running out of money? Keep in mind that this is the fact for *today's* retiree, but it doesn't mean it will be the same for future retirees. In just the three decades that I've been in this business, data used for planning has stretched out ten additional years. We used to believe that if we planned life expectancies to age eighty-five, then people would be adequately prepared. But the reality is that today there are plenty of healthy and active individuals in their late eighties and beyond. Long gone are the days when we would get a good rocking chair, sit on the porch, and watch the world go by. My own grandmother lived independently to age one hundred and two. The fastest-growing segments of our population are nonagenarians (those between ages ninety and a hundred) and centenarians (those over the age of one hundred), according to the US Census. These segments of our population have tripled over the past thirty years. Think about retirees in your own family. Chances are that you know someone who is in their nineties or even approaching one hundred. Longevity is a reality. I would make a strong bet that the future for your employees will look more like twenty-five years or more in retirement, versus the eighteen-year average of today. Biotech and medical science are advancing by leaps and bounds. Certainly, savings required to last twenty-five to thirty years demands a tremendous amount of capital as well as very careful planning. To save what you will need requires far more attention than just socking away a small percentage of your salary in a 401(k). Many people retiring today are truly unaware of their longevity risks.

Thirty-eight percent of Americans don't save anything for retirement. It's rather disturbing to know that roughly four out of every ten American workers are not saving for their retirement. It is a common misconception that our economy is dominated by megacorporations. In fact, 90 percent of the companies in the United States have fewer than one hundred employees each. While the megafirms offer the premium benefit packages, such as deferred compensation, supplemental retirement plans, pension benefits, profit sharing, and/or 401(k) with healthy employer-matching benefits, the majority of workers in the United States are not employed by these large companies. The small- to mid-size business market represents most of America, which means many workers may not even have access to an employer-sponsored retirement plan and/or may have no employer matching to incentivize savings or boost their retirement. While this is still no excuse for individuals failing to take responsibility for their own retirement, the truth is that most employees don't take action on their own. Your influence as an employer is significant in the world of retirement benefits. You have the power to drive change. You have the ability to change the status of our national retirement crisis. This is critical, especially for smaller employers, who represent most companies in the United States.

Median retirement savings is less than $40,000. According to the Federal Reserve, the median balance of retirement accounts held by Americans who are saving for retirement amounts to less than $60,000. However, according to the National Institute on Retirement Security, almost forty million households have no retirement savings at all. Therefore, if we account for everyone, including the 38 percent of workers who aren't saving anything for their retirement, the national median retirement balance is below $37,000. The Employee Benefit Research Institute estimates that Americans have a retirement savings deficit of $4.3 trillion. Look at your company 401(k) average balances and see how these figures compare. My guess is that they aren't too far off. With average balances insufficient to provide for more than a few years of income, you can easily see the gap in your own company's retirement plan.

Sadly, the future is even bleaker for women. Studies report that we have less than half the savings of the average man, yet women live longer and therefore need more capital than our male counterparts. As for affluent investors (those with at least $250,000 in investible assets), the average retirement savings is $350,000, which is still too low relative to their income. And, finally, if we remove affluent investors from the measure, the national average account balance falls to less than $20,000 for the typical worker.

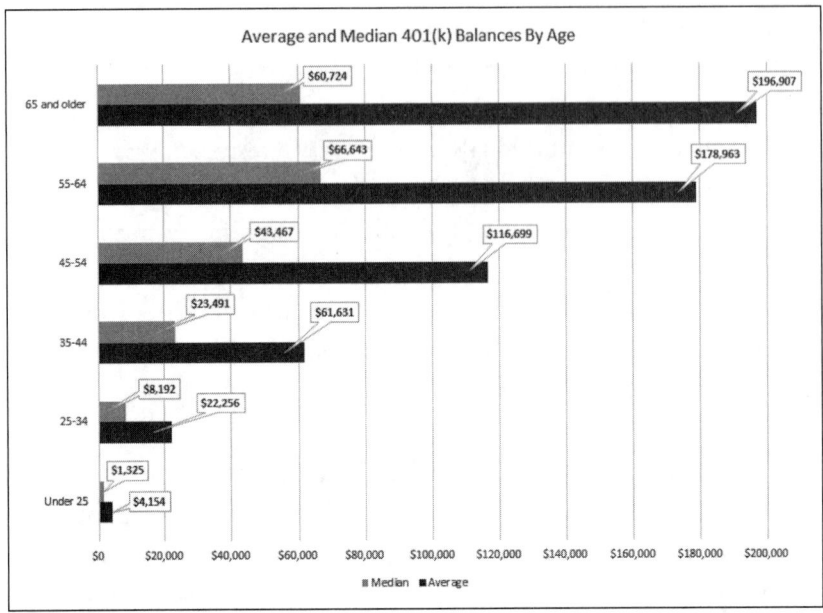

Figure 1.1. Source: Vanguard, 2017

Figure 1.1 highlights the average 401(k) account balance by age for those who are saving as compared to the median account balance, which accounts for those who do not have savings, as of 2017.

Eighty percent of Americans between the Ages of Thirty-Five and Fifty-Four Do Not Believe They Will Have Enough Money for Retirement. This is sad statistic: eight out every ten middle-age workers have no confidence in living the American dream. The good news is that this suggests employees have more realistic expectations about their future. But knowing reality is not going to help secure anyone's future—not yours, not mine, and not your employees'. The question is, what can be done to change this? Working longer seems to be the consensus, and with Social Security full-retirement age pushed up to sixty-seven, it probably makes sense. Indeed, the days of retiring at age fifty-five seem to be long behind us. This is largely because we are starting our careers later. Longevity and a delayed retirement may be a fact of life for all of us, but this is a relatively new concept, one that not all workers have embraced. We still must face the fact that Americans are ill-prepared for the costs of aging. Many are retiring today without adequate knowledge of how to sustain an income for life. Cashing out a bucket of money in a 401(k) at retirement is vastly different from receiving a monthly pension check guaranteed for life. Most retirees today have no idea what a reasonable and sustainable withdrawal rate is or should be used when transitioning their 401(k) into retirement income. And whereas a person had no access to their capital in a pension, it is easy to spend down a 401(k) to nothing.

Thirty-Six Percent of Retirees Today Only Have Social Security Income. Of course, Social Security was never designed to be the primary retirement plan. It is an insurance program, intended to be a part of a retirement plan, yet for more than one-third of our retirees today, it is their retirement. I'm less concerned about the viability of the program, despite what you may hear. For sure, we should expect changes to the system, including later full retirement ages for future generations. But most importantly, what quality of life is social security alone going to provide? Social security was not designed to provide an adequate replacement income for workers when they become elderly. According to the Social Security Administration as of June, 2018, the average social security retirement benefit paid is $1,413 a month. I can't imagine how that will afford anyone a happy retirement, let alone a decent quality of life.

Retired Couples Will Need at Least $260,000 for Health Care. Fidelity's Retirement Health Care Cost Estimate reveals that a couple both aged sixty-five and retiring this year can now expect to spend an estimated $260,000 on health care throughout retirement. This estimate includes premiums, deductibles, copays, and prescription drug prices as set by original Medicare. However, this estimate does not include long-term-care costs, which is an increasing risk as we age. Further, it's fair to say that this out-of-pocket cost is more likely to increase as life expectancies continue to expand and health-care costs continue to rise. Our government is under pressure to care for our growing elderly population, especially when it comes to health care, yet with federal debt today over $20 trillion, where is this money to come from?

If these facts aren't disturbing enough, a study by the University of Michigan found that Americans fifty-five years of age or older now account for 20 percent of all bankruptcies in the United States. That's one out of every five bankruptcies! Surprisingly enough, the leading cause of these bankruptcies among this age group is not housing costs or credit card debt. The number one cause is medical bills. That's right. According to a report published in the American Journal of Medicine, medical bills are a major factor in more than 60 percent of all personal bankruptcies in the United States. And even more disturbing is that of those bankruptcies that were caused by medical bills, approximately 75 percent of the individuals actually *did* have health insurance.

RETIREMENT IS A CONCERN FOR AMERICANS

Survey after survey shows that retirement security is among the top worries for Americans. With the many layers of risks to the average worker today, this comes as no surprise. As an employer, you can be a leader in addressing this crisis by helping and encouraging your employees take steps to save more, invest better, improve their financial health, and protect themselves against longevity risk.

Americans are struggling to prepare for retirement and, even worse, are losing ground with each passing year. Figure 1.2 indicates the rising percentage of households at risk of outliving their retirement savings, highlighting an increase of over 65 percent since 1983.

Four clear trends, in particular, illustrate to what extent Americans are underprepared for retirement:

1. Too many workers are saving absolutely *nothing* for retirement, neglecting their needs.
2. Of those who do save, they are not saving enough, and most have no idea how much they ought to be saving.
3. Wealth-to-income ratios are stagnating even though life expectancies are increasing.
4. The percentage of Americans at risk of having insufficient retirement income has been rising steadily since the responsibility has shifted from employer to employee.

NATIONAL RETIREMENT RISK INDEX
Share of households at risk of not havng enough money to maintain their standard of living in reitrement

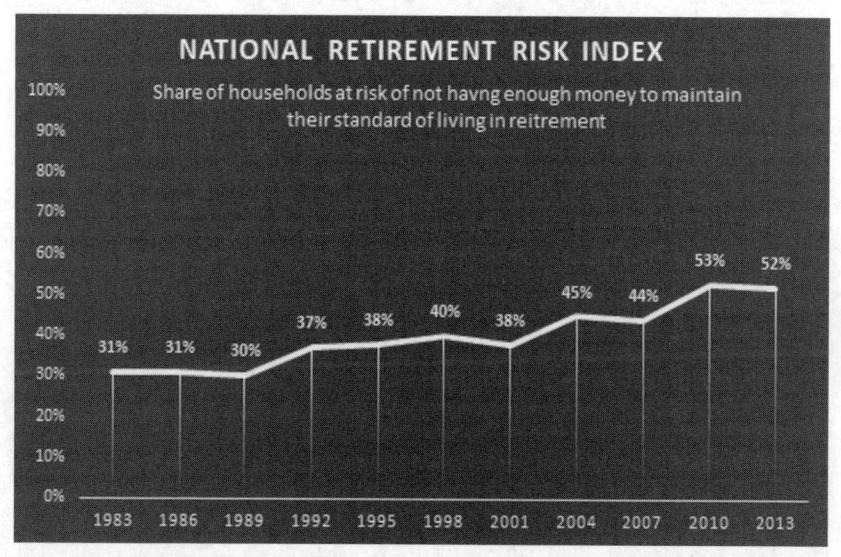

Year	%
1983	31%
1986	31%
1989	30%
1992	37%
1995	38%
1998	40%
2001	38%
2004	45%
2007	44%
2010	53%
2013	52%

Figure 1.2. Source: Alicia H. Munnell, Wenliang Hou, and Anthony Webb, "NRRI Update Shows Half Still Falling Short," Center for Retirement Research at Boston College.

You may not have the ability to change the national statistics, but you do have the ability to change the statistics for your employees. You can help them pursue financial security by being a champion of your retirement plan and supporting retirement success. I have no doubt if each and every one of the nearly thirty million businesses did this in the United States, our national retirement health would improve dramatically. We might even be able enjoy the American dream.

As a sponsor of a 401(k) or qualified retirement plan, you have the ability to change the lives of not only your employees but also of their spouses and beneficiaries. You have the ability to boost confidence, reduce financial stress, and change the future for perhaps hundreds, if not thousands, of people. *Retire Ready* is about your most valuable asset—your employees—and how to lead them toward retirement success.

BACKGROUND

In 1875, the American Express Company created the first corporate pension plan. The general idea: put a portion of workers' income in a collective account, invest the money, and use the proceeds to provide employees with a guaranteed income in retirement. This became known as a *defined benefit plan,* with the retirement payment—a percentage of the worker's final average salary—*defined* in advance. Such plans provided a monthly retirement income for life. The employee never had to worry about funding the plan, making investment choices, or running out of income. All he had to do was live within the budget provided by the pension check, and that (later coupled with a small Social Security benefit) enabled most retirees to enjoy a simple, yet secure, retirement.

Pension plans grew tremendously in popularity. At their peak, nearly half of all workers were covered by a pension benefit. Pension plans provided a staple to our retirement infrastructure for almost one hundred years, and while they didn't provide a life of luxury, they did provide income continuity for employees as they transitioned out of the workforce. However, challenges developed in the 1960s as life expectancies increased and abuse and mismanagement of pension funds revealed the fragility of these plans. Pension bankruptcies became a growing crisis that captured the attention of Congress and impacted workers across the country.

On September 12, 1972, NBC aired a documentary called

Pensions: The Broken Promise that highlighted the depth of the pension crisis and featured interviews of employees who were casualties of the calamity. "I think it's a terrible thing in this country where men who worked forty-five years have to eat yesterday's bread," remarked former employee Stephen Duane. "You wake up in the middle of the night in a cold sweat knowing all your work, all your life, has gone down the drain. I was just a number." Thousands of companies failed to fulfill their pension promises. From large companies like Studebaker Corp. and Eastman Kodak to J.C. Penney, Westinghouse, and TWA to smaller firms, millions of workers across the United States who were promised retirement income benefits found themselves approaching their sixties, out of a job and with no company retirement benefits—hardworking employees who'd dedicated their entire career to a single company, giving up other job opportunities largely because they were promised a secure retirement.

In 1974, President Gerald Ford signed into law the Employee Retirement Income Security Act (ERISA), which dramatically changed the way Americans saved for retirement, codifying the rules for how companies managed retirement obligations. It also paved the way for a new type of savings plan: the individual retirement arrangement (IRA). A few years later, in 1978, IRS Code 401(k) was written. Originally applicable to only highly paid executives as a "tax-favored savings account," the 401(k) eligibility eventually expanded to all employees. Thus, the defined *contribution* approach to retirement savings was born.

With the 401(k), also known as a *defined contribution* plan, no longer did we face the lifelong indentured servitude required to qualify for pension payments. The traditional pension required employees to remain with the same company for decades, thereupon limiting employee growth and income potential. The perceived value of the pension had diminished as Baby Boomers saw their parents struggle in the aftermath of the failed pension, and this younger generation of workers preferred to pursue career advancements. Many workers felt their opportunities were hampered by archaic management styles of larger corporations and sought to advance by taking chances with newer, dynamic organizations such as Apple, Commodore, and Microsoft. This was also the beginning of the tech era, and small technology companies were all too eager to recruit and attract talent away from the Xeroxes and IBMs of the world.

The 401(k) enabled employees to seek better opportunities and "job hop" while funding their own retirement. The employee controlled the funding and the investing, and, unlike the pension, the portability of the 401(k) plan allowed the individual to determine his or her own destiny. In fact, the 401(k) even gave us a chance to avoid relying on the tenuous promise of Social Security since we could control our own wealth accumulation. We didn't need big brother—whether in the form of the paternal corporation or government. We finally had the chance to do as Thomas Jefferson said and "declare our independence"!

The enthusiasm and zest for the 401(k) initially was widespread. Employees were thrilled to be empowered with a sense of control and freedom they had never experienced before. Many employees had never invested in the stock market and had no idea such opportunities were so easily available until the 401(k). This new awakening and potential to amass fortunes propelled the 401(k) to be one of the most sought-after employee benefits of the 1990s. The fervor for these plans, coupled with fantastic market performance, bred a confidence that compelled employees to believe they would never need the boring lifetime income payments of the traditional pension. At the same time, employers were being forced to freeze costly pensions because they were grossly underfunded, largely due to inaccurate performance assumptions and life expectancy calculations.

But wait - if 401(k) plans were so great, what the heck has happened? Why are we facing a national retirement crisis? What, you may be asking, went wrong?

Well, the original notion of the 401(k) plan may have lured everyone into a false sense of confidence. First, it was exciting. Let's admit it, the ability to make our own investment decisions and watch our accounts grow was far more enticing than the boring pension arrangement that pooled accounts. With a pension, the employee never saw an account balance, only a statement that showed a modest monthly income payment stated so far into the future that he or she felt no connection between his or her current situation and the retirement income benefit. It was far more energizing to see the money grow in the 401(k) and watch the balances compound. Second, the 401(k) was easy to see and easy to understand, compared to the defined *benefit plan*, where the benefit or income payment was based on complicated formulas that didn't make sense to employees. A 401(k) plan, by contrast, was simple. Even though the only guarantee was the contribution—generally made by the employee—the 401(k) appeared to be a great solution for retirement. It gave the employee control of his or her investments, thereby affording workers of all income levels the opportunity to build more. The plan gave employees portability, so employees were able to seek bigger and greater opportunities. Even though the future income benefit was not guaranteed, no one cared about this as the stock market boomed. While the pension plan rewarded employees for tenure, the days of staying with the same company over a working lifetime began to vanish nearly as quickly as the pension plans themselves. Besides, there was something appealing and quintessentially American about empowering individuals to be the masters of their own financial destinies.

Today, fewer than 20 percent of US workers have traditional pension plans, and most of those are working for government agencies. However, unlike the pension, which requires no funding from the employee, the 401(k), of course, is *driven* by employee contributions. Unfortunately, we have since learned that when left to their own devices, most Americans would rather spend their money today than save it for tomorrow. Spending, after all, is the American way. This is the era of high debt, relatively easy credit, grand lifestyles, and instant gratification. *Why wait and save to buy what you want (and probably don't need) when you can borrow the money and get it now?*

Remember layaway? If we needed a major item in my family, my mother would go to Montgomery Ward and put the item on layaway. Every week she would stop by and make a little payment on a new couch or a needed major appliance. The entire family would anxiously await the day when, at last, it was paid in full and we could take the major purchase home. It was a treat for all of us because of the weeks and weeks we all had cut back to make that major family purchase. The family was engaged in the process, and unbeknown to us, layaway and the attendant sacrifice taught all of us to appreciate possessions just a little bit more.

These days when families need a new washer or dryer, they go to Best Buy and purchase it immediately on credit. We think we're buying smart because we signed up for zero interest for twelve months. The kids come home from school, and suddenly there's a new set of appliances that they may not have even known were in need of replacing in the first place. No one in the family thinks twice about it. But, of course, the store and the bank are acutely aware of the deal. Indeed, interest and credit charges could cost the family as much as 200 percent of the purchase price because, as the banks know, most buyers fail to pay the balance off in time to enjoy the zero interest charges or avoid late payment fees. Some homeowners even refinance their credit card and personal debt into a thirty-year mortgage and end up paying thousands of dollars more for their consumer purchases.

National Institutue on Retirement Security Figures
Shares of households not meeting retirement savings target by age

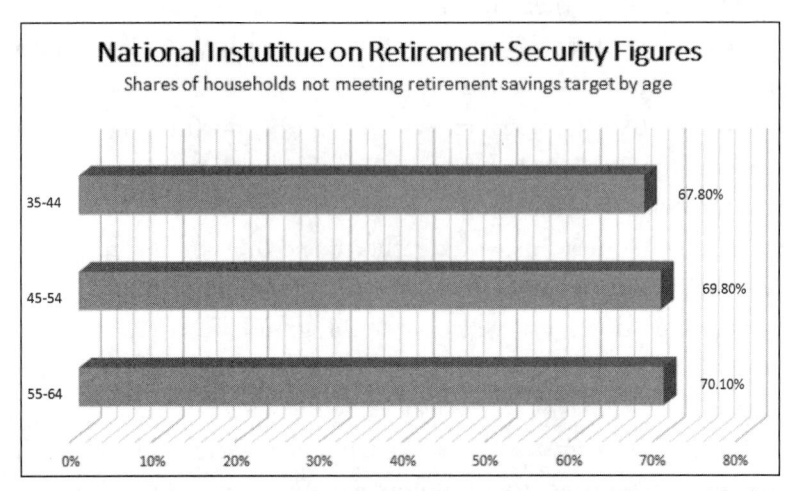

Age	%
35-44	67.80%
45-54	69.80%
55-64	70.10%

Figure 1.3. Source: "The Retirement Savings Crisis: Is It Worse Than We Think?" Washington National Institute on Retirement Security.

The consequences of a consumer-driven economy is that families are laden with debt and there's ultimately very little left over to fund retirement. It's hard to save for one's future when spending and living for today is so convenient. It's easy to be impulsive and careless. Statistics show that half of 401(k) plan participants have less than $10,000 in their accounts. This is a sad figure when you consider the magnitude of the dollars needed to secure even a modest retirement. And figure 1.3 highlights the very scary reality that nearly two-thirds of Americans are not meeting their savings requirements. It's no surprise that most Americans report that they are worried about their prospects for retirement. They should be!

When 401(k) plans were first introduced, they were quickly embraced by employers and employees alike as the cure-all for retirement needs. Employers didn't have worry about funding or investing, and employees gained all the control. Of course, what everyone failed to realize is that employees are often ill-equipped to properly manage their retirement. They aren't financial or investment experts. With pensions, employers hired money managers and actuaries to help them properly manage plan assets, and even still, they couldn't get it right. How are untrained employees expected to be better prepared to manage their retirement? Most employees don't know the difference between a stock and a bond. How many of your employees have schooled investment knowledge? How many of your employees have a rudimentary understanding of economics? I think you'd be surprised to know how little most people understand about finance. I studied finance in college and learned how to read financial statements and studied macroeconomics, and yet, I wasn't schooled on sound investment principles. Nonetheless, in the 1990s, within a span of about ten years, there was a direct and powerful shift that declared the employer nearly totally free from the responsibility of retirement obligations. This shift has burdened employees with the full sum of the task—all the while without providing the employee with any real preparation, education, or training on the fundamentals of retirement planning, finance, or investing.

Well, actually, some employers did offer enrollment meetings to promote participation in the plan, and still others may offer some education. But have you ever sat in one of those meetings? Generally speaking, they are boring, with a *capital B*! Or they are overly complicated. They are often repetitive, uninspiring, and—how many different ways can you say the same thing? For those who get it, they are already saving. For those who don't, hammering the same message over and over hardly motivates or inspires a call to action. The only ones who get excited perhaps are the new employees who have never heard the presentation before. But after enrolling, what do participants do? *Nothing!* Inertia. They keep the same investments, the same contribution rate. They don't track their progress. There is little to no method to the madness. In their defense, they simply don't know what they should be tracking, or why or how. Sure, they may monitor performance, but that's just measuring year-over-year returns—and annual returns are largely beyond one's control. Retirement planning is not a set-it-and-forget-it process. No one will build a solid retirement without diligence and hard work. With all due respect to providers, the content of the material covered tends to be only the basics of enrollment, not the steps and process required to build a secure retirement.

After one or two of those meetings, employees lose interest. The impact is lost because the meetings fail to *engage* the employee. Most educators fail to build a base of financial knowledge to truly empower employees to properly manage their retirement. A push to enroll does little to help existing plan participants address their growing financial needs. Workers are stretched with their time and money. Your employees have children and are worried about college costs. They want to buy a home, they have massive debt, they are getting divorced or married, or they have health challenges in their families. They have aging parents they are caring for, student loans to pay. They have old 401(k)'s with former employers that they don't know what to do with. They are concerned about current economic or political events and the impact on their portfolios, be it rising interest rates, recessions, elections, or global problems. Their financial needs extend well beyond simply enrolling in the 401(k).

I will admit that some education is certainly better than none, but the financial burdens and retirement responsibilities placed on everyone today is so great that your employees need more than a retirement savings 101 lesson. *This is a crisis we all face!* This is not to say the employer is entirely responsible; after all, employees demanded these 401(k) plans and continue to do so to this day. No different than with the IRA that requires the individual to make investment choices, we may have failed to consider the critical importance of adequately empowering employees with the tools and knowledge they need to build their own secure retirement. Now, thirty years later, we are scrambling to figure out how to solve this predicament. Unfortunately, the current structure of our retirement system did not come about by conscious design. Rather, we arrived here by happenstance. And now it is up to all of us to work together to fix it.

What do your employees need? After all, you can't *force* your employees to participate in your plan. You can't *make* your employees be more responsible with their finances. They already have tax incentives, convenient payroll deduction options, and perhaps even free matching dollars. They more or less have a general awareness for the need to have retirement savings, certainly far more than any other generation has had. What more can be done? Admittedly, motivating employees to sufficiently fund their retirement is a tougher job than it seems. After all, you would think that encouraging them to save now to secure their futures would be quite easy. But the idea of giving up some of their paycheck today simply does not appeal to everyone. Now, in truth, rarely does an employee totally dismiss the notion. Who, in their right mind, can dismiss the need? No, rest assured that most employees understand the need, but they do not understand the *sense of urgency*. They procrastinate. After all, when is it ever convenient to save money? It's far more rewarding to spend. Most employees do have a sincere desire to start saving "someday." The problem is, they don't understand the time value of money and that "someday" cannot wait.

As the 401(k) plan sponsor, it is up to you to help your employees understand the plan and what they stand to gain from it. It's up to you to promote the fact that their savings has the potential to be magnified by matching contributions and the magic of compound interest. Even then, not all your employees may be able or willing to contribute to the plan. Studies prove that much more must be done to change the future for the United States. I'm going to define some of those strategies in an easy-to-implement program. Together, we can aim to empower employees to retire ready.

WHY EMPLOYERS NEED TO CARE ABOUT THEIR EMPLOYEES' RETIREMENT HEALTH

The US labor market hit a major milestone: the median age of working Americans—*half the working population*—is forty or older, according to the Bureau of Labor Statistics. Furthermore, AARP research shows that nearly 80 percent of Baby Boomers (those over the age of fifty-four) expect and want to work in retirement. The top two reasons for remaining in the workforce are income and health insurance. As more people near retirement age and realize the inadequacy of their financial preparedness, more are likely to choose continued employment. Why should you as an employer care about this?

You should care because a healthy company retirement plan is a function of a healthy company. Some employers think retirement planning is an employee need, not an employer necessity. Certainly, with the adoption of the 401(k) over the past three decades, employers have been switching from being benefits *providers* to being benefits *facilitators*. But this hasn't made the risks of an aging workforce go away. Having retirement-ready, financially healthy employees isn't just "something nice"—it's essential. Not only can it reduce stress on the job and help increase productivity, but it also may help ensure your business's viability. There is software available that will show you just how substantial the costs can be of having an aging workforce unable to afford retirement. You should know that the liability for not helping your employees retire at their normal retirement age can potentially cost your organization millions of dollars.

The impact on your company's bottom line includes higher labor costs, increased health-care premiums, and lower productivity due to financial stress, age, and health risks. A precise diagnosis of the health of your retirement plan will uncover your true forecasted costs, analyzing your employee data and your employees' level of retirement readiness. By measuring your employees' retirement readiness, insight can be gleaned about future trends and forecasts for your business. Considering that an estimated thirty-two million Baby Boomers (about the size of California's population) may never be able to afford to retire, and considering that today 76 percent of all workers expect to delay retirement, we can't help but wonder what kind of impact this might have on businesses. Analysis shows it's far more concerning than you probably realize.

When employees work past normal retirement age, employer costs become unpredictable. Higher health-care costs and higher salaries can add up. Of course, those employees who are financially prepared but *choose* to work past age sixty-five are typically excellent employees to have and well worth the added costs. Senior employees can bring an invaluable and immeasurable level of experience, maturity, judgment, and perspective to a firm. However, employees over the age of sixty-five who are working because they can't afford to retire are very different. When older workers have no choice and they hold onto their jobs because they lack alternative income, feelings and attitude about work are distinctly unlike those of employees who want to be there. Costs for these employees who simply would rather not be on the job could be very high. Beyond health care and salaries, liabilities and absences may increase, while morale and productivity could decrease. Employers need to be mindful of the implications. And certainly, the more an employer can do to help his or her employees with retirement readiness, the better off everyone will be. As they say, *take care of your employees and they will take care of you.*

Building a strong retirement and financial wellness program may seem straightforward on the surface, but integrating it into the 401(k) and ensuring that your education and support is multidimensional to benefit diverse stakeholders can be challenging. A well-executed retirement plan strategy is an investment in employee and organizational performance. The first step is agreeing to the engagement, making the commitment, and setting priorities. I hope you embrace this challenge and take your employees' financial health and retirement readiness seriously, not only because it is the right thing to do, but also because it can have a significant impact on the health of your organization.

THE FUTURE

Some people fear the government is going to claim the 401(k) and confiscate their assets. First, while this idea makes for entertaining headlines, the government cannot confiscate your assets. It's unconstitutional. What the government can do, however, is establish a guaranteed retirement fund that is backed by the full faith and credit of the US government as a mandatory investment option an employer must offer in the 401(k). The purpose of this would be to provide some infrastructure for or stability to the employee's investment options. The federal government can choose to offer a 401(k)-like supplemental/alternative plan, which many state governments have already decide to adopt for those workers who do not have access to an employer-sponsored 401(k).

Some think this is only the beginning and that in due time such a plan will be a forced savings, similar to Social Security. It's far too speculative to say whether such a prospect would be more or less favorable than the dire straits we are headed for, but it's doubtful any supplemental option would override the 401(k). What I see happening sooner is perhaps a push toward stricter penalties or consequences for early withdrawals and more incentives to compel companies to share in the funding. I also anticipate more disincentives to use the plan for something other than retirement savings.

If it makes you feel any better, you might care to know that the situation isn't a whole lot better in other countries. According to an HSBC study, 48 percent of respondents across fifteen countries have never saved toward their retirement, with more nonsavers in high-income countries such as the United Kingdom, France, Canada, and Australia. According to the survey, people on average expect their retirement to last for eighteen years, but their retirement savings is set to last for only ten years. This is a crisis in many countries around the world. The developed world is struggling with aging populations, not just the United States. Nonetheless, our retirement system earned a C grade in the 2017 Melbourne Mercer Global Pension Index, which ranks thirty countries on the adequacy, sustainability, and integrity of retirement benefits.

Some of the possibilities for improving our system include a risk-sharing principle, which means the employer and employee could share in the risk of funding and investment returns. Another potential is a mandatory contribution requirement or an auto-IRA-like vehicle. Countries like New Zealand and Sweden have mandatory retirement savings over and above social security programs. There are pros and cons and other substantial considerations that must be made in light of any of these possibilities. Indeed, the system continues to change and there are many moving parts, as well as multiple perspectives to consider: that of the individual saver, the employer, the government, and the wider public interest, as well as that of the financial industry, each of whom have a great stake in our retirement infrastructure. For sure, the future is uncertain and our retirement system will be continuously evolving. The good news is, there are things you can be doing now to move toward making a difference so you and your employees can retire ready.

HOW EMPLOYERS CAN LEAD CHANGE

As a 401(k) plan sponsor, let me ask you a candid question: are you proud of your leadership role? You have the distinguished privilege of leading and participating in the very core of your employees' financial success. The fact is, retirement success starts with you and your leadership team. Do you have a desire to make a difference? If you don't, you probably won't be able to lead change. Plan stewardship is defined as the careful and responsible management of the retirement dollars your employees have entrusted to your care. Now you may not see it as such, given that your employees are making their own contributions and investment elections. However, as I will explain more in this book, you are caring for their money in many very important ways.

Our national economic health cannot and will not be improved without good stewardship. If you look at the massive amount of 401(k) fiduciary breach that has been illuminated through litigation and DOL audits, you will easily conclude that too few employers have truly embraced this privilege. This is not to suggest companies are intentionally negligent. I believe most firms do care about their employees' welfare. But I also know many employers view managing the 401(k) as a nuisance, an inconvenience, or a disruption (particularly for small business owners). Indeed, it is additional work. It can certainly be a headache and a burden to plan sponsors. And heightened regulations have only increased the workload. The 401(k), sadly, has been treated as an afterthought by many plan sponsors. Because of this, plan oversight has been lacking. Too many employers have not made their 401(k) a priority. If you do not have a competitive, current, productive plan in place, your employees will find it very difficult to achieve retirement success.

I understand, particularly if you are a small business owner, that you have limited time and a litany of other priorities, such as how to keep up with customer demands, keep your doors open, and keep your employees employed. But as you will soon learn, with the right 401(k) team, stewardship does not have to be compromised because of your limitations. If you are committed to protecting the long-term interests of your employees, you can help them retire ready. If you have a passion for your business, I presume you also have a passion for your employees since they are instrumental to helping grow and maintain your success. After all, you can't build a thriving business alone. Your employees are vital to your sustainability. Therefore, your discipline and commitment to protect their long-term interests (such as their retirement) must be built into the core values of your organization.

Great leadership doesn't happen without a defined purpose. If you identify retirement readiness as a key component to the long-term success of your company, you must be attentive to the needs of your employees. This means taking leadership in a way you may never have before. You need to be deliberate, practical, and proactive in your approach to managing your retirement plan, not just because the law requires it, but mostly, because your employees need it. That includes seeking new ideas and avenues for support as we face a heightened regulatory environment. It also means being action-oriented and accountable. Do you have the ability to inspire your employees to achieve retirement success? You absolutely do! Your plan design, your employee communications, and your 401(k) team can serve as the backbone of your stewardship.

Ignoring the risks and consequences is not going to help you advance in the growing competitive world in which we all live. At the very least, you can no longer ignore the rules, regulations, and requirements as a fiduciary. The risk of a plan audit or litigation is too great today. But more than that, your regard for your employees will hopefully lead you toward a governance that rewards them for their years of service and loyalty. Building trust among your customers is probably a top priority. Is building trust with your employees also a priority? I certainly hope so, because a lack of ethics or regard can be infectious and breed grave internal conflicts. Assuming trust is important, remember that leadership, not compliance, builds trust. Even if you are fulfilling your fiduciary duties, is that enough to build trust for your retirement plan? Probably not. It is your leadership, your direction, that matters. If your management team is failing to drive genuine enthusiasm and confidence in your 401(k), you will be unable to drive retirement success.

Let me ask you another question: how important is employee

loyalty to your business? You probably don't like turnover. It's costly and time-consuming. Having a code of ethics, not a code of conduct, helps build loyalty. Being ethical is much more than merely following rules and regulations. What sort of ethical obligation do you feel you have in helping your employees retire ready? If you feel you ought to do what you can to ensure your employees are securing their retirement, one potential strategy to making this happen is to break out of your status quo and engage the right team. Retirement success is driven by developing and adhering to a prudent process that goes well beyond compliance.

Building retirement readiness within the framework of your firm's limitations may appear as a cumbersome, laborious task. It may seem like an unobtainable or unrealistic goal. I've heard the pushback from CFOs, CEOs, and HR managers or directors. "Our employees are living hand-to-mouth or "We can't offer an employer match, so we can't drive success." Others have lamented, "I don't have the time to promote the plan." Or there's the complacent ones who claim, "Our plan seems to be just fine." Some say helplessly, "I don't have the time for that." Others retort, "Our employees would rather have a pay raise than a 401(k) contribution." Still some naively declare, "I don't think our employees would value this." And I heard one HR manager actually say, "I don't want to promote investing in the 401(k) when the markets could fall and employees could lose their money." I've heard CFOs assert, "Our employees are different from most!" as if they don't need retirement wellness. Or even worse was on the one who said, "Our employees are not financially savvy enough for a retirement plan." And small business owners often complain, "We don't have the staff to do this." The fact is, the excuses are endless. For sure, great things don't happen without hard work.

You may have difficulty leading a successful plan if you don't have the passion to help your employees retire ready. If you don't view your leadership role as a privilege, you may struggle to change the retirement outcomes within your firm. If every employer in the United States dismissed their power to influence change for retirement wellness, we are all likely destined for problems. We cannot afford to have employers wrought with complacency. We must work together to make a difference, and it starts with you. And it starts now.

Chances are your employees admire and respect your success and trust your judgment. Therefore, with your encouragement, most of your employees will likely take heed of your guidance. Intuitively, they know your 401(k) is a smart plan for them, but they need your leadership to instill the confidence necessary to recognize how powerful this plan can be. Keep in mind, you can easily outsource the process, so it's not really about your time or work. It is about your mind-set. Retirement success cannot be built within your organization without a genuine desire for such success from you and your management team. I have led far too many retirement education meetings where leadership has been totally absent and disengaged. What message does this send to your employees? While your schedule may not permit you to sit for full meeting, you should insist at least one senior manager participate in your 401(k) workshops. Even better, an appearance from your CEO/President would make a strong statement. Remember, your employees look to your leadership for direction. So, I encourage you, as the employer/owner or senior executive, to make an appearance at these meetings and show you care. When you are present, it shows you support the plan, you believe in it, and you care about their welfare. However, when you are absent, uninvolved, or preoccupied, it says this information is not important. Believe me, your employees pay far more attention than you may realize to your leadership. I have spoken with thousands of employees over the years. It's no coincidence that the most successful plans I work with are those with the most-engaged management.

Good stewardship means stepping out of your comfort zone or casting off complacency to working toward building a strong retirement plan. I hope you embrace the desired rewards. Your business will likely benefit from reduced financial risks, lower employee costs, and increased productivity. You can do it! And remember, you don't have to do it alone. A great 401(k) team can do most of this for you. Follow the guidelines outlined in *Retire Ready* and you should be well on your way.

CHAPTER 2
THE 401(K) PLAN

Joel is forty years old with three children and a nonworking spouse. He is managing director of your Indiana facility, earning over $250,000 a year. Although he is paid handsomely, he just received $4,000 in corrective distributions from your 401(k). Once again, your plan did not pass the discrimination testing, so as a highly compensated employee, he was returned his excess contributions, which are now subject to federal and state income taxes. He is rather upset because he cannot maximize his tax benefits and prepare properly for his retirement. He worked for a major company previously and did not have this problem before. His wife, Karin, is also quite concerned about their future. Their dear friend has been trying to recruit Joel, and although the pay is slightly less, the competitor offers a fantastic retirement package. Joel seeks you out as CFO and asks what you are doing to fix the 401(k) so the executives may be able to max out their contributions. What do you tell Joel?

The 401(k) is not the only type of employer-sponsored retirement plan, but I believe it is one of the best ways for your employees to save for their retirement. There is a reason why over $5 trillion is currently invested in these plans. For sure, the 401(k) has become an important part of our national retirement system. Employees are told they need to save money for retirement, and the 401(k) offers an easy way to do this with nice tax incentives. Congress knows Americans need a little encouragement to save money for retirement. The tax benefits, self-directed focus, portability, matching incentives, convenience of payroll contributions, familiarity, and simplicity all support its widespread use. There is a reason it is so popular. It works well for those who take advantage of the plan and use it correctly. Unfortunately, we know, based on statistics, that not enough workers are using the 401(k) to seek to maximize their retirement success. But as an employer, providing the means for your employees to get started is the first step. I believe every employer should find a way to offer a retirement plan, and the 401(k) is one of the most efficient options.

It's not just about the employee, of course. There are many benefits to setting up a 401(k) for the employer as well. The 401(k) allows employers to provide a graceful transition for an aging workforce. Aging employees can be expensive, and they may be less productive. The ability to provide an incentive for your employees to exit the workforce with dignity and enjoy their senior years is the very essence of why retirement plans were started over one hundred years ago. The 401(k) also helps employers attract and retain talent. A 401(k) is relatively simple to set up and is relatively low maintenance and low cost, particularly when compared to other options. Employees are very familiar with these plans and may already have assets in them. To be competitive in today's market, employers must consider ways to address their workers' need for retirement savings, and the 401(k) often fits the bill.

Of course, to boost your retirement benefits, you may want to add other qualified plans to complement your 401(k), such as a Profit Sharing or Employee Stock Ownership Plan (ESOP). Or you may find that layering a defined benefit or pension can provide additional valuable tax benefits for executives, owners, and/or key employees. If discrimination testing or plan costs are a hurdle, nonqualified retirement plan options may be worth considering. Such plans can offer flexibility and provide golden handcuffs to retain key employees. There are many options employers can utilize to create a solid retirement benefit for their employees. And while there is no one-size-fits-all solution, the 401(k) is a good plan to build a retirement foundation for companies. It provides valuable benefits at a relatively low cost. Because of this, over the past thirty years the 401(k) has grown to become one of the core retirement plans in the United States. If you haven't yet set up a plan for your company, this chapter will help you begin by addressing the key components of the 401(k) infrastructure. If you have already set up a 401(k), this chapter provides a review of the mechanics of your plan as a good start to learning how to drive retirement success.

Once you decide to set up a 401(k), the process is quite easy. You will need to get plan documents drafted, choose your custodian (where the money will be held) and select an investment or financial advisor, sign documents, get employees enrolled, and maintain the plan. Although easy, the process is not necessarily simple, and maintaining the plan according to the regulations requires far more knowledge than most employers realize. This is because there are rules for maintaining the tax-favored status of the plan, compliance requirements, and stewardship duties (since you are taking care of your employees' money). However, most employers would likely agree that the work involved in maintaining a 401(k) is well worth the benefits.

THE NONPROFIT 403(B) PLAN

Because nonprofits are equally concerned with providing for their employees' welfare, I would be remiss if I didn't briefly mention the 403(b) plan. A 403(b) plan is a tax-advantaged retirement savings plan only available to public education organizations, hospitals, churches, and 501(c)(3) nonprofits. Since 2009, the 403(b) and the 401(k) essentially have operated and functioned the same way. In the past, 403(b) plans were easier to administer, but today ERISA 403(b) plans and ERISA 401(k) plans are subject to essentially the same rules and requirements. Consequently, with limited exceptions, the information written in this book is the same for plan sponsors of a 403(b) as it is for sponsors of 401(k) plans.

In fact, more nonprofits today are choosing the 401(k) over the 403(b) because of its popularity and employee familiarity. Plan sponsors will find there are more 401(k) providers from which to choose and a more diverse array of investment options. Therefore, pricing may be more competitive in the 401(k) market. In some rare cases, a 403(b) plan can qualify as a non-ERISA plan, which reduces compliance work significantly. However, many common elements found in retirement plans—including offering a company match—immediately disqualify a nonprofit from offering a non-ERISA plan.

Giving your employees a broader set of lower-cost investment options is a compelling reason to consider switching your plan from a 403(b) to the modern 401(k) plan. It is likely worth your time to benchmark your plan's investment options and pricing against what is possible with a 401(k). However, you should consult an ERISA attorney or other expert before making a change.

THE TEAM

One of the most common misunderstandings I hear from plan sponsors is who does what and why within a 401(k) plan. *Why can't my provider do the plan administration? Do I need a financial advisor? Should my administrator be doing more? My financial advisor seems to collect a fee, but I never see him. Should my employees be getting more support from our provider? Who should be taking charge of my plan?*

Retirement is a destination, and a long-distance one at that. Imagine that your employees are in Los Angeles and they need to get all the way to New York. That's a long journey. While today we enjoy coast-to-coast travel in a matter of hours, once upon a time, settlers risked their lives traveling cross-country. The covered wagon only made eight to twenty miles a day, depending upon weather. That means it took six months or more to get across the country, and many pioneers lost their lives in the pursuit. Food rationing, weather, illness, attacks from Native Americans, and a whole host of challenges made the journey very dangerous and difficult. Fortunately, those days are long gone but long-distance journeys still have their own challenges. As a long-distance goal, retirement planning has its own risks and obstacles. It requires a working lifetime of diligent saving, planning, and preparing. And many roadblocks are bound to be met along the way. Nevertheless, the 401(k) can be an excellent vehicle to help toward building a secure retirement. Of course, it is not the only vehicle that can accomplish this, but it is an effective one. Just as there are a variety of vehicle options from which one can choose to travel from LA to New York (such as a plane, train, car, bus or bicycle) employers can choose from a variety of retirement vehicles. The 401(k) is one vehicle of choice because it is very efficient, just as a jet airplane is today's choice for long-distance travel.

Think of your 401(k) recordkeeper (also known as a plan provider) as your jet airplane. The recordkeeper is the manufacturer of the vehicle used to help you and your employees reach the retirement destination. Just as Boeing manufactures the 737 and Airbus manufactures the A320, your recordkeeper simply creates the product built to accumulate retirement savings. While the role of the provider (used interchangeably with the term *recordkeeper* henceforward) can be confusing because some do more than others, the basic job of the provider is to provide the chassis needed to support your retirement plan.

Because 401(k) plans involve more complexity than a basic checking or savings account, there is more involved in the construction and maintenance of the plan. Likewise, there's far more complexity involved in the making of a plane compared to a bicycle. Within the 401(k) world, the difference is mostly related to reporting and recordkeeping. Your provider keeps track of the money; therefore, in its simplest form, the 401(k) is a vehicle built and designed by a recordkeeper to accept money (sent from the employer through elective salary deferrals), direct the funds to individual accounts established for each employee, and then invest it as per the employees' chosen allocations. All of this is done within an IRS tax-favored arrangement that requires both you and the recordkeeper to adhere to specific laws and regulations. To be compliant, your plan provider must maintain records (thus the term *recordkeeper*), track money sources (such as salary deferrals, employer matching, rollover contributions, and after-tax contributions), move deposits into the allocated investments, print and mail account statements, process transactions, provide retirement tools and calculators, produce enrollment and educational materials, and provide a customer service line. Of course, a jet airplane is much more than just a bunch of aluminum and passenger seats. Likewise, a 401(k) is much more than just an account with a selection of investments.

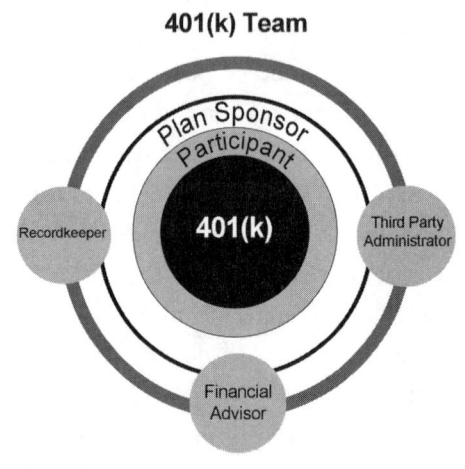

401(k) Team

Figure 2.1.

Just as a vehicle you own requires maintenance, your 401(k) also needs to be maintained. If you have a corporate jet, you know what this means. You need an aircraft mechanic and crew responsible for maintaining the mechanical and avionics equipment that will ensure your plane is safe to fly. Without a good maintenance crew, your trip may be a disaster for you as the jet owner as well as any passengers you have onboard. Likewise, your plan administrator (Third-Party Administrator, or TPA) is important because they will inspect and maintain the structural and mechanical elements of your 401(k) using various tools. Without a good qualified TPA, your plan may not be operating safely and that could be a disaster for both you and your employees.

Think of your plan administrator as the maintenance crew for your 401(k). The TPA's primary responsibility is to ensure your plan meets IRS guidelines in order to keep it compliantly operating as a *qualified* retirement plan (meaning tax qualified). Your 401(k) permits everyone who participates to contribute dollars before federal and state income tax and allows any earnings to compound without current taxation. The Internal Revenue Service is forsaking current tax revenue in order to incentivize retirement savings. Because of this, there are rules that must be followed to retain the tax-favored status. It is the job of your TPA, or plan administrator, to help ensure you are adhering to the rules so as to retain the tax benefits afforded by the 401(k).

It is difficult, if not impossible, to run a compliant 401(k) plan without a solid maintenance crew. Plan administrators should also perform regular reviews of your plan design to help you consider if any adjustments or repairs are needed. This is especially true if you have organizational structural changes. You want to keep your plan operating at optimal capacity or efficiency, and your administrator can help ensure this happens. For example, an increase or decrease in your payroll may directly impact your plan's testing results. Changing any matching arrangement or experiencing a significant change within your salary deferrals can affect the mechanics of your plan. For a small company, if there are any ownership changes such as a partner sells out or retires, or a new partner is added, or you take on new highly compensated employees, your discrimination testing results can be affected. To avoid unexpected potentially unfavorable surprises, proactive plan reviews and periodic conversations with your plan administrator are essential. Chapter 4 will address the specifics of providers and administrators

Finally, you need a pilot. If you've ever seen the cockpit of a plane, you know there is an abundance of very complicated electronics called flight instruments. Levers, buttons, switches, gauges, and displays that make up the control panel are complex, and most people would have no idea how to use the instruments to get the plane off the ground, let alone get it safely to its destination. Even still, pilots specialize in flying different types of aircraft. For instance, it takes far more training to be a commercial pilot and fly complex aircraft than it does to be a recreational pilot or helicopter pilot. Think of your financial advisor as your 401(k) pilot. A financial advisor is professionally qualified to help you pilot your employees toward retirement. However, not all financial advisors have the same level of training or expertise; for this reason, the type of advisor you should select for your 401(k) is one who is trained and has proficiency in the full operation of ERISA-based retirement plans. This is including but not exclusive to the investments. Without a qualified financial advisor, you may find it challenging to help your employees get safely to retirement.

The job of the financial advisor is to help ensure every passenger (employee) gets to their destination (retirement). This is no easy task, since each employee manages his or her own account. However, through plan design assistance, plan sponsor support, and employee education and guidance, the advisor can help ensure your employees are able to navigate confidently to their destination. Your advisor should work with you at the plan sponsor level to help you ensure your plan is operating at optimum capacity and also work with you at the participant level to help your employees understand their responsibilities so they can pursue a secure retirement.

It's really no surprise that employees are failing to be retirement-ready. They are making major mistakes with their basic planning, and when things go sideways, they really fall off course because they don't know what to do. Without direction, they do what *feels* right, not what *is* right. It feels right to jump up and panic during turbulence on a plane, but the right thing to do is to stay seated. It might even feel right to jump out of the plane, but clearly that is not the right course of action. Have you ever noticed it is the pilot who comes over the PA to address the passengers when there's turbulence? It's not the flight attendants, even though they are certainly capable of providing the instructions. It's that kind of leadership your employees need. Admittedly, I am biased toward the need to have a financial advisor, but this is because I have seen the difference between good advisory leadership and no advisory direction. Frankly, our national retirement crisis indicates your employees likely need professional help—more help than plan providers can give on their own. Refer to chapter 10 for more information on the role of the financial advisor.

Finally, to get a plane off the ground you need fuel. While the fuel consumed by an aircraft varies with the size and type selected for the trip, you cannot get an aircraft to the desired destination without fuel power. Think of salary deferrals, employer contributions and investments as the fuel that propels your 401(k) plan to the desired retirement destination. It is important the right kind and correct amount of fuel is used to go the distance of the trip. I fear too many employees are destined to run out of fuel mid-flight because they may not be making the best funding and investment decisions for the distance required. As a plan sponsor, your responsibility is to offer a suitable menu of investment options to help ensure they have sufficient "fuel" required for their goal.

Now that you understand the general structure of the 401(k) and the role of the plan provider, TPA, and advisor, let me turn to the details of the documents and processing requirements for plan administration. It's a good idea to plan ahead and be aware of important dates, relevant rules, and information so as to follow procedures as defined by the IRS and the Employee Retirement Income Security Act (ERISA).

PLAN ADOPTION AGREEMENT

Once you decide to establish a 401(k), the first step is set up your Plan Adoption Agreement, which is typically written by the Third Party Administrator. The Plan Adoption Agreement is a legally binding agreement that allows you to choose and define the provisions you will include in your retirement plan. For instance, who will be eligible to participate, and at what age and after what period of time of employment? How many hours must an employee work in order to be eligible? And what types and amounts of contributions will the plan allow? Will you offer a matching formula or make any employer contributions? And if so, what will your vesting schedule be? How will loans be handled? If you choose to include loan privileges, you can decide how many outstanding loans will be allowed at any given time. And what will the interest rate be? It must be set at a reasonable and competitive rate.

There are many plan provisions to consider. A plan expert can help guide you to determine the provisions that make the most sense according to your needs and goals. Keep in mind, you can change or modify your provisions after you have established your plan. In fact, it's a good idea to review your plan provisions occasionally to ensure they continue to meet your company's needs and plan objectives. You also want to review the agreement periodically to be sure your provisions are consistent with your understanding of the plan. I have seen plan sponsors unknowingly allow enrollment sooner than their plan adoption agreement allowed or include a certain class of employees when these were specifically excluded in the documents. Failing to follow the terms of the agreement is a violation. If you don't understand the specific terms or have a new staff member handling the plan, it's a good time to review the documents with your advisor to be sure you are following them correctly and that they are aligned to your goals and objectives.

For instance, you may have a one-year waiting period for enrollment, which might be inconsistent with your desire to promote and encourage participation. You may want to adjust the interest rate charged on your loans in light of the current environment of lower interest rates. Perhaps it is time to add some of the newer provisions to your plan, such as the Roth 401(k) option. As you do with any legal document, you will want to review your Plan Adoption Agreement with your 401(k) team every few years and update it accordingly.

Your adoption agreement is accompanied by the Basic Plan document, which provides in-depth details of how the plan should operate in accordance with the rules and guidelines in order to qualify as a tax-qualified plan. The valuable pretax benefits of the 401(k) must be preserved by abiding by current rules. There are prototype agreements that can be used, or you can write a customized document with the help of a plan expert and an ERISA attorney. However, most plan sponsors find the turnkey documents provided by recordkeepers to be easier to use since they are written with the legalese necessary to comply with the laws. A plan administrator (TPA) can help keep your plan documents current and consistent with IRS guidelines to avoid disqualification. The point is to know and understand the details of your agreement and the rules and the stipulations, including those that you can control to improve the effectiveness of your plan and those you cannot change.

TRUSTEE SERVICES

Once you set up the Plan Adoption Agreement, trustees must be appointed to administer the plan in accordance with the documents and for the exclusive benefit of the plan participants and their beneficiaries. This means the trustees are responsible for ensuring the plan does not engage in "prohibited transactions" as described by ERISA. Knowing these rules is obviously important for compliance. The trustees should also monitor the value of the plan assets, allocations, and vesting to ensure appropriate reporting and tracking. Most companies appoint an internal officer or employee as trustee, but you may be able to outsource this responsibility if you want to offload the work. Often, some of the responsibilities are outsourced, whereas others are conducted internally in order to retain some control. Speak with your 401(k) team about options for trustee services to determine what approach is best for your firm.

Obviously, trustees must not engage in prohibited transactions such as self-dealing (using plan assets for their own account) or act in any transaction that creates a conflict of interest. If a trustee breaches any of his or her responsibilities, obligations, or duties as imposed by ERISA, the trustee will be personally liable to reimburse the plan for any losses resulting from the breach and may be subject to remedial relief as deemed by the courts. Should the Department of Labor find fiduciary breach, a civil penalty may be assessed. Therefore, the trustee role is to be taken seriously. The consequences of misconduct can be quite costly.

A common trustee duty is processing loans and distributions. This includes ensuring loans are qualified and adequately secured, along with establishing a systematic repayment schedule. Trustees may also review distribution requests, including hardship withdrawals, to be sure they are qualified. These are services you may choose to outsource to streamline your workload, but not all TPAs or recordkeepers provide these services, so be sure to speak with your 401(k) team about your options and think through the time and responsibilities involved when you consider acting as a trustee in-house. If you process withdrawals and distributions in-house, it is imperative that you clearly understand the rules and guidelines to avoid conflicts. Also, it is important to understand what duties cannot be outsourced and to be prepared to follow the guidelines for trustee services as a fiduciary.

RECORDKEEPING

The recordkeeper is responsible for maintaining the records for the plan, investing the deposits as directed by the participants, preparing statements, performing daily accounting, and providing support services. The question you must answer is, who keeps track of the money? The person who does this is called a recordkeeper or plan provider. Recordkeeping services can be performed in-house by a third-party administrator (TPA), by a separate recordkeeping firm, or by a bundled service provider (recordkeeper–TPA combined). Usually, the recordkeeper is an investment company, bank, or insurance company engaged as recordkeeper for the safety of assets and protection for your employees. Although it is an option, it is generally not a good idea to perform recordkeeping in-house, unless perhaps you are a very large company, because of the time involved in performing such duties.

The most important job of the recordkeeper is to track the money so it can be properly reported. This requires meticulous accounting practices, as there are numerous records to monitor and track, including determining how much each employee is contributing to stay within the IRS guidelines, distinguishing matching contributions and profit-sharing dollars for vesting schedules, and identifying and tracking Roth contributions, rollover contributions, and so on. As its name implies, recordkeeping is critical to ensure every participant's dollars are recorded properly and the records checked for accuracy. This includes daily investment pricing and dividend reporting, among other things. It is also critical that investment earnings are recorded accurately and timely.

These days, most recordkeepers' duties are automated, so recordkeepers generally make a significant investment in technology. Therefore, selecting the best recordkeeper is often tied to finding the best technology available to support you. For example, some of the key services provided by recordkeepers include maintaining a website so you can make transfers and manage the plan as a plan sponsor. You will want to walk through a demonstration of the recordkeeper's website to observe its capabilities and determine the ease of its user applications. Recordkeepers also provide access for your participants so they can to view and make changes to their individual accounts, so a demo of the participant-level technology should also be a part of that which is scrutinized during your selection process. Mobile apps for employees and other technology benefits may be important to consider.

In addition to the website, recordkeepers print and mail statements to employees, process trades and other transactions within participant accounts, produce enrollment kits and educational materials, and maintain a toll-free customer service line for both plan sponsors and participants. You want to be sure they have adequate staffing to handle the incoming calls from your employees. You will need the recordkeeper to be responsive and attentive to your needs, furnishing you with materials in a timely manner.

The provider is responsible for ensuring recordkeeping

requirements are fulfilled as per regulations and in compliance with the laws. Your provider should help you market your plan to attract greater participation, provide employee communication documents, and so on. The role of the recordkeeper is to help make the management process of your 401(k) run smoothly, consistently, and easily. Recordkeeping is considerably more complicated than it appears, but as already noted, providers invest tremendous resources into automation; therefore, they can use their size and scale to provide all the support you need at a relatively low cost. Recordkeeper fees are generally paid by the participants in the plan, either as an asset-based fee or a flat fee. It is important to note these fees are not typically billed to the employer, which makes your fiduciary duties and liabilities very important to understand.

Due diligence should be performed rigorously to ensure that all IRS and ERISA rules and requirements are satisfied to safeguard your retirement plan and keep it in full compliance. Tracking and monitoring the activities in your 401(k) plan is no different from tracking and monitoring the activities within your own bank account. While it is not your responsibility to monitor participants' individual accounts, you do have the duty to review the plan account assets and ensure funds are posted and allocated to your participants correctly. I encourage you review chapter 3 to understand your fiduciary duties, which include fee monitoring.

THIRD-PARTY ADMINISTRATOR (TPA)

A Third Party Administrator (known as TPA henceforth) is a company hired by you, the plan sponsor, to run the administrative duties of your 401(k). As already mentioned, 401(k) plans require plan administration, but such services may be bundled with your recordkeeper, or you can set up a separate arrangement with an independent firm. Administrative services include writing, amending, and restating plan documents, assisting in the processing of distributions, loans, calculating participant vesting percentages, preparing annual returns and reports required by the IRS (such as the 5500 filing), and fulfilling other government agency requirements.

Perhaps the greatest service a TPA provides is compliance testing. Each year, your plan must pass specific tests to be in compliance with all IRS nondiscrimination rules. Many bundled plan arrangements (where the recordkeeper also acts as the TPA) offer only prototype plan documents that generally do not allow the plan sponsor to customize testing methods to help you meet discrimination requirements. Consequently, the plan may have to contend with "corrective distributions," which means the plan must return pretax dollars as taxable distribution for highly compensated employees. A TPA, by contrast, can help you apply different testing methods and determine if there are other means to maximize the tax benefits for owner–employers and/or highly compensated employees. In other words, an independent TPA may be able to help you run a more tax-efficient plan.

If you are struggling with corrective distributions, it is probably time to get a second opinion. In many cases, it's simply a matter of making a few minor adjustments. In addition, the personalized service provided by a good TPA is generally a better overall experience than the boilerplate administrative services included in a bundled plan. However, there are plenty of bundled providers who do offer great support, so it depends upon the size of your plan and your circumstances whether a small TPA arrangement in an "unbundled" plan is better or if a bundled plan makes more sense, measured by cost, service, and value.

NONDISCRIMINATION TESTING AND TOP-HEAVY PLANS

The Employee Retirement Income Security Act (ERISA) requires several tests each year to prove 401(k) plans do not discriminate in favor of highly compensated or key employees. Therefore, once you establish a 401(k), you must go through a process of nondiscrimination testing. Congress does not want the considerable tax breaks to be enjoyed only by highly paid employees, so nondiscrimination testing is the way the government ensures you work diligently to ensure that everyone is encouraged to participate in your plan or that your employer dollars are serving to support all employees, not just those with the highest incomes.

According to IRS guidelines, a plan may be top-heavy when the total value of the plan accounts of key employees is more than 60 percent of the total value of the plan assets. The rules are designed to ensure that the lower-paid employees receive a minimum benefit. Therefore, when a 401(k) plan is top-heavy, the employer must contribute up to 3 percent compensation to all non-key employees. You can set a vesting schedule subject to IRS requirements, but it is important to know that top-heavy plans require mandatory employer contributions to non-key workers.

Top-heavy tests must be reviewed each year. The process is a bit complicated. First, all key employees must be identified. This includes any employee who is an officer making over $180,000 (as of 2019), an owner of the business with more than 5 percent ownership, or an employee owning more than 1 percent of the business and making over $150,000 for the plan year. When determining ownership interest, family aggregation rules apply. Therefore, it's important to identify the family ownership interest of all company stock and to forward that information to your TPA, your advisor, or the person performing the nondiscrimination tests. Your TPA can also discuss options that may help to work around top-heavy rules.

It's common for a 401(k) plan to be top-heavy, especially for smaller plans and plans with high turnover. If you've been operating a 401(k) plan covering only you and your spouse but you hire other employees who become eligible under the plan, keep in mind that you'll probably have to make required minimum contributions for these new hires if they are non-key employees. It's also important to note the distinction between *key employees*, who count for top-heavy purposes, and *highly compensated employees*, who count for another set of discriminating tests, the ADP (Actual Deferral Percentage) and ACP (Actual Contribution Percentage) tests.

For the purposes of ADP/ACP testing, your employees are divided into two groups—highly compensated (HCE) and non–highly compensated (non-HCE). For the 2019 tax year, highly compensated employees are those who earn more than $125,000 or anyone who owns 5 percent or more interest in the company. In its most simplistic form, the average contribution of your HCE as a group cannot exceed the non–highly compensated employees' contribution by more than 2 percent (excluding catchup contributions). For example, let's suppose your average HCE is deferring 8 percent and the average non-HCE is deferring 4 percent. The differential is 4 percent, which is more than the 2 percent allowed. If you can get the deferral rate for non-HCEs to average 6 percent, your plan would generally be able to pass the test, but otherwise, failing the discrimination test means your HCEs will not be able to maximize their contributions. Using a Safe Harbor Plan option will eliminate this testing hurdle, or perhaps an employer matching schedule that encourages employees to hit the 6 percent deferral may be an effective solution. Another option that may help your employees secure their retirement is to promote retirement readiness. If you cannot afford to offer a matching solution, you may want to apply the auto-enroll and auto-increase features discussed in chapter 5, which can serve to build more retirement readiness within your company.

There are other testing hurdles and different testing methods that can be used, so you may still be able to pass the discrimination test in the example above given other factors. Work with your TPA to determine how best to meet the testing requirements. You may be able to exclude certain employees or utilize other testing methods, such as what is called a "cross-tested" method, to help HCEs defer their desired amount. Or you may want to consider a Safe Harbor Plan.

According to Judy Diamond Associates, nearly sixty thousand plans failed their nondiscrimination testing, resulting in over $800 million in contributions returned to highly compensated employees, called "corrective distributions." Such distributions create additional taxable income to the highly compensated employees and reduce their retirement savings. If your plan does not pass your testing hurdles, you may have to return excess contributions and disqualify your key employees from fully participating in your plan. Not only does this present a tax hurdle for your executives, but also it can handicap their ability to save adequately for their retirement. If your plan is suffering from corrective distributions, I highly encourage you to seek a second opinion with a plan expert to review some options and potential remedies. I have been able to fix problems for plans that were struggling with corrective distributions in excess of $250,000 where my competitors were unsuccessful at finding a solution. With diligence, you do have options.

THE SAFE HARBOR PLAN

The "Safe Harbor" plan is a popular 401(k) arrangement because such plans make it easy for small business owners to maximize their own contributions while reducing some of the limitations associated with adhering to IRS nondiscrimination testing. With a safe harbor plan, your 401(k) is structured in such a way that it automatically passes the nondiscrimination test or avoids it altogether. It is relatively easy, but the requirement is that you must make employer contributions to each employee's account, either based on employee participation via a matching arrangement or by making a "nonelective" contribution for everyone.

To have your plan qualify as a safe harbor plan and to avoid testing hurdles or eliminate the risk of a top-heavy plan, employers can select a matching contribution or a fixed contribution arrangement. The advantage of a matching arrangement is simply that the employer dollars are allocated only to those who participate in the plan. The basic matching formula can be a dollar-for-dollar match of the first 3 percent of compensation, plus a 50 percent match up to the next 2 percent of compensation (for a total of 4 percent maximum). Review the comparison in figure 2.2. As an example, we will assume the owner is maximizing his or her benefits and there are five employees, one of whom is considered highly compensated. Suppose employee 1 defers 10 percent of compensation, employee 2 defers 5 percent, employee 3 defers 3 percent, and employee 4 defers nothing. The employer match for employees 1 and 2 would be 4 percent; for employee 3, 3 percent; and for employee 4, zero. The aggregate average basic match for safe harbor is 3.7 percent in this example.

	Compensation	Deferral Percentage	Deferral Dollars	Basic Match	Enhanced Match	Non-Elective
Owner	$275,000	Max	$18,000	$11,000	$11,000	$8,250
Employee 1	$150,000	10%	$15,000	$6,000	$6,000	$4,500
Employee 2	$75,000	5%	$3,750	$3,000	$3,000	$2,250
Employee 3	$50,000	3%	$1,500	$1,500	$1,500	$1,500
Employee 4	$30,000	0	0	0	0	$900
Total	$580,000		$38,250	$21,500	$21,500	$17,400

Figure 2.2.

You can use any enhanced formula that is at least as generous as the basic matching formula defined under safe harbor rules. Therefore, if you wanted to keep it simple, you could opt for a 100 percent match of the first 4 percent of compensation. In that case, unless employees 3 and/or 4 changed their contributions, you employer match would be the same based on this census. (Note the "enhanced match" option in figure 2.2.) Of course, employer matching does incentivize employees to contribute enough to enjoy the maximum contributions, so you will likely find employees are more apt to increase their contributions accordingly. As a result, employee 3 may bump his or her deferrals to 4 percent, and employee 4 may start participating in the plan with a match incentive.

By comparison, a nonelective or fixed contribution provides benefits to *all eligible* employees, even if they don't contribute with their own dollars. In figure 2.2, all the employees, including employee 4, will get a 3 percent employer contribution regardless of their own salary deferrals and irrespective of their elective participation (including owner–employees). A nonelective contribution can result in lower employer outlay, as in the foregoing example. The advantage is that not only may the nonelective contribution require fewer employer dollars, but also it can provide a more predictable outlay. However, it is important to note that only 47.4 percent of the allocations are directed to the owner, compared to the matching safe harbor option with over 50 percent allocation to the owner. Either way, a safe harbor plan eliminates testing hurdles.

If you want to overcome your testing hurdles and limit the amount of your employer out-of-pocket costs, have a TPA or plan specialist evaluate your employee census to give you estimates of the costs for the different options. If you have very little participation in the plan, for example, such an arrangement may not cost much but will allow you to maximize your tax-favored benefits. Keep in mind, matching benefits drives behavior, so you may see an increase in deferral rates if you offer a safe harbor matching formula. But, of course, this is effective if you seek to drive retirement success for your employees.

It is important to consider the implications of these different methods as they relate to profit sharing contributions and any other plan arrangement you may have. Changing from 3 percent fixed safe harbor to 4 percent matching could adversely impact other allocations to highly compensated or non-HCE employees.

Based on standard ADP/ACP testing, the company illustrated above would not pass testing without a matching option. The deferral for non–highly compensated employees is 3.38 percent, compared to 7.76 percent for HCEs. Therefore, by adding a matching safe harbor option, the owner–employee and employee B can contribute the maximum to their own accounts (and not be penalized with corrective distributions), and a large allocation of the contributions may go to the owner–employee if it is a small company. In the above example, more than 50 percent of the employer contributions are allocated to the owner–employee, putting the plan at risk of being top-heavy. Therefore, paying $10,500 a year in order to ensure optimum participation in the plan is a small price for what is essentially insurance that the owner–employee and highly compensated employees can fully participate in the plan. Since these are likely the key employees, the value of the safe harbor arrangement likely exceeds the cost. Plus, the employees are getting a benefit that may help you attract or retain valued people.

By comparison, the nonelective option requires less capital outlay but allocates only about 47 percent to the owner–employee. The plan sponsor must carefully consider options against goals. Either way, the safe harbor arrangement enables more tax-favored contributions to the HCEs.

Unlike a traditional matching formula or top-heavy mandatory contribution, both of which allow a vesting schedule, a safe harbor plan requires immediate vesting. This means employees will be immediately entitled to their share, even if terminated. However, depending upon your employee census, the safe harbor plan may be a small price to pay for insurance that will ensure you and your highly compensated employees can secure your retirement. On the other hand, a traditional matching option should be considered and compared as well.

A safe harbor provision can be attached to a 401(k) at any time, provided there is sufficient employee notification. If you are struggling with testing hurdles, this may be a smart solution to consider. If your plan includes a non–safe harbor matching contribution, you may already be safe, but it makes sense to at least review this option with a plan expert to decide the best structure for your plan based on your company's needs. The goal is to maximize contribution limits for you and all employees, including your key people. There are various ways to do this, so it pays to consult with specialists. Of course, the safe harbor 401(k) tends to work best for companies with predictable revenue streams. If your business has difficulty finding matching funds on a consistent basis, other arrangements, such as profit sharing, may be better than the safe harbor option. The point is to know you have options.

SUMMARY PLAN DESCRIPTION

As the name implies, a summary plan description (SPD) is a summary of the plan adoption agreement, outlining features of your 401(k) plan in a condensed format so it can be distributed to all your employees and participants in the plan. Your SPD will define rules such as when your employees are eligible to participate, the vesting schedule for matching contributions (if applicable), the formula for matching contributions (if applicable), how to qualify and apply for loans, and how to initiate hardship withdrawals. It also includes participants' rights under ERISA, among other things. These are the key rules your employees need to know and understand as participants in your plan. Obviously, it is important that you and any internal plan administrators clearly understand the terms of the SPD for compliance. The SPD is the important document your employees need to refer to when they need to get to their money. It spells out the rules for distributions, including how beneficiaries can make a claim to the benefits. Although it's generally written with legalese, the intent is that the document be understandable by the average employee.

As a plan sponsor, you will be provided with an SPD by your administrator or 401(k) provider. The SPD, which may be written based on a template to save costs, ensures all the legal points are covered. It is an important reference document for plan participants. Federal law requires plan sponsors give employees a copy of the SPD when they enroll in the plan and distribute the SPD when there are changes made to the plan, or at least every ten years. You are also required to provide a participant or his or her beneficiary a copy of the SPD anytime such person asks. Some companies post the SPD on their employee website so it's always available. However, distributing a copy of your SPD is a legal requirement. Your employees should be given a copy rather than be required to know or be assumed to know how to go find it. You can send out the SPD in hard copy or electronic copy, but please know it must be distributed regularly. Since it is a legal requirement, you should also have a system for tracking and documenting your SPD distribution to demonstrate you are complying with the law if your plan is ever investigated. See 29 CFR § 2520.104b-2. Because the SPD outlines the terms of your participation in your 401(k) plan, it is part of a legally binding contract. You, as the employer, are required to follow the terms laid out in the SPD. Therefore, it is a good idea to review your SPD to ensure its accuracy and be certain it reflects your objectives for your plan. After all, it is the key to your employee communications. In the event your plan document says something different from your SPD (which can happen if your plan documents are amended, for example), the plan adoption agreement is always considered the definitive word.

ELECTIVE DEFERRALS AND CONTRIBUTION LIMITS

For 2019, the maximum annual total elective salary deferral for plan participants is $19,000 or 100 percent of compensation, whichever is less. This means each employee can defer no more than $19,000 into the plan, in any combination of traditional or Roth 401(k) (if applicable). But if an employee exceeds this limit, the difference is included in the employee's gross income and the employee is disqualified from the plan. For employees age fifty or older, catchup contributions may also be allowed, with current catchup contribution limits set at $6,000. So, employees age fifty or older can contribute a maximum of $25,000 into their 401(k) for 2019 calendar year. Keep in mind, these limits do not include employer matching or profit sharing contributions.

If your plan document permits, you can make matching contributions and/or discretionary nonelective contributions or profit sharing contributions to your employees' accounts. The maximum allocation is the lesser of 100 percent of the participant's compensation or $56,000, which includes employer and employee contributions. Therefore, as an owner–employee, if you meet the proper discrimination testing rules and plan allocations, you may be eligible to contribute $19,000 as a salary deferral, plus an additional $37,000 (2019) as an employer match / profit sharing allocation, for a total of $56,000 pretax 401(k) contribution. This amount can be as high as $62,000 for those employees over the age of fifty with catchup contributions. As you can see, it can be quite advantageous to review profit sharing and supplemental plan options to optimize owner–employee benefits. Of course, this will require allocations to your employees as well. Therefore, a cost analysis should be performed by specialists before you make any final decisions about your plan design.

Once you initiate payroll, you must deposit your employee contributions into your retirement plan's trust or individual accounts as soon as you can reasonably segregate those dollars from your general assets. The DOL provides employers with a seven-business-day safe harbor rule if there are fewer than one hundred participants, but it should be done sooner if possible. In today's tech world, it usually can be done within three days. If you have failed to deposit employees' elective deferrals as soon as you could have, you should find out how to correct this mistake with your recordkeeper or plan administrator.

PARTICIPANT NOTICES

If there is one thing plan sponsors seem to find overwhelming and confusing, it is the participant notices. Once you set up a plan, you must give your employees certain written information about their retirement plan. Some of this information must be provided regularly and automatically, whereas other kinds of disclosures must be made available upon written request. You may provide these notices to participants electronically (online) if the communication meets certain conditions. The following description is not inclusive of all participant notices, but it does provide an overview. It is a good practice to review required participant notices with your 401(k) team to be sure you are in compliance with current laws. All notices distributed should be documented in your ERISA file and stamped with the date and method of distribution.

Fee Disclosure. Every twelve months, you must provide all employees, whether they are active participants or not, with a Participant Fee

Disclosure notice. New hires should be given this notice with the enrollment packages upon eligibility for the plan or within ninety days of entry date.

Safe Harbor, QDIA, and Automatic Annual Notices. By December 1 of each year, you need to distribute the QDIA Annual Default Investment Notice required to satisfy qualified default investment alternative (QDIA) rules and take advantage of the 404(c) protection to which you are entitled. Also, if you have any of the automatics included in your plan (e.g., auto-enroll or auto-increase), by December 1 of each year, you need to distribute the ACA—an annual notice of right to opt out of the automatics. If you have a Safe Harbor Plan, such notice should also be distributed annually by December 1. These notices listed should always be provided with new hire packages or within ninety days of plan eligibility, along with the Summary Plan Description (SPD).

Summary Annual Report. By September 30 of every year, you should distribute the SAR (Summary Annual Report) if you file your 5500 on time. If you file an extension, the SAR must be distributed by November 15.

Event-Related Notices. Should you ever add, remove, or replace investments in your investment menu, a thirty-day Fund Change Notice should be sent to all eligible employees and participants with balances in their plan notifying participants of upcoming changes in the plan's fund offerings and providing them with any required disclosure information, such as mapping information or instructions about how the change impacts the participants. These notices must be sent thirty days in advance of any changes.

Should you have any fee changes, an updated Participant Fee Disclosure form should be distributed 30 to 90 days *before* such change takes effect. If there are any modifications to the Plan Adoption Agreement, a summary of material modifications (SMM) update should be provided and accompany the Summary Plan Description (SPD) within 210 days following the plan year the amendment takes effect. This is also the same for any SPD restatement.

Electronic Notices. As of this writing, you may provide online notices instead of paper format provided your communication is conveyed in a manner that is as understandable as if given in a paper document. The point is not to confuse the language or make it difficult for the employees to understand the notice. Obviously, the employee needs to be able to easily access the notice. Although you can offer a link to the documents, it must be easily obtainable by all employees. You cannot remove the web page or change it once it is distributed, unless you provide additional notice. You also must be sure the employees understand they may request the notice in paper format, and it's always a good practice to be sure your employee's consent to receive the notice electronically beforehand. Usually this can be accomplished by adding such language in an enrollment form or online account access agreement. You don't want to have an employee file a complaint for not receiving proper disclosures. Please be sure to refer to the DOL rules for notice requirements since the rules can and do change over time

DISTRIBUTION RULES.

Generally, distributions of 401(k) contributions cannot be made until the participant turns fifty-nine and a half, has a severance from employment, dies, becomes disabled, or incurs a financial hardship. Of course, in the event you terminate the plan and have elected not to establish a successor plan, the plan assets are eligible for taxable distribution or qualified rollover. A plan provider change will not trigger a distribution. You can move plan assets from one recordkeeper to another without prompting distributions.

Depending on the terms of the plan, participant distributions may be full or partial and made as a lump-sum or periodic distribution, such as installment payments. In most circumstances, the plan administrator must obtain the participant's consent before making a distribution. This means that if you have a terminated employee, you cannot just cut a check and force a distribution, except as noted below. While it might be nice to force out former employees rather than tracking them down to provide statements and disclosures, consent is required to do this, unless one of the conditions noted below is met. Also, depending upon your state, the plan may require the consent of the participant's spouse as well.

There is an exception to participant consent if the participant has terminated employment with an account balance of less than $5,000 (excluding any rollovers he or she made into the plan). This is called a forced distribution. If the balance is over $1,000, the funds must be transferred to an IRA with a notice sent to the terminated employee advising such person of his or her right to transfer the funds from the IRA to another retirement plan. It is generally a good practice to work with your plan administrator to help move assets or encourage that assets be moved out of your plan for terminated or even retired employees. Otherwise, you must keep track of addresses and employee information as long as the assets remain in the plan. You may find yourself tracking employees who haven't worked for you for a decade or more. Therefore, it is a good idea to consider forcing out small account balances to potentially save you lots of extra work. It's also a good idea to provide transfer information and documents to any terminated or retired employee and perhaps incorporate that dialogue into the exit interview process. Having transition packages for terminated or retired employees helps facilitate this. Remember, you are still responsible for terminated employees' accounts, so by educating them about transition options, you may help reduce your fiduciary risk. Your financial advisor can help you streamline that process.

HARDSHIP DISTRIBUTIONS

Because employees do not have access to distributions or withdrawals unless they retire or terminate service, employers may offer hardship distribution options within their plans. Hardship distributions can be taken at any time regardless of participant age, provided the hardship is due to an immediate and heavy financial need and must be the result of a severe and unforeseen need. You can choose to permit hardship distributions within your plan or not. However, by law, such distributions are limited to the amount of the employee's elective deferrals and employer matching contributions only (qualified matching contributions [QMACs], qualified nonelective matching contributions [QNECs], and investment earnings may not be distributed on account of a hardship). Check with your plan administrator to determine if your matching contributions are QMAC or QNEC.

In addition, hardship distributions are subject to taxation and penalties, as per distribution rules, and cannot be rolled over into another plan or IRA. Finally, the maximum amount allowed should not exceed the amount necessary to satisfy the financial need, but it may be adjusted to account for taxes or penalties that may result from the distribution. For example, if your employee needs $7,000 to pay medical bills, you can only provide $7,000 plus a reasonable adjustment for taxes and penalties.

Eligibility for hardship withdrawal must be determined by relevant facts and circumstance. To date, there has been very limited federal guidance regarding what constitutes an unforeseen financial emergency. For instance, there is no guidance to make clear what is meant by the terms *severe* and *unforeseeable*, but a hardship distribution is quite obviously not likely to qualify if funds are used to purchase a boat or a vacation home. The hardship may be the result of medical care not covered by insurance, tuition or education expenses, or imminent foreclosure of a primary residence, but a hardship is not granted to pay credit card debt or "nonsevere" obligations, such as for a vacation or rental property. It may be allowed to cover water damage to a home not covered by insurance, or funeral costs for a dependent, but it is up to the plan trustee to determine the qualification of the hardship. This can be difficult if you don't understand the guidelines.

The decision to either allow or deny a hardship withdrawal application is subject to the trustee's interpretations of the rules. To make it easy, your recordkeeper may limit hardship withdrawals only to specific hardships. The prevention of foreclosure or eviction from primary residence, tuition or related fees for postsecondary education for the participant, spouse, or dependent, funeral expenses for the spouse or dependent, or medical expenses not covered by insurance are typical. Because of the ambiguity, be sure to understand your plan documents and, more importantly, your recordkeeper's rules for hardship withdrawals, which may be more limited than your documents. Each participant's financial emergency hardship withdrawal application must be carefully evaluated. Without specific rules defined in your SPD or by your provider, qualification may be based on the unique facts and circumstances of each participant's particular situation. The fact is, a 401(k) should be considered only after funds from other types of accounts are found not to be available in order to preserve the integrity of the retirement savings. The key to administering financial emergency hardships is to apply the rules and procedures for these distributions to all participants *consistently*.

Hardship withdrawals are not loans and cannot be processed as loans. Nor are they available to terminated employees (terminated employees can take taxable distributions). Like with ordinary distributions, hardship withdrawals are subject to taxes, including 20 percent mandatory withholding tax, and any applicable penalties for early withdrawal. The 10 percent penalty tax may be waived depending on the type of hardship; however, it is best to refer employees to their tax advisors for potential tax implications since each situation is different. As a plan fiduciary, you must exercise great care in handling these hardship qualification decisions and be mindful of the language used to communicate to your employees. Plan sponsors have run into conflicts when processing hardships incorrectly or inconsistently because they have misunderstood the rules.

Regardless of how you choose to handle them, hardship withdrawals are costly to the employee's retirement security and should only be allowed in extreme cases. It is customary to prohibit contributions to the plan for at least six months after receipt of the hardship distribution, in order to discourage such distributions.

FILING REQUIREMENTS

The Internal Revenue Code and Titles I and IV of the Employee Retirement Income Security Act (ERISA) deal with the collection and review information about employee benefit plans, including health and retirement plans. ERISA Form 5500 was created so the government can assess the financial condition, investments, and operations of all employee benefit plans. Consequently, each year your 401(k) will be required to file Form 5500 with the IRS. The purpose of Form 5500 is to provide the IRS with an annual valuation of your 401(k) plan's assets. In most cases, your TPA will help you complete the filing. If you have fewer than one hundred eligible participants, you will file a short form (5500-SF). If you have more than one hundred eligible participants, you will file Form 5500 (which will also require a CPA audit; see below). Regardless, when you are preparing your Form 5500 is a good time to do a checkup of your administrative responsibilities and retirement plan needs.

Form 5500 contains essential information including the type and details of your plan specifications, eligible participants, plan assets and liabilities, service providers and plan fees, fidelity bond coverage, named plan fiduciary, plan loans, intent to comply with 404(c), and whether or not your plan is self-directed, among many other details. It is important to take the time to understand and review your 5500 form before you file it. Often, plan sponsors rely on their plan administrator to complete the form and neglect to conduct their own 5500 reviews. An analysis by Deloitte Consulting for the US Department of Labor found that nearly 22 percent of Forms 5500 had discrepancies when referenced against the filing's various schedules. Form 5500 filing is the basis used for many DOL investigations and IRS plan audits and as a legal framework for your plan in the event of litigation. Inaccurate or incorrect information can subject you to a plan audit. Additionally, it is important to file your form in a timely manner, as the federal government may impose penalties for noncompliance with filing regulations. Consult your tax advisor, your plan administrator, the IRS, or the Employee Benefits Security Administration (EBSA) of the DOL if you have any questions.

CPA AUDIT

Your employees place a great deal of trust in you when they allow you to withhold their hard-earned dollars from their paychecks and deposit these funds into their retirement accounts. They trust that you are withholding the correct amount, depositing it into their accounts in a timely manner, and, if you offer employer matching, calculating the match in accordance with the plan agreement. Your employees place significant trust in you to protect their retirement savings. Hence, the focus of a required CPA audit is to protect the plan participants. Understand that a complete audit process provides an important means of oversight of the plan's operations. The audit serves to identify that the plan is operating within the framework of DOL and IRS compliance.

If you have under 100 *eligible* participants starting at the beginning of a plan year, your plan is considered a small plan and the audit requirement is waived. This number includes employees who are eligible to participate but are not active participants. However, once your plan reaches 100 *eligible* participants at the beginning of a plan year, your plan becomes a *large plan* and generally must have audited financial statements, with the 80–120 exception described below. A plan audit means you are required to hire a CPA to review your plan's internal controls and financials and that you must attach audited financial statements prepared by an independent certified public accountant to your Form 5500 when filing.

There is an exception to the 100 eligible participant limit. It's called the 80–120 Participant Rule. If you have between 80 and 120 eligible participants and you filed as a small plan the year before, you can continue to do so after going over 100 eligible participants and avoid the CPA audit requirement. But once you reach 120 eligible participants at the beginning of a plan year, you must file as a large plan and file Schedule H along with your 5500. This means you must hire a CPA to perform a plan audit.

While most employers and plan sponsors have nothing but the best intentions when establishing a retirement plan for their employees, the fact of the matter is that many times the administration and the upkeep of the plan take a back seat to other aspects of the business. As noted in *Retire Ready*, it is important to take the administration of your plan seriously; the IRS and Department of Labor certainly do. Therefore, your CPA audit is there to work with you to ensure your plan meets compliance and regulatory requirements and to resolve any issues that may arise during the audit. Of course, you are responsible to hire the auditor, but the auditor's ultimate responsibility is to your plan participants. Keep in mind, CPAs must follow a code of ethics written by the American Institute of Certified Public Accountants, so they have a duty to serve the public interest. The goal of an audit is not to "catch" the employer doing something wrong or reprimand plan sponsors for improper actions and/or inaccurate recordkeeping. It's merely a duty to fulfill your fiduciary responsibility for compliance and ensure your plan is operating correctly.

If you are well prepared and organized, the process of conducting a 401(k) audit can be straightforward. With the right amount of planning and a competent auditor, you may find that a plan sponsor should get through the audit process relatively quickly and efficiently. Of course, if you are disorganized, it can be messy. If you have never experienced an audit before, it's a good idea to plan ahead. Your TPA and 401(k) team, along with your CPA, can serve as very helpful guides throughout the entire process. To ensure a smooth and efficient audit process, it is important to start with an auditor whom you trust and who can be your partner throughout the review. It goes without saying, the more prepared you are in planning for the audit, the more orderly the work process will be. Having good internal controls could potentially save you time and money. For plans with calendar year ends, most 401(k) audits are done during the summer months, so you will want to begin preparing earlier in the year.

The audit will focus on several different areas such as participant-related transactions and activity including salary deferrals, employer matching, plan loans, investments, and plan financials. A financial statement will need to be prepared. Because salary deferrals belong to the plan participants and do not ever belong to the company, deposits and transactions must be handled with prudence. Therefore, the CPA will need to understand how your plan accounting works, review your internal controls over the plan, and identify any risks associated with the plan.

Auditors consider several questions in their analysis, including the following:

- Do all eligible employees have the same opportunity to participate?
- Are assets of the plan fairly valued?
- Have contributions to the plan been made in a timely manner?
- Are participant accounts fairly stated?
- Were benefit payments made according to the terms of the plan?
- Were there any issues identified that may impact the plan's tax status?
- Have there been any transactions made that are prohibited under ERISA?

The completed independent auditor's report, along with the plan's financial statements and necessary schedules, are attached to Form 5500 and ultimately filed with the Department of Labor. For those plans requiring an audit, the audit and the complete Form 5500 must be filed electronically with the IRS by July 31. Extensions, permitted under a few circumstances, can delay the deadline until September 15. The other option is to formally extend the Form 5500 itself, which yields an automatic extension until October 15. However, to avoid the penalties for failing to complete Form 5500 or ramifications of filing late, plan sponsors should take the time to understand the requirements for a 401(k) audit well in advance of the July 31 deadline.

PROHIBITED TRANSACTIONS

The 401(k) plan assets are not the assets of the company, but rather assets owned by the employees. Therefore, as a good investment steward, plan fiduciaries and company owners or officers must exercise great care when handling other people's money. Prohibited transactions are not allowed unless an exemption is available. The IRS defines prohibited transactions essentially as any self-dealing transactions between your retirement plan and the plan fiduciaries, direct or indirect owners, or company officers and their family members or service providers. You cannot use the plan assets for your own benefit, for the benefit of your firm, or for personal gain. It should be obvious that plan sponsors cannot borrow or lend money or extend credit from the 401(k) assets. Of course, 401(k) assets are employee assets, so no one can use them for any reason other than benefits to which you are entitled as a plan participant or beneficiary. For instance, if a plan fiduciary wants to take a loan from his own 401(k) as a participant and with the same terms and limits that apply to all participants and as defined by law, such action is allowed and is not considered a prohibited transaction. But if the owner of your company is using plan funds to cover payroll or make a lease payment, the transaction is prohibited and subject to excise taxes. In the event of a prohibited transaction, the transaction must be immediately corrected and an excise tax be paid. The amount is 15 percent per year if the transaction is corrected in the same tax year, but if the transaction is not corrected within the taxable year, additional penalties are imposed. It goes without saying, misappropriation of funds is taken very seriously with 401(k) plan assets by the IRS, the DOL, and the courts. As a fiduciary, you are held to the highest level of the law to safeguard your plan assets.

IN SUMMARY

Your employees know they need to save for retirement, but although they have the ability to do so on their own with IRAs and investment accounts, very few take the initiative without being prompted. They depend upon you to help them not only enjoy a paycheck but also provide benefits to secure their financial well-being, such as medical and life insurance as well as a retirement plan. Consequently, your care and stewardship of your company retirement plan is critical to drive your employees' financial security. Although they have an obligation to understand the plan, to participate, and make prudent decisions, you have a greater responsibility to oversee your plan and ensure it is being run in a manner that puts your employees and their families' best interest first and foremost. It's an honorable responsibility. If every employer embraced this duty with respect and comprehensive regard, I'm confident we could transform and conquer retirement in America.

Wouldn't it be great if everyone could enjoy their golden years with dignity and financial confidence? If you work together with the right 401(k) team who aligns you and your employee's goals and objectives to the plan and follows a diligent and prudent process, you just may be able to give your employees the priceless gift of being retire ready.

CHAPTER 3
FIDUCIARY

Mason is your new production manager. You are delighted to have recruited him from a major competitor who offers a very strong benefits package, including a large 401(k). Having a great deal of experience as a participant in the 401(k), Mason reviewed your investment options and noticed you offered some fund that were class A shares and others that were class R shares. He was unfamiliar with these share classes, but upon conducting his own research, he learned that class A shares are retail shares. Given the size of your company and 401(k) plan assets, he presumed he would be entitled to wholesale (or institutional) pricing on his investments. He approaches you to inquire why the firm didn't negotiate for better investment pricing on your 401(k) options. He is concerned that he isn't being treated fairly as a participant. As a plan fiduciary, your duty is to protect the interest of your employees. Therefore, how do you reply?

Suppose your dear aunt was suddenly placed in a nursing home and she had designated you as trustee of her $15 million estate. You are now tasked with the responsibility of prudently managing her assets, not just for her but also for her named beneficiaries, who consist of about a hundred different relatives and friends. Under the law, you are a fiduciary, which means you have a legal obligation to act in the best interest of your aunt and the best interest of each and every one of her named beneficiaries. It also means you must act as an investment expert, since you are now managing her money, and follow the duties of loyalty, care, and prudence.

Having authority over a qualified retirement plan or 401(k) is really no different. You must act in the best interest of your employees and their beneficiaries. You must act as an investment expert. *But wait a minute,* you say. *My employees make their own investment choices. In fact, they even make their own contribution decisions. All I do is offer them the ability to participate in the plan.* Yes, but because you offer a plan and control many aspects of that plan, you are deemed a fiduciary. Anytime you *manage other people's money,* you are likely to be a fiduciary under the law. For instance, who decides from which menu of investments your employees can choose? You do! Who decides and negotiates the fees that your employees must pay for the plan? *You do!* Who decides the terms and conditions under which your employees can access their money, their loan options and interest rates, their eligibility, and more? *You do!* With control comes liability and responsibilities.

I realize many plans were started on the basis that the 401(k) is "free" and "easy." Unfortunately, sales representatives who sold these plans often oversimplified the process. While in general 401(k) plans may be low cost to the employer, they certainly aren't "free." Someone has to pay to operate these plans. You may pay administrative costs and perhaps audit fees, but it is typically the employees who pay the bulk of the costs of running the plan. Because you select the provider and vendors who charge the fees to your participants, you have the duty to follow a due diligence process to ensure the fees are fair and reasonable, just as you would if those plan fees were paid by you or your firm.

While the 401(k) is easy to administer compared to the traditional pension plan arrangement, it is certainly not without work. You have several responsibilities as a fiduciary. If you have ignored these duties thus far without any consequences, you should be aware that the regulatory world is changing quickly and enforcement of these rules is increasing. Your chances of a DOL audit or litigation may be greater now than ever before. Therefore, not only should you take your fiduciary duties seriously, but also you should consider taking additional steps to help you manage your financial liabilities.

One of the easiest ways to manage your risk is by complying with safe harbor provisions under 404(c), which is discussed a little later in this chapter. Be sure to follow the guidelines to enjoy limited ERISA safe harbor relief. You may also want to consider fiduciary insurance. If you already have fiduciary insurance, you should review the policy regularly. See chapter 11 to learn more important details of fiduciary insurance. Of course, you do have to purchase a fiduciary bond, and you want to be sure you understand the correct coverage required. Additionally, if you hire an advisor to help you run your plan, check whether the advisor is a stated 3(21) or 3(38) fiduciary. This will allow you to engage a co-fiduciary to share in your investment-related liability. However, keep in mind that fiduciary status is based on the *functions performed for the plan*, not just a person's title. There may be individuals within your firm who are acting as fiduciaries that you are not aware of, and that means added liability for your organization.

The primary duties of a plan fiduciary include (1) to operate the plan in the best interest of the participants and their beneficiaries; (2) to act with the care, skill, prudence, and diligence that a knowledgeable person familiar with such matters would use in managing the plan; (3) to operate the plan in strict adherence with the plan documents; and (4) to offer the participants a diverse range of proper investment options to choose from and oversee the investment options available under the plan. Of course, more specific duties arise from these general duties, including the duty to monitor the plan's service providers, to ensure plan fees charged to plan participants are reasonable, and to ensure the plan documents remain in compliance with changing tax laws and respond to participant claims in strict adherence to the plan's claims procedure as mandated under ERISA. The fiduciary standard of care under ERISA is one of the highest fiduciary standards in US law.

WHO IS THE FIDUCIARY?

A 401(k) must have at least one fiduciary named in the written plan, and this is usually the owner or CFO. This individual has signing authority and retains discretion in administering and managing the plan. He or she is also stated as a fiduciary in the plan documents. But as already mentioned, fiduciary status is based on the functions performed for the plan, not just based on one's title. There are typically multiple people acting as fiduciaries within a company, even if they are not identified in the plan documents. A plan's fiduciaries will ordinarily include the trustee, investment advisors, individuals exercising discretion in the administration of the plan, all members of a plan's administrative or investment committee, and company officers. Attorneys, accountants, and actuaries who are not employees of the firm are not generally fiduciaries when acting solely in their professional capacities. The key to determining whether an individual or an entity is a fiduciary is whether they are *exercising discretion or control over the plan*. If you are an HR manager and you are influencing plan decisions, even if you aren't the plan's trustee, you may be considered a fiduciary under the law. Signing authority does not define the fiduciary role, but the actions of the employee do. Employers should know who is acting as a plan fiduciary and be sure those individuals ought to be acting as such, because the liabilities and risks fall on the employer as plan sponsor, and they could also fall on employees acting as fiduciaries.

For a fiduciary, there's one simple rule: *always act solely in the best interest of the plan participants and their beneficiaries*. Now that's easier said than done because unintentional fiduciary breach is a common violation. While this has gone unpunished in the past, the DOL and courts are not tolerating negligence these days, even if it's unintentional. In today's world, ignorance is not bliss. You have important responsibilities when you sponsor a 401(k). You are subject to a standard of conduct because you take care of *other people's money*. And, contrary to what anyone may tell you, *you cannot* abdicate your fiduciary responsibilities and liabilities to anyone else, not to a financial firm, not to a CPA or TPA—and not even if you relinquish your discretionary powers to someone else. This is because you always have the right to hire and fire your vendors as wells as change or terminate your plan. Consequently, no matter what you may hear, you will always remain a fiduciary and have the highest level of responsibility.

HOW CAN YOU BE A FIDUCIARY IF YOU AREN'T MAKING THE INVESTMENT CHOICES FOR YOUR EMPLOYEES?

Many plan sponsors ask how they can have liability when their employees are making their own investment choices. It's a fair question, but keep in mind that you have direct control over the list of investment options offered to your employees. Some employers don't even realize they have control over the list of investment options. Some employers simply offer the entire gamut of funds available through their recordkeeper, not realizing they have a duty to carefully select their investment menu to align with the best interest of their employees. You can offer a narrow range of only a handful of investments, or you can offer hundreds. But keep in mind, your liability for investment monitoring does not decrease simply by offering more funds. In fact, it could arguably increase.

Your employees are selecting allocations from this menu of options, but you have the privilege and responsibility of determining what that menu will be. Therefore, you are exercising control, and with control comes responsibility and liability. For instance, suppose your investment menu offers two different large-cap stock funds that are benchmarked to the S&P 500 Index. The five-year average return for fund A is 7%, and the five-year average return for fund B is 5%, yet the S&P 500 Index has averaged 11% over this same period. It may be argued that your employees are not able to competitively participate in the large-cap market because your menu of options is underperforming. Who should ask why there is a 4–6% return differential and determine what should be done about it? You. It is your duty to identify laggards as well as other nuances within your investment menu and take action accordingly. Your employees have limited power. In this example, they have to choose one of the two large-cap stock funds in your menu if they want to participate in this asset class within your plan even though these funds are underperforming. As a plan sponsor, you ultimately control the investment options, and you have the authority to remove those underperforming funds and replace them with superior options. Doesn't it make sense that you ought to ensure the funds in your investment menu are competitive?

Of course, that may beg the question, why not let your employees choose from a self-directed brokerage account and allow them to access the entire open market so they can control their own investments rather than be restricted to a menu of twenty or thirty funds? Oh, if it were only that easy. Most employees are financial novices. They are not investment experts. The DOL knows this, as do the courts and attorneys. Most plan participants do not know the difference between an income stock fund and a high-yield bond fund, let alone how to select suitable funds from the entire investment universe. To give them complete open investment options would mean they would have to know how to prudently select suitable investments from the entire financial universe, representing perhaps hundreds of thousands of securities. If you offered such a strategy, many of your employees would likely find the options overwhelming and confusing and would be even more prone to making costly mistakes. As a steward of your employees' welfare, you cannot escape liability and abdicate your responsibilities simply by establishing a do-it-yourself arrangement.

ERISA requires that you act responsibly for the benefit of your employees, and that includes managing risks. Therefore, a plan sponsor must carefully consider what investment options ought to be included in their plan and why as well as what ought not to be included, and why. Think about how you would manage your dear aunt's $15 million estate for her and her one hundred beneficiaries. Fiduciaries of a 401(k) must always consider the potential implications of any and all investments made available to their employees. For instance, offering sector funds may add pizzazz to an investment menu, and more-experienced investors may understand limited exposure to, say, technology or energy stocks, which may provide the potential for higher returns without unnecessarily increasing risk if strategically allocated, but a novice investor may be compelled to put a large portion of his or her account balance in a sector fund if he or she sees stellar results, having no understanding of the risk. They've read that past performance is not a guarantee of future results, but most employees really don't understand what that truly means. Sectors tends to fall in and out of favor and are subject to wild market swings. An employee may not only be making the mistake of a concentrated position but also, even worse, be allocating the bulk of her retirement dollars at the peak of a cycle, putting retirement savings at great risk.

Remember the dot-com bubble? I can't tell you how many employees naively thought it was okay to have all their retirement savings in tech stocks because "technology is never going to die." Yet, when the NASDAQ fell, it took over fifteen years to return to its prior high. And what about the staggering number of Enron employees who held 100 percent of their 401(k) savings in Enron stock? Where did they find themselves? Broke.

Scrutinizing investments and supporting your employees' needs based on their experience or lack thereof is paramount if you are to fulfill your fiduciary duties. And if you want your employees to retire ready, they absolutely need help.

It makes sense to exercise care and prudence when it comes to investment oversight for the sake of your employees. Why wouldn't you want to seek to create the best investment menu possible? Consider that there are nearly ten thousand mutual funds available these days. Not all of them are top performers. Indeed, simple math suggests half will be average to below-average performers. According to Morningstar reports, the difference between a fund performing in the top quartile and a fund performing in the bottom quartile of its peer group can be as much as 3–5% per year, and sometimes far more. Compounded over time, this can amount to hundreds of thousands of dollars lost by sitting in subpar investments. Poor performance can be extremely harmful to retirement success. While it seems that plan sponsors and the DOL are caught up in the difference between 0.25 percent and 0.50 percent in fees, inferior investment performance can represent a far greater cost to your participants.

This is not to suggest it is prudent to chase past performance. On the contrary, this has proven to be rather ineffective. Frequently adding or removing investment options within your plan's menu not only can be a cumbersome task but also can create confusion for your participants. Of course, this is not a reason to avoid such changes if they are necessary. The key is to follow a *sensible* monitoring process that is in accordance with your Investment Policy Statement. A due diligence process and a defined Investment Policy Statement can help you ensure there is a routine, systematic process followed for evaluating, measuring, and acting when investments in your menu fall below acceptable levels. Everyone involved in running your plan will understand the process when it is written out in an Investment Policy Statement. There is more to scrutinize than just performance, of course. Risk, style drift, management, and many other things must be considered before adding or removing investments. A sound due diligence process will provide a systematic method to investment monitoring.

As you can imagine, there are more responsibilities to properly overseeing a plan than just monitoring investments. There are still many different obligations to ensure ERISA compliance. Going beyond compliance, there is much more to do to help drive retirement success for your employees. But you cannot run a successful plan unless it is compliant, so understanding and fulfilling your fiduciary duties is the beginning. However, it is certainly not the end. Logically, it is critical to mitigate the risk to your firm and to you personally.

IMPLICATION OF BEING A FIDUCIARY

Fiduciaries have important responsibilities and are subject to standards of conduct. Because you act on behalf of your employees and their beneficiaries, you have a duty to act prudently. This means you have a duty to have expertise in a variety of areas, including investments. Lacking that expertise, you will want to hire someone with the professional knowledge to carry out those responsibilities. You can read about investment oversight in chapter 6. The focus of a fiduciary should always be on prudence; therefore, you should have a consistent process for making decisions on behalf of your employees. It is wise to document all decisions as well as the basis for those decisions. For example, not only should the decision to change providers be in writing, but so should the rationale and the selection process made to compare providers. This is the only way to demonstrate your standard of conduct. And keep in mind, there is personal liability at stake, which can include restoring any losses to the plan if you fail to follow, or fail to demonstrate that you've followed, a prudent process.

Suppose you decide to change recordkeepers because your nephew works for a plan provider and he told you he can offer you a better plan. You like your nephew, you think he's a good guy, and you want to help him out. You're not enamored with your plan provider, and since your nephew is working for a well-recognized firm whose name you trust, you agree to give him the business. Without a process for comparing his proposal with that of your current provider and the performance of the overall market, you have failed to act prudently for your employees. While this might seem obvious, you would be surprised how frequently this sort of thing happens. Acting on the basis of trust because it is your nephew, friend, or personal advisor does not amount to a due diligence defense. Imagine years later, the DOL investigates your plan and determines your provider fees are excessive—or even worse, a lawsuit ensues from a disgruntled employee. The suit claims your plan has excessive fees and has caused financial harm to the plan participants. How do you defend that claim if you don't know and understand your plan fees and how they compare to the market? Declaring you made the decision on the basis that you trusted your nephew (or financial advisor, friend, or anyone else) is probably not going the be a strong defense.

In that same scenario, had you shopped the market, interviewed candidates, asked each contender the same questions so as to act in an objective matter, and after careful review determined your nephew offered the best plan, you would have documentation showing you were objective in your decision. Although I am not an attorney and make no claim of being able to interpret the law in this example, ERISA has made it very clear that it holds fiduciaries responsible for the *process*, not the results. You don't have to be perfect, just prudent. The later example demonstrates a form of prudence. Additionally, conflicts of interest, such as doing business with a relative, should be disclosed and openly addressed. The law does not say you cannot do business with a friend or relative. It says you must follow a due diligence process and act objectively. It is imperative that plan sponsors understand the scope of fiduciary duties, including but not limited to plan fees.

Plan sponsors should also be aware of others who serve as fiduciaries within their plan. The law says all fiduciaries have potential liability, *including personal liability* for the actions of their co-fiduciaries. Therefore, if you conceal or do not act to correct a fiduciary breach, you may be putting yourself at risk. For example, suppose your boss floats employee contributions for his personal use, but you do nothing about it. Although you are concerned, he says it's being used to cover operating costs. And because the funds always get repaid, you decide to ignore it. As defined by ERISA, you may be deemed as knowingly participating in this breach of responsibility, and consequently, you may share in any potential liability. If you suspect your firm is intentionally holding back employees' 401(k) deferrals beyond a reasonable processing period, you must act to correct the problem, or perhaps it might be best to consult with legal counsel.

Suppose the CEO insists on hiring his personal financial advisor as your plan advisor, whom you know collects an excessive fee from the plan and provides little to no service. But because of the business, the advisor gives the CEO a big discount on his personal loans and investments. This is a conflict of interest and may also be a fiduciary breach. Neglecting to correct the problem could put you at financial risk.

Although these are just hypothetical examples that may or may not lead to liability, the US Department of Labor has published specific compliance guides that clearly state fiduciaries have potential liability for the actions of their co-fiduciaries if a fiduciary knowingly participates in, conceals, or does not act to correct another's breach of responsibility. The point is, the significance of being a fiduciary is substantial enough to warrant careful consideration, which may include forming a retirement plan committee to ensure all fiduciaries understand their roles and requirements and comply with the rules.

RETIREMENT PLAN COMMITTEE

As they say, teamwork is "less me and more we." Without a retirement plan committee, I believe it is difficult to adhere to a disciplined process of 401(k) plan management. One person alone cannot effectively make decisions on behalf of all your employees. Therefore, the goal of having a retirement plan committee is to provide the foundation for your plan governance and oversight. It helps to have different sets of eyes overseeing administrative issues such as plan fees and employee communications, as well as investment decisions and basic procedures set forth within the plan. There are many steps employers should be taking to ensure their retirement plan is in compliance both with the IRS and the DOL. A regular review of these issues and a focus on internal controls may help prevent costly fines and fees. I am often asked by plan sponsors, "How can we reduce the liability associated with managing our 401(k) plan?" Well, one of the most effective ways to reduce personal and firm liability is to establish an investment or retirement committee to work together to collaborate on plan management. Candidly, retirement readiness is difficult to achieve without a committee or team of people who are engaged in driving retirement success for employees, regardless of how big or small the company.

Larger companies may find that having as many as five committee members is efficient, whereas smaller companies may need only two or three. Regardless of the size, the systematic methodology followed by a committee can help mitigate risk. A committee may not prevent lawsuits, since anyone can be sued for any reason. But for many reasons, it makes good sense to have one. However, it is not good to have a committee if they never meet or if they fail to follow their own rules. Plan sponsors have been able to reduce personal liability and run an effective plan by having specific operating standards and following best practices. Therefore, if you desire retirement success, you should follow best practices, and utilize the power of a retirement committee. Having different eyes and ears allows for valuable input and enables plan sponsors to think more like plan participants.

If you already have a committee, is it formally established? Just as a corporation adopts bylaws to create a governance structure and operating rules, a retirement committee should adopt a charter to structure its operations in writing and to define its purpose and objectives in the bylaws, including the appointment and replacement process of its members. If you don't yet have a committee, it may be time to start the process. How many should be in your committee is dependent upon what is deemed necessary by you and your organization. The importance here is that the committee be clearly defined and formalized. Committee members should formally acknowledge their acceptance of the appointment in writing, and each member ought to formally recognize his or her role as a fiduciary. Members also should be able to resign from their roles. But, of course, there are those who should be permanent members, such as leadership from finance, HR, and possibly legal if you have in-house legal counsel.

COMMITTEE MEMBERS

Sponsors can take different approaches to appointing a fiduciary committee. Who should be appointed and how many should be appointed is a decision that should be carefully considered. The optimal number of committee members depends on the size of your plan, but keep in mind that if your committee is too small, you may not receive enough input to make informed decisions. On the other hand, if there are too many members, your committee may not function productively. Also, it may be smart to consider seeking an odd number of people in your committee to avoid ties when voting on challenging issues.

Refer to figure 3.1. Although the Chief Financial Officer and Vice President or Director of Human Resources are obvious choices, you want to seek representation from a mix of departments to contribute diverse viewpoints. This helps your committee consider its decisions from varying perspectives. In addition to executive members from HR, finance, and operations, you may want to think about those with related experience: benefits, accounting, legal, or finance.

COMMITTEE MEMBERSHIP

When choosing committee members, consider senior employees with relevant experience who can understand ERISA's fiduciary responsibilities. An industry-reported best practice is to number each group at approximately five, including:

- ☐ A trustee, as long as it is not an institutional trustee;
- ☐ An expert in human resources (HR)/employee communications;
- ☐ An expert in finance/investments;
- ☐ An expert in business affairs; and
- ☐ An expert in legal matters.

Figure 3.1

The committee should be prepared to make decisions and take action accordingly. Remember, under ERISA, members of the committee are personally liable for their fiduciary decisions. To limit personal liability, it is critical that fiduciaries conduct themselves with an exceptional level of care—and to the extent that you have included middle- to lower-level management, senior management must provide appropriate oversight to the deliberations and decisions. Directors and officers of publicly traded companies are responsible for ensuring that the persons they have appointed to positions of investment fiduciary responsibility understand their roles, responsibilities, and obligations and have the ability to carry out their duties with integrity and competence.

It goes without saying that all committee members should be educated on the fundamentals of ERISA. This should include an understanding of a fiduciary's duties, plan procedures, and service providers' contracts. The three main facets of their duties are regulation, governance, and stewardship. This means anyone appointed must understand how to operate the plan in the best interest of participants, understand how to operate the plan so it is consistent with the goals and objectives of the organization, and uphold the responsibility to make decisions on the basis of participant loyalty and trust. Your advisor should be able to help provide fiduciary training to your committee members, or you should enlist the services of an expert to help ensure members have the knowledge required to fulfill their duties.

COMMITTEE OVERSIGHT

Whether you are just establishing a committee or reviewing your current committee, now is a good time to review your management process. Do you have an appointed committee chairperson and secretary? It is a good idea to have this formally adopted. Your financial advisor is usually the one to help prepare the meeting agenda and coordinate the meetings, but you can appoint a chairperson to perform this duty and/or other leadership duties if you feel that such a setup might be better suited to your organization. The chair and secretary should have the same vote as other committee members in all decisions, but the chairperson should also be the designated agent for the service of the legal process. The secretary is responsible for keeping minutes of the meetings and is usually the official custodian of records for the committee. Figure 3.2 highlights a sample meeting minutes format.

The chairman and secretary should be authorized by the committee to execute any instruments necessary for the committee to conduct business. In light of this, it is not uncommon to see the CFO act as chair and the HR director to act as secretary, although you should appoint your members based on the resources of and needs within your organization.

> The Investment Committee Meeting minutes should include:
> - ☐ Who attended each meeting
> - ☐ What was discussed
> - ☐ What was decided
> - ☐ What prudent processes and rationales were used in forming decisions

Figure 3.2

If you engage a qualified financial advisor, he or she can help you establish, assemble, and facilitate your committee. This can include providing ERISA education, sharing best practices, keeping current on hot topics, providing important benchmarking reports, and supporting the much-needed investment expertise required to run your plan. A qualified financial advisor may also have access to an ERISA attorney for input when needed. In short, your financial advisor should be a valuable resource to help ensure your committee is focused on good plan stewardship.

At your first meeting or, at least once every year or so, the agenda should include a review to ensure that all members understand the purpose and objectives of the committee. The committee should establish a formal prudent process for managing the plan's investment strategy; initiate and implement investment decisions; analyze, monitor, and document the plan review; understand the role and duties of service providers; have a general knowledge of products offered; and understand fees and related expenses as these pertain not just to your plan but also to the overall market.

ROLES AND RESPONSIBILITIES

Confirm the fiduciary roles of the plan committee(s), the plan sponsor, the administrator and any nonfiduciary employees.

- ☐ Ensure fiduciaries are educated about their roles.
- ☐ Provide ongoing education and training to committee members.
- ☐ Designate other committee member roles and functions, such as someone to monitor providers, investments and plan compliance; also, name a plan secretary to take detailed meeting minutes, documenting discussions and decisions.
- ☐ Designate roles of employees to act on behalf of the committee. Committee members may allocate specific fiduciary responsibilities, provided that this delegation is in writing and the terms and limitations are specified.

Figure 3.3.

A professional advisor can help lead plan and investment discussions, proficiently answer technical questions raised by the committee, and provide valuable insight to help with the objective oversight of the plan. As the plan "pilot," the advisor should be a lead liaison as expert consultant, but in most cases, the committee should ultimately make the decisions. To do this, the committee should ask difficult questions including how, what, and why; evoke challenging discussions and thoughts about current processes and what can be done to improve the plan; and determine what is working well and how the firm can better help employees pursue retirement success. To run a good plan, the committee needs to be actively involved, deliberate and offer rationale on all decisions made for the best interest of the plan participants and their beneficiaries. In other words, members should be not passive listeners but, rather, active leaders. Figure 3.4 provides an example of committee procedures. I have found it is usually most time-efficient to vote on matters during the meeting to resolve outstanding issues rather than deliberate at a later time, because efficiency is key. Plan reviews can be easy if the committee handles the process proficiently. I've discovered that when decisions are delayed, inefficiencies often develop and risks of inaction increases so I highly encourage committees resolve issues during the meetings.

Usually these meetings occur once every trimester or quarter, depending upon the complexity and size of the plan. Committees for small plans can generally meet semiannually to fulfill their review. When you consider the amount of assets in the 401(k) under your care, you see that dedicating a few hours each year to review the functionality of the plan is not a substantial investment of time. However, this review can provide a substantial benefit to the employees as well as help the employer manage potential fiduciary conflicts. Of course, plan reviews are separate from other management duties such as vendor searches, fiduciary training, and ERISA compliance self-audits.

Finally, if you are forming a new committee or re-engaging a committee, it is probably a good time to review the plan documents, including the Investment Policy Statement. All members should understand the plan's investment strategy and the process for vendor and investment selection. Members must understand that ignorance, bad communication, or inexperience is not an adequate legal defense should the plan fall into question. ERISA requires that plan fiduciaries manage the plan with care, skill, prudence, and diligence. Exercising fiduciary duties is a standard of conduct measured against the conduct of experienced fiduciaries exercising prudence, not against laypersons. As a fiduciary, you are held accountable as a "prudent expert," regardless of your experience. Of course, as already noted, the committee can delegate some duties to "prudent experts." However, outsourcing does not abdicate the plan sponsor from the oversight function.

Remember that the IRS's and Department of Labor's job is to protect your participants and their beneficiaries, not to protect you.

COMMITTEE PROCEDURES

Adopt procedures for committee meetings.

- ☐ Include procedures in the plan charter to help ensure the rules are followed.
- ☐ Conduct quarterly or semi-annual meetings.
- ☐ Create meeting agendas.
- ☐ Document committee meeting attendance.
- ☐ Designate mandatory vs. optional attendance at meetings.
- ☐ Document issues are considered, and decisions made.
- ☐ Have a system for storing minutes.
- ☐ Rotate participant member responsibilities annually.

Figure 3.4

MEETING YOUR FIDUCIARY RESPONSIBILITIES

The duty to act prudently is one of your central responsibilities under ERISA. It requires expertise in a variety of areas, including investments. Lacking that expertise, you will want to hire someone with the necessary knowledge to carry out the investment selection and monitoring, as well as other functions. Prudence focuses on the *process* for making fiduciary decisions, not on the outcome of those decisions. For instance, let's suppose you engage a new payroll provider and the sales representative declares that his firm can cut your 401(k) plan costs and save the plan money. What sounds like a more prudent process – take his proposal at face value and make a decision or spend the time to seek out a variety of providers, ask the same questions of each (including your current provider) and request the same information from every candidate before carefully evaluating the options? Clearly, the later makes far more sense but you may be surprised how often plan sponsors make decisions without conducting the proper due diligence. I understand due diligence requires work and takes time, but it is the only way to place your participant's best interest first and foremost. If, in the end, the provider you choose does not meet your expectations, you are generally not liable for making a bad decision when *you can show you followed a diligent selection process.*

LIMITING LIABILITY

With fiduciary responsibilities comes potential liability. However, fiduciaries can limit their liability in certain situations. One way is to demonstrate you have carried out your responsibilities properly by documenting the process used. Another way is to give participants control over the investments in their accounts. That means being able to choose from a broad range of investment alternatives. Under DOL regulations, there must be at least three different investment options to enable employees to diversify investments, including a fixed account, a stock fund, and a bond fund. Also, participants must be allowed to give investment instructions to change investments at least once a quarter. If you meet these criteria, you may qualify for safe harbor relief under 404(c), which is addressed later in this chapter.

Plans that automatically enroll employees can be set up to provide fiduciary relief from any plan losses that are the result of automatically investing participant contributions in certain default investments. There are four types of investment alternatives for default investments as described in DOL regulations, which I address a little later under "Qualified Default Investment Alternative" (QDIA). An initial and an annual notice must be provided to participants. They must have the opportunity to direct their investments to a broad range of other investment options and be provided information on these options to help them do so. However, while a fiduciary may have relief from liability for the specific investment allocations made by participants or automatic investments, the fiduciary retains the responsibility for selecting and monitoring the investment alternatives that are made available under the plan, including the QDIA.

PLAN BENCHMARKING

Litigation over excessive fees has been pervasive. In 2015 three long-running fee litigation cases settled for over $220 million because of the plan sponsor's failure to use bargaining power to negotiate for lower fees. It may be disturbing and hard to believe, but recordkeepers and plan providers have not been completely transparent with their charges. In fact, litigation in the early 2000s exposed flagrant abuse from recordkeepers who were charging excessive fees, collecting redundant fees, and concealing charges within the many layers of ambiguous expenses. Unfortunately, it is not the provider or the open market that is held responsible for offering fair and reasonable fees, although some providers did get swept up into the lawsuits. It is the plan sponsor's duty as a fiduciary to be sure the fees charged based on the plan selected by the plan sponsor are fair and reasonable.

Even if you don't want to change providers, your fiduciary responsibilities should involve a process called *benchmarking*. Benchmarking is simply a method of ensuring your plan is competitive, whether this be with fees, benefits and services, or investments. When it comes to fees, you should be shopping every few years to ensure your plan is competitively priced. Your findings should be documented and the records maintained to demonstrate your due diligence *process*. Keep in mind, you are not required to change plans if you are pleased with the service and overall support you are receiving, even if the fees are higher than average. However, you are required to ensure the fees are fair and reasonable *relative to the services provided*, and to do this you must know what the going rate is for the services you are getting. So even if you are content with your plan, you should benchmark fees or follow some method to periodically review plan charges to the open market. You must be able to justify the fees. You may be able to negotiate fees with your current provider so they are deemed fair and reasonable.

As your plan assets grow, the pricing will likely come down. But your provider may not voluntarily reduce your fees without your prompting. Some providers have pricing on older contracts that is substantially more than they would bid on a new contract. In other words, if you were a new customer, you would get a lower price. But if you don't benchmark your plan, you have no way of knowing how your plan's pricing model compares to the market, and your participants could be paying more than they should. Since fees impact investment outcomes, this is an important step for you to take, not only because it is important for you as a plan fiduciary but also because it helps drive retirement success.

Benchmarking your plan and discussions around the results should be addressed with your committee during committee meetings. While the chair or secretary may be appointed to conduct the vendor search, your financial advisor can be very helpful with the process. The committee should be presented with the information needed to make a sound decision for plan management. When such a matter is deferred to a committee, a more comprehensive thought process is likely to be followed, compared to, say, a CFO or HR Manager gathering proposals and selecting the best plan based on his or her own judgment. Again, ERISA is focused on the *process*, not the results. Although a committee is not required, you can see that it certainly may promote a more consistent and more thorough compliance process. Figure 3.5 highlights the core fiduciary requirements.

The DOL has described this in a regulation as requiring that a fiduciary:

1. Engage in an objective, thorough, analytical search with the purpose to gather relevant information;
2. Appropriately consider the information;
3. Reach a documented conclusion based on the information and analysis; and
4. If necessary, engage independent advisors to help with the process.

Figure 3.5.

Fiduciaries have an obligation to engage in an objective, detailed process that not only considers competing providers' fees, services, and products but also considers the needs of the plan and its participants. By using the basic framework outlined in this chapter, fiduciaries should be able to make reasonable decisions and satisfy their fiduciary obligations. The goal is to engage in a prudent selection and monitoring process. I highly recommend that you consider engaging an independent qualified advisor to help with the process.

Providers are not deemed fiduciaries at this point, unless you have a specific fiduciary contract, and even so, they may only be investment fiduciaries for example. Keep in mind, representatives from your provider are inherently going to focus on serving their interests first. Providers are in the business of making money by keeping you in their plan. You will not find providers offering provider searches, and if they did, you must consider the potential conflict of interest. Any reports you use to assess fees need to allow you to conduct an objective analysis, which is why outside sources may be better for this review. I have seen providers who offer in-house investment experts overweight investment menus with proprietary funds (funds managed by the provider that tend to create the highest revenue for themselves), which can create a conflict. Therefore, engaging an outside advisor who stands to enjoy no financial gain by the choice of recordkeeper, TPA, or investment options probably make far more sense and may be more apt to reduce your risk.

Although in the past retirement plan oversight was considered an arcane responsibility, it is not anymore. In-house plan administrators need to be well trained and have an audit checklist that will at a minimum show due diligence in managing the plan. Employers are well advised to review and strategize the requirements for due diligence with their retirement plan.

PLAN FEES

Understanding and monitoring your retirement plan's fees is not just a fiduciary requirement; it's also a good practice. This process has been enforced through DOL plan audits and high-profile litigation. Fees can be grouped into several categories: recordkeeping, administrative, legal, plan advisory, investment, and education and communication. The principal reason fees have been thrust into the limelight is that plan participants often bear most, if not all, of the cost of running the plan. The purpose of compliance is not for the regulators to determine if your plan fees are reasonable, but rather to ensure you follow a process or method for monitoring fees and assessing their fairness. In fact, the DOL has been silent on the issue of what amount is fair and reasonable, which affords you, as plan sponsor, the opportunity to determine the most appropriate structure for your plan based on your needs and demographics. But the law clearly states that you must understand your plan fees. I have seen too many cases where plan sponsors have neglected to understand the scope of the expenses being charged to their participants.

In concept, the fee benchmarking process is to enable you to compare your plan's fees to those on the open market of comparable plans based on size, assets, and plan demographics. The objective is to know that what your participants are paying is fair and reasonable *relative to the market*. The process, in reality, is no different from the due diligence you would follow when making any major purchase. When you bought your last car, did you pay the MSRP, or did you shop around, compare prices at different dealerships, and then negotiate? Of course, the difference with the 401(k) is the complexity and intangible nature of the product. This makes it very difficult for the layperson to understand and properly assess value. In the absence of this knowledge, value is limited to price and price only. Unfortunately, I find that too many plan sponsors or retirement committees make decisions without considering the sum of the services, and after a tedious plan conversion process, they learn they ultimately get what they pay for. Are you going to buy your teenage son or daughter the cheapest car you can find? Probably not.

The fee analysis is an opportunity to be sure you understand all fees and expenses, including any "hidden" fees such as revenue sharing. In chapter 7, I review all aspects of plan fees. In order to fulfill your duties as a fiduciary, you need to understand how your plan fees are being charged, why they are being charged, who is paying them, and what comparable plans of similar size and service models are charging. The objective is to avoid excessive fees. If you monitor and negotiate your plan fees as if you were paying them out of your own pocket, you will surely ask tough questions and be sure to have a clear understanding of all charges. That, along with good documentation, will enable you to conclude and substantiate what is best for your participants in a similar manner as you would do for yourself. If you treat your plan with that level of care, you will more likely inherently follow a prudent due diligence process.

INVESTMENT BENCHMARKING

How do you know if your investments are performing great, okay, or poorly? Your duty is to ensure not only that your participants are not being overcharged excessive fees but also that they have a reasonably priced and competitively performing investment menu. If you are like most, you compare your investment performance to the broad indexes such as the S&P 500 or the Dow Jones Industrial Average, and you may feel satisfied so long as your investments appear to be meeting or exceeding the benchmark returns. You may also conclude that if your participants aren't content, they can merely change their investments to other options within your menu. But in doing so, you may be ignoring or discounting underperforming funds and that means you may be putting your participants at a disadvantage.

Investment benchmarking is a process of measuring your investments against the corresponding index or comparable peers in terms of return and risk, among other important metrics. There are literally thousands of possible benchmarks available, so no matter what the composition of your individual investment menu, you should be able to find meaningful comparisons for each fund you hold in your menu. For accurate assessment, your funds should not all be measured against the same index. Perhaps the most important value of investment benchmarking is that comparing a portfolio's returns to a benchmark is a way to measure your portfolio manager's skill. It answers the question, "What value was added by the manager's decisions?" Obviously, this works well for actively managed funds.

Benchmarks not only measure returns but also help measure risk and determine whether the return adequately compensated shareholders for the risk involved. Keep in mind, investments should be benchmarked against their peers and their corresponding index. For instance, you want to compare each fund to other funds of similar objective and also against the index that would most adequately align to that fund. Of course, you wouldn't compare the performance of a US stock fund to that of the European stock index or the performance of a short-term US government bond fund to one that is part of China's stock market. While that seems obvious, plan sponsors are usually quite bewildered as to how to properly track and monitor investments. This is why engaging a financial advisor as an investment expert makes good sense.

Monitoring reports and analyses provided by third-party specialists instead of those provided by your recordkeeper's proprietary software may help prevent any appearance of conflict and better enable you to be fair and reasonable in the evaluation. Provider or proprietary software may not provide that impartiality. As a plan fiduciary, you need to be careful in your objectivity. I recommend you consider using third-party information to analyze investments. We often provide second opinions and benchmarking analysis reports, which can differ dramatically from proprietary evaluations. Morningstar is the leading provider of investment research used by many institutions. It is a trusted source of information on mutual funds, stocks, and so forth, and one that many plan sponsors use as a tool for evaluating their investments. Although it is not without flaws, it is considered a trustworthy and reliable industry source.

Perhaps one of the greatest controversies in the investment world is the argument for passive versus active management. Passive managers often argue that active managers frequently fail to match or beat their benchmark, and they question the reliability of active managers' methods for recognizing and predicting trends. Active managers argue that the lack of downside risk in an index fund subjects shareholders to sharper losses and compromises results because ultimately investors are more concerned with risk than they are with returns. Instead of siding with either of these controversial views, it is generally deemed best practice to remain objective and include both passively and actively managed funds in your investment menu. There is truly no right or wrong answer when it comes to the active approach versus the passive approach; it's rather a matter of opinion. Some participants prefer the low-cost index method, while others want a management team at the helm. If you define your process through your Investment Policy Statement (IPS), your committee will know what types of investments you will include in your investment menu. It's a good idea to note whether both active and passive investments are to be included. A well-written IPS also defines the monitoring process.

INVESTMENT POLICY STATEMENT

An Investment Policy Statement (IPS) provides the framework for sound investment management. Having your management policy formally documented not only helps you follow a prudent process for choosing and evaluating investment options but is also one of the most powerful tools available for reducing your fiduciary liability. The Department of Labor even states, "If an investment policy statement has been properly formulated and memorialized, all prudent procedures covered will fall into place. This is predicated upon the fact that liability usually occurs when the fiduciary has failed to act in this area as opposed to acting improperly."

Such strong language from the DOL makes it quite clear that a well-written Investment Policy Statement can help you manage your fiduciary obligations. Of course, the objective is to have a "properly formulated" IPS, which means the language must be carefully considered. Additionally, your IPS should unite your company vision and mission and the investment objectives of your plan. Because the IPS can serve as the cornerstone to regulatory and legal compliance and provide the documented justification of the plan's mission and investment objectives, the wording is especially important. Engaging an ERISA attorney to help you write or review your IPS is probably wise. Keep in mind, an IPS is written primarily to provide a discipline for evaluating and monitoring your investment's performance. Therefore, the statement should include specific language about that process.

That being said, ERISA does not state that having an Investment Policy Statement is required. However, it is difficult to build an investment strategy for a plan without one. Having an Investment Policy Statement is a best practice; nonetheless, 20 percent of all plans do not have an Investment Policy Statement in place, and nearly one-third of all plans under $10 million in assets lack this document, according to a recent Deloitte Consulting 401(k) survey. It's difficult to fulfill your investment management duties without defining a prudent process. The IPS is a great tool to help you accomplish this. It should also be noted that if your plan gets investigated by the DOL, on the list of items for review is your Investment Policy Statement, which makes a rather strong statement of its importance to the regulators.

What does your Investment Policy Statement say? When was the last time you reviewed it? You need to review your IPS regularly and be sure it is written consistent with the guidelines you follow and set as your plan objectives. Your IPS should define your plan's overall investment philosophy and investment objectives; clearly identify who is responsible for choosing and monitoring the plan's investments; explain how the plan will construct its investment menu and how it determines what investment options to offer, including which asset classes were chosen and why; identify how the plan will evaluate the investment funds offered and under what circumstances the plan will remove investment funds or managers; and indicate how that process will be managed.

Investment Policy Statement
Framework for Sound Management

QDIA
Identify your selected QDIA

Education
Procedures for trustees' and participants' education and advice

404(c)
The plan's intent to be compliant with ERISA Section 404(c)

Responsibilities
A documented structure of roles and responsibilities that can be understood by all interested parties

Modern Portfolio Theory
Specific methods used to apply the Modern Portfolio Theory (MPT) and identify the limitations of MPT

Investment Selection Process
A well laid out identification of the method of selection, evaluation, periodic review, "watch list"

Timeline
An explicit timeline to regularly review and updated the document

Participant's Risks
A proper accounting of real risks as they pertain to the plan's exact demographics

Vision and Mission Statement
Reiteration of your firm's vision and mission statement

Declaration
A declaration that the IPS is consistent with the institution's corporate goals

Objectives
A statement of plan objectives

Investment Menu
"The current investment menu and asset allocation goals

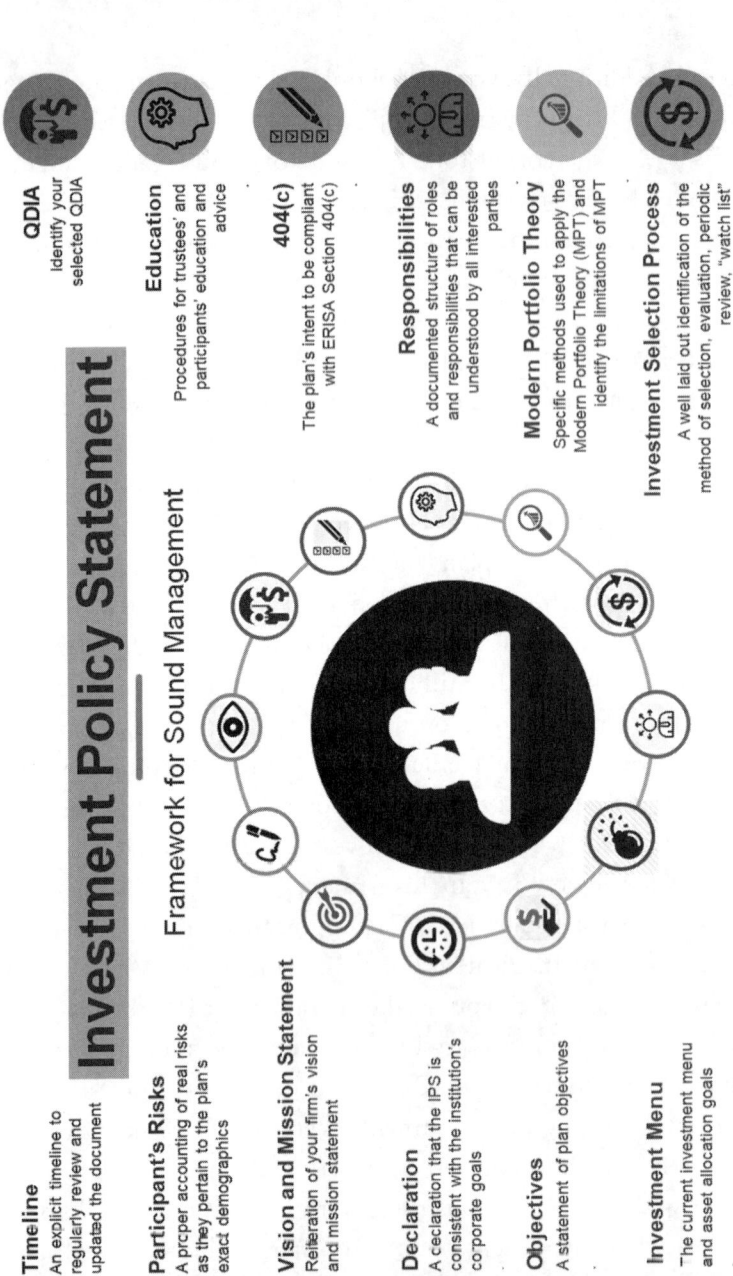

Figure 3.6.

When you consider the depth of this process, ask yourself: *How well am I following this process for my plan right now?* Are you relying on your plan provider to do this for you? If so, does that follow the prudent process of being objective? Probably not. Does that fulfill your fiduciary duties? Not according to the law. Has your own advisor neglected to discuss the value and significance of your IPS? Is your plan weighted toward proprietary investments (those managed by your provider)? Is that consistent with your IPS? How are you monitoring potential conflicts of interest for your participants with the funds selected in your menu? You should know there has been much litigation around the area of proprietary funds. Are these funds monitored appropriately against their true benchmark and peer group?

Without a written statement in place, plan sponsors may be less effective in evaluating their investments uniformly. Now is a good time to review your IPS and ask: *Does my plan have all the elements of an appropriate Investment Policy Statement, or do I only think I have all the elements?* There is no one right way to develop an investment policy. The aim is to have criteria for evaluating investments and to follow them. The regulators are less likely to hold plan sponsors accountable for investment performance, but you will be held accountable for your management process. If you do not have an investment policy in place, it may be difficult to corroborate your process. Of course, if you have an IPS, you must follow it. This is not something that should merely be written and filed away.

Figure 3.6 highlights some key components of an effective Investment Policy Statement. Keep in mind, having a statement is important, but if you don't follow it, it is useless. In fact, probably the only thing worse than not having an IPS is having one and not adhering to it.

Once a year I review the IPS with every plan committee I work with. This helps remind everyone of the process, the purpose, and the end goal. We always have the IPS available when we review the investments, as we often may refer to it as a guideline when adding or removing investments. Now is a good time to review your statement and ensure you understand the language and follow the written protocol. You may find it is time to rewrite your IPS to align it to your organization's objectives and capabilities.

404(C)

Section 404(c) is a largely misunderstood but important benefit within ERISA. The potential impact here is substantial. As already mentioned, you have a legal responsibility for the investments in your 401(k). The law clearly states that you must select investments that minimize the risk of large losses, and this is even true for "participant directed" plans such as the 401(k). The general rule is that as an ERISA plan fiduciary, you are liable for all aspects of investment selection and monitoring of plan investments and are on the hook for any participant who claims fiduciary breach should something go wrong. But section 404(c) provides a limited exception to this general rule that can help mitigate your liability.

Section 404(c) only applies to individual account plans, such as a 401(k), where participants can direct investments within their accounts. If your 401(k) satisfies 404(c), plan fiduciaries will not be liable for any claim of a breach related to a participant's investment selection. For example, let's say your employee ignores the principles of proper diversification and invests all of his assets in your plan's China fund. The fund subsequently loses half its value in one year. The participant cannot make a claim for fiduciary breach related to his selection of the fund *unless* he can successfully claim that the plan did not properly follow 404(c). Of course, the participant could claim a fiduciary breach citing the fact that your plan offered this particular fund on its investment menu in the first place, provided it can be proved that your selection and/or monitoring of the fund was imprudent. Consequently, the relief from fiduciary liability offered under 404(c) is limited in scope. But it costs nothing to enjoy this limited relief provided you follow the rules for compliance. In today's litigious world, I think you would agree that every little bit of liability reduction helps.

If the requirements of ERISA section 404(c) are met, fiduciaries are not liable for any loss or for any breach that results from a participant's or beneficiary's exercise of control over assets in his or her account. If, in a plan that meets the requirements of ERISA section 404(c), the participant imprudently selects investments that lose money, plan fiduciaries generally are not liable. Thus, 404(c) frames the duty to monitor investments in a unique way. Clearly, a plan sponsor wants to monitor for continued compliance with 404(c), but if the fiduciary is satisfied that the plan complies with 404(c), then your obligation to monitor *individual* participant investment decisions is in effect eliminated. However, this is not entirely true, because you still have an obligation to monitor for the ongoing prudence of the inclusion of the funds in the menu, as discussed above.

COMPLIANCE WITH 404(C)

To be compliant, a plan, according to ERISA section 404(c), must provide a "broad range of investment alternatives." This means a plan must offer at least three investment alternatives, as follows:

1. These investments must be diversified.
2. They must have materially different risk and return characteristics.
3. They should enable participants to achieve a portfolio with aggregate risk and return characteristics at any point within the range normally appropriate for the participant.

Note that when combined, these investments should reduce the overall risk of a participant's portfolio.

In its most simplistic form, a money market fund, bond mutual fund, or stock mutual fund could fulfill these requirements. However, most plan sponsors today use target date funds to fulfill this requirement. Please refer to the section of chapter 6 on investment menu options for additional information.

Regardless of how you choose to comply with 404(c), please keep in mind that the initial decisions with respect to these issues should be reviewed from time to time. For instance, the plan fiduciary should (re)consider if the plan has at least three investment alternatives that in the aggregate enable participants to "achieve a portfolio with aggregate risk and return characteristics at any point within the range normally appropriate for the participant."

404(C) IS THE EXCEPTION, NOT THE RULE

In order to qualify for 404(c) safe harbor relief, three categories of requirements must be met, as highlighted in figure 3.7.

Investment Menu Requirements → Plan Design and Administrative Requirements → Information and Disclosure Requirements

Figure 3.7.

ERISA 404(c) states you must offer a broad range of investment alternatives with differing potential for investment risk and return. Only three investment options are required to meet the requirements, and this can be satisfied by offering funds that cover equity, fixed income, and capital preservation asset classes. You will probably want to go beyond that and offer an array of stock, bond, and money market funds in your investment menu. Whichever the case may be, the rules are quite clearly stated in figure 3.8.

It is important to note that the 404(c) safe harbor must be formally elected in your plan document and indicated on your Form 5500 filing in order for you to benefit from the liability relief under 404(c). You also must offer a broad range of investments within your investment menu and provide all participants the opportunity to control their investments. Most plans follow these investment requirements, but it's a good idea to check to be sure your plan documents declare your plan is treated under 404(c). It never ceases to amaze me how many plan sponsors unknowingly neglect to note their intent to be 404(c) compliant on their 5500 filings or how many plan sponsors acknowledge the intent and then fail to comply with the rules. Either way, you may not truly enjoy the benefit of the protection if you don't follow the requirements.

INVESTMENT MENU REQUIREMENTS

ERISA section 404(c) generally requires a plan to offer a "broad range of investment alternatives."

- ☐ The investments available under the plan are sufficient to provide the participant a chance to materially affect (i) the potential returns in his or her account and (ii) the degree of risk to which it is subject
- ☐ The plan offers at least three investment alternatives that:
  - Are diversified
  - Have materially different risk and return characteristics
  - Enable the participant to achieve a portfolio with aggregate risk and return characteristics at any point within the range appropriate for the participant
- ☐ When combined with the others, each tends to minimize risk to the portfolio through diversification
- ☐ Participants are given the opportunity to diversify their accounts sufficiently to avoid large losses

---

Figure 3.8.

However, declaring that your plan is 404(c) elected is not enough. You must also provide the required disclosures to your participants, including a notice that the plan is a 404(c) plan. Such notice is mandatory. It needs to declare that a 404(c) plan may relieve the trustee of responsibility for investment losses. Your disclosure must also provide a description of investment choices and risks involved, provide a description of fees, and define procedures for, and limits on, participant-directed investment instructions. However, as already noted, 404(c) is an exception and not a rule, so keep in mind that plan fiduciaries remain liable for the selection and monitoring of all investment options made available to the participant based on the prudent care law.

QUALIFIED DEFAULT INVESTMENT ALTERNATIVE

Since you cannot force an employee to make his or her own investment elections, you should consider having a "default investment." Called a "Qualified Default Investment Alternative" (QDIA), this is designed to reduce liability for plan sponsors when participants fail to make their investment elections. The default investment option applies to all plans but is especially important if you have auto-enrollment, a safe harbor nonelective plan, or a Profit Sharing plan. This is because when employees neglect to make their own investment allocations, you fall in to the role of decision maker for them, which could subject you to fiduciary risk. However, by directing those contributions to your QDIA (provided your plan designates a Qualified Default Investment Alternative), you will not be held liable for any potential losses resulting from the investment performance.

The intent of directing a suitable QDIA is to encourage employees to invest in assets that are suitable for long-term retirement savings. If a plan sponsor fails to designate a QDIA or fails to fulfill the QDIA requirements, it is critical to know fiduciaries can be held responsible for losses when a participant neglects to direct his or her investments. The Department of Labor's regulations governing QDIAs identify three "types" of investments that would be considered a QDIA. It can be a balanced or risk-based fund, a target date fund (TDF), or a professionally managed account. Since very few 401(k)'s offer individual professionally managed accounts, the standard QDIA is either a target date fund, asset allocation, or balanced fund. Whichever you select, know the rules state funds that do not have fixed income allocations do not qualify as QDIA, nor do funds that lack equity exposure. Some older plans may have the money market or stable value fund as their default fund, which does not meet current requirements. Consequently, now may be a good time to ask your advisor what your QDIA is. I do occasionally run into plans that have not updated their QDIA since the rule change in 2007. This means some plan sponsors are exposed to undue risks.

PLAN DESIGN AND ADMINISTRATIVE REQUIREMENTS

ERISA section 404(c) generally requires a plan to allow participants the opportunity to control their investments:

- ☐ Under the terms of the plan, participants are given the opportunity to give investment instructions to an identified fiduciary who is obligated to follow those instructions (except in certain defined circumstances, such as prohibited transactions, etc.)
- ☐ If participants do not give investment instructions in writing, they must be given an opportunity to receive a written confirmation of their instructions
- ☐ Participants have the ability to change investments with a frequency appropriate in light of the volatility of the investments

---

Figure 3.9.

IN SUMMARY

Our national retirement crisis has the potential to impact everyone. Even those who are adequately prepared for retirement may be impacted by deteriorating investment returns, inferior health care, and higher taxes. Businesses could be impacted by diminished consumer spending capacity and rising operating expenses. Workers may be impacted by rising health-care costs and increased Social Security and Medicare taxes. The government will likely be faced with growing deficits. Our nation is at risk to be adversely impacted economically, fiscally, and socially. We must work diligently, responsibly, and earnestly to strive to change the future for America.

While ERISA does not require that you establish a 401(k) or any type of employer-sponsored retirement plan, it does say that if you do decide to sponsor a plan, you are held to the highest level of the law as a plan fiduciary. The Department of Labor is responsible for enforcing ERISA compliance, and believe me, if you are not following their guidelines, you will have a hard defense if you ever need one. The nation's lack of retirement readiness has gained government attention, and because of this, DOL audits and litigation are on the rise.

Financially, it just does not make good business sense for plan sponsors to ignore their 401(k) plan or shirk their fiduciary duties. At the very least, the liability is too great, but more importantly, your employees need your advocacy. Keep in mind, your 5500 form is public record, and anyone can review it online. For professionals in the industry, it is quite easy to recognize inconsistencies on the 5500 forms, which may identify targets for potential fiduciary breach. In fact, the Department of Labor reviews these filings regularly.

Over the past several years, some large law firms have enjoyed tremendous success suing plan sponsors, to the extent that now smaller law firms are using the same process and replicating this model, both with smaller 401(k) plans and nonprofits and universities. Success breeds duplicity. Because your fiduciary requirements are no different from those of any other plan regardless of your company or plan size, you should be aware. Large firms may appear to be targets for lawsuits, but they have been working toward compliance over the past several years. Smaller firms, on the other hand, lack the resources, time, and knowledge to dedicate to their 401(k), so they can be easy targets for fiduciary breach. That is why having the right 401(k) team working in partnership with you is so important in today's regulatory environment.

You have a duty to act in the best interest of your participants. This is *your* duty, not the duty of your plan provider or recordkeeper. This means that you need to be a prudent expert and follow prudent procedures. If you are not an expert, you need to go out and find one. That is arguably the benefit and value of a good financial advisor. The financial advisor should share in your responsibilities, duties, and risk, not just collect compensation from the plan. As a co-fiduciary, your financial advisor can help lead you toward fiduciary compliance and help your employees pursue retirement success. In the absence of a qualified advisor acting as a plan fiduciary, you bear the sole responsibility to ensure you are following the rules, fulfilling your duties, and managing your plan solely for the benefit of your participants and beneficiaries.

CHAPTER 4
PROVIDERS AND ADMINISTRATORS

Mitch recently joined your firm as the employee relations advisor. His job is to make sure everyone is treated fairly and to seek to protect the employer from undue risks. He understands employment law and serves as a liaison between managers and employees to help resolve employee conflicts. He had some concerns about the investment performance in your 401(k), having noticed the funds seemed to be underperforming. Upon further investigation, he noticed the plan fees and fund expenses seemed to be higher than normal. Also, several employees had commented that the provider service was lacking. He has approached you, the CFO, to ask for documentation showing why you chose the provider you have and showing a comparative market analysis of fees. He further expressed concern about the investments and wanted to see your latest benchmarking report. As CFO, how do you respond to Mitch?

Plan sponsors have many choices when selecting providers for their 401(k) plans. The challenge for many businesses, especially smaller businesses, is in finding the time to search for the right provider and even to know what a good provider looks like. Recordkeepers can vary significantly with service models and cost, but most plan sponsors are not familiar with the variety of providers and service models that are available. Even if your plan is set up perfectly today, your needs may change over time. Plan assets grow, and the number of participants can change. As your assets grow, your pricing may be able to be reduced. Likewise, as the number of participants increases or decreases, your service needs may change. Therefore, it is good practice to review your plan regularly to see if plan design changes can be implemented to improve the plan. It is your fiduciary duty to make sure that plan costs are fair and reasonable. If your plan has changed dramatically since you started with your recordkeeper, it could call for a complete change in providers. However, you may find this is a task that can quickly become overwhelming. This chapter will discuss the different providers and administrator options plan sponsors have and how to evaluate vendors.

TRUST VS. GROUP ANNUITY PLATFORM

Retirement plans are typically held at either a mutual fund company, brokerage firm, bank, or life insurance company, and they are either classified as a "trust" or "group annuity." The differences between the two arrangements are nearly indistinguishable in most ways. Mutual fund companies, brokerage firms, and bank platforms are known as "trusts" and generally allow for direct investments into mutual funds via share purchases, whereas the insurance company 401(k) platform is called a "group annuity" contract where assets are invested in funds via separate accounts and acquire "units" of the funds that are held separate from the general assets of the insurance company. For the most part, there is little difference between the two, and one is not necessarily better than the other.

There is generally said to be no cost advantage to one over the other, although group annuity contracts may carry additional expenses, including withdrawal and transfer charges. You may find group annuity contracts offer a more restrictive share class option. This means your participants may pay retail pricing versus institutional pricing. While not all group annuity contracts have these restrictions or impose withdrawal and/or transfer charges, it is important to understand, review, and compare all fees on your proposals. To confuse the layperson even more, it is important to know that group annuity contracts have nothing to do with individual annuities. Individual annuities are a completely different product. In fact, usually group annuity 401(k) platforms do not even offer retirement annuity options for your participants. By annuity, I mean the ability to generate an income via lifetime or guaranteed payments as opposed to lump-sum withdrawals or discretionary distributions. This alternative distribution option may be attractive for employees who don't want to have to continue to budget and manage their savings through retirement.

An income annuity is similar to a pension income. Regardless, the distribution options available to your employees are governed by your plan adoption agreement. If you decide you would like to allow income distribution options, such an arrangement would be in addition to lump-sum distribution options available upon termination or retirement. I discuss this arrangement more as a part of plan design in chapter 5.

However, in the 401(k) world, typically group annuity contracts do not have any insurance or income riders. Therefore, 401(k) contracts are for the sole purpose of enabling insurance companies to provide recordkeeping services for qualified retirement plans. Both the trust and insurance platforms are designed to provide your employees with a means to accumulate tax-deferred retirement assets and invest in pooled investments, and in both cases the money stays in the participant's account until withdrawn. Starting early and saving more is the goal for retirement success. A 401(k) provider who can offer you the most supportive role in accomplishing that goal, with fair and reasonable fees, should be the focus, regardless of the platform.

Funding your retirement plan through a trust platform or an annuity contract is a decision that should be based on the same criteria—plan costs, investment options, service models, and features and benefits. The difference between the two platforms is otherwise largely immaterial to participants and plan sponsors. What really matters to your participants are fees, technology, and investment access.

OPEN ARCHITECTURE PLANS / INVESTMENT OPTIONS

As you review your current plan or shop plan providers, you will discover that a distinct difference between vendors may lie in the investment access. While initially you may not have given much thought or consideration to the importance of the investment options, as you dig deeper into reviewing your plan and understand how to compare plans, you will likely quickly discover how critical investment access can be.

Open architecture plans provide access to nearly unlimited mutual funds or even exchange-traded funds (ETFs) and may include collective investment trusts (CITs). Having access to literally thousands of fund options and a wide range of share class alternatives with complete independence, fee transparency, and without proprietary fund investment requirements can be a very valuable benefit. However, it also can be quite overwhelming, especially if you are not engaging an investment expert (i.e., financial advisor) on your 401(k) team. In general, you will only find open architecture offered through trust platforms (i.e. mutual fund, brokerage, or bank plan providers). While insurance platforms tend to offer a more restrictive list of investment options, they have been expanding those options over the past several years. Unlike open architecture, insurance companies typically provide some level of prescreening of fund options for monitoring purposes. While this may not replace your fiduciary due diligence requirements, smaller plan sponsors may find the condensed list of options available via insurance platforms easier to manage. The trade-off, however, is having less access to potentially superior investments.

All providers or recordkeepers generally offer a menu of investment options that typically have limits. It can range from as few as forty or fifty funds to as many as two hundred fifty or six thousand or more. Regardless, as a plan sponsor you ought to avoid confusing your participants by opening up the full list of options to them. Best practices suggest funds should be narrowed down in your customized investment menu specifically selected for your plan from your provider's list of options to a more manageable figure. Some plan sponsors are offering the full gamut of investments to their employees, which could be two hundred different options. One of the largest providers in the small plan market (an insurance platform) says their average plan sponsor has fifty-one investment options available in their investment menu. However, too many investment options have been proven to be overwhelming and confusing for participants. ERISA best practice trends indicate fiduciaries consider limiting the number of options so as to prevent participants from taking investment missteps. Remember, the DOL recognizes that most plan participants are investment novices and prone to making mistakes. Your job as a fiduciary is to place your participant's best interest first. Knowing that your participants are not investment experts and given that most are unskilled and inexperienced investors, are you putting their best interest first when offering fifty or more different investment options? How many of your employees know the difference between a stock and a bond—let alone the difference between the "Melbourne Total Market Index Fund," the "Coleman S&P 500 Index Fund," and the "Dynasty Equity Fund?" Do *you* even know the difference between the funds within your menu?

I realize some of your employees may like having the broad array of options and enjoy a sense of control by having so many choices. But the truth is, too many choices tend to stymie most employees. If you look at your participant elections, the odds are that the majority of plan assets are in target date funds or similar asset allocation funds. If so, this is very telling. Most participants want to set it and forget and let professionals manage the money. Offering too many options can cripple employees and compel them to make bad choices, enticing them into performance chasing or even a day-trading mentality. ERISA does not set limits on the number of investment options you can or cannot offer your participants, so if you feel offering an abundance of options fosters success, it is your decision to make. It is also your decision to defend should you ever be challenged. The US

Supreme Court says 401(k) plan sponsors have a duty to monitor the investment options they offer, which means you will be held liable for monitoring and managing your full investment menu. Managing and monitoring a robust investment menu of fifty or more options puts more work and more risk on you as a plan sponsor. Furthermore, you may want to consider the fact that the courts favor a more manageable list of options as being better suited for plan participants.

Therefore, the objective when comparing service providers is to review the list of options available in order to determine if that list is sufficient to properly manage your investment options for many years into the future. While your plan may only need one or two large-cap growth funds, you will likely want to be able to choose from a robust selection of large-cap growth funds to have the flexibility to change the funds in the future in order to maintain a competitive menu. You might feel it is best to have a more stable growth fund available to your employees with low stock turnover rather than that high-flying superstar fund of the year. Or you may feel the high-turnover, consistent top-quartile performer fits within the rest of your investment menu. Perhaps you would rather have the largest growth fund in terms of assets; a name your employees might be familiar with. Or maybe you believe your participants would rather benefit from a smaller but strong-performing fund that may be more nimble. Do you have sufficient options with your current recordkeeper from which you can choose? Keep in mind that if your selected fund underperforms and you want to replace it, it makes little sense to have access only to a small handful of replacement options. This is the same consideration you must make for each of the important asset classes you wish to include in your menu. A provider with a limited investment menu may not fit the bill because the objective is to carve out your own selected list from your providers' options to offer your participants adequate and suitable investments aligned to your Investment Policy Statement and plan goals.

Once you establish the right mix of investments, you can and should be adding and/or removing funds based on your due diligence.

Of course, you must consider the availability of investment options through your recordkeeper, which is why having access to a larger pool of investments creates better opportunities for investment success. You and your committee can work with your investment expert to create and seek to maintain a superior investment menu that can help your employees retire ready. Of course, any investment selections should follow your Investment Policy Statement (IPS) and your IPS should cover all the core asset classes to be sure your employees can individually create a competitive investment portfolio that aims to build retirement security based on different ages and risk temperaments.

If you have participants (namely, executives) who want even more investment flexibility, you may consider adding a self-directed brokerage window option. This provides access to trade in the open market within the plan on an individual basis. The employee opens up an online trading account specifically designated through your 401(k) provider, and he or she can then buy and sell securities on his or her own, typically with very little restriction. Your recordkeeper is still responsible to track and record activity on the statement, etc. But those assets are held outside the plan and are typically billed separately. To protect your liability and for better risk management, most plan sponsors or providers limit the percentage of the account that can be invested in an SDO (self-directed option) to no more than 50 percent, although less might be even wiser. Of course, there is much debate over offering a brokerage window option and the fiduciary liabilities involved. The costs typically are much higher, and since you cannot discriminate in whom you offer this option to, you do have the risk that inexperienced participants could turn their retirement savings into a bit of a poker hand and undermine their retirement. But this option is usually available by most providers so if you think it is in the best interest of your participants be sure to ask about it. You can read more about investment menus and brokerage options in chapter 6, where I address the pros and cons of this approach.

When negotiating for a new recordkeeper, access to quality

investment options should be a key factor. Unfortunately, many plan sponsors (not being investment experts themselves) are not mindful of the disparity of returns within specific investment asset classes. While most all plan sponsors these days want to be sure to have access to large-cap stocks like the S&P 500 Index, and while they want to offer active and passive funds, additional choices to invest in small-cap stock funds as well as international stocks and so forth need to be carefully considered. There ought to be much scrutiny of the actual risk–return metrics of the individual investment options. A large part of the recent litigation has been centered on investment options, performance, and share classes. As a fiduciary, you must not ignore or discount an underperforming fund. And certainly, don't assume a fund is underperforming because of market conditions. It may be underperforming because of poor management. Also, don't neglect your duties to monitor on the basis that your participants can just move their money around to different investment options. You cannot mitigate your liability by offering five different small-cap funds. ERISA makes it very clear that there must be rationale for why each investment is included in the menu and that you must conduct ongoing documented investment reviews.

To fulfill your fiduciary duties, you need the flexibility to exchange your investment menu so as to eliminate inferior-performing funds. Having access to a full investment menu of alternative options available through your provider is critical to do the best job you can for your participants. A five star-performing management team based on past performance is not necessarily going to continue to be a star-performing team in the future. While your employees may choose a "plug and play" approach, if you follow that same method, it could put you in fiduciary breach. Consider that management turnover or poor management decisions can directly impact not only performance but also cash flows. An underperforming fund is less likely to attract new investment dollars; therefore, it may be further handicapped by having to sell securities in order to meet redemptions. This can exacerbate losses, especially in a down market.

The difference in fund performance between comparable funds can be substantial. There could be a significant difference in returns between top-quartile and bottom-quartile performers. Although returns are not the only factor you should consider when selecting investments, investment performance is clearly a key driver to retirement success. Therefore, it is important for plan sponsors or retirement committees to keep a watchful eye on the investment performance and have access to sufficient alternative options without having to change providers should the current portfolio managers fail to deliver results.

Average investment returns can make the difference between your employees retiring sooner or running out of money in retirement. Over a thirty-year or longer period of time, even a small differential in compounded returns can translate into significant dollars in retirement accounts. Too often, I find plan sponsors ignoring the value and importance of investment access and monitoring. While larger plan sponsors have instituted investment monitoring policies, smaller plan sponsors often take a "set it and forget it" approach to their 401(k)'s. If you have not reviewed your investment menu since you initially set it up, or even in the past year, it is time to review your options and consider adding or removing funds. It is not good practice to assume your funds are competitive just because your vendor offers them, even if the vendor provides some screening services. Some vendors may tout investment monitoring as a value-added service, but this is not a substitute for your own evaluation. Vendor investment screening, if it is performed at all by your provider, is certainly unlikely to be scrutinized with the same goals or guidelines within your Investment Policy Statement. The ability to remove lagging investments and replace them with a more competitive option is important, and the greater the investment access and more attentive you are with your oversight, the greater chances you have of helping your employees achieve retirement readiness.

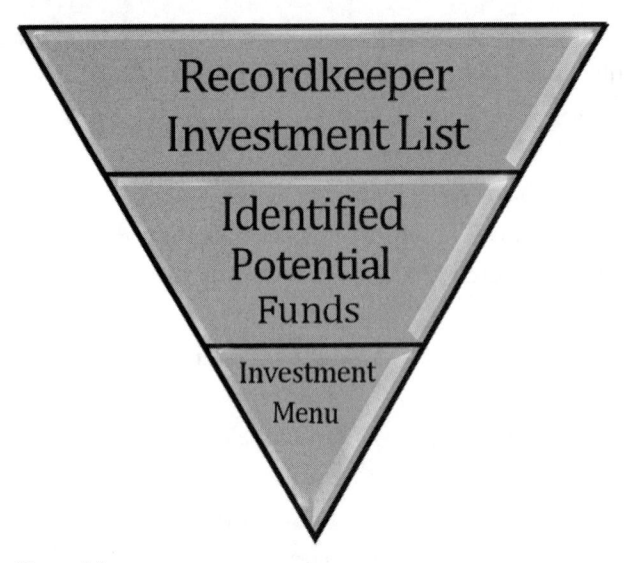

Figure 4.1.

This is not to say that open architecture is a mandate for a superior 401(k). It is important, however, to realize that the ability to customize your fund lineup based on the needs of your participants is central to their ability to grow their savings and that having limited access may restrict your ability to craft a superior investment menu. In general, just as there is an ideal number of investments to include in your investment menu to give your participants sufficient means to diversify and properly asset-allocate their retirement savings, there is an ideal number of investments available by a good vendor that allows you the flexibility you need to maintain a competitive menu for your participants. What that number is depends on the size and needs of your plan, however suffice it to say that you need a robust list of options. Open architecture certainly gives you the greatest liberty, but admittedly without the help of an objective professional investment expert, such vast options can be daunting for the plan sponsor and retirement committee to sort through.

THIRD-PARTY ADMINISTRATION—BUNDLED VS. UNBUNDLED

One of the important components of setting up and managing a 401(k) plan is your plan design and administration. A Third Party Administrator (otherwise known as a TPA) can not only help you determine who will be eligible to participate in your plan (a notable consideration in order to pass discrimination testing requirements) but also help you design your plan features and benefits, as well as provide additional valuable services. Having the right TPA is crucial to making your life much easier and ensuring your employees, especially your key employees, can fully participate in your plan. A good TPA works with you on important compliance issues and provides advice and services you need to efficiently operate a successful plan. The right TPA will also know how to communicate with you on technical matters in a way you can easily understand.

Plan administration primarily includes IRS compliance to ensure your plan meets the qualifications to remain eligible for the tax-favored benefits. Testing your plan contributions to ensure there is no discrimination in favor of owners or highly compensated employees is a primary component of IRS compliance. You may have found yourself or other key employees unable to fully participate in your plan because of discrimination testing hurdles. Nothing is more frustrating than to receive "corrective distributions" at the end of the year, which is a return of salary deferral contributions that are now taxable to the employee because of the inability to pass testing requirements. When highly compensated employees cannot fully contribute to the plan, such employees are severely handicapped in their retirement readiness. They will need to replace a greater percentage of their income with their own savings since Social Security will provide a cap income benefit. You should know there is flexibility in how your plan is structured, and it may be possible your TPA can use creative plan design strategies to help you overcome these testing challenges. For this to happen, however, you may need the talent and capabilities of a skilled plan administrator who understands plan design at a very high level and can write a custom plan. Bundled administrators do not typically have this ability. A plan administrator will also prepare the 5500 tax forms and provide a summary annual report for you, among other compliance services. Plan administrators may also help you process distributions such as loans, hardship withdrawals, QDROs, and termination distributions.

When you shop plans, you will find there are two main options—*bundled* and *unbundled*. This means the plan administration is either bundled in the plan by the vendor (and such administration is priced into the total plan fees provided by the recordkeeper) or *unbundled*. If you select an unbundled plan, you will hire a separate third-party plan administrator to perform the administrative duties, the fees will be charged outside of the provider model (usually paid by the employer), and services will be performed independent of the provider. Although the TPA and recordkeeper will need open communication and sharing of information to complete their work, an unbundled plan means this service component is outsourced and, therefore, can be moved or changed separately.

While there are specific advantages and disadvantages to each arrangement, the arrangement that is best suited for you depends upon your service needs, the size of your plan in terms of number of eligible participants and assets under management, and the projected growth of your organization. Smaller plan sponsors often face discrimination testing hurdles, and the customized services provided by an outside administrator may prove to be far more valuable than a lower-cost option of a bundled plan, whereas larger plan sponsors with several hundreds or thousands of participants may not be able to take advantage of the custom plan design options because of their size and may be better off with a bundled plan option to reduce overall plan fees and simplify their workload.

BUNDLED

The bundled model is where one single vendor provides all recordkeeping and administration services. Bundled service providers are able to provide the entire range of administrative services to a plan sponsor from within a "one-stop shop." Costs, integrated with the provider fees, are typically paid by the plan participants and may be lower than those of an unbundled arrangement. However, bundled plans do not typically offer strategies to maximize the tax benefits for owners and highly compensated employees. Bundled plans tend to offer more generic turnkey plan designs and testing formulas that work best for larger companies. Bundled plans also tend to have account or customer service representatives who are more process-oriented than consultative. This means the service, while still friendly and pleasant, may be more reactive than proactive.

A bundled plan may be desired because it may be able to take a large portion of the workload off the plan sponsor. This can be especially helpful if you are a small business. If you are burdened with tracking eligibility, sending out enrollment information, prepping and managing the audit process, verifying compliance tests, and processing QDROs, loans, hardship withdrawals, etc., a bundled plan may be worthwhile to consider. For sure, bundled plans offer a convenience, but keep in mind that the trade-off is lack of flexibility. With a bundled plan, if you are not pleased with the administrative services, you will likely have to move the entire plan since provider and administration are integrated into the contract. There is little to no ability to carve out special services or enjoy customized support. A bundled plan may also lack consulting expertise with respect to any plan design and solutions that you may need now or in the future. Such an arrangement is more systematic and streamlined to be handled in-house by the provider. Finally, smaller plans may discover fewer competitively priced plans in the bundled space.

UNBUNDLED

The unbundled model allows freedom for the plan sponsor to utilize an independent service provider for each critical task. It allows for maximum control and enables you to select a team that is the "best of the best." On the other hand, if you select a bad TPA, you may find yourself embroiled in administrative nightmares. However, the ability to separate your administration from the recordkeeping allows you greater control and flexibility. You can easily change TPAs without disrupting the overall plan if you aren't pleased with the results. Indeed, the more moving parts you detach, the more freedom, control, and flexibility you enjoy, but such freedom requires more work. Keep in mind, changing administrators may still require compiling data from both TPAs the first year, unless the change is timed perfectly with your plan year. By comparison, a bundled plan is far more convenient and simple. But smaller TPAs are generally consultative in nature and help provide solutions that meet your needs rather a delivering a one-size-fits-all, "check the box" type of arrangement. If you choose to hire your own TPA, be sure to shop around and scrutinize their pricing and service models. Following a due diligence process will help you avoid costly mistakes. Your financial advisor may help with this process and save you time and work, as he or she may already have strong working relationships with qualified plan administrators capable of doing the best job for you.

Is It Time To Change Providers?

Signs that it may be time to consider changing providers:

- ☐ Statements or administrative reports that don't arrive in a timely manner
- ☐ Errors on reports or statements
- ☐ Delays in distributions
- ☐ You or you HR team has to field calls your provider should be handling
- ☐ Nonresponsive provider

Figure 4.2

PROVIDER EVALUATION

Is your provider fulfilling their duties? Are you satisfied with the service? support? fees? How do you know if your plan provider is competitively priced? How do you know if your provider is competent? Familiarity may breed comfort, but that does not determine quality or fairness as these relate to your plan participants. If you haven't shopped providers in three years or more, it is time to fulfill your fiduciary duty to ensure your provider is delivering the needed support at a fair cost, relative to the market. Even if you are happy with your provider and you don't want to change, or you determine after shopping that you are satisfied with your current recordkeeper, due diligence is an ongoing fiduciary responsibility and cannot be ignored based on contentment.

Your employees need your diligent attention and effort to enable them to build the most they can for their retirement. They need a sound retirement plan to help them track toward retirement security. Your advocacy is critical to their ability to retire ready. Participants need to be assured they are paying fair and reasonable fees so as not to compromise the growth potential of their savings. They need a strong investment menu to boost their retirement values, and they need a great education program to achieve the results required to pursue retirement success. If you find that your provider is not offering the best plan for your organization, you owe it to your employees to consider other vendors.

Having said that, I will caution you that changing providers is no easy task. You may be inclined to put up with a situation that is not totally satisfactory rather than enter into the search process. A vendor search requires scrupulous detail work, and the process of finding and changing vendors can be time consuming. Evaluating providers can be difficult. You may not know how to properly assess and measure the quality of candidates. The Department of Labor (DOL) says that "selecting competent service providers is one of the most important responsibilities of a plan sponsor." Yet, there are no specific procedures defined by ERISA for how to go about this. What you do need to know is that 401(k) provider services can vary dramatically in breadth, depth, and fees. This variability can make it difficult to select providers with services that match your plan's needs at reasonable costs. That is why engaging the professional services of a 401(k) expert can be invaluable. Not only can a financial advisor save you time, but also you will be more apt to find a provider who best meets your specific needs.

Of course, you don't want your participants paying for extra or unnecessary services they won't use. Consequently, you need to understand the service options before you start shopping and comparing plans. Unfortunately, most plan sponsors do this backwards—they start shopping before they understand their options. This can lead to selecting a plan that is overpriced. Sales representatives may oversell frills or benefits you don't really need or won't use, or even worse, you can miss important factors in the prudent selection process that compromise the quality of your provider selection. These mistakes may be at the expense of your participants and can impact their retirement readiness.

Recordkeepers need to be efficient in supporting you as a plan sponsor. They also need to be able to properly support your plan participants. Your needs, as a plan sponsor, are likely to be different from your participants' needs. For example, your participants probably need a good diverse selection of investments, retirement planning support, and technology to help them easily manage and monitor their accounts. You, on the other hand, might need ERISA compliance support, administrative assistance, ease of payroll integration, flexibility with reporting, and a marketing budget. The decision to change providers must be made for the benefit of your participants, but if you are not getting the support you need, a case can be made that it's time to go on a vendor search.

Does your current provider expect your system to change to meet their requirements? Is the company experiencing too much staff turnover that requires you to work with new people or inexperienced representatives? Has your provider promised services they haven't delivered? Do they fail to keep you apprised of upgrades you may be entitled to? Has your provider neglected to adjust your plan fees as your plan assets have grown? Has your participation rate stagnated, fallen, or failed to increase over an extended period of time? Are the investments underperforming? Are your investment options available through your recordkeeper too limited? If the answer to any of these questions is yes, you may have outgrown your 401(k) provider. Figure 4.2 highlights signs that it may be time to consider a change.

CHANGING PROVIDERS

If you have already established a 401(k) plan, you know the process was not exactly easy or simple. Just finding the right team of advisors and the best provider fit was probably laborious and complicated. If the idea of changing plan providers seems daunting, that is because moving a plan is, indeed, involved. Yet, the primary reason plan sponsors change plans today is poor service.

Sponsors are least satisfied with provider communications and education programs, according to 2017's PLANSPONSOR Defined Contribution Survey. Plan sponsors are seeking on-site meetings and participant support, which I am excited to see. It wasn't too long ago when plan fees were the main impetus for change. As I've already mentioned, plan fees can be compressed only so far before service is ultimately compromised. With demand for participant support rising, plan fees will likely follow suit. We just may see the pendulum now settle in the middle between a demand for value—a balance between good service and support—and fair and reasonable costs. Ironically, a study noted in *"The Way the Brain Buys"* by the Economist indicates that cost represents only 16 percent of all consumer purchase decisions. But, of course, when purchasing intangible products such as a 401(k), it's very difficult for plan sponsors to consider quality and value. If you were shopping for a new car and were presented with two different cars for purchase, car A being priced at $13,000 and car B being priced at $30,000, would you automatically choose car A? Probably not. There's not enough information to make a smart buying decision, and therefore you would likely ask more questions, such as make and model, engine size, features, and warranty. With new cars, it is proven that more people choose car B based on average car prices. Clearly a $30,000 car is going to offer more value and you probably feel a little wary of a $13,000 car. But when it comes to selecting 401(k) plans, how much consideration is weighted on price versus value? If you were presented with 401(k) plan A at a cost of 1.15 percent or plan B at a cost of 0.65 percent, which would you choose? More often than not, I see plan sponsors put the majority (perhaps up to 84 percent) of their buying decision on cost, which is totally contrary to how we decide on almost all other purchases. There is not enough information to know if plan B is a better selection, yet employers often automatically favor plan B because of price. It's as if we completely discount value when we consider intangible products or services.

If you are not enamored with your provider because of service, fees, or any other issue, it may be time to shop providers, but there's far more to consider than just fees. Generally speaking, most recordkeepers have a "target market" in terms of an ideal plan size that fits their pricing and support model. A financial advisor who specializes in this area and works extensively in the 401(k) industry can help you sort through the maze of options to narrow down your candidates and find the best fit based on these alignments. Advisors specializing in 401(k) communicate regularly with a wide array of providers to better understand their models, pricing, etc., meaning that this collective intelligence will save you time and money. It makes sense to shop those plans that are best aligned to your specific needs and plan attributes and not waste your valuable time on those outsides of your scope.

On the other hand, if you decide to tackle this task without the support of a qualified advisor, you must do your homework and be very careful. I have seen many plan sponsors choose providers based on limited knowledge and, ultimately, come to regret their choices.

As already stated, changing plans is a bit of a nuisance and can involve a tremendous amount of time and work. Since time is money, you don't want to waste your time or make a bad decision. I know of a CFO who didn't enlist the assistance of a professional when he started his provider search and ended up selecting a provider that was totally incapable of meeting the services and providing the support he and his participants needed. He unknowingly selected a recordkeeper who specialized in start-up plans, yet his company's plan had over $25 million in assets. Consequently, he endured years of frustration because the recordkeeper was unable to support the needs of his larger plan. If you have the wrong recordkeeper, it's potentially better to move forward with another provider, even if it's inconvenient to change again. The right thing to do as a fiduciary is to correct the mistake.

If you have a provider who is not meeting your needs, do not settle. Do not risk compromising the needs of your participants, and certainly do not settle for poor service. While I do recommend working with a professional advisor to simplify the process and create a more satisfying experience, you may still want to better understand the process. Engaging a financial advisor in the provider search is somewhat akin to engaging a realtor or broker in a real estate search. Realtors know the market. They are educated and experienced, they have insight on listings, they have negotiating skills, they act as buffers, and they can help with the legalities of the sale or purchase. Their job is to connect buyers and sellers to properly align the goals. The job of a financial advisor with a 401(k) provider is similar. And inasmuch as it doesn't make much sense to hire an out-of-state realtor to help you with your local home purchase, you'll probably want to hire a financial advisor who works in your area and specializes in the 401(k) market. Keep in mind, there are many fields in which an advisor can practice in the financial services industry, just as there are different fields of medicine. You wouldn't go to a podiatrist if you had an earache.

As a plan sponsor, you know that the world of 401(k) plans entails a never-ending learning process. If it has been many years since you conducted a provider search, it will likely be even more confusing and challenging. Therefore, the more questions you ask when you begin your search, the more confidently you will be able to choose a provider who will be a partner in ensuring your employees' retirement success. Engaging the right professional early in the process could save you time, money, and work.

Whether you decide to engage a financial advisor to help you with the provider search or decide to tackle this on your own, a request for proposal (RFP) may help initiate the process. A professional advisor may create the RFP for you. There is a sample RFP that may be helpful listed on our website, but before you begin this process, I think you should consider the mistakes plan sponsors frequently make when initiating the RFP, be it with an advisor or on their own. Some of those mistakes are listed here:

> **Failing to Ask Tough Questions.** If you decide to hire a financial advisor to help with your search process, be sure to ask plenty of tough questions about their qualifications. Also, be sure to ask if they have any conflicts of interest. For instance, does their firm offer its own product? And if so, are they compensated more to sell that plan? Are they able to shop a broad array of providers or just a limited scope? Is their compensation tied to the provider selection? If so, does the compensation vary by provider?
>
> If you are tackling this provider search on your own, be sure to ask tough questions beyond the basics, including details on fees and administration. Who will be servicing your account? Will you be assigned a dedicated account representative, and if so, where is that representative located? Are you going to be directed to a call center, and if so, what are the hours? How does the online access and support compare to what you have now? How long does it take to process

loans and distributions? What kind of employee support and communications does the provider offer? Is there a marketing budget to promote the plan? Does the provider provide trustee services, and if so, what are the fees? Does it make sense for you to outsource that work? Does the provider offer co-fiduciary support, and if so, what do those services look like? How many investment options can you access to construct your investment menu, and how often can you add/remove investments? Is there a limit to how many fund options you can offer in your plan? There are many components that go beyond costs to ensure long-term satisfaction with a provider.

Failing to Shop Around. The 401(k) marketplace is very competitive, and features and benefits offered vary greatly. It generally pays to shop around to distinguish the different services so as identify what is important to you and, most of all, to your plan participants. Seek to learn more about the ideal plan size a particular provider under consideration can accommodate and why one may be better than another. You may not get objective information from the provider's sales representative, so it pays to shop and do your due diligence. Your retirement committee can also help raise key questions and considerations to help in the decision-making process. Remember, selecting your vendor is a serious fiduciary obligation. That is why engaging a financial advisor first can help save you a lot of headaches and mistakes.

Confusing Salespeople with Consultants. Most 401(k) vendors distribute their product through an in-house sales force, and these salespeople are often quite good at their jobs. But remember, their job is to sell a product. Plan providers are not consultants, so be careful about relying on them for objective information and guidance. If you hire an advisor, on the other hand, you are hiring a consultant and as such he or she should have no financial gain in selling you a product. A financial advisor can help you with the vendor search by screening providers for you with great scrutiny. The advisor is likely charging a fee for the vendor search or is getting paid through an asset-based fee arrangement to provide *advisory* services. Therefore, an advisor will typically do most of the work for you behind the scenes and ultimately present a few provider options for you and your committee to consider. An advisor should be looking at many different proposals but narrowing down the options to present to you for your decision. Of course, an advisor will only do this in earnest after hired. You may find an advisor will offer you a soft market comparison of plans when proposing an engagement. At my firm, we often do this to demonstrate how to defray our costs. But a true vendor search cannot be done by a financial advisor when the advisor is not properly compensated.

 A good practice is to ask your advisor to bring in three salespeople representing three different providers that are considered a good fit and let them make a presentation to you and your retirement committee so you can make an objective decision. Your advisor should be educating you about the differences between the plans presented and helping you negotiate fees and services based on what's most important to you and your plan's goals. But he or she should not be selecting the plan for you. By prescreening providers, you will have the opportunity to consider plans that are distinctly different from one another but aligned to your needs. In the end, the decision as to whom you select ought to be your (and your committee's) decision. Your decision should be made independent of the advisor, although naturally you will be leaning on his or her expertise and guidance.

You will want to know there is no conflict of interest in his or her recommendations (meaning there is no additional or hidden compensation or incentives for the advisor based on the options presented). In the event that conflicts of interest exist between your advisor and a vendor, these should be immediately and voluntarily disclosed by the advisor. This may not preclude you from selecting the vendor, but a sound decision can only be made with full disclosure. If your advisor has a conflict of interest (such as incentive compensation) and neglects to disclose this voluntarily, it may be wise to seek a different advisor. Full transparency is essential to building trust in a consulting relationship. You should not have to ask about conflicts that may influence recommendations or guidance. An advisor who abides by a good code of ethics would never hesitate to do this forthright. Ultimately, you are responsible as a fiduciary for selecting the right plan for your participants and for knowing why you selected a specific provider. Clearly, you cannot do this without transparency. You must follow a diligent process to meet your legal obligations. This process should be carefully documented to demonstrate your process and fulfill your fiduciary duties, and your advisor should be helping you as a co-fiduciary with full disclosures. Again, such a conflict may not necessarily be a deal breaker *if it is fully disclosed in advance*, but you and your committee need to be able to consider all information when making a decision. If you learn, after the fact or through other sources, that your advisor withheld pertinent information, it would likely be wise to reconsider your relationship with the advisor. Plan sponsors generally greatly rely on the advisor's guidance, so the relationship must be based on trust. If your doctor failed to disclose important information regarding your health-care options or side effects of treatment that put you at risk, would you keep relying on him or her for your health care?

Reducing the Buying Decision to Only Fees. Fees should never be your primary reason for selecting a provider or anyone on your 401(k) team. As previously noted, fees are one of many deciding factors, and while they are an important part of the buying decision, they should not be the sole motivation for selecting a recordkeeper or service provider. Basing your selection simply on who has the lowest cost is shortsighted and may have long-lasting negative repercussions. Service and support are as important, if not more important, than fees. Acting in the best interest of your participants involves considering *value*. As a fiduciary, you must proceed with caution and care for your employees.

Bells and Whistles. When evaluating participant services offered by a provider, plan sponsors should be wary of too much emphasis placed on bells and whistles such as fancy statements, websites, and sponsor-level branding. These added features may be nice, but they don't ensure value. Instead, concentrate on the issue of plan efficiency and retirement readiness and what kind of support and dedication the provider can offer in this area.

PROVIDER SEARCH QUESTIONS

Below is a list of questions you may want to consider asking prospective providers:

1. What are your ideas to help us increase participation rates?
2. What administrative functions will and won't you perform?
3. Do you provide trustee services and if so, at what fee?
4. What compliance functions will and won't you perform?
5. How can we decrease plan costs?
6. Do you function as a fiduciary? If so, what are the limitations?
7. Do you recommend and assist us in monitoring investments? What kind of reporting will you provide for our documentation? Is it proprietary or third party research?
8. What are the management fees of the funds proposed and are there other share class options available?
9. What are the revenue sharing arrangements and how are those revenue sharing dollars allocated?
10. Is there an ERISA account option?
11. How often do you review and consult on plan design and updates?
12. How many investments options do you offer and how do you screen these investments?
13. Is there a proprietary fund requirement?
14. What kind of employee education do you provide and how often? Is it just enrollment meetings or retirement wellness subject matter?
15. How will you help us increase contribution rates?
16. How will you help participants manage and/or reduce stock market risk?
17. Do you offer stable value funds or money market funds?
18. Do you offer Collective Investment Trusts and if so, why or if not, why not?
19. How do you help Plan Sponsors promote retirement readiness?
20. Do you offer customized materials with our logo/branding?
21. Will the successor custodian accept the investments from the predecessor custodian or will they need to sell the investments?
22. Will the successor custodian map the investments to similar investments or will participants need to make a new allocation election? Who will recommend the mapping?
23. Who will be preparing and sending notices to the participants regarding the transfer and blackout dates?
24. Is there a conversion/transition representative leading the provider change?
25. What is the step-by-step process for the plan conversion and what steps should I anticipate requiring our time and attention?

This is just a short list of the many considerations a fiduciary should factor into a vendor selection.

Figure 4.3.

Failing to Consider Compatibility. Request references for plan sponsors of similar plan sizes and demographics, and seek to glean insight from those who have had both positive and negative experiences with the provider. Not all providers are suited for a small or start-up plan where the sponsor may need more hand-holding, just as not all are suited for a complex plan with multimillion-dollar account balances. Providers tend to work in niche markets and are usually the most competitive within their space, typically driven by plan size. Do you really want to be a small fish in a big pond? You might like the large recognized names of some providers, but how important are you in their eyes when it comes to service and support? You may find, as I have seen many times over, that providers who serve the megabillion-dollar plan market are not very service-oriented or accommodating for average- or smaller-size plans. Likewise, a provider who specializes in the small market will likely be unable to meet your needs if your plan is one billion dollars in assets. How do you know what the right fit may be? Ask questions and do some homework. Or work with an advisor who specializes in this area.

When plan sponsors evaluate various providers' final presentations, the offerings typically look alike—the providers present similar slides and give similar answers to questions. But in actuality, the recordkeeper's services may be very different. For this reason, customize your RFP (if you decide to use one), and be sure to address your plan's goals and provide information openly. This is essential to getting the results you need to improve your retirement plan. An advisor should be able to help you identify the differences, but in the absence of engaging an advisor, knowing what is most important to you will help you ask the right questions. In figure 4.3, I provide a short list of questions you may want to consider as you make your vendor selection.

PLAN CONVERSION

Once you select a vendor, you will begin the transfer process, which is not difficult but is involved. The first step is to sign documents with your new vendor, which will likely include a Plan Adoption Agreement along with vendor-drafted plan documents. You will also likely need to provide a current employee census, Plan Asset Statement, an IRS Favorable Determination letter, a valuation statement for the recent year, 5500 filing forms, and a few other documents that may be requested by the new provider.

You might incur start-up, takeover, or transition costs. You may be able to negotiate these costs or have them waived, but it is typical to make a required payment of some amount to get the process rolling. You must also provide a written notice to advise your current recordkeeper that you are terminating your plan with them.

Your new provider will then initiate opening accounts and prepare for the transfer of assets. Your new provider will likely also help you prepare a blackout notice, which must be distributed to all your employees thirty days before the transfer occurs. The purpose of the notice is to advise your employees of the plan change. During a stated window or period of time, no changes may be made to the investment allocations, and no loans or distributions may be taken. This blackout period is only typically a matter of days with today's technology, but your employees need to be aware of the restrictions and be given ample opportunity to review their investment allocations ahead of time to determine if they want to make any changes in advance.

The entire conversion process may take 90–120 days. Figure 4.4 highlights the process. Your current provider may be the one to determine how swiftly your plan is transferred since they must release both information and assets to the new provider. Although it is generally a smooth process, some vendors are not as efficient as they ought to be with plan transfers. Therefore, it's a good idea to be in communication with both your current and new provider to help facilitate the transition. With that said, often delays are caused more by plan sponsors neglecting to provide needed documents than by vendors.

Once the new provider receives the funds, the process is nearly complete. Typically, plan assets are delivered to the new provider via wire transfer. Once the funds are received, the new provider will have to reconcile them against a liquidation statement and align them to participant data to ensure all vesting information, deferral rates, loans, and so on are transferred correctly. The data must be audited because all the historical data for every participant must be transferred to the new vendor for tracking purposes. You will also want to review this information for accuracy.

Either the new vendor will receive cash, which will then be reinvested according to the predetermined mapping schedule or selected default funds, or there will be an in-kind transfer of the securities (this is less common these days). The majority of the time, assets are mapped to like-for-like investments, which means the funds are liquidated by the former provider and reinvested by the new provider in similar funds based on your selection. Again, your advisor can help with the new investment selection and mapping process. It may take several days to get the wire transfer and reinvest the funds, and during this time your participants may be out of the market. It's typically just a few days, but it is important to understand the process, which should be clearly stated by your new recordkeeper. The process and information transferred should be reviewed and understood by plan fiduciaries. The recordkeeper change must be disclosed to participants, both active and inactive, via the blackout notice.

Once the transfer is complete and the information is reconciled, the new vendor will pick up where the former vendor left off with all recordkeeping and account management services. You should have online access to view your plan through the new provider and be able to tend to any service or fiduciary work uninterrupted. During the transition time, you will want to get acquainted with the new provider's software and learn how to generate required reports, etc., for your own recordkeeping. The vendor should do a demo or walk-through of the website to ensure those involved in the plan sponsor administration are comfortable with their ability to perform their ongoing duties, including processing deposits into the plan.

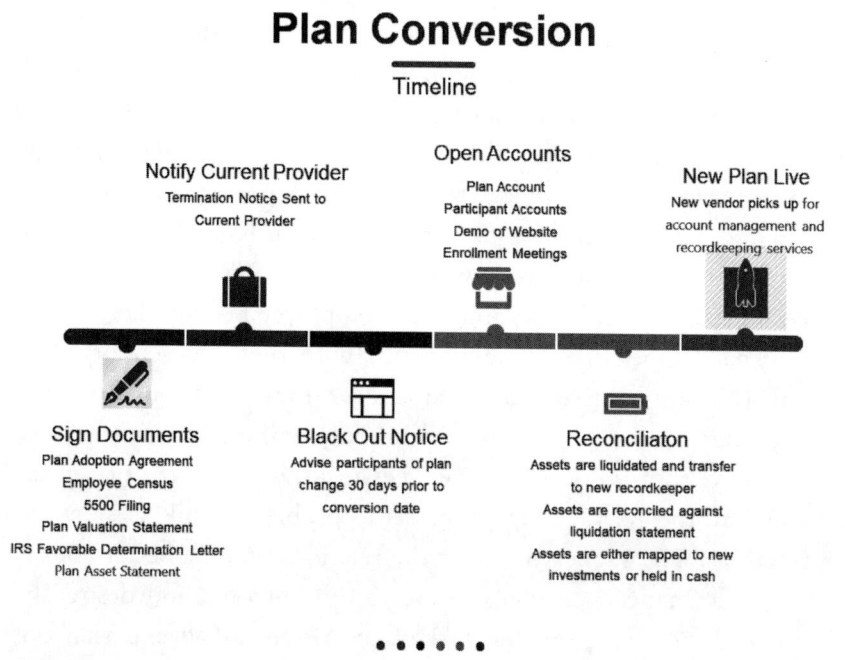

Plan Conversion
Timeline

Notify Current Provider
Termination Notice Sent to Current Provider

Open Accounts
Plan Account
Participant Accounts
Demo of Website
Enrollment Meetings

New Plan Live
New vendor picks up for account management and recordkeeping services

Sign Documents
Plan Adoption Agreement
Employee Census
5500 Filing
Plan Valuation Statement
IRS Favorable Determination Letter
Plan Asset Statement

Black Out Notice
Advise participants of plan change 30 days prior to conversion date

Reconciliaton
Assets are liquidated and transfer to new recordkeeper
Assets are reconciled against liquidation statement
Assets are either mapped to new investments or held in cash

Figure 4.4.

Your new vendor or financial advisor ought to also provide an education meeting to address the vendor change with your employees, encourage new enrollment, and ensure a smooth transition by answering questions and addressing important information for your participants. They may also offer an online demo of the participant website so employees can be more comfortable with the change. Your employees need to learn how to navigate new software and understand the scope of the functions they can perform online. This is also important for a smooth transition. You will want your employees to feel confident and capable to easily and readily access their accounts and perform their own maintenance such as beneficiary changes, investment changes, and tracking. Let's face it, plan changes create anxiety for everyone involved. The more hands-on support your 401(k) team can provide, the better the transition will be received by everyone. If you have engaged a financial advisor, he or she should be taking the lead with employee education.

In due time, everyone will adjust to the new system. The overall experience should result in a more positive outcome and greater advancement toward retirement success. Change creates opportunity and brings a new start to what may be a stale plan. If you find your 401(k) lacking or failing to bring excitement and value to your employees, a change of vendors may be just what you need. Reinvigorating your plan with a new vendor or new advisor often renews the energy put into what should be a very important employee benefit plan.

What happens if your experience with the new vendor is not ideal? Is it possible that you have made a mistake and come to regret the change? Although this experience is rare, if it is determined that the new vendor is not meeting expectations, you should not hesitate to review the relationship, discuss the problems, and set new expectations. The sooner you reset the relationship on a better course, the better chance that you can create the outcome you desired by initiating the change in the first place. Often, a bad experience is the result of poor communication, and a service reset can help get the new relationship on the right path. This may mean requesting a change of account representatives or having your advisor intervene to address the concerns. But if you made a mistake and find the new vendor failing to meet your needs, consider cutting your losses and starting over with your vendor search. While it is time-consuming to find a new vendor, staying with a vendor who is providing bad service and causing aggravation is not worth the frustration. I've known of plan sponsors who switched vendors only to return to their former providers a short time later. Obviously, you want to try to avoid this extra work by shopping carefully in the first place. It is important to fully review and assess your current vendor arrangement objectively before you jump in. And be sure to scrutinize new vendors carefully. While this sort of misstep is rare, it should be noted that it does happen. Should you find yourself unable to recalibrate your vendor relationship, don't fear the transfer process. In the end, a great provider and 401(k) team is worth fighting for.

BLACKOUT NOTICES

Blackout rules were established by the Sarbanes–Oxley Act of 2002, which manifested because of the Enron scandal. If you don't know the Enron story, it is an extraordinary one. Enron was believed to be one of the most financially sound companies in the country during the 1990s. Located in Texas, Enron became one of the world's largest energy companies. However, in 2001 it went bankrupt as the result of fraud and deception, including misrepresenting earning reports to shareholders. Enron wasn't the only company charged with accounting scandals at the time, but it was among the worst offenders. Enron executives committed fraud, including embezzlement and illegal manipulations of the energy market. In fact, sixteen executives were sentenced to prison. Former CEO Jeffrey Skilling is currently serving twenty-four years. The debacle also brought down one of the largest accounting firms, Arthur Andersen, which was found guilty of criminal charges as auditor of Enron's financial statements. The malfeasance impacted thousands, if not millions, of people.

In order to prevent this type of fraud from occurring again, the Sarbanes–Oxley Act (SOX) was written to close accounting loopholes and increase transparency. The Enron failure was not just about a company that had gone from being one of the largest, seemingly most successful companies in the United States to become the most striking example of corporate greed. It was also about being the first company where as many as twenty thousand employees lost roughly one billion dollars in 401(k) retirement savings. You see, Enron's 401(k) offered employer matching contributions, but these were only paid in the form of Enron stock. And to that end, the shares were restricted for liquidations or reallocations until the employee reached age fifty. To make matters worse, management encouraged employees to purchase Enron stock with their own contributions (at artificially inflated prices based on misstated earnings). Indeed, many employees had their entire retirement account balances invested exclusively in Enron stock. Curiously, during the time that Enron's financial problems were becoming public knowledge, the company decided to change 401(k) providers, and thus investment access was frozen for three weeks while Enron stock plummeted. This was a further grave misfortune for Enron employees. Ultimately over $375 million in settlement claims were charged against Enron's bankruptcy proceedings, and another $37.5 million were settled by Northern Trust Company, the administrator of the Enron plan, but it is unknown how much, if any, of those dollars actually were paid to participants and beneficiaries.

The purpose of the Blackout Notice is to provide written notice to participants of the reason for the downtime, the expected beginning and length of the downtime, and specific details of the suspended activities. This notice is required to not just the alert participants of the temporary investment freeze but also give them the opportunity to make changes to their allocations prior to the freeze if they feel it is necessary to do so. The notice must be distributed to all participants at least thirty days but not more than sixty days in advance of the plan change. If there is any change to the original information provided, including a conversion date change, plan sponsors must provide participants with an updated notice explaining the reason for the change.

If you fail to comply with blackout notice requirements, you may incur civil penalties assessed by the Department of Labor to the tune of $100 per participant *per day*. So, if you have two hundred participants and you fail to provide proper notice to your participants for fifteen days, you could be facing $300,000 in penalties! So please recognize that blackout notices are important and are not to be ignored or disregarded.

IN SUMMARY

A 401(k) recordkeeper's responsibilities are to value investments on a daily basis, maintain accurate records of the various contributions your participants make to the 401(k) over their working lifetimes, credit investment earnings, and track amounts distributed. The recordkeeper must provide your employees with statements at least quarterly and, ideally, provide online access. They also process distribution checks and answer service questions for your participants, among other things. By comparison, a Third-Party Administrator (TPA) is responsible for creating optimal plan design and performing the annual IRS compliance administration, such as filing the IRS 5500 form and maintaining legal documents.

Both your recordkeeper and your TPA must also maintain records of employee deferrals and after-tax voluntary contributions as well as records of employer matching, qualified nonelective, and Profit Sharing contributions. Your administrator is required to do this for IRS compliance, whereas your recordkeeper must maintain these records for participant-level services. While you can perform these recordkeeping duties in-house, it is generally not advisable because of the laborious work and responsibilities. Banks, investment companies, and insurance companies provide this service at a fair cost.

A good plan administrator will ensure more employees are eligible to participate in your plan and help keep your plan qualified for the tax-favored benefits, but it is your recordkeeper who provides the chassis for your 401(k). They provide the means by which your employees can seek a financially secure and successful retirement. While investments might provide the fuel to get the plan going, the recordkeeper provides the sound vehicle to help your employees get to retirement. Without a good platform, your employees' future may be compromised. Take the time to monitor your vendors, and ensure you maintain a competitive team so your employees can build and secure their retirement. The right recordkeeper, administrator, and advisor can make the difference—and your team matters to everyone involved in your 401(k).

CHAPTER 5
PLAN DESIGN

Ava was just hired as your new office worker in March. She is eager to participate in your company 401(k). She was told she won't be eligible until July 1, and then she will have to wait for open enrollment in January. She is concerned about the timing because she wants to roll her former 401(k) over into your plan. Plus, she doesn't want to miss this year's pre-tax advantages. She regrets not asking questions before she started, as the ten-month prolonged wait may have influenced her decision to accept the job offer. She asked her supervisor why she must wait so long to participate and was told she should talk to you, the HR manager. What do you tell Ava as to the rationale for delaying her participation?

Plan design can have an important effect on participation in your 401(k) and help promote or handicap retirement potential. Your plan design can impact participation, contribution rates, asset allocation, and investment performance. Specifically, your design decisions influence employee behavior. Frequently, many of the problems employers face in relation to their plan can be fixed or minimized by restructuring or redesigning their 401(k) plan. If you have employees who are not participating in your plan, I hope you are asking yourself what can be done to encourage participation. After all, we know everyone should be saving for their retirement. Additionally, if you have participants deferring less than 10 percent of their paycheck, they are not likely to be able to retire ready. What can you do to change this behavior? Take a closer look at your plan design. You have far more control than you may realize.

Because 401(k) plans place the burden of ensuring adequate retirement savings on the employees, employers need to understand that the design or structure of their 401(k) can either accelerate or impede their employees' retirement readiness. Although the government places some limits on how companies can structure their plan's, you actually have a great deal of discretion when it comes to the design of your 401(k). Consequently, making good plan design decisions requires an understanding of the options and the relationship between these options and participant savings outcomes.

Your 401(k) plan is a useful retirement tool only to the extent that employees actually participate in the plan. If your employees don't participate, it doesn't do much to promote retirement readiness. Since participation is voluntary, you must carefully consider influences you have over behavior, and that starts with how your plan is written. A key behavioral question is your enrollment protocol. How long it takes before employees are enrolled or eligible to participate in your plan is a significant determinant of the driver for retirement preparedness. Too many plans have restrictive eligibility requirements. If your plan is one of these, now is a good time to ask the question why. Matching contributions are another behavioral influence that can help drive participation, including your matching formula. Or how do your employees enroll? If your plan requires an active election to initiate participation, it may take longer to enroll new employees and get them on track for retirement. There are several plan design features you can take advantage of which will help drive positive retirement outcomes and spur action even if your employees lack motivation. If your ultimate goal is to drive retirement readiness, your plan design needs to be structured to help the progress. Inherently, employees have a natural resistance to forsaking money today to secure their future. We live in a world where instant gratification takes precedence. Therefore, any actions you can take to help promote savings will only serve to enhance the financial welfare for both your employees and your business.

Financial stress is a sadly widespread amongst workers, and the proportion of people overstretched financially has only been increasing over the years. Financial troubles are linked to health problems like depression and sleep deprivation, which negatively affect not only your employees' personal lives but also their job performance. Living paycheck to paycheck or being debt-ridden can be a major distraction. Studies report that more than half of all workers feel some degree of financial stress. A large majority of those surveyed are worried about meeting future financial goals, including their retirement. Unfortunately, many feel unable to save sufficiently to meet their future needs because they are so bogged down by today's financial demands. In all my years of helping employees, I have never heard a soon-to-be retiree say they regretted saving money in their company-sponsored retirement plan. Conversely, though, I have heard many declare they wished they had saved more and started sooner. Helping your employees think differently about money is a great step toward driving retirement health. Did you realize you can influence retirement outcomes with just your plan design?

If your plan participation rate is low, it is definitely time to review your plan design. You may not be taking advantage of the important plan features that can help increase participation. If your plan contribution rate is below what it should be for retirement preparedness, now is the time to determine if you need to realign your plan features and benefits to enhance contribution rates. Your 401(k) advisory team can help you utilize plan design features to address your plan's retirement-readiness inhibitors. Oftentimes, a few adjustments can make the difference between a thriving plan and one that has stagnated. This chapter will address some of the important plan design issues and ways you can structure your plan to help overcome some of the greatest challenges employers face when seeking to drive results. It's never too late to amend your plan to promote retirement success.

ENROLLMENT ELIGIBILITY

Twenty years ago, nearly 75 percent of all 401(k) plans required at least three months', but perhaps up to a full year, waiting period for an employee to be eligible to participate in the plan. And even still, the employee had to wait for the open enrollment window, which may have only been twice a year—January 1 and July 1. So, if you were a new employee hired in August, you had to wait six months to be eligible, and then wait until July 1 for open enrollment, which meant you could be without retirement savings for nearly an entire year. Given that every time an employee changed jobs, he or she had to wait another full year to resume retirement savings, you can see this was quite a major setback. With job hopping today, the average worker could lose five to ten years of retirement savings just by waiting for enrollment. Clearly, that is totally contrary to ensuring your employees are able to retire ready.

Fortunately today, 62 percent of all 401(k) plans allow for *immediate* eligibility, and this includes nearly half of those with matching incentives. In fact, today fewer than 30 percent of plans require a year of service before eligibility. If you want to promote your plan and perhaps attract better talent, it is time to consider making it easy for your employees to gain entry to your 401(k).

Is every employee eligible to participate in your plan? *Should* they all be eligible? As a plan sponsor, you can control, at least to some degree, who is eligible to participate in your plan and who isn't. While you may want to open up the plan for all employees, know that discrimination testing hurdles, administrative workloads, and costs may not make it feasible or practical for you to include *every* employee. For example, does it make sense to include employees under the age of twenty-one? If you are a cupcake shop and you hire young workers, it may not be practical to open up your plan to these employees. They may only be making minimum wage and may likely have no interest in participating; yet, by including them, it may hurt your discrimination testing calculations. Remember, discrimination testing pertains to those *eligible*. The law says you can exclude employees under the age of eighteen or twenty-one. You can also exclude employees who do not work at least one thousand hours a year. So, if you have a lot of part-time employees, you are not required to make your 401(k) available to them.

Why wouldn't you want to include part-time workers? Again, part-time employees may impact your ADP/ACP testing since these workers are less likely to participate or contribute sufficiently to support your testing requirements. You need employees to make meaningful contributions to your plan for their own benefit and for the discrimination testing requirements. Part-time and/or younger workers are often working more to spend money than to prepare for retirement. Additionally, the turnover of this segment of your employee base can put quite a workload on you. Remember, every time an employee terminates the job, you have to keep track of their addresses if they have a 401(k) account balance or process distributions. This can be quite cumbersome for plan administration. The law also says you can exclude nonresident aliens as well as those covered by a collective bargaining agreement.

Once you decide *who* will participate, you then need to consider *when* you would like your employees to become eligible. You can set your eligibility immediately or use any time frame up to twelve months. Again, you must consider your administrative capacity as well as the goals and objectives of the plan. You also must consider testing challenges, if applicable. If you offer a matching contribution with a long vesting schedule, you may want to encourage participation as soon as possible. Or if you aren't offering an employer match, it may be best to allow immediate participation. But keep in mind that an immediate enrollment may increase your workload because of processing. The majority of plans today offer immediately eligibility, but 27 percent offer sixty- to ninety-day service requirement; 3 percent require six-month service requirements; and 8 percent require a full twelve-month service requirement. Before taking any definitive steps to change your plan design, your 401(k) advisor or plan administrator can back-test your plan and run estimations to determine any impact to your discrimination testing results. However, there should be a way to find a balance so you can promote retirement wellness. As noted, a long waiting period for enrollment can be a handicap for your employees.

The next plan design question is about your plan entry date. Once an employee meets eligibility criteria, the entry date is determined. The entry date is the time when an eligible employee can enter your plan, such as the first day of the next month or the first day of the next quarter. Once upon a time semiannual enrollment window dates were popular, but today most plans allow monthly or quarterly entry. Regardless, as soon as an employee is enrolled in your plan and an account is set up by your recordkeeper, you have the job of processing the payroll accordingly. Clearly, monthly enrollment is best for promoting retirement readiness; however, if monthly entry is too burdensome for your payroll workload, you can set entry dates quarterly or semiannually. Remember, plan language matters here, so choose carefully. Most recordkeepers and payroll companies make it easy to make salary deferrals into the plan, so this is not likely to be a problem. However, if your company doesn't have sufficient administrative staff to support the added workload, you may want to consider your plan entry date judiciously. As a champion of your 401(k), your goal is to get employees enrolled and participating as soon as possible and help them maximize their benefits. If you seek to help your valuable employees overcome our retirement crisis, a little extra work is a small cost.

If you are setting up a new plan or restating an existing plan, you can include an amnesty date. This waives the eligibility requirements for all existing employees and makes it so that only new employees are subject to the eligibility and participation requirements. You can also limit the frequency with which employees can make changes to their deferral elections to avoid additional workload. In most cases, plan sponsors don't place any restrictions on these changes, as restrictions may unintentionally dissuade participation. However, if you want to ease the administration of the plan, you can limit deferral changes to, say, quarterly rather than monthly.

TO MATCH OR NOT TO MATCH, THAT IS THE QUESTION

Employer matching contributions are important. Forty-three percent of employees surveyed by Fidelity Investments said they would settle for lower pay if it meant they would receive a higher employer contribution to their retirement plan account. In fact, only 13 percent said they would take a job with no company match *even if it came with a higher pay level*. So, yes, I think it's fair to say employer matching contributions are very important. Don't underestimate how valuable this benefit is to your employees just because you may have never heard an employee say they were changing jobs over a 401(k). Survey after survey shows that employees are deeply concerned about their retirement, and they are well aware of the advantages of boosting their retirement security potential with employer contributions.

Employer contributions play a vital role in helping Americans reach their savings goals, and offering an employer match is one of the most significant factors in whether or not employees choose to participate in your plan. The good news is that more than half of all plans offer some form of employer matching arrangement, and many participants contribute enough to get the full match. Still, I'm amazed when employees pass up the opportunity for free money. However, an employer match is not enough to meet funding requirements. National average deferral rates in 401(k) plans are still far lower than necessary to build enough capital for sufficient income replacement at retirement. Studies show that younger employees should be deferring at least 10 percent, whereas older employees who are behind may need to save 15 percent or more to meet their future income needs. Therefore, if you offer a match, consider what more you can do to drive results with your matching incentive formula. By designing your matching schedule to impact retirement readiness, you may help make a difference in the quality of life your employees enjoy in retirement. Many firms have found it effective to encourage their employees to stretch in order to reach the maximum match. I think this makes sense because, as I have found by speaking with many employees, they tend to stop at the amount required to get the match, even if it is insufficient to meet their needs. When I ask employees "How did you arrive at the 5 percent deferral rate?" I am stumped by the frequent response.

"Because that's what is required to get the maximum match."

"Have you ever thought about what you actually need for your retirement goals?" I query.

"No. I never thought about it that way."

You may be surprised to learn that many employees respond that they figured the matching rate was set at 5 percent, for example, "because that is the amount the company thinks I should save." Naturally, that is not the way plan sponsors generally think when they design their matching formula.

Indeed, you do have a tremendous influence on employee behavior. Most employees don't think about what they need to save; they only think about what they feel they can comfortably afford based on their idea of what "makes sense." And most employees understand that getting free money certainly makes sense. There is a wide range of company matching formulas used today. A typical arrangement might be 50 percent of employees' contributions up to the first 6 percent of employee deferrals. Or a company might set its match as a dollar-for-dollar benefit up to the first 3 percent. These examples are the same cost to the employer, but which one do you suppose is going to be better at helping the employee retire ready? The former option of 50 percent up to six percent. However, it's still not enough to build full retirement readiness. What would happen if you offered, say, a 25 percent match up to 12 percent?

Suppose you can't afford to offer a match? Is your 401(k) still a valuable benefit? You bet! Employer matching is not required. Naturally, conveying the importance of the plan in the absence of a match could be a bit of a challenge, particularly if leadership doesn't have great confidence in the plan. It is your 401(k) advisory team's duty to help communicate this benefit. Indeed, you may find many employees have a mental roadblock when it comes to saving, so without the matching incentive, some will just not feel inclined to participate. Therefore, they must understand that *their* actions, not yours, drive results. This means your employees need good education. It's possible to boost participation and drive retirement success without a matching incentive. Granted, it may be more of a challenge, but it is not impossible to build a secure retirement fund in the absence of an employer match.

A participant who learns how to make better investment decisions has the potential to build as much as or more than one enjoying a match but who's making poor investment decisions. Studies have proved employees left to their own devices are more likely to experience inferior investment results. We know many employees are not educated about investments. They are not financially savvy. Even those who are more astute are still subject to making emotional decisions. This is especially true with money. I have seen some of the most brilliant and accomplished CEOs, CFOs, and academic professionals making illogical errors with their finances. Many employees are terribly unschooled in investment principles, and it shows in their outcomes.

For example, take two employees, employee A and employee B. They are both thirty years old and contribute the same amount to their 401(k)'s over their working lifetime, except employee A also gets a 3 percent employer match. However, this same employee doesn't happen to make the best investment decisions. He buys when things are going well (after prices have gone up) and sells when things turn sour (after prices have fallen). He chases past performance, and he makes decisions that are too conservative or too aggressive at the wrong times. He ends up generating an average rate of return of 4% over thirty-five years. Don't scoff; evidence supports that long-term average past returns for most investors are even lower, despite far superior stock and bond market results over this period.

End of Age	Employee A Without Employer Match at 4% Growth	Employee A Without Employer Match at 8% Growth	Employee B With Employer Match at 4% Growth	Employee B With Employer Match at 8% Growth
35	$14,618	$16,091	$23,389	$25,745
40	$34,732	$42,296	$55,572	$67,675
45	$61,904	$83,772	$99,046	$134,036
50	$98,091	$148,159	$156,946	$237,054
55	$145,746	$246,756	$233,193	$394,810
60	$207,930	$396,257	$332,689	$634,012
65	$288,463	$621,289	$461,540	$994,063

Figure 5.1. Based on a starting age of thirty with a $50,000 income, with 5% salary deferrals and 3% annual COLA. Assumed growth rates are not guaranteed. Employer matching dollar-for-dollar up to the first 3%. This is a hypothetical example and is not representative of any specific situation. Your results will vary. The hypothetical rates of return used do not reflect the deduction of fees and charges inherent to investing.

By comparison, employee B does not get an employer match. Instead, she learns how to be a disciplined investor through a strong employer-sponsored education program, and she is able to earn a thirty-five-year average return of 8%. Which employee has more in his or her account thirty-five years later: employee A with the employer match, or employee B with no matching but better investment results?

The answer is employee B, of course—the one who made better investment decisions. Certainly, employees with both a good investment education *and* matching contributions will be in better position to pursue a secure their retirement. But the point is, investment performance is often overlooked or discounted when, in fact, it is arguably as important as the value of matching contributions. In the example highlighted in figure 5.1, a thirty-year-old employee earning $50,000 a year with a 5 percent deferral can accumulate $159,749 more than an employee with employer match, simply with better investment performance (8% growth rate versus 4% growth rate). That could translate into an additional $665 or more in monthly retirement benefit. But, of course, as also highlighted in figure 5.1, for a reasonably cost, you can provide your employees with an enormously valuable benefit if you add a matching benefit. The same employee earning 8% growth could accumulate potentially $372,774 more at retirement with an employer match, and that could amount to an additional $1550 a month in retirement income. Of course, the value of any matching benefit needs to be communicated effectively to your employees so they can appreciate and truly understand it, and naturally the rate of return and time compounded will determine just how substantial it will be. An older employee, for example, will likely get far less for the same matching dollars. Nonetheless, I strongly encourage employee education as a staple part of your ongoing financial wellness plan to help convey the significance of compounding growth and/or employer matching. It is still baffling to me why plans with matching benefits do not have a 100 percent participation rate. I attribute this more to lack of sufficient education than to employee procrastination. Everyone can afford at least a 1 percent or 2 percent contribution, and although that is by no means sufficient to secure a retirement, it is a start. All employees should be taking at least minimal steps on the path of retirement success.

Still, as figure 5.1 highlights, the power of investment earnings cannot be ignored. When an employee earning only 4% on his or her investments with the benefit of free employer dollars has less for retirement than an employee without matching but who has better investment results, the power that employees have to control their investment outcomes must be acknowledged as a critical component of retirement success.

With that said, if you can afford to match, it is highly encouraged. Employees value it. And if you want to be a true champion of your 401(k), matching incentives are a big motivator. Most employees do take matching seriously, and so should you. The magic of that small benefit has the potential to translate into better morale, productivity, and employee retention and can help in recruiting talented workers. Plus, depending upon how your plan is structured, it may reduce or eliminate discrimination testing hurdles. I have seen companies that were not matching offer very small fifty-cent match up to 2 percent of pay significantly improve participation.

Matching contributions is *behavioral finance* at its best—where emotion and psychology influence decisions. Employees are greatly motivated when there is free money on the table. Consequently, it is important that you consider how your matching arrangement is structured and that you ask yourself if it is structured to help influence your employees to drive optimal retirement readiness. Statistics show that of those plans that do offer match, over 80 percent have matching formulas that fail to properly incentivize a sufficient savings rate for retirement readiness. We know that a 10–15 percent contribution rate is the commonly cited targeted deferral rate for retirement security, yet many matching arrangements are structured to "max out" at 5 percent or 6 percent salary deferrals. Typically, as already noted, employees will contribute only enough to get the "free money." A 50 percent match up to 6 percent contribution translates into a 6 percent deferral incentive. Therefore, if an employee maximizes the plan's benefits, he or she will still fall short of the needed target. The longer the employee misses this targeted savings rate, the greater the potential shortfall. While a mere 1 percent doesn't sound like much, when compounded over twenty or thirty years, it can add up to a substantial amount of lost capital, possibly forcing the retiree to work several years beyond his or her targeted retirement date. Why have an arrangement that influences employees to fall short?

If you have a safe harbor plan, you cannot change your matching formula, so unfortunately there is little you can do to compel your employees to stretch to the targeted savings rate. However, if you do not have a safe harbor plan, I strongly encourage you to review your employee census, because you will likely discover your plan is weighted toward a contribution rate aligned to your match formula. If your formula is like that of 80 percent of all plans, it is failing to drive retirement readiness. You may be unintentionally encouraging your employees to fall short.

Fortunately, employers are finally starting to figure this out. We are seeing more matching arrangements targeting higher contribution rates, causing employees to stretch to that 10 percent goal. Examples of this include 25 percent match up to 8 percent, or 25 percent match up to the first 6 percent and 50 percent match thereafter, with a 10 percent cap. There are a variety of ways to reconfigure your matching formula to drive results without incurring more employer costs. The key is to work with professional advisors who can help you create the arrangement and communicate it productively when rolled out to your employees. You also want to be sure you don't unintentionally discriminate with a matching formula that happens to make it too difficult or unrealistic for your rank-and-file employees to enjoy the full extent of the benefit. Be sure to address any concerns with your advisory team. Adjusting your matching formula to gradually stretch toward a 10 percent contribution rate is easy and very effective for promoting retirement wellness.

Since nearly half of all plans do not offer matching contributions, if you are a budget-minded employer, you may want to consider some economical alternatives for your plan. This may include Profit Sharing or a Safe Harbor plan. Of course, as already stated, you have limited control over the matching formula with these options.

VESTING SCHEDULES

A vesting schedule is set up to determine when your plan participants will be eligible for employer contributions. Vesting means ownership. Employee salary deferrals are always 100 percent vested, meaning that those dollars are employee-owned. Rightfully so, their contributions are always their money. However, if you offer employer contributions either via matching or a profit sharing arrangement, you can determine when your employees will vest, or own, your share of the employer contributions. You can use a vesting schedule to reward, motivate, attract, and/or retain employees. Once an employee is 100 percent vested, all the current and future employer contributions belong to him or her. In other words, you cannot recant, or take back, the vested funds for any reason. However, if the employee terminates employment (willfully or otherwise), amounts that are not vested will be forfeited. In other words, those dollars will come back to you, the employer, and can be used to offset plan costs.

When nonvested money is forfeited, it is placed into a suspense account. Your plan should have language and administrative procedures in place designating how your forfeiture account will be used, which is generally either to pay for plan expenses or provide for future employer matching contributions. The Internal Revenue Code does not allow for forfeitures to accumulate within the plan for several years. Such action would be in conflict with Rev. Rul. 80-155, which requires all funds be allocated in accordance to your contribution formula annually. Consequently, it is recommended the forfeitures be used in the year in which they occur.

Should you inadvertently hold funds in a suspense account for too long, the proper correction is to reallocate the forfeiture to participants who would have been entitled to the contribution had it been exhausted in a timely manner, including terminated participants who have received distributions from the plan. Your plan administrator can help you file using the Self-Correction Program (SCP) of the Voluntary Correction Program (VCP) as per the IRS's Employee Plans Compliance Resolution System (EPCRS).

MOTIVATING EMPLOYEES WITH A VESTING SCHEDULE

Employers can determine how generous they choose to be with matching employer contributions or discretionary profit sharing allocations made to their 401(k)'s. The funds aren't truly the employees' until they have complied with the plan's vesting schedule. Before you define your vesting schedule, it might be good to consider why you are making employer contributions to your plan. If you are making contributions to encourage loyalty, you will want to be sure your vesting schedule incentivizes tenure. On the other hand, should you desire to attract talented or key employees, you may want to consider full and immediate vesting. But keep in mind, a vesting schedule, to some extent, can help reduce employee turnover. A plan design expert can offer an analysis of options and relevant factors that you ought to consider. The point is to make the plan a reward but not overly complicated or difficult for you or your employees.

VESTING SCHEDULE OPTIONS

There are basically three types of vesting schedules, each of which is described below.

> **Immediate Vesting.** Employees gain 100 percent ownership of the employer's contribution as soon as it is posted to their accounts. According to the National Compensation Survey, roughly one out of every four 401(k) plans with a matching incentive offers an immediate vesting schedule, largely because this is required if you choose a safe harbor plan, which avoids the ACP/ADP testing hurdles. Beyond the safe harbor advantage, the benefits of immediate vesting is the ability to more easily recruit employees to join your firm. The disadvantage is that the dollars you contribute are immediately available to your employees should they terminate their services, even if within a short period.
>
> **Cliff Vesting.** Cliff vesting transfers ownership all at once, but after a specified period of time not to exceed three years according to the Pension Protection Act of 2006. If you choose this schedule, your employees have no rights to the employer contributions if they leave before the specified period of time, but the day they reach that date, they own it all. For example:

- After one year of service, the employee is 0 percent vested.
- After two years of service, the employee is 0 percent vested.
- After three or more years of service, the employee is 100 percent vested.

The advantage of this type of arrangement is that it's simple and yet still short enough to attract employees. Roughly 22 percent of all plans with a match offer a cliff vesting schedule.

Graded Vesting. Nearly half of all 401(k) plans offer a graded vesting schedule. This schedule gives employees gradually increasing ownership of your contributions as their years of service increase. Therefore, if an employee leaves before being fully vested, he or she gets to keep a percentage of the employer contributions, but not all. According to the Pension Protection Act of 2006, there is a six-year maximum time frame on graded vesting schedules. Your vesting schedule can be more liberal, but it must not be more restrictive than the schedule listed below:

- After one year of service, the employee is 0 percent vested.
- After two years of service, the employee is 20 percent vested.
- After three years of service, the employee is 40 percent vested.
- After four years of service, the employee is 60 percent vested.
- After five years of service, the employee is 80 percent vested.

- After six years of service, the employee is 100 percent vested.

The reason graded vesting is so popular is because this schedule focuses on employee retention. However, if you are struggling with participation and testing hurdles, you may want to consider a more liberal vesting schedule. Remember, if you opted for a safe harbor plan, employer contributions must always be immediately vested.

CHANGING VESTING SCHEDULES

Periodically, as you review your plan design, you may conclude it is time to change your vesting schedule to better align with your organizational goals or needs. Generally, you can change your vesting schedule, but you cannot reduce the vesting percentage for existing participants. For example, if you have immediate vesting currently and you seek to change it to graded vesting, your existing participants will remain fully vested. Consequently, the graded vesting schedule would only apply to new participants. Additionally, regardless of what schedule you change to, employees with three or more years of service can elect to choose the previous vesting schedule. They will have an election period beginning no later than the date of the adoption of the amended schedule and ending either sixty days after the modified vesting schedule is adopted, after the modified schedules is made effective, or after the participant is provided a written notice of the change. Because more restrictive vesting changes will impact very few employees, it is best to select the right vesting schedule when you start your employer matching program.

Finally, it should be noted that vesting schedules start based on *hire date*, not plan inception date or date of the inception of matching arrangement. Therefore, if you institute a matching arrangement today with a three-year vesting schedule, eligible employees with tenure of three years or more will be immediately vested, even if they just began participating in your plan.

OTHER VESTING ISSUES

When determining years of service for vesting schedules, know that a year of service is any vesting computation period in which the employee completes the number of hours of service (not exceeding one thousand) required by the plan. Typically, the vesting computation period is the plan year, but it may be any other twelve-consecutive-month period.

In certain circumstances, employer contributions are required by law to be 100 percent vested. These circumstances include attainment of normal retirement age (as defined in the plan), termination or partial termination of the 401(k) plan itself (this does not mean transferring the plan to a different provider), and when there is complete discontinuance of contributions to the plan. Additionally, though not required by law, nearly all 401(k) plans provide for 100 percent vesting upon the participant's death or qualifying disability.

AUTOMAGIC!

Quite possibly the biggest threat to retirement success is inaction. Why does a person resist taking steps that will help secure his or her future and build wealth? Human nature. We naturally tend to resist doing the things we *need* to do to and instead opt to do things we *want* to do. Do you like to go to the dentist? I had one of those scary dental experiences when I was a child. The dentist was an old man with bushy eyebrows and hairy ears. He dug and poked in my mouth, using all sorts of frightening-looking instruments, needles, and drills. He didn't explain a thing, didn't care to take the time to comfort or reassure me. The Novocain wasn't very effective, and I kept jumping because of the pain, but in response, he would just poke more. I was traumatized. Even though I have had wonderful dentists since—and I'll admit a dental appointment is not a big deal anymore—I still cringe when I get that reminder notice in the mail. I put off my checkups until the dental office is hounding me. Whether it's doing taxes, getting a colonoscopy, or even doing laundry, there are some things that many of us just put off doing until we absolutely cannot postpone any longer.

Let's admit it, spending money is far more enjoyable than saving it. When would we file our taxes if there were no April 15 deadline? Probably never. Have you ever had to fight with your kids to eat vegetables? How about eating candy? Do you have a gym membership card that just sits in your wallet? Doing the right thing is almost always harder than doing what is enjoyable. When it comes to saving for retirement, the motivation doesn't hit some until they realize they are getting older and may not want to work forever. Unfortunately, that point of realization is usually far too late to begin saving sufficiently to create a comfortable income for life.

Our financial values are, for the most part, learned. If your parents were good financial stewards, you almost certainly place a higher value on savings than someone who grew up in a home where the family was not as careful with money. What we are taught as children about money shapes our attitude about spending and saving as adults. That is why income or financial status has no relevance to one's financial values. A low-income family can be just as prone to teaching their children about bad spendthrift habits as an ultrahigh-net-worth parent. A wealthy family can teach strong financial values just as easily as a low-income family who struggles. My mother lived hand-to-mouth, and although we weren't low income, we certainly didn't have an extravagant lifestyle. However, every time she got her hands on a tax return or bonus, she spent it on a new car or a fancy vacation, Granted, she always made sure her kids were taken care of and our needs were met, but she rationalized, *I don't have much, so when I get a little extra, let's indulge!* Believe me, that mindset shaped how I thought of money and I found myself indulging too often and was laden in debt at a very young age. Fortunately, I learned quickly about the value of savings thanks to getting into this business.

I know of very wealthy families who are conscientious recyclers, even reusing foil and disposable food containers. I also know of poor families who save and recycle every resource they can. Likewise, I also know of those who spend recklessly. I'm sure you, too, know of some who spend money like crazy, perhaps even in your own family. When your brother drives up in a Tesla Model S or your best friend sends you amazing pictures of his exotic travels to the Bay of Kotor, Montenegro, you can't help but feel disadvantaged. Spendthrifts justify their indulgences by saying, "I make it. Why not enjoy it!" But living rich is less about how much you make and more about how much you keep. People can earn seven-figure incomes and still not keep much in the end. It happens all the time. Just look at the number of celebrities who file bankruptcy. There's a reason why so many lottery winners end up broke and poverty-stricken. Money doesn't grow on trees, and those who treat it as if it does eventually face the day of reckoning.

The peace of mind that comes from financial independence, on the other hand, is priceless. Unfortunately, most people don't understand this until they have made sacrifices and *earned* financial security. Most don't realize financial windfalls are not necessarily blessings. There's no substitute for hard work and sacrifice. But, the first step is usually the most difficult, especially for those who were not taught values of prudence. Procrastination is often the biggest culprit. Of course, most all of us, at least to some degree, are victim to procrastination. However, when it comes to securing retirement procrastination can be devastating. Young workers are typically not motivated to think about retirement savings because it seems like a lifetime away. Then they get married and buy a home, and their mortgage becomes the priority, pushing retirement savings out to a "better time." Shortly thereafter, along come kids, and, indeed, kids are expensive. I understand it is certainly hard to save for retirement while supporting a family. Will it be better to save when the kids are older? No. Because not only will we lose precious time but when the kids are older, there's college expenses and wedding costs, and of course we want to help them buy a house and give them all the things we never had. Then there's grandchildren. Suddenly, it seems, we are approaching our sixties and are *finally* ready to make retirement a priority, only it's impossible to finance a twenty-five- or thirty-year income in just a handful of years. It takes us thirty years or more to pay off our mortgage, and retirement is an even greater expense than a house! For sure, workers need help to understand the importance and value of time and money.

You have the power to help your employees overcome their own self-imposed limits. Most 401(k) plans require employees to *choose* to put money into the plan. But since the Pension Protection Act of 2006, many employers have instituted "automatic enrollment," which means they automatically initiate employee salary deferrals unless the employee opts out of the plan. That is, with automatic enrollment the employee doesn't have to choose to put money in the plan; *they have to choose not to*. Under the Pension Protection Act automatic provisions, 401(k) participants can still exercise control over their individual accounts if they want to, but these automatics counteract the power of inertia:

- Automatic Enrollment
- Qualified Default Investment Alternative
- Automatic Increase
- Automatic Re-Enrollment

As a plan sponsor, you should consider taking advantage of the automatic options and decide which ones you could implement to help your employees work toward retirement success. Unfortunately, since these automatic features were introduced in 2006, many employers, especially those with fewer than one hundred employees, still have not become comfortable using them. Yet, this may be the greatest power you have to help your employees.

Consider the historically low participation in 401(k) plans. Companies that offered these plans didn't know what to make of the lackluster interest on the part of employees—until researchers identified the problem: sheer inertia. Most employees have the best of intentions. If you ask employees who are not currently participating, most of them will tell you they intend on enrolling—*eventually*. Sadly, many fail to get around to doing it. They simply procrastinate. So, rather than asking people to actively sign up, let's assume they want to do the right thing to pursue a secure future.

AUTOMATIC ENROLLMENT

When you get your driver's license, you are asked to check a box if you would like to donate your organs upon your death. Recent data suggest that in any given year there are generally more than 118,000 people on the organ transplant waiting list in the United States, but only about 7 percent undergo transplants of organs from deceased donors. The reason? Because we simply *don't check the box*. Conversely, countries with a "presumed consent" law don't have this problem. Austria, Belgium, and France have a nearly 100 percent organ donation rate. What's the difference? They assume their citizens want to be organ donors. Of course, you can choose not to, but to do so you must *opt out* by checking a box. In the United States, you are assumed *not* to be an organ donor, so it's no surprise that over 45,000 Americans die each year waiting for a donor. But in France, it is assumed you will be an organ donor, so ultimately there is over 90 percent consent. Simply a difference in phrasing can literally save the lives of potentially tens of thousands of Americans.

What about your 401(k)? Do your employees have to take action to participate? Why should we assume workers don't want to save for their retirement? Shouldn't we assume they do want to save? After all, that is the responsible thing to do. It certainly ought to be automatic for all workers. Do we have a choice with Social Security? No! As soon as we earn our first dollar, Social Security and Medicare taxes are assessed. We ought to be leading employees to practice the same for saving for their retirement, don't you agree?

The Pension Protection Act of 2006 includes a provision that allows employers to set their employees up for immediate enrollment in their company-sponsored retirement plan. The intention is to encourage workers to begin saving for their retirement early on so that they are financially capable of retiring. If an employee decides not to participate in the company's plan, he or she can simply opt out. However, automatic enrollment means we are going to assume everyone wants to prepare for their retirement. Employees agree that enrolling in a retirement plan is easy to put off doing, but when it's done for you, you have to actually say, "I know I should be doing this, but I'm not going to." Instead of opting out, however, most employees keep contributing—and they are likely glad they did!

Through auto-enroll, your employees have to take action in order *not to save*. Therefore, if they succumb to inaction, inertia will work in their favor. And it has. According to study after study, auto-enrollment programs have substantially increased 401(k) participation. While the employee "thinks about it," they are putting their money to work for their retirement. Without automation, the inclination to procrastinate, hesitate, or hem and haw will often undermine the employee's retirement security. To thwart inertia and encourage retirement readiness for your employees, take advantage of automation in any way you can.

There was a study by the Employee Benefit Research Institute (EBRI) not too long ago that indicated 18 percent of eligible workers were not participating in their company retirement plans, which is only adding to our retirement crisis. Auto-enroll is a way of getting people to start the retirement savings habit early in their careers. In 2003, about half of workers age eighteen to thirty-four participated in available 401(k) plans. In 2013, thanks to auto-enrollment, plans reached *87 percent participation* with these younger workers, raising awareness and developing the savings habit that many older employees undoubtedly wished they had done earlier.

If you choose to set your plan for auto-enrollment, you will need to set a default savings rate. This is usually relatively low, typically 3 percent, although as recently reported, some plans are bumping that up. Because as a general rule of thumb we suggest employees save at least 10 percent to pursue retirement success, help your employees get there by establishing auto-enrollment at a level that will help them work toward retirement security. You may want to start with 5 percent rate and add auto-increase (described later) or align your default savings rate to maximize your matching contributions, if you offer them. The percentage automatically withheld must apply uniformly to all employees covered by the plan and must not exceed 10 percent of salary.

AUTO-ENROLL CONTRIBUTIONS

How does it work? If you elect auto-enroll, you must first notify all employees who are eligible to participate in the arrangement thirty to ninety days prior to the beginning of the plan year. Suppose your plan is running on a calendar year. If you send out a notice on October 1, employees will have until November 1 to opt out, and by January 1, those who don't opt out will be automatically enrolled. Of course, employees can still change their decision, but until or unless they do so, they participate in the plan and save for their retirement. According to surveys, only 15 percent of employees opt out, meaning 85 percent of those employees who were not participating before remain in the plan. You can set it up so your provider will do an auto-enroll for those not participating every year.

Newton's first law of motion states that every object will remain still unless compelled to change its state by the action of an external force. This is the normal definition of inertia, and this law applies to human behavior as well. Auto-enroll forces action. Employees who have not been participating in their company-sponsored plan for years have been compelled to change because of auto-enroll. It has been quite effective at raising 401(k) participation rates. If you follow statistics, you know that averages suggest approximately 15 percent of employees will opt out of your plan. If your participation rate is currently 60 percent, you could potentially boost your participation rate to over 80 percent with auto-enroll. That is more than a 30 percent increase in participation rates.

For new employees, if you decide to automatically enroll new hires immediately upon eligibility, you will need to give them notice on their date of hire or before the eligibility date, which means you must provide notice to the employee before the pay date for the pay period in which the employee becomes eligible.

What happens if you have an employee who was auto-enrolled but wants his money back? If written into your plan as an Eligible Automatic Contribution Arrangement (EACA), you may allow an employee to withdraw automatic-enrollment contributions and earnings without penalties, provided said employee makes this election within ninety days of the first automatic contribution. With this feature, the employee can withdraw her own contributions from the plan without incurring a tax penalty. Of course, she will forfeit any company matching dollars, and the amount of the withdrawal will be included in her income for the taxable year in which the distribution is made. Furthermore, the market value may be more or less than the actual contribution based on investment performance.

AUTO-INCREASE

Sadly, inertia (our tendency to do nothing) is more powerful than the threat of poverty in our old age. That's why automatic acceleration can encourage higher 401(k) savings rates. Not only can you auto-enroll your employees to get them into the plan, but also you can auto-increase or "auto-escalate" their contribution rates to help them move toward retirement preparedness. Many employees are not contributing enough to provide sufficient income continuity in retirement. The "set it and forget it" mind-set is resulting in a severe lack of retirement readiness. Many employees don't realize it, but when you have twenty-five years or more before retirement, a small contribution difference may make a big difference in the end. As a result, auto-increase could help your employees get to the target deferral rates to help drive results.

401(k) Future Value Based on Different Deferral Rates				
	4%	6%	8%	10%
AGE 25	$729,118	$1,093,674	$1,458,231	$1,822,790
AGE 30	$489,468	$734,199	$978,931	$1,223,666
AGE 35	$322,775	$484,160	$645,547	$806,934
AGE 40	$207,526	$311,287	$415,050	$518,813
AGE 45	$128,461	$192,691	$256,921	$321,152
AGE 50	$74,768	$112,152	$149,536	$186,920
AGE 55	$38,798	$58,196	$77,595	$96,993
AGE 60	$15,144	$22,717	$30,289	$37,861

Figure 5.2. Assumes a $60,000 salary with no employer matching starting from scratch, with no other retirement savings; 7% annual net average rate of return, 3% COLA. Age 65 retirement. This is a hypothetical example and is not representative of any specific situation. Your results will vary. The hypothetical rates of return used do not reflect the deduction of fees and charges inherent to investing.

In figure 5.2 you can see the difference over time on a 1 percent deferral for a hypothetical employee. In this example, a 1 percent salary deferral doesn't make a tremendous difference for an employee close to retirement; however, the 1 percent differential for a thirty- to thirty-five-year-old employee can represent six figures. And the difference between a 5 percent deferral and a 10 percent deferral can represent a substantial sum, especially for younger workers. This is an example of an employee earning $60,000 with various deferral rates, earning 7% net average annual return on his 401(k). Of course, income and/or return differences will represent different outcomes, but employees over the age of fifty starting this late in their working years may be forced to work beyond normal retirement age, while having to save more and enjoy far less.

Of course, 10 percent is the target in this example, but I understand it's not easy to go from zero savings to 10 percent all at once. There is where auto-increase can be especially valuable. Suppose you have a thirty-year-old employee currently deferring 5 percent into his 401(k). If we can get him to increase to the 10 percent target by utilizing auto-increase by the time he's thirty-five, he will be at 10 percent salary deferral. This could enable him to have $994,013 at age sixty-five (the growth of his account with auto-increase), compared to $403,466 had he remained at 5 percent. Which outcome is going to be better at attempting to provide a secure retirement?

New research, including studies done by Harvard University, shows that employees are apt to be as happy with a 5 percent to 9 percent deferral as they are with the more traditional 3 percent or 4 percent salary deferral. Unfortunately, the lower contribution rate is just not enough to fund retirement these days. Most employers at larger companies have adopted both auto-enrollment and auto acceleration for their retirement savings plans, according to a study by Hewitt Associates. At most larger firms, not only will you automatically become part of the plan through auto-enroll but also you will see your contribution increase every year automatically unless you actively opt out by signing a document. Auto-escalate and auto-enroll can be set to occur every year, so if an employee opted out this year, next year he or she will need to opt out again or be automatically enrolled or automatically increased. With these automatics every year, sooner, rather than later, many employees will overcome procrastination. You are also sending a very powerful message when you implement these auto features: We care about your retirement success and want to help you become retire ready.

The auto-increase or "automatic escalation" program may be the most effective of the automatics because it can be extended to *all workers*, not just new hires or those not participating. Unless the majority of your employees are contributing 10–15 percent to the 401(k), they are unlikely to be retirement ready. The auto-increase can help them get there.

If you implement auto-increase, your provider will simply send out a notice each year informing participants that their contributions will increase on a stated date, such as January 1, and if they do nothing, they will be one more year closer to their targeted savings goal. As with all auto features, they will be given sufficient notice and have plenty of time to opt out. But if you give pay increases on January 1, this may be timed perfectly. With the automatics, you can help your employees overcome one of their biggest challenge to their retirement—properly funding it.

DEFAULT INVESTMENTS

When you set up your plan, your provider is going to ask you what fund you would like to designate as your "Qualified Default Investment Alternative" or QDIA. This is the default investment selected for those employees who fail to make their own investment selections. Having a default option in place is important for many reasons, particularly if you elect automatic enrollment.

If your plan has been in force prior to 2006, you ought to review your default investment option, because it may not be qualified under the current law. Prior to the Pension Protection Act (PPA), plan sponsors were not relieved from liability for investment losses held in a default investment option. Therefore, the standard default option was a cash preservation fund or money market account. Today, the PPA offers safe harbor for fiduciaries provided you meet specific criteria, which starts with selecting one of the three types of investments that would be considered a Qualified Default Investment Alternative as defined by the regulations: balanced or life-cycle funds, target date funds, or managed asset allocation accounts. Notice that money market and cash preservation funds are not included. This is because the regulators realized it is important that participants have their retirement assets invested in a manner appropriate to their age and risk tolerance, not focused on capital preservation.

Figure 5.3 highlights the key elements required for Qualified Default Investment Alternatives (QDIA). While this may be a life-cycle fund or a balanced fund, Target Date Funds (TDFs) have emerged as the predominant choice among plan fiduciaries these days. In fact, TDFs were identified as the QDIA selection for nearly three-fourths of plans surveyed by the Plan Sponsor Council of America. One of the unique components of TDFs is the glide path concept (i.e., the systematic reduction of equity exposure over the participant's time horizon). There are a wide variety of glide paths available in the marketplace today. While there is general consensus across TDF providers that younger participants should typically be invested in a more growth-oriented manner, there are significant differences between TDF glide paths in the years leading up to retirement, at retirement, and during retirement. I encourage you review chapter 6 to learn more about target date funds to be sure you understand your QDIA options.

QDIA requirements include:

- ☐ A QDIA may not impose financial penalties or otherwise restrict the ability of a participant or beneficiary to transfer the investment from the qualified default investment alternative to any other investment alternative available under the plan.
- ☐ A QDIA must be either managed by an investment manager, or an investment company registered under the Investment Company Act of 1940.
- ☐ A QDIA must be diversified so as to minimize the risk of large losses.
- ☐ A QDIA may not invest participant contributions directly in employer securities.
- ☐ A QDIA may be a life-cycle, target date fund, balanced fund or professionally managed account.
- ☐ A QDIA must be either managed by an investment manager, or an investment company registered under the Investment Company Act of 1940.
- ☐ A QDIA must be diversified so as to minimize the risk of large losses.
- ☐ A QDIA may not invest participant contributions directly in employer securities.

Figure 5.3

Don't forget to monitor your QDIA carefully and ask your advisor to keep you current on trends and developments with these types of accounts, especially if you institute auto features. If employees neglect to make their investment elections, you will want to be sure you qualify for the safe harbor for your plan's default option.

AUTO RE-ENROLLMENT

A significant driver to retirement success is certainly going to be proper funding. However, investment performance is also critical. Poor investment choices or, even worse, poor timing choices can sabotage retirement security for even the highest contributors to your plan. Over the years, I have met many employees who had the right intentions when participating in their company 401(k) plan, only to find disappointment with their investment performance and soon grow discouraged to the point where they stopped contributing, stopped monitoring their accounts, and even stopped opening their statements.

Auto *re-enrollment* helps to address the growing concern about the retirement readiness of American workers and helps keep the progress going by focusing on seeking to improve investment results. Re-enrollment can help promote improved investment outcomes. At the very least, re-enrollment could help correct investment election problems. The name is actually a misnomer since participants are not required to literally re-enroll in the plan. It should probably be called "re-election" because the approach means that participants are required to make new investment decisions, even if they have previously given investment instructions. Each participant can decide to leave his or her investments "as is" or select different investments, or if they do nothing, their funds will be defaulted into your qualified default investment alternative, or QDIA, which is presumed to be properly allocated between the different asset classes.

You might be surprised to find participants are very confused about their investment choices. Ideally, they will define their own personal goals, identify their rate-of-return needs, and perform their own risk tolerance analysis before making their investment elections.

But, of course, you know many employees are simply unskilled in finance and don't know how to define their goals and determine the right investment strategy. Therefore, it is not usual to find that some of your participants' fund choices are not the best. Often they are either too conservative, too aggressive, concentrated in one or two similar funds, or just not effectively allocated. Re-enrollment can help correct these imbalances.

I find that most participants intend to review their 401(k) each year; however, life tends to get in the way, and they forget. They simply don't understand how important it is to review their accounts and rebalance their portfolios periodically. They may have allocated their contributions when they initially enrolled in the plan, but if that was many years ago, those allocations may be too risky for their age now. Then there are the participants who are too conservative with their allocations who may not even have a fair chance at building a sufficient retirement fund. There is a cost for assuming risk, but there is also a price to pay for a "risk-averse" strategy. I received a call from a participant not too long ago who asked why his account wasn't moving even though the market was going up. I asked him if he had selected any stock funds in his 401(k), and he replied, "I don't know." This was an employee who earned over $250,000 a year. As it turned out, he didn't realize he had allocated his 401(k) contributions to a money market fund. Fortunately, the market rally spurred him to take a look, but he could have been sitting in a low-interest-paying money market fund for a very long time and not realized it.

To help correct these problems, you can initiate a re-enrollment, which realigns your participants' investments to a more balanced allocation and generally a more appropriate level of risk-taking. Why would you do this? Very simply put, your QDIA, if selected correctly, should be properly balanced for both growth and risk management. In the case of Target Date Funds or life-cycle funds, these are aligned with the age of the employee and follow a path over a lifetime of shifting risk. Your QDIA aims to ensure your participants are investing strategically for their retirement. It's what I call the Goldilocks story—not too hot, not too cold, but just right. More of this topic is covered in chapter 6.

Re-enrollment also helps with inertia. If the employee does nothing, his or her account will automatically be reallocated to your balanced fund or to the appropriate Target Date Fund aligned to his or her age. If the employee wants to opt out of this rebalance, he or she must go online and review his or her investment selections. Hence, re-enrollment is a call to action. If you notice your participant-directed investment allocations are out of whack, you may want to institute a re-enrollment.

The process is not complicated. A notice must be given thirty days prior to the date of the re-enrollment (the day the plan assets will be automatically defaulted into your QDIA). Specifically, employees are notified their investments will be reallocated *unless they opt out*. If you follow this process, you can facilitate a rebalance of investments with full participant knowledge and implied consent. However, in the event the participant fails to pay attention to the notice, he or she can still change how the account is invested after being notified that the default took effect, or at any later time. In the meantime, the assets are moved to a more balanced asset allocation strategy. Consequently, re-enrollment requires your plan participants to stop and think about their investment strategies. At my firm, we often do re-enrollment alongside an investment meeting to help remind the employees of the value and importance of asset allocation.

A number of plan sponsors re-enroll all participants into their QDIA default funds annually. If you have never re-enrolled your participants into your QDIA default funds, you may want to seriously consider doing so this year. Studies have shown that more than three-fourths of all participants accept their reallocated account balance. Of course, before you do this you should consider benchmarking your QDIA or Target Date Funds to be sure they are aligned to your Investment Policy Statement. Because the objective of re-enrollment is to create a better alignment between participants' asset allocations and their retirement goals, fiduciaries ought to be confident the QDIA is suitable. Of course, this is a fiduciary requirement regardless, but if the goal of your plan is to help your employees become retirement ready, this auto feature may improve the likelihood that your participants can pursue greater financial security and avoid amateur investment mistakes.

"I DON'T WANT TO FORCE MY EMPLOYEES!"

Some employers worry the automatics are forcing employees, but I have found these employers often have a misunderstanding of what the automatics do. They do not *force* anyone to do anything; rather, they create an *opportunity* for employees to be able to work towards a more secure retirement. In fact, research is indicating that employees are showing overwhelming support for the automatics. In one survey, 85 percent of women said that automatic enrollment helped them start saving earlier than they would have otherwise. As more companies adopt the automatics, employees will become more accustomed to the process, and they might even begin to expect it. Employees always have the right and the ability to opt out of any automatic. But to do so, they must make an effort, which is more than they may be doing currently. That alone will undoubtedly motivate them to rethink their own retirement.

The auto-enroll helps give a boost to employees who may not have taken the time to seriously consider their needs for retirement savings. If an employee doesn't want to save for his or her retirement, he or she can simply opt out of the auto-enroll. On the other hand, without auto-enroll, the employee has to proactively initiate action and make decisions. It is proven that these decisions can stymie action. When employees go online to enroll or fill out paperwork, just a simple question like "How much would you like to contribute?" can cause an impasse.

Gee. I don't know. How much should I contribute? What should I do? I can definitely do 3 percent. But maybe I should put in 5 percent. Hmm ... I think I should just wait and see what I have left over at the end of the month before I decide.

And thus, the enrollment postponement begins. If that doesn't stop the employees, they are likely to hit a block when it comes to the section of 'Select your Investment Allocations.'

"Where should I invest? Oh, gee, I don't know. There sure are a lot of choices. And it seems the returns are very different. Gee, I'd better wait and talk to my spouse or do some research."

If we get lucky enough to get past this point, there's the beneficiary designation section that can cause a standstill.

"Who is going to get this if I die? Well ... I need to think about that. My parents are a bit old, and my sister is not being very responsible right now. I don't have children, and since I'm in the middle of a divorce, I guess I'd better hold off until I figure this out."

For employees who are not really familiar or comfortable with the 401(k) and the concept of financial planning, these basic decisions can be serious roadblocks. However, the auto-enroll makes it easy. The employee gets a notice that says this is how much is going into your 401(k) and here is how it's going to be invested *unless you want to change it*. The employee doesn't have to give it any further thought. But keep in mind, many employees look to you for leadership and direction. They may believe the automatic deferral rate is the "recommended savings amount," when it is usually just a starting point. That is why auto-increase in addition to auto-enroll may be effective. The auto-increase helps employees get on track in a slow but gradual manner. But as with all the automatics, if the employee doesn't want to increase contributions, he or she can simply opt out.

Finally, the auto re-enroll helps encourage your employees to *revisit* their investment decisions. If a participant wishes to keep his or her investments as is, he or she can simply indicate that preference, and the account will not be changed. But if the participant fails to do anything, his or her account balance and future contributions will be invested in your QDIA and effect a portfolio rebalance. Re-enrollment also reduces fiduciary risk since it provides plan fiduciaries with QDIA safe harbor protection. Re-enrollment is flexible and can address the particular needs of a plan. It may not be available on all plans, but now may be the time to review the automatics with your 401(k) team.

5 + 1 = 10™ SYSTEM

Did you know 5 + 1 = 10? It certainly does! It's simple. In fact, we have found this process to be so helpful, we trademarked it. We teach employees about 5 + 1 = 10 and it really seems to resonate. It's easy to implement, easy to understand and very effective. So effective, in fact, we have found employees talk about it with their spouse, their kids, friends and even extended family members. Here's how it works. Start with 5 percent contribution. Most employees can handle that or stretch to get there if they aren't currently. Then, every year, increase their contributions by 1 percent until they get to 10. Within five years, they will be on track toward hitting their targeted funding rate.

As a plan sponsor, you can impart the benefit of 5 + 1 = 10 for all of your workers very easily. By setting up an auto-enroll at 5 percent and then extending auto-increase at 1 percent a year, within five years you should have most of your employees deferring 10 percent of their salaries, which means you should have most of your employees started on their way toward retirement readiness. Imagine that! You can potentially improve the health of our national retirement just by following 5 + 1 = 10. Not only that, but also think about what it can do for the future of your business. By providing a graceful exit for your aging employees, you can save your company potentially substantial dollars in excess compensation and insurance costs. Indeed, if every employer instituted the 5 + 1 = 10 system, we might be well on our way to a bright future in the United States. With 5 + 1 = 10, we just may be able to change the future for our next generation of retirees and promote economic prosperity. Employees will talk about it because they will see the difference in a relatively short period of time. We find that senior employees even share 5+1=10 with new hires at the water cooler and we've noticed it can become quite a mantra within an organization.

Wait. Isn't that coercive? Should you really *force* your employees to drive retirement results? Are you reluctant to turn the auto-increase into a default option? If so, you should know only about 10 percent of workers opt out of increasing their contributions. That means nearly 90 percent of those who are defaulted into an auto-enroll and auto-increase program tend to stay there.

Some studies indicate your employees need to save 10 percent at a minimum to have a chance at an enjoyable retirement. If you asked your employees to save 10 percent right now, many of them would say, "I can't afford that. After all, it is never convenient to save money, least of all *10 percent!*" So, instead, employees select a more "comfortable" rate of 3 percent, 4 percent, or 5 percent. And ultimately, they stay at this rate. They may never end up resetting their funding. Certainly very few stretch up to the 10 percent range, and this means they potentially miss out on the real magic of compound interest and the time value of money. If your employees do not hit their retirement targets with adequate funding, it will be all but impossible for them to enjoy a secure retirement.

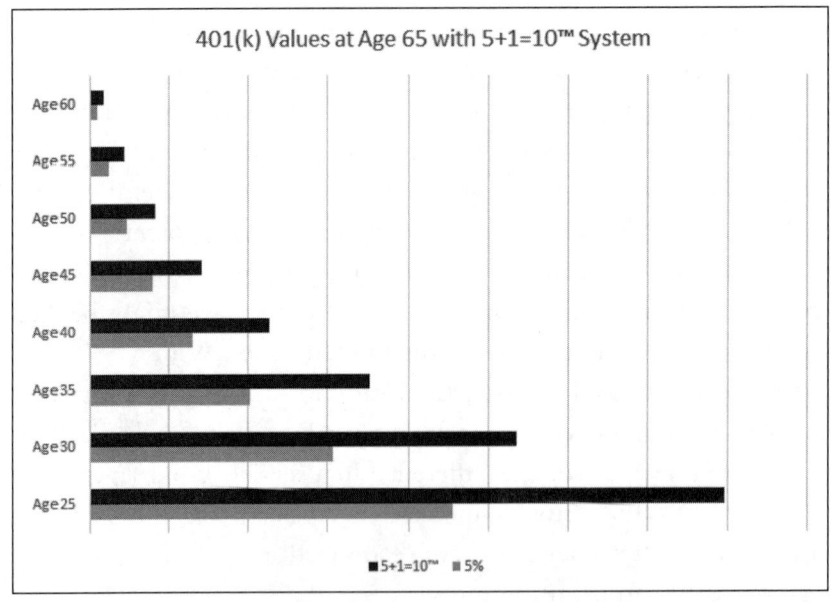

Figure 5.4. Assumes $60,000 salary with 5% deferrals, no employer match, 7% annualized rate of return with 3% COLA adjustments. This is a hypothetical example and is not representative of any specific situation. Your results will vary. The hypothetical rates of return used do not reflect the deduction of fees and charges inherent to investing.

I realize it's difficult to go from 0 percent to 10 percent in salary deferrals. And that's why 5 + 1 = 10 works. Of course, the sooner employees get to 10 percent, the better, but I understand a 10 percent deferral may be too much to take on at one time. It may cause anxiety or financial strain, which is why I developed the 5 + 1 = 10 approach. You can see in figure 5.4 just how significant this system can be, particularly for younger workers. The black bar represents the 5 + 1 = 10 system at work, compared to the gray bar, which represents a 5 percent fixed contribution rate. It may make the difference between being able to retire ready or being ill prepared. First, start with auto-enroll and get your employees started in the plan, then follow with auto-increase. Periodically auto-reenroll in an effort to ensure your employees are investing correctly, and your participants will be started on their way to retirement success.

If you are reluctant to initiate the auto-features, consider this: when taxes go up, do your employees refuse to pay it? Do they come to you to demand an explanation as to why their taxes went up or do they just pay it and manage to get by on the rest? They pay it of course! Why? *Because they don't have a choice.* But, sadly, when they do have the choice to pay themselves first and take the step necessary to seek to secure their future, they often choose not to. Rest assured, workers don't *want* to sabotage their future. It's just never "convenient" to save money. It's certainly always more enjoyable to spend it. But when "tomorrow" becomes ten or twenty years later, the cost of lost opportunity can be quite substantial and may even become irreparable. With 5 + 1 = 10, as you can see in the chart in figure 5.5, your employees can get to 10 percent savings rate within just five years.

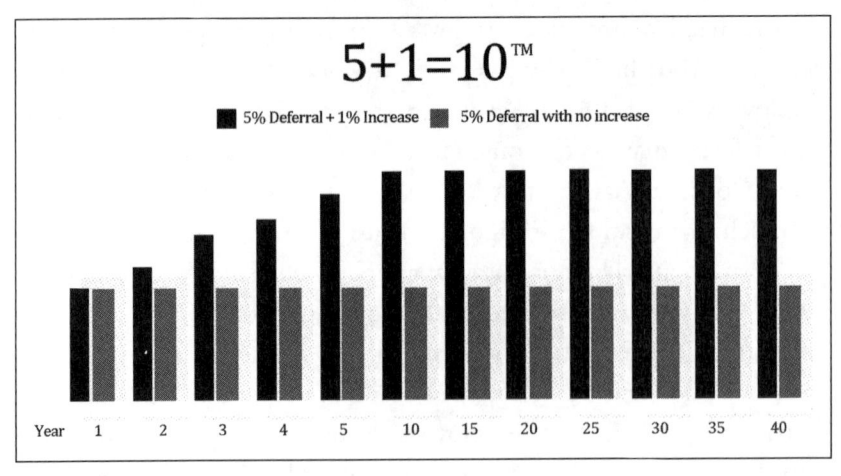

Figure 5.5.

You can see the gap created in wealth between the 5 + 1 = 10 approach and the 5 percent flat savings rate over time. While very few of your employees might be able to start out with 10 percent savings, all of your employees have the potential to get there with 5 + 1 = 10. It's about developing good habits and helping your employees move toward seeking favorable outcomes. You have the power to do this!

THE ROTH 401(K)

In a traditional 401(k) plan, employees contribute pretax earnings to their retirement plan. However, plan sponsors may choose to amend their 401(k) plan document to include the Roth 401(k) option. In doing so, participants can allocate all or a portion of their retirement plan contributions to the Roth 401(k) and enjoy future income tax-free retirement benefits. This means employees can contribute as much as $19,000 *after-tax* instead of pretax (or any combination of the two up to the limit – based on 2019 limits). Participants over age fifty may also use catchup contributions for either traditional or Roth 401(k) contributions ($6,000 limit currently). Employer contributions, however, must always be pretax, or must go into the traditional 401(k).

The difference between the traditional and Roth 401(k) is purely a matter of tax. The investment options, administration, and operation of the Roth 401(k) is essentially the same otherwise. Roth 401(k) salary deferrals are made with after-tax contributions, so the employee does not benefit from current tax benefits. However, instead, the Roth 401(k) allows for tax-free growth potential *and distributions*, provided the contributions have been invested for at least five years *and* the account owner has reached age fifty-nine and a half. The Roth 401(k) is far more advantageous than the Roth IRA, which has lower contribution limits and is subject to Adjusted Gross Income (AGI) restrictions. High-income earners are generally disqualified from the Roth IRA, but the Roth 401(k) is available to any eligible plan participant.

By definition, the key difference between a Roth 401(k) and a traditional 401(k) is that contributions to the Roth are taxable but future retirement income is tax-free, whereas the traditional 401(k) contributions are pretax and future retirement income is fully taxable as ordinary income. While many employees are still opting for the pretax traditional 401(k) and prefer to enjoy current tax benefits, there may be a very attractive advantage of the Roth 401(k), especially for younger or highly compensated employees.

According to *Consumer Reports*, more than 60 percent of 401(k) plans offer a Roth option, but fewer than 20 percent of employees actually use it. So, would paying taxes today be more advantageous? The question is, do you believe your federal and state income taxes are more likely to go up in the future, go down, or stay the same? If you are absolutely convinced your tax rate in retirement will be the same as, or lower than, your current income tax rate, a traditional 401(k) contribution makes good sense. However, the reality is that taxes are ever changing. We live in a period of tax uncertainty, with massive federal debt and an aging population, which only increases the uncertainty with growing Medicare and Medicaid liabilities. Indeed, if you look at history, you can see that taxes have predominately been rising, even for lower-income earners.

Since it's difficult to know exactly what your income will be in retirement, the ability to incorporate tax certainty into your retirement plan has good merit. Having some money in a Roth will give you more control over your taxable income in retirement. This is because qualified withdrawals from a Roth 401(k) are not included in AGI. Consequently, you can reduce your potential tax on Social Security income, and for high-income earners, this can help reduce Medicare premiums in retirement based on current tax laws. There are also no mandatory distributions required at age seventy and a half, which may prove to be a great advantage for higher-income workers.

A Roth 401(k) plan is considered to be most advantageous to younger workers who are currently taxed in a lower tax bracket but expect to be taxed in a higher bracket upon reaching retirement age. The thought is that higher-income workers prefer a traditional 401(k) plan because they are currently taxed in a higher tax bracket and will, presumably, be in a lower tax bracket in retirement. However, with rising Medicare costs, there is reason for high-income earners to rethink their future retirement strategy and take a closer look at the Roth 401(k) alternative.

We all know health care costs have been escalating. Employers have been working diligently to try to curtail the costs, but we are all feeling the impact – employers, employees and even doctors. The health care challenge has not been any easier for retirees. Once an individual retires and reaches age 65, he or she must enroll in Medicare. It's a mandatory requirement. It may be important to know premiums for Medicare are based on your modified adjusted gross income (MAGI) and this means the more *taxable* income you have in retirement, the more you will pay in Medicare premiums. Since inception, in 1965, Medicare premiums have increased at an average annual rate of 7.73%, *which is more than double that of the national inflation rate.*

Figure 5.6 highlights today's costs of Medicare for those over the age of 65. You can see, based on today's premiums those with the higher incomes pay substantially more for Part B coverage. For example, a retired individual with $130,000 MAGI will pay twice as much as a lower income retiree, but an individual with over $160,000 MAGI will pay 220 percent more. If we project out these costs with inflation adjustments, the highest income earners could pay over $1900 a month just for Part B Medicare in 20 years. This doesn't include the costs for Medicare supplemental insurance, dental, vision, co-pays, deductibles, co-insurance or any out-of-pocket expenses. With life expectancies increasing to age 90 and beyond, the rising costs of Medicare based on IRMMA brackets could potentially consume nearly all of one's Social Security benefit, at least for those with high incomes in retirement. This is an example of a redistribution of wealth that is happening without most Americans even knowing it.

MEDICARE INCOME RELATED MONTHLY ADJUSTMENT AMOUNTS (IRMAA BRACKETS 2018)

Individual MAGI	Couples MAGI	Part B	Part D
< $85K	< $170K	Premium	Premium (varies)
$85k - $107k	$170k - $214k	$187.50 (40%)	Premium + $13.30
$107k - $133k	$214k - $266k	$267.90 (100%)	Premium + $34.20
$133k - $160k	$266k - $320k	$348.30 (160%)	Premium + $55.20
$160k	$320k	$428.60 (220%)	Premium + $76.20

Source: Medicare.Gov

Figure 5.6.

There are only a few income sources that are not included in IRMAA, and one of those excluded income benefits is – you got it - Roth 401(k) distributions. Another excluded income benefit is from Health Savings Accounts (HSA). If you have a high deductible medical plan, you may want to look into adding a Health Savings Account option for your employees. If you anticipate an above-average income in retirement you may want to consider incorporating the Roth 401(k) into your plan.

Not only will you be able to enjoy tax-free income that is excluded from IRMAA (under current tax law) but also, keep in mind as already noted, Roth 401(k)s have no age 70½ required minimum distributions (RMDs). Traditional 401(k) plans are subject to age 70½ distribution rules, which means you must take taxable withdrawals based on IRS mortality tables once you reach age 70½ to force tax recovery of your account. Consequently, RMDs could increase your MAGI thereby possibly resulting in escalating Medicare premiums. Thus, for highly compensated employees, the Roth and HSA can be a valuable strategy to help you pursue the lifestyle you desire in retirement.

If you haven't figured it out yet, there are very complex issues that one must consider with retirement planning. It's not just about *accumulating* wealth. It's also about protecting it. And for affluent or high-income workers it's becoming increasingly more difficult to mitigate the impact of our government's redistribution of wealth strategy. As we continue to face the realities of the aging population, with over 8,000 Baby Boomers turning age 65 every day for the next 11 years, we should be prepared for continued challenges. Our national retirement crisis is a growing concern that will impact us all.

You can offer the Roth 401(k) to your participants as a way to enable them to prepare accordingly, as per their own individual needs and approach to retirement planning. The Roth 401(k) allows participants to hedge against the risk of rising taxes. Since we have no idea what taxes will look like over our lifetime, tax diversification can prove to be an effective strategy. There is no perfect option, so it is possible a split between Traditional 401(k) and Roth 401(k) may be a wise approach toward retirement wellness.

PROFIT SHARING

Adding a profit-sharing option to your 401(k) can be a powerful tool in promoting retirement readiness and rewarding your employees for their contribution to your success. Profit-Sharing Plans are a valuable option for smaller businesses because they offer flexibility and could enable owner-employees a greater share of the allocations. But even larger firms have found benefits to Profit-Sharing Plans. As an employer, you can choose how much contribution you wish to make each year, if any at all. Unlike the 401(k) matching options, which are nondiscretionary employer contributions, profit-sharing contributions are completely discretionary. This means you can decide each year whether or not to make contributions to the Profit-Sharing Plan.

As the name implies, these plans are based on your choice to share profits. Actually, profits are not really relevant in that you can contribute during years of no (or low) profits, or not contribute during periods of high profits. The value of the Profit-Sharing Plan is the flexibility in the yearly contributions. You need not have ever reported profits to make contributions. So, Profit-Sharing Plans are not really oriented toward annual company earnings. But by being *profit-driven*, you reserve the right either to share profits with your employees or not. Whichever the case may be, if you do decide to make a profit-sharing contribution in a given year, the company must follow a predetermined formula for deciding which employees get what and how much. You can use discretion when it comes to making contributions, but you cannot discriminate in terms of who receives the benefits. Employee allocations are typically determined as a percentage of pay, and if you so choose, contributions may vest according to a set vesting schedule.

Naturally, you must also set up a system that tracks contributions, investments, vesting amounts and distributions, and file an annual return with the government. A plan administrator will do this work your behalf, so it is a relatively simple arrangement offered by most 401(k) providers and typically incorporated into your existing 401(k) plan. Although you cannot discriminate, you have some flexibility to choose which employees can participate in the Profit-Sharing plan, when they will be eligible, and how contributions are allocated to participants. As mentioned, you can also add a vesting schedule, somewhat akin to that of 401(k) matching contributions, so the plan can be structured to reward tenure.

Profit-Sharing Plans can be a part of a 401(k) or they can be stand-alone plans. They need not have to be a part of an existing 401(k), but since these plans don't allow for employee contributions, it may be best to include them alongside a 401(k). Employees really don't have much control over a Profit-Sharing plan except to elect their investment allocations. That is why it is recommended to layer a Profit-Sharing Plan onto a 401(k) to allow for employee salary deferrals as well. If you already have a 401(k), you may want to consider adding a Profit-Sharing Plan to help you attract and retain talented or key employees.

If you don't have any qualified plan yet established, consider the benefits of a 401(k) *with Profit-Sharing*. You can use a Profit-Sharing Plan option in lieu of employer matching or in addition to it. Either way, it's a great way to boost your retirement benefits and retain flexibility.

401(K) ANNUITIES—QUALIFIED LONGEVITY ANNUITY CONTRACT (QLAC)

A key benefit of the former pension arrangement was the ability to enjoy a check for life in retirement without ever having to worry about running out of income. Every month, the retiree received a check very much like Social Security, which continued essentially uninterrupted for the individual's entire lifetime, whether he lived five years or fifty. Of course, one of the challenges that led to the demise of most private pensions (and that public pensions are now facing) is the increased life expectancies. Preparing actuarial assumptions with longevity can be difficult. If the assumptions are underestimated, it can prove disastrous. To protect against this risk, insurance companies offer annuity payouts that function very much like pension checks, backed by the insurer. Since insurance companies are rather adept with actuarial assumptions, they tend to provide a great deal of stability for those seeking income-for-life benefits. However, as with everything, there are trade-offs.

While our parents or grandparents may have enjoyed the peace of mind that comes with a guaranteed lifetime retirement income, they lacked control over their investment results. They also did not enjoy inflation adjustments to their income and they lost the ability to leave behind an inheritance for their children. Today, employees may not have pension benefits but they can turn their retirement savings (or any other capital for that matter) into the same type of income-for-life benefit in the form an annuity, but of course with the same trade-offs.

Annuities have been around since 1812. In fact, in 1905 Andrew Carnegie founded the Teacher's Pension Fund, which in 1918 became the Teacher's Insurance Annuity Association (now commonly known as TIAA-CREF). Annuities haves been long used as retirement income options, which can include the income-for-life option.

Although the income-for-life benefit can provide peace of mind, it does come with restrictions. Workers must relinquish their capital in exchange for the income benefit. However, within a 401(k), an annuity option does not have to be an "all or nothing" approach. Employees can choose to allocate a portion of their retirement savings to provide an income guarantee on some of their funds, while the remaining assets can be left in the traditional investments for more flexible wealth accumulation pool. Since most employees do not like leaving their retirement to chance, the ability to guarantee a certain amount of income at retirement may be attractive.

In a 401(k), employees know they are investing in the financial markets, which offer no underlying guarantees. If they choose the right investments, they may be able to adequately fund their retirement; however, if they don't, they could risk not having sufficient assets to support their retirement. Thus, the goal of the annuity option is to build a future income guarantee into their retirement plan, much like one may view Social Security. In this case, however, the insurance company makes a promise that for a stated amount of lump-sum money, it will provide the retiree a check in a fixed amount payable every month in retirement. This provides workers with a way to attack retirement planning from multiple angles and potentially increase the odds of living a comfortable life.

This is known as a Qualified Longevity Annuity Contract (QLAC) and it may be purchased within a 401(k). But it does have restrictions and, frankly, it may not be the most ideal solution. For instance, the annuity can only be a fixed contract, meaning the earnings are based on interest rates set by the insurance company and guaranteed by the insurer's general account. The annuity allocations cannot be invested in the stock market or accounts of the employee's choosing. Thus, the rate credited is based on current interest rates set forth by the insurance company, which may be a lower earnings rate than alternative investment options. This means the assets could be at a greater risk of being eroded by inflation. Also, QLACs are not permitted to offer a cash surrender option, meaning that once it is allocated to the annuity, the employee will only receive an income at retirement. There will be no lump-sum option for that portion of the account. Contracts are purchased based on lump-sum amounts, which cannot exceed the lesser of 25 percent of a participant's account balance or $130,000 (based on 2019 limits, subject to cost-of-living adjustments).

Payments from a QLAC typically commence upon retirement but can be extended to no later than age eighty-five. Thinking strategically, this means an employee could avoid the age 70½ required minimum distribution (RMD) for those assets in a QLAC. Although most of your employees will likely need the income sooner, higher-net-worth executives may find the QLAC to be a strategic tax-planning tool.

Upon a participant's death, if the payments received have not exceeded the principal originally paid, the difference may be paid out to the designated beneficiary, provided this option was elected by the participant when the annuity was purchased. But, since the primary objective of the annuity is to provide a guaranteed income benefit for the participant, there is typically little to no benefit left for heirs. These income arrangements are not new, but only since 2014 has the Treasury Department made them available for retirement plan participants. Thus, they have not taken off in popularity as of yet, and there are plenty of questions to ask the insurance provider if you decide to include an annuity option in your plan. For instance, the insurance company is guaranteeing the contract, but what happens if you decide to change vendors? There may be added fees to carry the annuity contract in a new plan. Will the internal charges be increased in the future? Can participants borrow against the QLAC in an emergency? What happens if an employee leaves the company? Will the annuity contract roll over to an IRA? Will there be a surrender fee, and if so, who will pay it?

Given the complexity of these contracts, the impact on employers who sponsor this option in retirement plans may be considerable. Offering plan participants the opportunity to purchase a QLAC inside their 401(k) provides another tool to help them enjoy a steady income at retirement, but plan sponsors should know QLACs erect a new fiduciary hurdle that must be carefully managed. Annuity contracts can be very complicated, so the selection and monitoring of annuity providers and contracts, subject to ERISA due diligence requirements, can be rather involved and time-consuming. In fact, employers may be reluctant to offer lifetime income options because of fiduciary and legal risks. Furthermore, finding a recordkeeper who offers the QLAC option may not be an easy process. In the event you decide to include the annuity as an option within your plan, given the complexity of annuity contracts, it is advised to engage an expert to assist in assessing annuity providers. The market is evolving and the government and financial institutions are both seeking alternative solutions for workers, so it's important to keep current on the trends and weigh your options carefully help your employees. The annuity option may be new but in due time, it could grow to become more common within the 401(k).

IN SUMMARY

Plan sponsors need to find the most appropriate way to structure their 401(k) plan based on their goals and objectives, which do change over time. Therefore, plan design is not something to consider only when you initially write your plan. In fact, if you haven't reviewed your plan design in a while, it is time to take a closer look at the details of your plan, including its features and benefits. For example, the idea that employees must wait before enrolling in their 401(k) is slowly losing traction. By allowing immediate enrollment, you enable employees to pick up saving for retirement where their prior firm may have left off. You also help ease the process for employees rolling over their former 401(k) accounts so they can consolidate if appropriate.

One of the biggest impacts you can have on your 401(k) is to offer an employer match. If you haven't considered this yet, keep in mind that this is a critical component to motivating your employees to take action and build retirement savings. And if you do have a matching option, it is certainly important to consider the incentive and target the right matching formula that will get your employees on track toward a secure retirement. Plan sponsors are using more creative formulas to drive results. One such plan offers 100 percent match up to the first $4,000 of contributions for all employees! While that might sound like a hefty obligation for some companies, if everyone saved $8,000 a year for their retirement, we would surely make a good impact on our national retirement crisis.

Automatic enrollment and automatic escalation are two behavioral-based design elements that every plan should consider. These are great tools that are designed to get your employees saving for their retirement today and get them to save more. Such incentives may go far to ensure your employees can retire ready. You may worry that automatically deducting money from your employee's paycheck will upset them, but if you do not take action to help your workers save more and invest appropriately, they will likely be more distressed if they discover they can't afford to retire. There is much you can do to be a good steward. The Pension Protection Act of 2006 gives you excellent tools to help you do your part to promote retirement readiness.

CHAPTER 6
INVESTMENTS

Liam is a new participant in your 401(k). He is forty years old and finally making a good salary, so he decided to contribute to the 401(k) plan this year and allocate all of his contributions to stock funds because he considers himself a long-term investor. Suddenly the stock market drops unexpectedly, and his portfolio falls sharply. He has become very anxious. He is no longer thinking like a long-term investor. Instead, he is checking his account online multiple times a day. He fears he will continue to lose money if he stays invested. He is confident the market will eventually come back up, but he figures if he gets out now, he will buy back in after the market hits bottom. He is sure this is a smart move. In passing, he tells you his plan and mentions that he is even thinking he will stop contributing for a while and wait until things get better. What do you say to Liam?

More than sixty-one million people participate in self-directed employer-sponsored retirement plans, including the 401(k). Unfortunately, an overwhelming majority of them don't have expertise in portfolio management, yet the rate of return earned on their plan is critical to retirement success. It can make the difference between a secure retirement and a vulnerable one. When it comes to 401(k) investments, although the bulk of the responsibility is placed on the participant, plan fiduciaries do have some responsibilities and liabilities. Even though the 401(k) plan is self-directed (i.e., the employees make all the investment selections), the plan sponsor has a duty to follow a prudent process of selecting, monitoring, and maintaining an adequate investment menu from which participants can choose to direct their contributions. In short, you have the power to help your employees build strong investment portfolios by offering them quality fund options. Your careful management and oversight can enable them to seek superior investment results, which is why ERISA requires plan sponsors to monitor their investment menu. Some plan sponsors unintentionally or unknowingly handicap their participants by offering an inferior list of options. If you are not scrutinizing the investments within your 401(k), you should know unintentional negligence is not a defense against fiduciary breach.

When a 401(k) plan is established, the plan sponsor is tasked with the responsibility of selecting the menu of investments available to its participants. You will have a variety of fund options available. The investment options available should be a careful part of the recordkeeper consideration, as some recordkeepers have more limited investment access. Of course, investments vary based on objectives, performance, risk, type of securities held, and expenses. Some funds are actively managed, while others are passive funds. Some are domestic funds, while others are international. Some are traditional, while others are niche or specialty. What is best for your participants? Only you and your committee can make this determination since you know your employees better than a recordkeeper or outside administrator does. However, if you do not carefully select and monitor the funds offered to your participants, not only are you in fiduciary breach but also you may very well be unknowingly causing impediments that can inhibit retirement preparedness. The Department of Labor has emphasized the lost opportunity resulting from higher plan expenses, but what about the cost of inferior investment results? Do investment returns matter? You bet they do! Does risk affect outcome? Absolutely! Is there a cost to missed opportunities? Most definitely!

Did you know the difference in performance results between two similar funds can range quite substantially? From 2014 to 2017, according to Morningstar, a top-quartile-performing US stock growth and income fund averaged as much as +14.95% per year compared to a bottom-quartile fund of similar kind that averaged as little as −1.51% over the same period. That's a difference of nearly 16.5% a year! I would say those in the later fund certainly missed opportunities. *Why would you ever want to be invested in a bottom-quartile-performing fund (a fund beat by 75 percent or more of its peers)?* You wouldn't. Yet it happens. How do your funds rank against their peers today?

Of course, it's not just about performance. The difference between fund expenses of similarly managed funds can also vary widely. For example, actively managed funds may have expenses as low as 0.48 percent, while others may charge 1.58 percent. Even the same fund can have different expenses based on different share classes. The difference in risk or volatility of similar funds can potentially be swings of 10 percent compared to swings of 20 percent. And what about missing out on an important asset class that may not be included in your investment menu, such as global bonds or emerging markets? Is there a cost to that? Of course there is. As of this writing, we are in a rising interest rate environment. Traditional bonds tend to lose value as rates rise, but there are fixed-income funds managed to mitigate rising interest rate risk. Should you have nontraditional bonds included in your fund menu? Are you adequately preparing your participants with access to investments that can help them navigate through the ever-changing economic environment?

And what about your employees—are they paying close enough attention to their investment selections? Do they understand how rising interest rates impact their portfolios? Are they rebalancing to manage risk? Are they pursuing smart opportunities? Do they understand important investment strategies and principles that will enable them to have the best chance of optimizing their return potentials for the future? Or are they chasing past performance, making random investment selections based on their gut instincts, rumors, or speculation? Are they acting complacent about their investment selections and not even monitoring the results? Are they relying on your target date funds to help them achieve their goals? I suspect many are. Therefore, how confident are you that your target date funds are offering competitive returns? Where do your target date funds rank compared to their peers? Do your employees have too much allocation to cash, compromising their growth potential? Or do they have too much concentration in stocks, increasing market risk? How often do you monitor your participant allocations to ensure employees are making effective investment decisions in their quest for retirement security?

Your 401(k) advisory team should be helping you monitor your investment menu, educating your participants on sound investment strategies, and helping you monitor their investment elections periodically in order to promote retirement readiness. *Wait, you say, why should I monitor my employees' investment elections? I'm not liable for their choices!* So long as you follow the rules and comply with 404(c) requirements, this is true. However, investment performance is a key driver to retirement success, so if you want to help drive retirement readiness, you ought to be aware of your participants' behavior. Only then can you tailor education and support that can assist in building retirement success. Perhaps it's time to institute a re-enrollment to help your employees. It's hard to know what your employees need without monitoring their selections. Building a smart retirement plan means going beyond compliance and taking the time to identify the needs specific to your plan and its participants.

Too many investors focus on current returns, but what really matters are long-term *average returns*. A great year can help boost values, but average returns are what ultimately matter. Every year a participant earns an inferior return it will adversely impact his or her long-term average return. Speaking of which, what is the long-term average return of your plan overall? If you don't know, you should. Inferior returns can potentially present a problem for your plan and can cause eventual snags for you and your participants. If you ultimately seek to provide a graceful transition for aging employees, you need to be involved. Your participants might be the drivers of their investment decisions, but you have tremendous influence on the primary components that impact the end result.

Your advisor can help you monitor your plan's asset allocation, average returns, and risk, identify participants concentrated in just one or two funds or those who may be heavy in cash, and so on. This will enable your advisor and committee to custom-design an education program to encourage practicing sound investment principles. You cannot tell your employees what to do, and you should avoid providing investment advice or counsel yourself; however, your hired investment experts can provide education and promote a sensible investment approach. Granted, employees can dismiss the guidance, and it is generally not your liability if they choose to do so, but doesn't it make sense to have a defense in case an employee ever legally challenges your accountability? An education file can show dates that you sponsored educational meetings, who attended, and what topics were covered. In addition, your investment committee minutes will show plan reviews, discussions of participant behaviors, and your efforts to circumvent unintended consequences of participant inexperience. As they say, the best defense is a good offense. Of course, being an effective investment steward means demonstrating a desire and discipline to protect the long-term interests of your employees. A fiduciary may demonstrate that the best interest of the employee comes first, but being a good investment steward evokes a higher sense of purpose. So beyond fulfilling legal obligations, sound investment stewardship is about voluntarily committing to the purpose of supporting retirement readiness. It is about going beyond legal or regulatory oversight and recognizing that when it comes to the heart of your 401(k), your employees need investment guidance.

PLAN SPONSOR INVESTMENT CHOICES

The investor's chief problem—even his worst enemy—is likely to be himself.
         Benjamin Graham

When it comes to designing your 401(k), one of the most important decisions is selecting the plan's investment menu. I find many plan sponsors tend to discount this step, however this is paramount to promoting retirement readiness. Don't underestimate how critical it is that each fund option be carefully selected so that the list of options is aligned with your Investment Policy Statement. But your responsibilities don't end there. It is also required that fiduciaries regularly monitor their plan's investments. This means you must continue to monitor your list of options after you set up your plan. Your Investment Policy Statement (IPS) can serve as a guide to help you make decisions about asset allocation changes, fund changes, and whether funds need to be added or removed, or if other action needs to be taken. Remember, your employees are limited to the choice of options you make available to them; therefore, you have a lot of influence on the risks, returns, and potential success of the plan.

Recordkeepers may offer a list of prescreened, preselected investment options that can range from a small list to a rather extensive one, or they may have what is called an "open architecture plan." An open architecture plan essentially enables you to craft an investment menu from the entire universe of fund options, nearly without limitations. With some providers, the investment options may be limited to just their own funds (which are known as *proprietary funds*), or the recordkeepers may have requirements to include more of their own funds in your menu. The majority of reputable providers offer access to a broad array of different money managers since no single fund family has the best in all classes. I recommend careful consideration of proprietary-restricted plans. Admittedly, start-up or small plans may have limited options given their plan size and small company plan sponsors may find proprietary plans to be the most cost-effective way to go. In general, it is best practice to follow the same scrutinizing process of all fund options and make objective decisions with every selection while maintaining a broad array of fund families.

Occasionally, I run across a plan where the employer has literally made available every investment offered by their recordkeeper to the participants, which in some cases means employees have a list of over one hundred different fund options to choose from. This is generally not a good practice for many reasons, the least of which is because on May 18, 2015, the United States Supreme Court ruled unanimously in *Tibble v. Edison International* that retirement plan fiduciaries have an ongoing duty to monitor plan investments. Do you really have the time to monitor one hundred different investment options? I think you'll find that employees don't really want to have to sift through a vast menu of choices either. Best practices recommend you select only those that fit the needs of your participants so they can create a diversified portfolio suitable for retirement savings. If you are offering your employees an expansive investment list of different funds, you may want to rethink your approach. While technology has created more opportunities, it has also made for more complexity, and too many options increase the risk of choice overload.

What we have learned from the boom-and-bust market cycle is that many employees don't really understand effective investment strategies, and they need help. Left to their own devices, some are at great risk of running out of money in retirement. Employees are largely unskilled and untrained as investors, so please carefully consider your role as an investment steward. Being a good steward of their welfare means you need to help prevent your employees from making unintentional mistakes. One way to do this is to monitor your investments. Another way is to help your participants gain the knowledge required to make sound investment decisions. I highly encourage you to do your best to help them learn how to enjoy and reap the many potential rewards of investing by utilizing the resources of your advisory team. Even still, we are all subject to making irrational and emotional decisions, particularly during times of market upset. Thus, while your fiduciary requirement is that you monitor your investment options, good stewardship means understanding behavior finance and how that influences investment behavior in order to be sensitive to employees' impulses. You can read about the emotions behind investing in chapter 9.

In fulfilling your stewardship duty, one of the first and most important things you can do is seek to make certain your employees have access to a suitable number of investment options and to those that are of the best possible quality. What is deemed the right number? Finding what is just right may be a process of both considering best practices by other firms like yours and understanding the makeup of your participant base. Whereas once upon a time three investment fund options may have been considered sufficient, today such limitations may not make sense What you don't want is to offer too few so as to restrict your diverse group of employees from creating their own custom portfolios suitable for their varying ages, personal risk tolerances, and growth objectives. Nor do you want to offer so many that your inexperienced or novice investors become overwhelmed and make poor allocation choices.

In the 1990s I was an advisor on a plan with over one hundred thousand participants. The plan was over $20 billion in size. Before I stepped in, they literally offered participants three investment choices: a stock index fund, a bond index fund, and a stable-value fund. Although I don't believe this is a good practice today, it didn't hold back participants from retirement success. In fact, I would say it was one of the most effective plans I've ever had the privilege of working with. It's hard to be paralyzed when you have just three options. Sometimes the "keep it simple" approach is infinitely more effective.

The financial markets are complicated and can be bewildering, even to experienced investors. It is better to consider the needs of your novice investors above all else. Indeed, the courts, knowing that most employees are not investment experts, have tended to lean toward favoring a smaller list of core options. However, if you have more-experienced participants complain about limited investment access, you may want to offer a self-directed brokerage option (SDO) alongside a condensed and defined investment menu; although, you should know research has suggested more employees will stick with the prescribed menu.

Remember, the goal is retirement success, not to develop master day traders or stock pickers. Frankly, that talent is not required to build a secure retirement, and the odds of that kind of activity paying off are slim. With that said, too many choices within your menu are more likely to hinder the real purpose of the plan. Therefore, if you feel the need to offer complex options, it is probably better to offer a restrictive menu along with the Self Directed Option (SDO). Some plan sponsors feel the need to cater to the desires of their more experienced investors, who also often tend to be the key executives. The self-directed option may be a better solution than providing everyone with a complex, extensive, and overwhelming investment list. Of course, you need not accommodate those who desire the hottest, most popular funds. Because the self-directed brokerage option comes with its own set of added liabilities and challenges for plan fiduciaries, you have the right to be steadfast in maintaining a narrow but sound list of diversified quality investments. I believe it is best to err on the side of caution with your investment menu and be most sensitive to the needs of your inexperienced participants so as to avoid creating additional liability. However, because approximately 20 percent of plans use this option, I will explain the Self Directed Option (SDO) a little later in this chapter.

It's also important that you understand at least some basic behavioral finance concepts because they affect each and every one of us, including the most skilled and knowledgeable participants. We are all subject to external and internal influences, natural tendencies, and biases. These behaviors may handicap success. It's normal to get emotional over one's financial security. Especially during times of market panic, no one is immune to irrational behavior. Behavioral finance goes beyond fiduciary requirements and seeks to understand the natural tendencies of investors so you can help avert hardships, conflicts, and problems that could compromise retirement security. How you define and manage your investment menu can also be influenced by behavior finance, including your committee's own biases and influences. Being perceptive of these behaviors can help avoid potential problems.

The industry best practices today generally suggest offering fifteen to twenty-five different fund options within your 401(k). When you consider that each mutual fund held in your menu may hold an average of two hundred or more securities, you can see that such a menu of options potentially provides the average participant access to a very broad number of securities that can help create a well-diversified and properly allocated portfolio. Common sense supports the notion that the ultimate aim for success is to make the retirement plan easy for the participants, rather than unnecessarily complicated. That is why I encourage plan sponsors to maintain a broad but simple menu of options. It's never too late to fine-tune your menu. Indeed, it ought to be a part of your ongoing management.

The first order of business is to request a list of the options available from your recordkeeper. Your financial advisor can get this list and help you narrow down your selections by providing research reports and guidance on what asset categories you should include and what options make sense to consider and discuss the rationale for documentation purposes. Your advisor can scrub the list to help you select the most suitable options based on performance, risks, and fiduciary scores. Plan sponsors may want to consider the following categories of funds:

1. **The default investment fund** – for participants who do not make an affirmative investment decision.
2. **Core funds** – designed to permit participants to make basic asset allocation decisions, including stocks, bonds, and cash equivalent funds.
3. **Index funds** – designed to provide a low-cost investment alternative for those who do not want active management.
4. **Special purpose funds** – such as company stock, socially responsible funds, funds remaining from prior plans that cannot be liquidated yet, and stable-value funds.
5. **Sector funds** – specialty or niche funds that may be desirable based on current market trends or because they offer more growth potential, which may include additional asset classes such as real estate, commodities, and energy or other sectors. Because sector funds carry added risk, you may want to add allocation limits or restrictions, such as 10 percent maximum.

As already mentioned, depending upon your plan provider, you may have access to a robust list of options or a limited selection of funds from which you may develop your own custom menu for your participants. Open architecture plans provide the greatest access to nearly any fund in the mutual fund universe so you can more easily include the most appropriate options in your menu. They may also offer some Collective Investment Trusts (CITs) or Exchange Traded Fund (ETFs) options. An open architecture plan gives you, as the fiduciary, free rein in crafting the most custom investment menu. Of course, an investment expert can help you follow a prudent process according to ERISA guidelines, so you may need to engage an objective investment professional to assist in this process. Especially with open architecture plans, a professional can help prevent you from getting lost in the sea of investment options.

If your provider does not offer an open architecture plan, you should still have a number of options from which to choose. Small proprietary plans may be more restricted, but you can easily find providers who offer several hundred to several thousand different options. Which type of arrangement that is sufficient for you to choose solid investment options depends upon your goals and objectives. As noted, open architecture plans offer more flexibility and choices, but there are plenty of good options within restricted plans. It is important to understand that you still need to craft your plan's investment menu and narrow the options down from whatever list is provided by the recordkeeper. Of course, if your recordkeeper does not offer a satisfactory selection, it may be time to consider changing providers. Your investment selection process should be defined in your Investment Policy Statement, and attention should be given to both designing the original menu and monitoring and realigning the menu once the plan is in place.

A word on proprietary plans. As previously mentioned, if you are setting up a startup plan or have a very small plan, it may be fine to start with a limited plan to save on costs and get the job done. However, once your plan has sufficient assets, it may be time to consider other recordkeeper options. Proprietary plans are those heavily weighted toward the provider's own investment funds. If you have too many funds of the same fund family in your investment menu, you should know there have been litigation conflicts because of the lack of impartiality. At the very least, incorporating different investment firms can potentially offer greater risk management, if not better overall performance. A firm's economic outlook can affect fund management behavior across all portfolio managers within the organization. For example, if the company's macro outlook is bullish (positive), it would be fair to reason every portfolio manager within the firm will be driven by more confidence as he or she makes buy and sell decisions. Conversely, if the firm's outlook is bearish (negative), one can likely expect the portfolio managers to be more cautious. In fact, if you do some research, you may discover that funds of the same company tend to have a higher correlation with one another than funds managed by different companies, and this includes even those funds with very different objectives. Therefore, incorporating different investment firms offers the opportunity to integrate different strategists and economic outlooks, as well as differing approaches or philosophies to asset management. In other words, diversifying fund companies may potentially reduce risk and increase return potential. In short, it simply makes sense.

Additionally, some firms are better at managing domestic equities, while others tend to be more effective at navigating international markets, and still others are more adept within the fixed income markets. There is no "one firm fits all." So different fund families can help seek to create "the best of the best" menu. If you feel your plan is too restrictive, it may be time to shop providers. You may discover that more options create the potential for greater risk-adjusted returns.

FIDUCIARY MONITORING

The universe of investment options can be overwhelming for anyone, including investment committees. That is why having your priorities outlined before you begin the investment menu selection process is helpful. A well-written Investment Policy Statement helps enable a smooth and straightforward process for your investment committee. To make a part of this process structured, your advisor can help you review fiduciary scores and fund analytics. Some providers or administrators have created their own fiduciary scoring system, but I suggest considering using third-party research firms that specialize in this practice. For example, Fi360 is in the business specifically to help financial intermediaries follow prudent fiduciary practices. That is all they do; consequently their Fi360 fiduciary scoring® is objective. In other words, they don't manage money or collect a fee for asset growth so they offer an impartial analysis. Additionally, while you may think performance or expense ratios are the most important considerations, there are many other factors to scrutinize as a fiduciary and good investment steward.

For certain, performance is important, and fees have been a hot topic over the last few years but there are many other careful considerations when monitoring options. For instance, it's important to distinguish investments that are not registered or that lack regulatory oversight, as well as those that are very small and have limited assets under management. While it may be okay to make bets on new or speculative investments for yourself, as a fiduciary, it's important to be sure the funds you are offering your employees are liquid and reliable. If the fund does not have a long enough track record to be properly assessed, it is probably better to exclude it from your menu, even if it has been touted or written up in a popular magazine for its potential. A new fund just opening may be administered by an investment company with a reputable name, however, any new or startup funds lack a track record for scrutinizing and may not have sufficient assets for liquidity.

It also may be better to exclude funds that have experienced recent management changes. The fund's history won't reflect the performance of the new team and since you can't reasonably assess the new team, it is probably not an ideal fund candidate. As you look at the fund details, you'll want to select funds that are consistent with their management style. For example, a growth fund should have quantitative data to support this objective. When you look under the hood, it's important that you see that management is consistent with doing what they say they are doing. If they should drift from their stated objectives this can create conflicts. While deviating from the core style may offer the potential to boost performance, it also can increase risk, consequently it could undermine your participant's strategy. Suppose, for instance, you have a dividend-focused fund that you discover drifts into non-dividend paying growth stocks. The performance may be superior, however, such a style drift could result in greater volatility than comparable dividend-focused funds. Also, if you find a fund that is outperforming its peer group by leaps and bounds, instead of assuming it must be a great fund with superior management, you should ask questions. How were they able to do so well compared to peers? Are they taking on more risk? Are they more concentrated in a few positions? Look at the specifics to be sure you can attribute the performance to management and not increased risk-taking. Comparing average market cap, price-to-earnings ratio, and beta and other risk metrics to peers can often shed important insight. It very well may be a great performing fund and, if so, there may be good reason to include it in your plan, but high-flying star performers are often one hit wonders, which is probably not what you want in your 401(k).

Having said that, you also should consider that peer rankings can be rather subjective, since they are based on past performance. You can really only take backward-looking information at face value. Even Morningstar says their star rating is a "purely mathematical measure of how well a fund's *past* returns have compensated shareholders for the amount of risk assumed," and by their own admission, they acknowledge backward-looking measures has its limitations. At best, the star rating may be an initial screen to identify funds worthy of further research. Fiduciary scores are also typically based on backward-looking data. When analysis is exclusively concerned with the past rather than the present and future, it could present an inaccurate picture perhaps akin to driving down the road only looking through your rearview mirror.

Your investment expert can play a valuable role in helping you look more comprehensively at your investment menu relative to the present market conditions and future outlook. For example, if you look at history, you find that market conditions change over various cycles. In a well-researched study by Vanguard, on average, only 39 percent of funds with a five-star Morningstar rating outperformed their style benchmarks for the three-year period following the rating, while 46 percent of funds with a one-star rating outperformed their benchmark for the same period. The point is to be cautious, because relying on the recent past to assess the present or future may be a costly mistake.

Finally, expense ratios and fees are important to consider. However, I believe too many people are paying attention to fees *at the exclusion of performance*. Recently I met a rather affluent, newly retired professor. He said he was very proud of his portfolio because was "only paying 0.324 percent in expenses." I must to admit, in all my years I had never heard anyone get so specific about their fees. He knew down to the thousandth of a percent what he was paying! Of course, with his being an academic, I wasn't surprised. Indeed, I was anxious to hear more about his knowledge of his portfolio, so I asked him how much it had averaged in the past three years. But to that, he replied dismissively, "Oh, I don't look at my portfolio that way."

Hmm. Let me try this again. "How much have you made year to date or over the past year?" I asked. I thought for sure he was going to have that defined as specific, but instead he waved his hand and again dismissed my question.

"That's not important to me," he replied.

Naturally, I was completely baffled. How can your earnings not be important? But apparently he felt that only the fees were important to monitor and control. I discovered through more dialog, he had spent so much time focusing on his fees that he had no clue what kind of returns he was making, let alone if they were positive or negative or how the returns compared to peers or the corresponding benchmark. Of even greater concern to me was the fact that *he didn't care.*

What is the purpose of investing anyway? *To make money!* Sure, there are going to be expenses and costs involved in the process. There are costs for trades, costs to generate statements, fees for recordkeeping and auditing, costs to create and maintain the software used to access the account online, and so on. This doesn't include the cost of professional management, research, advice, planning, etc. So, yes, fees are to be expected. There is always a cost of doing business, no matter what product or service you are buying. In mutual funds that cost is generally translated as "expense ratios." But the purpose of doing business with an investment firm is *to make money.* If you don't know what you're making and how it compares to the markets (relative to the risk you are assuming), you probably are not monitoring your portfolio in a way that is conducive to success. Even still, it's never just about fees, but rather about value, no matter what you are buying. Value is a function of the cost *relative to the benefit.* Buying the cheapest car may not necessarily give you the best value. In fact, someone once told me "Terri, good *things aren't cheap, and cheap* things *are rarely, if ever, good."* You don't have to be an academic to understand that.

Investment performance is the fuel that drives wealth accumulations. I'm amazed at how few plan sponsors, and even participants, pay attention to their investment performance. Let me clarify. We know that your employees are looking at their account balances, perhaps almost daily. They are also looking at their investments with somewhat less, but still arguably manic, frequency. But paying attention to your investment performance is a more involved process.

There's a clear distinction between investment performance and investor returns. I know most people don't think in terms of percentages so it can be quite confounding to follow. Let me give you an example, as depicted in figure 6.1. If XYZ fund averaged 10% for the calendar year (Jan 1-Dec 31) but you bought it on April 1, is your return also likely to be 10% for that year? Highly unlikely. Suppose that by year-end your performance for the same fund was −2%. *How can that be?* Well, that is an example of the difference between *investment return* and *investor return*.

	Jan 1 - Mar 31	Apr 1 - Dec 31	Jan 1 – Dec 31
XYZ Fund	+12%	-2%	+10%
Benchmark	+5%	+2%	+7%

Figure 6.1 hypothetical scenario.

If XYZ fund gained 12% in the first quarter of the year but you bought it *after* it had gone up, and then from April to year end the fund lost 2%, the investment would have a calendar year return of +10% (12 −2). However, since you missed out on the first quarter you didn't get the 12% gain, so your results were -2%. As if that's not confusing enough, XYZ Fund may still be a top-performing fund. Suppose, as you can see in figure 6.1, the benchmark gained 5% the first quarter and gained another 2% from April-December. The means the benchmark had a return of 7% for the year, which is less than XYZ Fund but from the time you invested, the benchmark had a positive return whereas you had a loss. Befuddled? You're not alone.

Of course, when you compare the quality of one fund with the quality of another, you certainly want to measure and compare performance over the same period. An employee lacking this knowledge may see his performance online and quickly lose faith in the fund, even if it is a strong performing fund. If the employee then hastily moves on to chase the next winner, such activity may result in costly mistakes.

This hypothetical example also illustrates why market timing is typically ineffective. Miss one quarter or one good month or even a good day and you could compromise a substantial part of your return. Said differently, in this example the shares increased in price quite substantially in the first quarter and which is often what compels investors to put more money into the fund -*after the price has gone up substantially*- and shortly thereafter the price fell (which is not that uncommon after such a rally) but since investors do not understand price movements, the investor may lose confidence in the investment as a result of the decline, hence causing investor returns to be less than the actual investment return.

Dalbar conducts ongoing quantitative analysis of investor behaviors. They reported that as of 2015, the S&P 500 twenty-year average return was 8.19%, but the average equity fund investor had only earned 4.67% over the same period. It got worse the longer out they went. Over the thirty-year period ending December 31, 2015, the S&P 500 averaged 10.15%, but the average equity fund investor earned only 3.66%. So, yes, there is a big difference between *investment* returns and *investor* returns.

Fortunately, fund performance is typically reported net of fees, and expense ratios are clearly stated on investment performance reports, so disclosure requirements make it easier to compare funds. Still, many people don't understand the significance here. Let's take a look at an example in figure 6.2. Let's compare two hypothetical funds. We will assume for the purposes of this illustration that these funds have the same investment objective and risk characteristics. Fund A has an expense ratio of 0.42 percent, and Fund B has an expense ratio of 1.12 percent. All else being equal, which fund is better? Obviously, if one were to just consider expense ratios, Fund A would appear to be a better fund. However, the performance (posted net of investment expenses) paints a different picture, doesn't it? Consistently, you can see that Fund B has been outperforming. If a shareholder of Fund A were to brag at a cocktail party "I'm only paying 0.42 percent on my fund!" it might make the shareholder of Fund B scratch her head and think perhaps she's overpaying. However, when you look at the results, you find that the shareholder of Fund B is certainly the winner. Unfortunately, some people never dig deep enough to understand the sum of product. The follow-up question should always be, *"But what have you made?"*

Fund	Expense Ratio	-Performance-		
		1 YR	3 YR	5 YR
A	0.42%	7.6%	5.4%	6.9%
B	1.12%	12.1%	8.6%	7.4%

Figure 6.2.

I occasionally come across an investor who balks about paying management fees. There are always those who think they should not have to pay fees for services and, for those investors, there are many do-it-yourself investment firms available. But we should not measure results in a vacuum. These investors often tell their friends they are paying too much if they get into such a conversation. However, that's like asking someone how much they pay in income taxes and then declaring they are paying too much. If I pay $150,000 in federal income taxes, for example, and you declare that's ridiculous! Really? How do you know? Ridiculous relative to what? A $200,000 taxable income. Yes, it is! But if that's what I paid on a $500,000 income, perhaps it is not.

The old adage "you get what you pay for" often rings true with most goods and services, including investment products, but I prefer the idiom "don't judge a book by its cover" as better advice. There are so many investments available, and certainly not all of them are going to be alike. This does raise the question; how do you evaluate your investments? Do you look at the performance compared to the stock market? What about funds that don't hold the same securities as the "stock market?" And what part of the stock market are you comparing – large companies to small companies? Or like kind to like kind? And what about risk? fees? Do you compare net performance or gross results? How do you know if your fund managers are the best? Do you compare the risk of two similar investments before you measure return, or do you ignore risk considerations? Do you monitor fees but disregard returns? When was the last time you compared share class options to determine if the same fund is available at a lower cost?

Participants commonly benchmark every investment in their account or in the investment menu against the best-performing position in their portfolio or within the menu of options. This is true even if the investment comparisons are stocks to bonds, small cap to large cap, or European stocks to Asian stocks. People don't understand they may be comparing apples to oranges. Many employees lack the investment skill and education, so they do what seems to make sense: sell the laggards and move to the winners. But chasing past performance is typically quite ineffective. Investments are intangible assets. We can't see them, touch them, or compare them except with the limited knowledge or information we have, which is past performance. Failing to take into consideration risk, including past risk compared to future risk, and past performance versus the potential future performance as well as other pertinent data that ought to be considered before making radical changes to a portfolio is a common amateur mistake that can potentially compromise retirement readiness.

Plan sponsors should be asking pertinent questions regardless of whether the returns are positive or negative, or whether the performance has been exceptionally high, mediocre, or terribly low. Questions like, how much risk is XYZ fund assuming compared to its peers? How does the performance compare to peers as well as the benchmark? Have there been any management changes that may impact performance? What is the standard deviation of the fund compared to peers? Have they drifted from the style of the fund, changing the risk exposure? The point is, everyone should be asking questions, but at the very least, plan sponsors *must* be asking questions. It's an ERISA requirement. It's called investment monitoring. It also makes good sense as an investment steward.

This type of constructive analysis should be conducted for every fund offered in your plan. Ideally, your committee reviews this together systematically with the guidance of a qualified investment expert. The goal is to collaborate as a team because interpreting the data is subjective. As noted, data used to measure past performance is not necessarily a reflection of what the future results or outcome may be. A committee, however, can review the data, consider the recommendations provided by your investment expert and discuss what is believed to be the appropriate course of action for the benefit of your plan participants. And, of course, you will want to be sure to document the discussion in meeting minutes to demonstrate your due diligence should you ever get audited. The monitoring process should follow the guidelines written in your Investment Policy Statement. Remember, fiduciaries are not responsible for the results but rather for the *process*. Therefore, plan fiduciaries will want to have a process for reviewing fund performance, comparing the fund against a peer group and/or benchmark, and have a system for removing funds that underperform. For instance, we use a "hold, watch, or remove" system that follows a defined strategy to seek to maintain an investment menu that is performing at least within the ranks of average, or, ideally, above-average. Should a fund fall below standards defined in the IPS we either put it on watch until the next review or replace it with fund that is deemed to have better potential. Of course, we seek to get above-average performance with each fund option, but that is not always achievable. However, with a disciplined and regular approach to investment monitoring, you can better assist your employees in their pursuit to be retirement ready.

I believe investment stewards need to approach their investment menu with far more care and caution than they may currently practice. Just because a fund was solid when you selected it initially does not mean it will remain as such over the course of time. Be sure to document your findings and retain your meeting minutes in the event of an audit. Every fund added to the menu creates an additional review burden. Therefore, having too many funds makes for more work. Additionally, funds that present unusual or hard-to-evaluate risks can be especially problematic to monitor. In the monitoring process, you should be satisfied that the funds selected meet a strict set of guidelines for suitability, sustainability, performance, and risk. Keep in mind, a large part of the recent litigation has been centered on investment options, performance, and share classes. Consequently, it is especially important to have a well-documented file supporting your investment monitoring and due diligence.

ASSET ALLOCATION OPTIONS

Asset classes are the broad types of investments that are available, such as stocks, bonds, cash, commodities, and real estate. These can be further broken down into "subclasses" such as large-cap, midcap, and small-cap stocks. Those subclasses can be divided yet again by management style into growth, value, or blend. From there, they can be separated as domestic stocks or international stocks, and then further defined into developed international markets and emerging markets. Now, that's just the equity markets. Overwhelmed? Well, perhaps so, too, are your employees.

Why is this important? Because asset allocation - the process of allocation one's assets among these different asset classes - — it said to drive over 80 percent of the long-term return we earn on our money. The best way to think about it is that asset allocation is really a risk reduction strategy.

With asset allocation, an investor will theoretically never get the highest returns. It is more likely than not that at any given time there will be some investments in the portfolio that will be down in value or out of favor. It stands to reason that if every investment in your portfolio goes up simultaneously, they will likely go down at the same time as well. Since the strategy behind asset allocation is about seeking to maintain a steadier, more consistent growth rate in a financial world that is volatile, inconsistent, and contradictory, asset allocation does not aim to have all the investments in the portfolio move in sync. While it may feel odd, when a portfolio is properly allocated to manage risk, we should expect to have investments that lose value at any given time. Overall, however, the portfolio should conceptually have a more stable yearly return. While asset allocation does not assure a profit or protect against loss, it is a system designed to reduce risk or volatility. More specifically, it is an approach to investing which seeks to optimize the return potential relative to the level of risk assumed. To try to reduce risk, we must incorporate asset classes that have a low correlation to stocks. Figure 6.3 identifies the different risk and return characteristics for various asset classes.

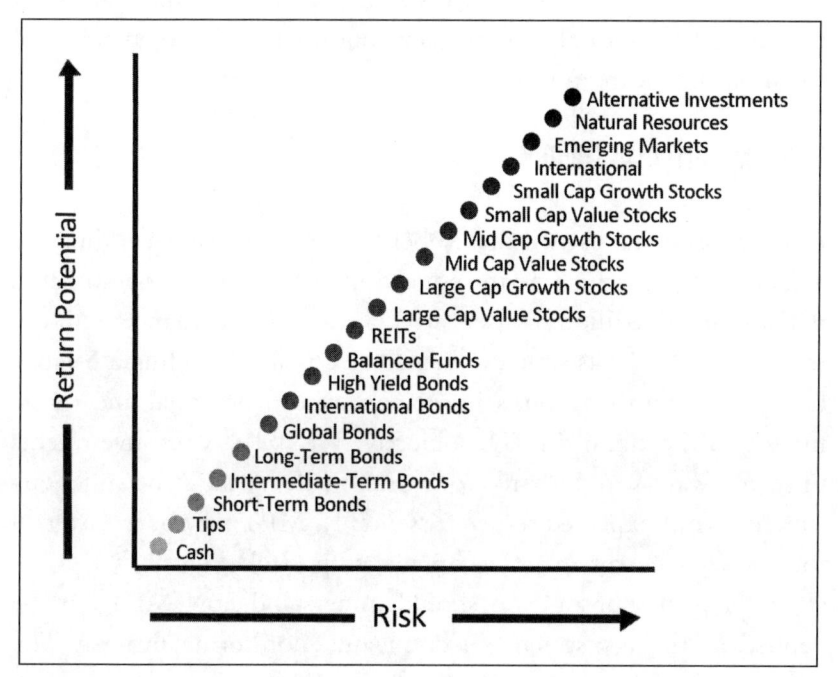

Figure 6.3.

Bonds are generally a lower-risk asset class. Of course, risk/return is relative, which means that lower risk translates into lower average returns. But history teaches us that adding bonds to stock portfolios can be an effective way of balancing risk and return. This doesn't always work, of course. For instance, during the 2008 credit crisis, investors fled to cash as the safe harbor. The massive sell-off of both stocks and bonds caused both asset classes to plummet in value simultaneously until eventually buyers changed their pattern. Since very few investors are comfortable stomaching market calamities, you may want to offer a robust selection of nonequity options in your investment menu. I find too few 401(k) plans offer an attractive list of nonstock funds. As your employee's approach retirement, they may be more interested in protecting their retirement funds. Because the financial markets are ever changing, it's a good idea to review your asset allocation options based on current market conditions and your plan demographics, and be sure you are offering a sufficient list of options to help your plan participants optimize their return potential based on the future, not the past.

MODERN PORTFOLIO THEORY

Harry Markowitz earned the Nobel Prize for the Modern Portfolio Theory (MPT), which he introduced in 1952. Today it is estimated that around $7 trillion in assets are managed in accordance with the tenets of MPT. In its simplest form, MPT is about finding a balance between maximizing one's investment return potential and minimizing the portfolio risk. The objective is to select your investments in such a way as to diversify your risks while, at the same time, optimizing your expected return. Essentially, MPT may be a powerful tool to complement an actively managed portfolio.

As a plan sponsor, you should understand how MPT can be applied to the investment selection and monitoring process. The purpose of MPT is to apply a mathematical discipline to construct an efficient optimum portfolio. Since your 401(k) includes a number of various funds, how your participants allocate their investments clearly determines outcomes. Academic research suggests asset allocation is the most important factor to impact return. In other words, it's not about market timing or individual fund selection but rather how you allocate among the different asset classes. Since it is considered to be the most important driver of success, MPT is worth understanding.

Although you are not making investment allocation decisions for your participants, evaluating the efficiency of your investment menu will better enable your participants the ability to build an optimum portfolio within the framework of your selected investment menu. Therefore, applying the discipline of modern portfolio theory to your Investment Policy Statement will provide a sound structure for managing your plan as a fiduciary. The modern portfolio theory is considered to be an effective method for efficiently managing an investment portfolio. It is a highly respected theory commonly used by many institutional investors.

Asset allocation is based on the theory that an efficient portfolio either (1) offers the highest expected return for a given level of risk or (2) has the least risk for a given expected return. Clearly, risk and return are linked with MPT. This is one of the most fundamental investment principles, known as the risk–return trade-off. Very simply put, participants who want a chance to enjoy greater returns will need to take more risk. There are no shortcuts to investment success, although many try though frequently with disappointment.

Investors typically feel the pain of loss more than they feel the joy of gain, so in an effort to reduce risk, the concept of MPT is to diversify across securities that do not behave alike. Even those seeking higher returns can seek to generate optimum returns by integrating securities that do not move in the same direction at the same time. Since your role as a plan fiduciary is to act in the best interest of your plan participants, it is your job to identify and determine the specific investments (and asset classes) which should be included in your plan menu. As such, ensuring your menu subscribes to the modern portfolio theory will enable your participants to have the potential to create an optimal, efficient portfolio commensurate with their risk tolerance and return target. Essentially, MPT focuses on asset allocation, so incorporating different asset classes into your menu of options may better enable your participants to advance toward retirement success.

While most people are quite familiar with the concept of diversification and the adage "don't put all of your eggs in one basket," the concept of asset allocation is still relatively new for laypersons. Asset allocation goes far beyond diversification. For instance, if you owned five different stocks such as McDonalds, Burger King, Chipotle, Domino's and Starbucks you might say you are diversified which would be true, but you would not have *asset allocation*. This is because you own all the same asset class (stocks). Not only that, but also you own all restaurant stocks, so there is not only a concentration of equities but also a concentration in the same industry. This is not an investment approach that will do much to mitigate or manage risk. The same is true for employees who diversify their 401(k)'s with a variety of equity funds, even if they include international stocks. This is because stocks tend to move in the same direction at the same time, in response to the same economic events. We are a global world so there is not enough variation in the sensitivity of these types of funds to significantly offset market risk.

Asset allocation is the process of going beyond diversification and holding assets of different types of investments. The core asset classes include stocks, bonds and cash equivalents. Since these assets generally tend to move differently to the same economic conditions, the goal of asset allocation is to seek to have your investments moving differently at the same time.

Core Asset Class Risks

Stock Risk		Bond Risk		Cash Risk	
	Market Risk		Interest Rate Risk		Inflation Risk
	Political/Economic Risk		Credit/Default Risk		
	Industry Risk		Liquidity Risk		
	Company Risk		Call Risk		Default Risk
	Currency Risk		Political/Economic Risk		
			Reinvestment Risk		

Figure 6.4.

To understand this, let's first identify various types of risks that most directly impact stocks, bonds, and cash. As you can see in figure 6.4, there are many different kinds of risk. Each investment is subject to different types of risk, although some risks overlap. For instance, all investments are subject to inflation risk, but this type of risk is most directly a threat to cash equivalents because lower returns more quickly erode the buying power of money. Therefore, inflation risk is indicated here as a predominant risk to cash. Bonds are more exposed to interest rate risk, although rising interest rates can also adversely impact stocks. Consequently, stocks and bonds have some of the same risks, which means they can move in the same direction at the same time. As a result, a mix of stocks and bonds will not create a negative correlation. Asset allocation does not seek to avoid losses but rather to manage the degree of risk assumed. Other asset classes such as commodities, real estate, and alternative investments are used to further diversify risk since these asset classes tend to have a lower correlation to stocks. Of course, alternative investments and commodities may not be suitable for all investors and should be considered as an investment for the risk capital portion of the investor's portfolio. This is because strategies employed in the management of alternative investments and fast price swings in commodities will result in significant volatility and may accelerate the velocity of potential losses. Nonetheless, for strategic reasons, target date funds may have a broad asset allocation mix of more than just stocks, bonds and cash and often include commodities and alternative investments.

History has taught us that investing in stocks will offer you the greatest opportunity to get the best potential return over the long run, but there have been numerous market upsets to withstand. Figure 6.5 highlights the historical volatility between stocks, T-bills, and ten-year T-bonds. Even though shareholders have been handsomely rewarded for patience and discipline over the past, the market drops continue to be a challenge for investors. Market declines are a normal part of the investment process. However, because investors do not tend to have a tolerance for sharp market drops and tend not to be able to withstand the instabilities arising from the uncertainties in the world, the process of asset allocation is to incorporate different asset classes in order to seek to reduce the overall portfolio volatility. By applying the modern portfolio theory, we can fine-tune the asset mix to dial in on a range of anticipated returns and market value deviation. The goal is to find an allocation suitable to the acceptable level of risk. Of course, investors cannot expect to earn stock market returns unless they accept full market risk. Therefore, the trade-off with the MPT is in forgoing the long-term upside potential of a given asset class in exchange for the ability to seek shorter-term stability. Thus, if a participant is not willing to ride through the ups and downs of the market and look toward a longer holding period, instead of jumping in and out of the market and subscribing to somewhat of a manic type of investor behavior, he or she may use asset allocation to find a balance between risk and return. By virtue of design, an asset allocation strategy will not mirror stock market performance. While everyone wants 10% returns, very few are willing to accept the real risk that comes with enjoying the potential of such return. There's no such thing as a free lunch. If you want the big rewards, you must have to have the courage to follow a disciplined strategy of tolerating wild market swings. In the absence of that courage, there's asset allocation.

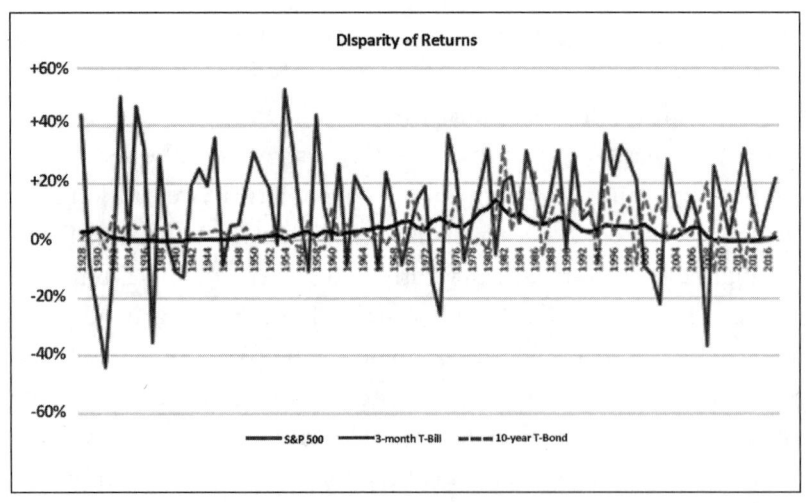

Figure 6.5. Source: Federal Reserve database (FRED), Saint Louis.

The more you and your 401(k) team can do to help your participants understand and accept a reasonable approach to investing, the more apt they are to achieve their goals. Building more certainty into a portfolio is important to many. Too many people want to be in when it's good but then they quickly jump out when it gets uncomfortable, and that is one of the great devastations of market timing. We don't want your participants hurting themselves by misunderstanding risk or setting unrealistic expectations. If participants apply asset allocation strategies to their 401(k) investment selections, they can seek to find the right balance between an acceptable and realistic return target in exchange for an acceptable and *realistic* level of risk.

With that said, as a plan fiduciary you should know that the Modern Portfolio Theory is not without its pitfalls. The premise for MPT is based on risk *as measured by volatility*. Volatility, also known as fluctuation, is defined as the degree of swing or variance in a return. We know most investors prefer fewer variances in their account values. Wide swings suggest instability, which causes more anxiety. Volatility is measured by what is known as standard deviation, which provides a tool to determine what has been a normal range of returns for the investment in question. The snare with MPT is that risk is measured on the basis of *recent* return variances. But volatility is not consistent, especially over shorter periods of time.

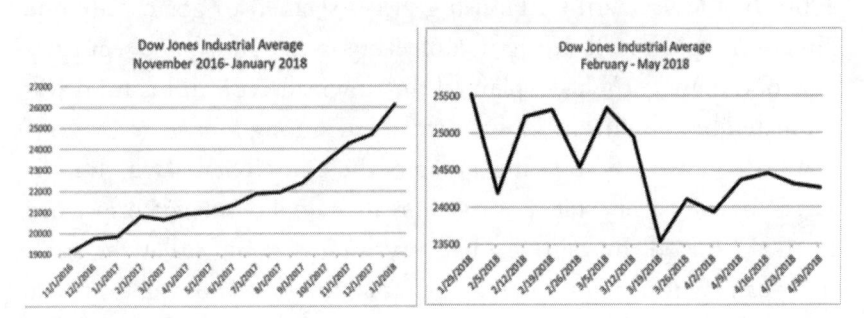

Figure 6.6. Source: Yahoo Finance.

For example, we will have periods when stocks are less volatile. From November 2016 to January 2018, the market did not experience one down month, as highlighted in figure 6.6. Clearly this does not accurately represent real stock risk. Consequently, measuring standard deviation over a period where stocks are unusually stable would present an inaccurate expectation or measure of risk. And indeed, as you can see in figure 6.6, from February to May 2018 volatility spiked. We should always expect higher risk if the investment has the potential for higher returns. Over time this has proven to be true. However, there are periods when higher returns are enjoyed with less volatility. Likewise, lower risk investments can have more volatility than expected. Said differently, over short periods of time, risk and/or return can be distorted, which further confuses investors. The markets are not efficient in the short run. When buyers feel confident, they buy more and drive prices up. That could create the illusion that the investment isn't volatile or is not risky.

Think back to the period between 1995 to 1999 for the NASDAQ. The volatility was actually lower for the aggressive tech sector than for bond funds over the same period, which, as per modern portfolio theory, suggested tech stocks were less risk than bonds. Even the Journal for Financial Planning printed an article that challenged the theory of asset allocation and suggested bonds were no longer important as a core asset class. But, of course, eventually everyone discovered it was not a "new economy" after all. Likewise, residential real estate in the 2000s had low volatility. Housing prices seemed to go in only one direction: up! I recall sitting in a meeting with a mortgage securities portfolio manager who explained the downside risk in his fund was mitigated because his fund was diversified among mortgages nationally. He followed by showing a map of the United States which indicated virtually every state positive in real estate. I perplexed him when I called him out by asking, "If everything is going up at the same time, can't it also all go down at the same time?" Of course, everyone eventually learned that housing prices don't always go up, and the risk was ultimately much greater than the recent past suggested. During the 2008 crisis, volatility in the financial markets was off the charts as investors made a mad dash to sell off everything for fear the sky was falling. The standard deviation suggested wildly increased risk for all securities, including bonds. Even price-to-earnings ratios were off the charts, implying stock prices were excessively high. What happened over the next three to five years? Let's just say results from 2009-2013 did not play out as the modern portfolio theory may have signaled.

Of course, as with any theory, there are flaws. There is no foolproof method of properly assessing risk and opportunities. And while you, as a plan sponsor, are not held responsible for outcomes, you do need to take risk and subjective information into consideration as you construct and manage your plan's investment menu. If you only consider MPT, your investment menu may not be aligned to current markets. Remember, over shorter time periods the markets are not efficient. Naturally, major market calamities such as the financial crisis of 2008 cannot be adequately anticipated, but the modern portfolio theory assumes the markets are efficient, meaning share prices accurately reflect their intrinsic value. While this has been true over long holding periods, over short spans of time, assets are absolutely not priced accurately. Investors will pay ridiculously high prices for securities just because they've gone up in the past and then sell them at insanely low prices just because prices have gone down. Plan sponsors, as investment experts, are supposed to be cognizant of this flaw in the modern portfolio theory. Of course, you may not be an investment specialist, which is all the more reason why hiring one to help you properly manage your plan through all market cycles makes good sense.

ASSET CLASSES FOR 401(K) PLANS

There are currently over 10,000 mutual funds in the United States with a total value over $16 trillion. In addition, there are approximate 2,000 ETFs (exchange-traded funds) that are worth approximately $2.5 trillion. The number of dollars under management and the number of options available in today's world is staggering. There are over 45,000 publicly traded companies globally, with roughly 55 billion shares trading hands on average every day. The United States ranks second in terms of number of public listings with 5,204 firms reported as listed on the New York Stock Exchange (NYSE) and

NASDAQ combined (as of the end of 2016). According to *The World Federation of Exchanges*, India had the largest number of public listing with 5,821 traded on the Bombay Stock Exchange, followed by Japan, Spain and Canada. With 56 different countries listed including those such as Morocco, Palestine, Sri Lanka, and Nigeria, we live in a complex global financial world that continues to evolve as new countries emerge and assume some semblance of Westernization and capitalism.

While we are all well aware of the industrialization of China, most of us don't think much about the economies in areas like Africa, eastern Europe, Latin America, the Middle East, Russia, or Southeast Asia, but these are examples of places that are transitioning, at least to some degree, to free-market-oriented economies. Indeed, many parts of the world are experiencing rapid developments of partial industrialization. While the United States continues to rank number one as the largest economy based on average GDP, other countries are growing fast. And as the world continues to become more competitive, our position in the world economies will continue to be challenged. According to IMF, World Bank, and United Nations lists, from 1960 to 1985 the Soviet Union ranked number two, but Japan soon moved into that spot, and Japan has since been replaced by China (since 2010). Germany, France, the United Kingdom, India, Brazil, Canada, and Italy are the others on the Top 10 list that have moved up and/or down over the years. The point is, it's an ever-changing global world; thus, your participants need access to a global investment portfolio that allows them to participate in the financial markets comprehensively.

Following is a list of different funds that you should probably consider including at a minimum, in your 401(k) plan investment menu. Keep in mind, investing in mutual funds involves risk, including possible loss of principal:

> **Large-Cap Stock Funds.** Large-cap stock funds generally have a median market capitalization of more than $5 billion up to $10 billion. These stock

funds are made up of the largest companies, otherwise known as "blue chips."

Midcap Stock Funds. Midcap stock funds normally have a median market capitalization between $2 billion and $10 billion. Midcaps are sometimes called "the sweet spot" in the market because these are companies that have more market share and capital than smaller companies, yet they still have strong growth potential. The prices of mid-cap stocks are generally more volatile than large cap stocks.

Small-Cap Stock Funds. Small-cap stock funds typically have a median market capitalization of less than $2 billion. These are smaller firms that have greater growth potential because of their small size and ability to grow market share, but they also have greater volatility because of their inexperience and limited capital.

International Stock Funds. International stock funds invest in equity securities of issuers located outside the United States. Generally this represents the developed markets including Europe, the United Kingdom, U.K., Canada, Japan and Australia. International investing involves special risks such as currency fluctuation and political instability and may not be suitable for all investors. These risks are often heightened for investments in emerging markets.

Global Stock Funds. This type of mutual fund generally includes at least 25 percent foreign securities in its portfolio, and the balance in domestic stocks, but the mix is usually 40/60 or higher.

Intermediate Bond Funds. These bonds are usually divided between longer maturity and shorter maturity. Short-term bonds are generally considered to be less risky than long-term bonds. Therefore, investing in an intermediate bond fund is especially smart during periods of declining interest rates. An increase in interest rates may cause the price of bonds and bond mutual funds to decline.

International or Global Bond Funds. Global bond funds hold bonds denominated in the currency of the place where the company is based. Since interest rate fluctuations differ from country to country, they help in diversifying currency exposure and seeking to protect assets against a long-term secular decline of value of in the US dollar. International bonds involve special additional risks. These risks include, but are not limited to, currency risk, geopolitical and regulatory risk, and risk associated with varying settlement standards. These risks are often heightened for investments in emerging markets.

High-Yield Bond Funds. High-yield bonds, otherwise known as "junk" bonds, are somewhat akin to small-cap stocks in that they are issued by smaller companies or by companies with no credit rating or with a below-grade credit rating. Because of this, they tend to pay a higher yield and be more volatile than other bonds. High yield bonds (grade BB or below) are not investment grade securities, and are subject to higher interest rate, credit, and liquidity risks than those graded BBB and above. They generally should be part of a diversified portfolio for sophisticated investors.

Aggregate Bond Funds. There are many different types of bond funds that may include an aggregate bond fund or perhaps even a "strategic bond fund." These are bond portfolios that own a variety of bonds that may include government, corporate, and/or global bonds, and they are generally intermediate to long term in duration or maturity.

Money Market Funds: Sometimes referred to as "cash equivalents," money market funds seek to preserve the value of your original investment. However, these funds are not guaranteed by the FDIC or any other government agency like a bank savings account would be, and the interest rate is generally lower than for stock and bond funds. It is possible to lose money in a money market fund.

Index Funds. These funds are invested to replicate an existing market index such as the S&P 500, which is an index of five hundred large US company stocks. They are not actively managed with a portfolio team buying and selling securities, but rather investors assume passive strategy of holding the positions in the index.

Company Stock Funds. If you are a publicly traded company, you may want to include your stock in your investment menu. Of course, company stock funds are not diversified investments, which makes them theoretically more volatile than a mutual fund but including them does promote employee ownership. (You may want to limit the exposure for your participants.)

Emerging Market Funds. These funds are made up of the stock of companies located in developing nations in regions including eastern Europe, Africa, the Middle East, Latin America, the Far East, and Asia. They involve special risks, including currency risk, geopolitical and regulatory risk, and risk associated with varying settlement standards, which are often heightened for investments in emerging markets.

Target Date Funds: A target date fund is a broadly diversified asset-allocated mutual fund geared toward investors presumed to be retired by the target date, resulting in a decreasing risk tolerance as they grow closer to their retirement or target date. The principal value of a target date fund is not guaranteed at any time, including at the target date, which is the approximate date investors plan to start withdrawing their money.

TARGET DATE FUNDS: "TO VERSUS THROUGH" GLIDEPATH

Not all Target Date Funds are created the same. The growing popularity of Target Date Funds warrants greater scrutiny and attention to the differences between these types of funds and how they are managed. Many fiduciaries have misconceptions about how these funds are structured and neglect to ask important questions, such as the following: How often do they rebalance? What is the level of risk involved at different dates, and how does this compare to other TDFs? Do the funds go to cash or bonds by the target date, or do they keep some stock market exposure into retirement? And, if so, how is that determined? Is the management of the fund properly diversified for the target date?

In the most simplistic description, Target Date Funds invest in stocks, bonds, cash and alternative investments following a strategic asset allocation strategy aligned to the investor's targeted retirement date. The mix of assets is automatically rebalanced over time, and as the employee nears the targeted retirement date, the allocations become less growth focused and more focused on income. That makes sense as a sound investment strategy, but perhaps the most ambiguous thing about these funds is whether the manager uses a "to" or a "through" glide path. In other words, does the allocation to equities scale down to the target date, or does it scale down over one's life expectancy? Which makes the most sense for your participants? How does your Target Date Fund glide path compare to other alternatives?

To understand the significance of this difference, we must first understand a glide path. The glide path is the heart of the target date series. The asset allocation is dictated by the glide path, which can be taken *to* retirement or *through* retirement. Most everyone understands that the allocation to equities will gradually decrease over time, but at what point does the equity exposure level out—past age sixty-five or past age eighty? That date can vary substantially depending upon the mutual fund family. Notice in figure 6.7 the difference hypothetical equity exposure from a "to" versus a "through" glidepath.

The slope of the glide path influences the asset allocation and therefore the risk and return metrics. As you can see in figure 6.7, the difference in risk could be substantially more in one target date fund compared to another. This is not a "one size fits all" solution so the real question is whether the postretirement glide path is right for your participants. A glide path should provide a large enough stock allocation to protect against longevity risk without exposing participants to excessive market risk. Of course, plan sponsors and fund families have different perspectives on what stock allocations best meet these goals. Nonetheless, a large part of the disparity in returns of target date funds reflects the difference in "to" versus "through" retirement glide paths, something that is rarely understood by plan fiduciaries. Inherently, a higher-risk portfolio should have a higher return during good markets and have more volatility during down markets.

Plan sponsors may prefer to focus on bringing equity exposures to lower levels as their participants approach retirement. In that case, you would want a "to" glide path. On the other hand, the "through" series are designed to meet retirees needs over their actual life expectancy. If you prefer to have your employees on a path toward capital preservation, consider aligning your Target Date Funds to the "to" strategy. If you believe your participants should focus on combating inflation and longevity risks in retirement, the "through" series may have a greater chance of accomplishing this, but the difference in equity exposure between two Target Date Funds can be quite dramatic based on their glide paths.

TDF Equity Glide Path "To" vs. "Through"

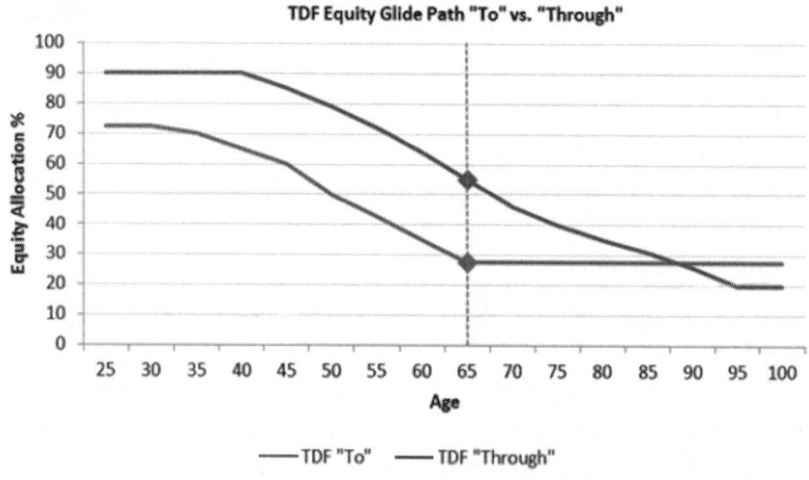

Figure 6.7.

For example, a 2025 Target Date Fund might have a 30 percent allocation if it is a "to" retirement glide path, compared to a 60 percent allocation if it is a "through" retirement glide path. That could translate into a substantial difference in returns as well as risk for your employees, and this can also distort expectations.

Not only should you understand how your Target Date Funds work and ensure the strategy aligns to your plan goals, but also you must ensure your employees understand how these funds work so as to align expectations. If it is believed employees are substantially reducing their market risk as they approach retirement age but your TDF is a "through" glide path, this lack of understanding could create a real conflict for your aging employees, especially during market drops. Of course, even older employees love to experience strong performance during economic expansions and will rarely complain about double-digit *positive* returns. And rarely will they ask questions as to why a fund expected to reduce to cash and bonds is competing with strong stock market results. Unfortunately, those questions will not get asked until the results turn bad, and then it might be too late. With 60 percent equities, a fifty-five- or sixty-year-old employee in a 2025 TDF could unknowingly face double-digit losses. That can quickly make for disgruntled employees.

This is not to say that a "to" glidepath is better. I, for one, argue that inflation risk is the greatest risk a retiree faces and having all of his or her retirement money in cash and bonds has historically demonstrated this to be ineffective. It may subject the retiree to spenddown risk. However, considering that capital depletion could take fifteen to twenty years, compared to a sharp drop of the stock market, which can happen in a matter of days, there may be more risk in misunderstanding a "through" TDF. Education is key. A good education and financial wellness program will help your employees understand the risk/return trade-off and help them feel confident making educated decisions based on their options. The goal of an education program is to empower your employees to make better financial decisions. Since there is no perfect solution, it is important your employees understand their options. Every option, including the "to" or "through" TDF, has pros and cons, thus perhaps the best remedy is to know what you want for your plan and provide good education to communicate to your participants.

SELF-DIRECTED OPTION

Within a 401(k), the self-directed brokerage option (SDO) offers participants a "brokerage window" where they can trade investments (stocks, bonds, mutual funds, etc.) that aren't in a plan's official investment lineup. The benefit of a brokerage window is that it can provide a participant more choices and better control than the limited options of their 401(k) investment menu. However, the brokerage window certainly isn't for everyone. For those with investment experience, time, and knowledge, the brokerage option offers the opportunity to fine-tune an asset allocation strategy. It can be a very efficient means for retirement accumulations because investors can choose from literally thousands of investment options. Of course, the sheer number of choices can make it more difficult for inexperienced investors to choose suitable investments.

The self-directed option offers all the same benefits, including pre-tax, tax deferral and the convenience of making contributions through payroll deductions, and if your recordkeeper offers it as an option, you may be able to add it as an investment alternative to your plan, if you so choose. If available, your recordkeeper will have an agreement with an online brokerage firm. Should you decide to offer this option to your participants, each participant would be responsible for opening his or her account with the brokerage firm, paying separate account fees as prescribed in the agreement, and paying trading commissions and any other costs involved in the "do it yourself" approach.

Because the SDO is a do-it-yourself process, it should be reserved for those who have experience with brokerage accounts. Of course, plan sponsors cannot discriminate and only make the SDO available to a certain class of participants, so you must consider the impact and implications should an inexperienced employee misuse the privilege.

Think of the SDO as a separate account within the 401(k) that is totally self-managed by the employee. The employee opens the account, moves money into it from your provider, and places his or her own buy/sell trades. What happens if the employee places a "buy" instead of a "sell" trade? Well, he or she is responsible for covering any market losses. What happens if the employee day-trades or buys speculative investments that lose value? You have given him or her free rein, so there is little you can do to intercede with aggressive trading or poor investment choices. With that in mind, you do have the option (and in many plans there are limitations) to restrict the percentage of an employee's account that can be directed to the SDO window. For instance, the recordkeeper may restrict no more than 50 percent of the account, but you may be able to set stricter limitations, say down to 25 percent for example if you choose, as an attempt to safeguard at least some of the participant's retirement assets.

Meanwhile, you should know the Department of Labor is believed to find fault with the SDO window, because studies show that larger numbers of investment choices confuse most participants. In addition, there is minimal guidance, if any, for selecting suitable investments. Therefore, I recommend you speak with an ERISA attorney before you add the SDO option to your plan. It is highly recommended that you consider the pros and cons of the risks and liability before offering this to your participants. Today, only about 20 percent of 401(k)'s make the SDO available. It was popular during the stock boom of the 1990s, but plan sponsors have learned that the importance of retirement preparedness means there may be no room for major errors. The DIY approach has not been considered to be very effective for participants overall, nor has it been shown to be necessary to benefit from building a secure retirement.

EXCHANGE-TRADED FUNDS

An ETF, or exchange-traded fund, is a bit like a hybrid of a stock and a mutual fund. It is a diversified portfolio, usually a basket of assets that tracks an index similar to an index mutual fund. But unlike a mutual fund, ETFs trade throughout the day like a common stock. The challenge with holding ETFs in 401(k) plans is twofold: First of all, intraday trading makes for pricing disparities. One participant could get a different price than another for purchases made the same day. This includes payroll deposits or reallocations. Secondly, unlike mutual funds, ETFs are not sold in fractional shares. This may make small acquisitions such as those typical within a 401(k) account challenging.

However, the ETF market is growing. There is an estimated $3 trillion in assets in various exchange-traded funds and over two thousand different ETF securities available. The advantage is that they provide efficient access to investments and strategies that previously have not been readily available. As ETFs gain in popularity, we may see more of them incorporated into 401(k) plans. However, to date there has not been an overwhelming case for ETFs. The absence of active management, the inability to trade in fractional shares, and the challenge of intraday trading makes them more difficult to navigate within the 401(k) market. There are a few providers who are making them available and have found ways to work around the limitations. If you have an interest in taking a closer look at incorporating ETFs into your 401(k), I suggest you understand how they differ within a 401(k) from those you may be familiar with outside your 401(k). An investment in Exchange Traded Funds (ETF), whether structured as a mutual fund or unit investment trust, involves the risk of losing money. An investment in ETFs involves additional risks such as lack of diversification, price volatility, competitive industry pressure, international political and economic developments, possible trading halts, and index tracking errors.

COLLECTIVE INVESTMENT TRUSTS

In 1955 the Federal Reserve authorized banks to combine funds from pensions, profit sharing, and stock bonus plans, and the IRS determined that such bank-pooled investments, called Collective Investment Trusts (otherwise known as CITs), could be exempt from tax. As a result, CITs became the popular choice for pensions. Of course, as pensions began to fail, CITs fell out of popularity. However, in 2000 the National Securities Clearing Corporation added CITs to its mutual fund trading platform, allowing CITs to trade daily and fluidly. The Pension Protection Act of 2006 approved CITs as default investment options for 401(k)'s. As a result of these changes, CITs have become an increasingly larger component of the 401(k) world, particularly for mega-size plans. CIT assets in retirement plans could soon surpass $3 trillion. Although a small piece of the estimated $32.5 trillion in all retirement assets, it is a growing piece.

Collective Investment Trusts are pooled investment accounts very similar to a mutual fund, but there are a few very notable exceptions. Unlike a mutual fund, CITs are not required to issue prospectuses or produce regular reports. Instead, the CIT spells out the terms and guidelines under which the investments of the trust are managed in a declaration of trust. There are no annual or semiannual reports. And unlike a mutual fund, a CIT has no trading ticker symbol, which means it is more difficult for an individual to track. Participants cannot download the investments on their phones or computers and monitor the price, because daily net asset values are not reported.

It is also important to note that CITs are not regulated by the Investment Company Act of 1940. They are regulated by the Office of the Comptroller of the Currency and subject to IRS and DOL oversight. They are also required to have an annual independent outside audit. But they lack transparency. Your recordkeeper will provide you with fact sheet disclosure and performance information, but it is very difficult to lift up the hood and see what's going on inside the investment. Morningstar provides a database of CIT performance data for more than one thousand CITs; however, this information is not available to the public.

The advantage for using a CIT is the ability to pool money with other investors' in retirement accounts and benefit from both scale and diversification. If the CIT is actively managed, ideally participants will also benefit from the skill of the manager. However, many are CITs are index funds, which means they are not actively managed. The lack of regulatory compliance costs and absence of retail investors means that CITs are designed to have lower costs than the average mutual fund, including passively managed index mutual funds. It is for this reason the large-plan market has embraced CITs. The increased fee litigation has compelled plan sponsors to seek lower-cost alternative investments.

In my opinion, CITs take us back to the days of no transparency, into the very heart of what caused the implosion of the pension. And it wasn't that long ago that hidden fees and ambiguity caused problems with 401(k) plan. With no dividend and capital gains distributions and no reporting, plan sponsor and participants simply have to trust that the accounting is accurate. We are left to hope the accounting firm is adhering to the rules and correctly auditing the financials since there is no annual statement or prospectus.

Candidly, I'm surprised by the growing popularity of CITs, especially in the wake of the Enron scandal, which brought down one of the largest accounting firms, Arthur Andersen. Enron used a variety of fraudulent accounting practices that ultimately wiped out more than $2 billion from pension plans. Anderson was found guilty of faulty audits of not just Enron but also Waste Management, Sunbeam, the Baptist Foundation of Arizona, and Worldcom, improperly accounting for more than $3.8 billion of expense. Andersen's failure to identify fraudulent activities is beyond bewildering. Indeed, with all the accounting and corporate scandals that led to Sarbanes–Oxley Act of 2002, I am perplexed by any potential option that lacks transparency as a solution to our retirement crisis. While I do believe most companies in America (be they investment, accounting, or any other type of business) are ethical and operate as fair and legitimate businesses, when it comes to investments, I think history has taught us caveat emptor—buyer beware. How can a participant perform due diligence without transparency? Low fees should be one factor but not the only factor to consider when selecting funds for your investment menu. The race to zero fees is resulting in momentum building within the Collateral Investment Trust space, since low cost is the key benefit of CITs.

IN SUMMARY

The 401(k) is one of the most common types of employer-sponsored retirement plans in the country, but it certainly isn't without its share of confusion and complexity. Perhaps that is no truer than with investment options and selections, not just for the employee but also for the plan sponsor. At the plan sponsor level, your job is to craft an investment menu of options that will provide enough suitable selections to meet the diverse needs of your employees based on their varying risk tolerances, ages, and overall goals. You will also need to be sure to cover the core asset classes needed to balance risk and return within the capital markets. Because recordkeepers can limit the list of options available from which you can select, or they can make available a whole open universe of investment options, the process can be rather involved and complex.

As a plan fiduciary, you must understand your role and responsibility for designing and monitoring your investment menu, regardless of the options available by your recordkeeper. Indeed, restrictive recordkeepers may make your job more challenging. You have a duty to maintain a process for ensuring your investments are competitive with fees and performance. At the same time, more options to choose from can make the process a bit daunting for an investment committee, just as it can be for participants. That is why it is valuable to engage an investment expert who can work diligently to help you seek to maintain an effective plan that can enable your employees to retire ready.

CHAPTER 7
PLAN FEES

Patrick recently joined your firm as the employee relations advisor. His job is to make sure everyone is treated fairly and also protect you from undue risks. He understands employment law and serves as a liaison between managers and employees to help resolve employee conflicts. He had some concerns about the investment performance in your 401(k) as he noticed the funds seemed to be underperforming. Upon further investigation, he also had concerns that the plan fees and fund expenses were higher than normal. Several employees had also commented that the provider service was lacking. He approached you to ask for documentation showing why you chose the provider you have and to see a comparative market analysis of fees. He further expressed concern over the investments and wanted to see your latest benchmarking report. How do you respond to Patrick?

In the 1990s, the number of companies starting 401(k) plans grew radically. From 1990 to 2000 over twenty million new participants joined the 401(k) savings trend (see figure 7.1). This was the era of the dot-com boom, and employees were eager to be able to participate in the stock market. It was no surprise why. Stock market performance was fantastic with annual returns of up to 20% not uncommon. Employees didn't pay too much attention to plan fees and expenses. The dot-com era built wealth with very little effort, even for the small investor. In no time, 401(k) plans became the staple retirement vehicle for working Americans.

These plans were promoted by insurance companies, investment firms, banks, and even payroll companies. They were frequently sold as a low-cost or even "free" substitute for the expensive pension plan. Of course, they were not free. But the expenses were embedded within the plans and often rather difficult to identify, even by professionals. Still today, we find assessing fees more challenging than it should be. Fees impact net results to the employees, and they should always have mattered. However, high demand for 401(k) plans in the 1990s overshadowed these concerns, and the consensus was buy first, ask questions later. Later came in the form of the dot-com bust, when from 2000 to 2002, the equity markets fell 40 to 70 percent in value. Suddenly, questions were asked and fees were illuminated, adding to the damage to retirement accounts.

To understand how this worked, consider a fund that has an average return of 12% (which was quite normal for a return back in the late 1990s). The investment expense ratio might have been 1.5 percent. There also may have been additional fees or charges that were not disclosed but that were deducted from the participants' accounts. Even at a fee of 1.5 percent, to average 12% return, the fund would have had to actually make 13.5%. Now, admittedly, few investors cared about paying 1.5 percent when they were enjoying the fantastic returns of the 1990s. At 12%, account values were doubling every six

401(k) Number of Active Participants

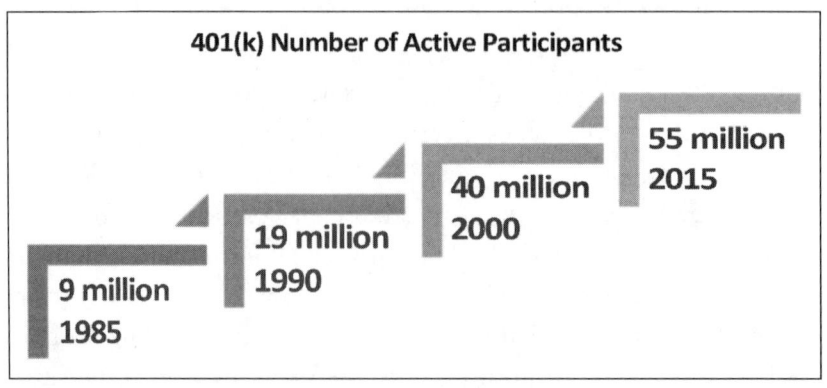

- 9 million 1985
- 19 million 1990
- 40 million 2000
- 55 million 2015

Figure 7.1. *Plan participation doubled during the decade of the 1990s.*
Source: US Department of Labor 5500 Reports.

years. An employee starting from scratch contributing $400 per paycheck to his 401(k) starting in 1990 could have had an account balance of as much as $300,000 by the end of 1999. At that rate, who would complain about fees? It was a big party! No one cared to question anything because everyone was enjoying the boom. But, naturally, when the party ended and the market fell, everyone began to ask questions, especially participants.

Prior to fee disclosure laws, the ambiguity in fee structures made it overwhelmingly challenging to determine if fees for the plan in question were fair and reasonable. What was disclosed was generally taken at face value, which meant only the management expense ratios were revealed. No one fathomed there would be a revenue sharing arrangement or additional fees. To be honest, even most financial advisors didn't understand the fees within a 401(k).

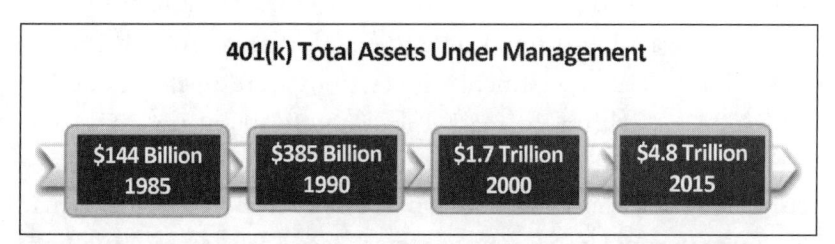

401(k) Total Assets Under Management

| $144 Billion 1985 | $385 Billion 1990 | $1.7 Trillion 2000 | $4.8 Trillion 2015 |

Figure 7.2. Assets increased approximately 350 percent during the decade of the 1990s. Source: US Department of Labor 5500 Reports.

But after the dot-com bust, plan fees began to fall under great scrutiny, and since that time they have continued to draw attention from the Department of Labor (DOL). Fees remain one of the primary subjects of litigation and DOL penalties.

Major firms with multibillion-dollar 401(k) plans found themselves buried in class action lawsuits. Many of these mega plans were paying retail prices when they could have, and should have, been priced at institutional levels, meaning that because of their size and structure, they should have received substantial discounts. Most plan sponsors didn't even know they had such options, but unintentional negligence does not abdicate a fiduciary from the law. It is not your provider's responsibility to ensure your plan fees are fair and reasonable. It is your duty.

Many firms were participating in revenue sharing arrangements, which created a conflict of interest. Some were using the revenues (or "kickbacks") to finance things like office equipment and executive retreats. Revenue sharing is legal, but any shared plan costs should be used to offset plan fees or be used for the benefit of plan participants, not the company or its executives. Some companies were faced with class action lawsuits because the revenue sharing was not being monitored by the plan fiduciaries, nor was it used for the benefit of participants.

While the dot-com bust caused more damage to 401(k) values than did fees, a dissection of the damages illuminated excessive fees relative to the services and work performed on the plan. Small plans were being charged as much as 3 percent a year against plan assets. At that rate, it was almost impossible to enjoy any real growth after the market bust. Once investment expectations were reset, fees quickly drew attention within the marketplace and for regulators. The stock market struggled throughout the remainder of the decade, and fees became a serious cause for concern. Competition in the 401(k) market spurred providers to promote lower fees as the attention quickly became about costs.

Originally, many employers ignored fees, perhaps mostly because there was not proper transparency, but also because they didn't have to pay them. Fortunately, investment management fees were disclosed because of SEC rules, so most employees understood there were fund expenses. What they didn't know was that there were also administrative fees and other charges taken out of their accounts. Even financial advisors and service representatives were not clear on the fees and how they were structured within these plans. The fees were often buried deep in plan documents and written ambiguously. I remember many times calling providers to get clear on fees, and with every call, I would get different answers from different representatives of the same plan! I don't believe anyone was truly seeking to withhold or misrepresent information, but I doubt the recordkeepers' own service representatives had easy access to this information. Plan providers were able to structure the fees in ways that eluded even their own employees.

Clearly, this highlights the lack of uniformity and a need for regulations. Nearly every plan, even within the same provider, can be priced and structured differently. Some have administrative fees as a separate line item; others don't. Some get paid from revenue sharing, while others don't. Some plans charge 12b-1 fees, while others do not. As noted, there is still not a uniform standard of pricing, but we are moving toward a more fixed-fee structure. At the very least, fee disclosure laws require that all fees be reported to plan sponsors and participants. Litigation, regulation, and competition has prompted and promoted transparency and lower fees.

However, lowering fees isn't enough. And, as I will point out later in this chapter, the focus on fees alone is not getting us closer to retirement success. Nonetheless, even smaller firms these days are being subjected to DOL investigations and assessed penalties because of excessive plan fees. Still today, many firms are confused over the fees and expenses charged within their plans. More specifically, I find many plan sponsors don't know what to do with the fee disclosure document beyond distributing it to the employees and filing it. That is not what you should be doing with your disclosure. If you don't know what you are being charged *in entirety*, how you are being charged, and why you are being charged, you are not fulfilling your fiduciary duties. You need to have a baseline in order to know how your plan fees compare to the market and to determine if your plan fees are fair and reasonable.

It is imperative that all plan sponsors regardless of size, large or small, understand how their plan fees affect participants and their retirement accounts. To understand this, you must be clear on the different types of fees and the different ways in which they are charged. As a fiduciary, you are responsible for following a *duty of loyalty*, which is the duty to administer your plan solely in the interest of your beneficiaries. In the case of your 401(k), this refers to your employees and their families. In order to help you understand how this duty fits with plan fees, let me provide some context.

In a 401(k) plan, an account balance will determine the amount of retirement income an employee will receive in the future. Certainly, we understand that contributions and earnings can increase the value of this account. Fees and expenses, on the other hand, may reduce the value and will impact the growth. Over time, this can substantially reduce the future retirement income. Consider this hypothetical example, assume that you have an employee with thirty years until retirement and a current 401(k) balance of $25,000. Let's further assume this employee contributes $5,000 a year to his plan and has a $3,000 annual employer matching contribution. If he enjoys a 7% return net of fund management expenses and your recordkeeper and advisor fees are 1 percent, his account balance will grow by 6% a year on average, which means he will have $820,000 at age sixty-five. But if your plan fees are 2 percent before management fees, this employee would only have about $600,000 or more than one-quarter less for retirement.

While actual results will vary, you can see how substantial fees can be when compounded over a long period of time. This was largely ignored for many years. However, because fees have a substantial impact on account values, employers have a specific obligation to consider all plan expenses charged to participants. You must follow certain rules when managing your plan fees according to ERISA. However, it is important to recognize that you are not bound to provide the *lowest-cost* plan on the market. It is not the Department of Labor's job to set fees or define what fees you should be paying. In fact, it is not the fee itself that the DOL is defining as fair and reasonable. It is the due diligence *process* you follow that matters to regulators.

Suppose you shop plans and get three proposals. Do you choose the lowest-priced plan? Good things aren't cheap, and cheap things are rarely, if ever, good. Be cautious when selecting the cheapest plan. The DOL does not prescribe what plan you must select, but rather that you provide reasonable rationale for your selection. For instance, there is nothing in the guidelines that says you cannot select the highest-priced plan and still fall within the fiduciary guidelines, *provided you can justify that the higher-cost plan best fits the needs of your participants.* The point is, you must be able to offer a rationale as to why your participants are paying the fees you have determined they must pay, regardless of what those fees are. Keep in mind, you are responsible for negotiating and selecting the fees, but the charges are actually incurred by your plan participants.

With that said, it may not be as easy to justify selecting the highest-priced plan. But in today's world the difference in plan fees is generally a matter of basis points (bps) rather than full percentages. A 10 or 25 bps differential is not going to have a significant difference in net results, provided you and your employees are getting a competitive plan. Why wouldn't you want a top-quartile investment menu and an advisory team who provides full financial support to you and your participants?

As with everything, however, cost is relative to value, so there is much more to consider than just fees when managing a plan. What ERISA does require, and the DOL enforces, is that you follow a due diligence process to ensure that plan fees are reasonable relative to the services. In other words, you must be aware of what the plan fees are, how they are paid, and why they are being paid. In short, the fiduciary standards set a process for management and oversight. Fees are not the only management consideration, but they ought to be one of the principal factors when reviewing your plan. Again, to reiterate, you should be following a process or methodology to determine the fairness of your plan fees. This is commonly known as fee benchmarking. The regulatory rules are such that it is your process that is scrutinized, not the actual fees themselves.

Of course, given all the industry attention paid to fees and expenses, competition in the market has resulted in cost compression. We are seeing 401(k) fees decline, so it is smart to be sure to negotiate your plan fees to keep in line with market standards, not just for ERISA compliance but also to promote retirement success for your employees. Clearly, even a small difference in fees can result in a sizable difference to one's retirement account. Compounded, fees can erode tens of thousands, if not hundreds of thousands, of dollars from accounts. Granted, if you are getting great service and support, those fees can make you more money by elevating your investment performance and participant behavior. But if you don't know what you are paying and how those fees compare to industry averages, you are not working in the best interest of your participants. Remember, your employees are relying on you to offer them a fair plan.

If you haven't monitored your plan fees or benchmarked your plan in the past few years, it is highly recommended you do so immediately. Not only is this a fiduciary requirement, but also it is relevant to the growth and success of your plan. However, it is not the fee itself that is the conflict creating the litigation and drawing attention. It is the fact that employers are not following a prudent process to ensure the plan is managed in the sole interest of plan participants and their beneficiaries. Many employers, still today, do not understand how fees are being charged and whether or not such fees are reasonable relative to the service model. So, let me take a moment to be sure you understand the primary fees and expenses associated with 401(k) plans.

ADMINISTRATION FEES

The cost of operating a plan involves expenses for basic administrative services. The day-to-day operations may include plan recordkeeping, accounting, legal services, and trustee services. They will also likely include access to an account representative, electronic access or plan sponsor and participant website, and/or telephone voice-response system. Your plan provider will provide the administrative services that will include daily valuations and reporting services for your employees, online transactions, and additional support for plan sponsor-level services. Your provider might also offer periodic enrollment meetings or educational seminars for your employees, webinars or podcasts, and access to online retirement planning software. You might benefit from quarterly, semiannual, or annual plan reviews to discuss the overall plan performance. Your provider may also provide numerous reports, including standard disclosures and plan health reports.

The costs of these services can be charged as a separate line item, or they may be wrapped in the investment management fees. When administrative fees are paid separately, such fees are either allocated among participants' individual accounts in proportion to each account balance or assessed as a flat fee. The asset-based fee method is more common because it is viewed as a fairer pricing structure since those with smaller account balances pay proportionately less in fees.

INVESTMENT FEES

By far the largest component of 401(k) plan fees and expenses is associated with managing investments. Fees for investment management and other investment-related services generally are assessed as a percentage of assets invested. As with all fees, you should pay attention to management expenses. Management fees can be broken down based on what is called passive management (i.e., index funds) or active management. Passive management is a lower cost because it is largely automated. Active management is when there is an individual or, more commonly, a team of portfolio managers and research staff collaborating on what securities to buy and sell based on the fund's objectives. In this case, the expenses are generally higher to cover market intelligence as well as the research, staff hours, and costs of conducting the due diligence work. Active management means daily oversight of the investments and usually includes a buy–sell discipline and an active investment strategy and may also include an asset allocation strategy. Advocates of active management declare that careful research, selective buys and sells, and attentive monitoring provides important downside risk to investors, particularly during volatile markets.

However, passive investing has become quite popular. Especially during bull markets it is typical for investors to question the rationale for the value of portfolio management and the justification for paying management fees. When the market goes up, why do we need someone at the helm? Arguably, you don't. However, the markets eventually turn, and it usually happens unexpectedly. But there are those who believe they can make their own adjustments, and they don't want to pay for active management. In that case, index funds or passive funds may be a good option. These are funds that follow an underlying index, such as the S&P 500. The fund company acquires the same positions as the index with the same weighted allocations and only makes changes as the index changes. Indexes are not managed for risk or performance but rather to represent the given benchmark.

The companies in the S&P 500, for example, are selected by a committee based on specific criteria that include market size, liquidity, sector, and financial viability, among other things, and selected specifically to represent industries in the US economy. Companies are removed only when they no longer meet the required criteria to be included in the index, unlike an actively managed fund, which may remove a company because of excessively high valuations, management changes, rising debt ratios, and so on. The fund company is merely acting as an administrator of an index fund, not a portfolio manager; therefore, the management fees are significantly lower. Proponents of index funds argue that most actively managed funds fail to outperform their respective indexes and that lower costs mean increased returns for shareholders. Of course, indices are unmanaged and cannot be invested into directly so index mutual funds are structured to simply mirror the holdings within the corresponding index. Index returns do not reflect fees, expenses, or sales charges. For example, the S&P 500 index would likely have different returns than a S&P 500 index mutual fund. Finally index performance is not indicative of the performance of any investment.

It is important to understand that one approach is not better than another. There are great portfolio managers, and there are less than stellar managers. Passive investing can be inferior to a good portfolio management team, or it can be superior to an average or below-average money manager. The debate will be long-standing, and there is no right or wrong answer. Of course, monitoring your funds should help boost the quality of your portfolio managers, but still, most plan sponsors have found offering both passive and active management will provide participants the flexibility they may want or need to navigate through various market cycles.

Investment management fees are almost always charged in the form of a bundled fee that is deducted from investment returns on a daily basis and expressed as an annual percentage. Generally speaking, returns posted on each participant's account are net of management fees, although they may not be net of other plan fees. The performance reports you may provide your participants are typically net of the management fees but are not necessarily net of plan administration or advisory fees. You will have to check with your 401(k) team to identify if its fees are bundled or charged separately.

Plan participants have some control over investment fees because they can choose to invest in funds within your plan that carry lower expenses, such as index funds and passive funds. But this still means you must be aware of the fees and how they impact your plan since their options may be restricted based on your selected investment menu.

ADVISOR FEES

If you choose to hire a financial advisor to assist you with investment monitoring, plan management, employee investment education, and other support services, such fees can be either lumped into the investment expenses or paid separately as an asset-based fee. A full-service advisor may help benchmark your plan for fees and investments, shop vendors, provide fiduciary training, help set up retirement committees, provide individual retirement consultations for your employees, and more. Including an investment expert in your plan can help ensure you are on your way toward retirement success, provided the advisor provides ongoing advice and assistance. Advisor fees may be paid in the form of 12b-1 fees or commissions, described below, or via an asset-based fee charged to the plan. Fee-based advisors will generally work for you under an ERISA 3(21) arrangement as co-fiduciary to help reduce your investment fiduciary risk or a 3(38) fiduciary as investment manager.

12B-1 FEES

There may be additional fees charged as part of your investment management expenses called 12b-1 fees. In the traditional sense, 12b-1 charges were used to offset broker commissions or marketing costs for retail mutual funds, but in the 401(k) market 12b-1 charges may be used to offset fees paid to cover plan administration or advisor services or may be paid as part of a plan's revenue sharing. You will find 12b-1 fees listed as a part of your investment management expenses, either via the prospectus or your fee disclosure document. Such fees are generally bundled into the fund expense ratios. It is important to assess your 12b-1 fees just like you would any other fees, as they are deducted from investment results. You may find different share classes available that do not include 12b-1 fees. Although this may lower investment costs, it may not lower plan fees. For example, if the 12b-1 fee was used to cover advisory services, the fee will still be assessed, but as a separate line item.

FIDUCIARY FEES

Some providers offer additional services for an added fee. An ERISA 3(16) plan administrator takes on fiduciary responsibility and liability for certain administrative functions. These may include transaction processing and participant notice distribution services. An ERISA 3(38) investment manager takes on full discretion and management of your investment menu. Or instead of hiring an ERISA 3(38) manager, you can hire an investment advisor who shares in your investment fiduciary responsibilities. This is called an ERISA 3(21) investment advisor. Some recordkeepers may offer 3(21) or 3(38) services. Fiduciary fees can be a separate asset-based fee or bundled within another fee structure. Regardless, you will need to identify these fees separately to access their fairness.

TRUSTEE FEES

Trustee administrative services can be outsourced or can be performed in-house by you or your staff. If outsourced, such services typically include processing receipts and disbursements such as approving hardship withdrawals, loans, QDROs, and rollovers. Some providers include these services in the administrative costs. Others charge a separate fee for this service.

TRANSACTION OR INDIVIDUAL SERVICE FEES

In addition to overall administrative expenses, there may be individual service fees associated with optional features offered under a 401(k) plan. There may be transaction fees charged separately to the accounts of participants who choose to take advantage of a particular plan feature. For example, individual service fees may be charged to a participant for taking a loan from the plan or for executing participant investment directions or access to investment research services.

REVENUE SHARING

Mutual funds were not designed specifically for retirement plans. The concept of a mutual fund goes all the way back to 1774 in the Netherlands, where the idea of pooling funds from investors of modest means to buy assets was conceived. In the United States, the first mutual fund was created in 1924. It, too, was designed to provide a means for people of modest means to participate in the capital markets. A part of the services provided by mutual funds is recordkeeping since the pooling of funds necessitates accurate accounting, including keeping track of share ownership. Additional costs of operating a traditional mutual fund include sales and marketing expenses. However, within the 401(k) plan, recordkeeping is performed by the plan's custodian and sales and marketing costs are not really required since the funds are not sold to the public. Because such services are not needed within a 401(k), revenue sharing was created to return such charges to the plan. These revenues generally either go to the recordkeeper to compensate for their services or go back to the plan and are used to offset other fees charged to participants. Revenue sharing is commonly used as a fee offset and, in such a case, may be utilized based on your choice as a plan sponsor. If it is paid back to your recordkeeper, you must be sure the revenues collected are not excessive. For instance, if the recordkeeper collects revenue sharing payments and also charges plan asset fees, the total paid to the recordkeeper must be considered and evaluated. This is where "hidden" fees have been uncovered and conflicts have been exposed. If your recordkeeper does not disclose revenue sharing arrangements, it is imperative that you ask questions.

Revenue sharing payments can be rather ambiguous, and they can vary based on the fund and share class, so fiduciaries need to be attentive as to how, why, and to whom revenue sharing monies are being paid. There are several potential conflicts of interest that result from revenue sharing. Keep in mind, revenue sharing is the result of fees paid by the plan participants in the form of investment expenses; thus, revenue sharing arrangements must return those benefits to the participants by way of fee offset.

You have already learned fees reduce investment returns and directly impact the value of retirement accounts. For example, if participants are being charged 1.2 percent for management fees and 0.3 percent of that is being paid back to the plan in the form of revenue sharing, fiduciaries need to be sure those funds are being used in a fair and reasonable manner. If a recordkeeper is retaining the revenue sharing, it should be disclosed and considered a part of the compensation to the provider. Suppose the recordkeeper is receiving

$25,000 in revenue sharing from your plan and your participants are also paying $30,000 as an asset-based recordkeeper fee. As a fiduciary, you must consider the total plan fees paid to your recordkeeper to be actually $55,000 (revenue sharing + asset-based fees). When you benchmark your plan and compare it to the market, you must account for the revenue sharing payments. If we further suppose the comparable fees in the market are $40,000 for a plan of similar size and benefits, we can easily see that your participants, in this example, are paying $15,000 above market. While paying fees that are above market is not a conflict in and of itself, fiduciaries need to rationalize the decision to pay more. Obviously, it can be difficult to justify if you are not aware of the revenue sharing arrangement. Additionally, if there are no extraordinary benefits or services provided with your plan to justify the extra costs, such fees may be deemed unfair and unreasonable. If you are unaware of the revenue sharing fees, you might mistakenly compare the $30,000 plan fee to the market $40,000 average range and incorrectly assume your fees are in the below-average range. While not all plans have revenue sharing arrangements, and not all funds participate in revenue sharing arrangements, this is an area that has gotten a lot of attention within the legal and regulatory environment.

One of the big revenue sharing drivers and points of conflict within litigation has been the use of retail shares. Retail share classes of mutual funds carry higher fees and, therefore, typically include higher revenue sharing arrangements. If your plan qualifies for institutional or retirement share classes, which have lower investment management fees, you must weigh your options very carefully to avoid overcharging your participants. Retail shares may or may not have revenue sharing, but at the end of the day, aligning the plan to the right share class is a direct benefit of the plan because it impacts participant net results. All plans should be analyzed based on share class options and total fees, including any revenue sharing payment. Only then can you properly assess the fairness of your plan fees and consider fee negotiations.

FEE BENCHMARKING: GETTING OUT THE YARDSTICK

As you can see, fees and expenses can be confusing and can easily become convoluted. To make matters more confounding, recordkeepers often structure their fees differently, so one may offer a bundled fee whereas another has separate fees, which makes it difficult to compare. Some fee arrangements are easy to understand, whereas others are layered with complexity. Plan benchmarking is a way to break down the different components of your plan and compare them to the marketplace, including to companies of similar size and similar demographics. Benchmarking is a generic term that can be used to compare plans based on different data such as fees, investment performance, plan best practices, service models, and even details like participation rates and contribution rates, among other criteria. Typically, when it comes to fee benchmarking, you will want to compare quality, results, and costs. The objective is to identify plans of similar kind and compare the performance or costs to those of your plan. The goal is to learn (or benchmark) how well your plan is performing by comparison and identify areas of improvement.

With the fee disclosure requirements and increased scrutiny, you are well advised to benchmark your plan fees periodically. The formal process of evaluating fees is called *fee benchmarking*. It is recommended that plan sponsors benchmark plan fees at least once every three years, although there is no defined time frame as per the regulators. It is important that you not just understand your plan fees but also identify the reasonableness of those fees relative to the market. As a fiduciary, you will need to be confident that your participants are paying fees that are fair relative to the services received. Fee benchmarking will help you identify what, if anything, needs to be done to make adjustments, such as negotiate better fees, shop providers, or negotiate for higher services.

There are many third-party service providers or financial advisors who can help you with this process. There is no single benchmarking process that has been universally adopted or required by ERISA. However, if you are ever subjected to a Department of Labor investigation, you will want to be sure your fee benchmarking and documentation reinforce your due diligence process of monitoring and managing your plan. It has been made very clear that it is not enough just to know what your plan fees are. You must also know that the fees are not excessive or unreasonable. So, while benchmarking is not a required process, it may be difficult to make a case for your plan fees without benchmarking.

DOES THIS MEAN I MUST ENSURE MY PLAN FEES ARE AVERAGE?

So, you benchmark your plan. Now what? Must you go back and tell your providers they need to lower their fees? Should you change providers to the one with the lowest cost even if you are happy with the services and quality of your team? Should you expect your service providers to negotiate their fees down to industry average? The answer is no. What is fair and reasonable is not measured by averages. For instance, the average priced vehicle today, according to Kelley Blue Book, is $33,560. But you may have paid substantially more for your car. You may have opted to drive a luxury car or a sports car or a fancy SUV. You may have opted for additional features and benefits, such as a larger engine, leather seats, a sunroof, or accessories. Plan benchmarking is not an evaluation done to demand lower costs. It's an evaluation to ensure fairness. Suppose you paid $50,000 for the same car your neighbor got for $43,000. While that happens frequently with auto sales, the financial industry is regulated differently, which means your requirement as a fiduciary is to seek to prevent this disparity. This does not mean you are required to select an average plan or expect your above-average service provider to reduce their fees to average rates. The purpose is to understand what is being paid and to use the benchmark as a basis for the evaluation of the plan as a whole, including services, support, and the quality of the product, to ensure your participants are not being overcharged.

Unfortunately, unlike a car, 401(k) plans are intangible, so they are difficult to assess in terms of value. Having a full-service financial advisor helping you pilot through the rules of ERISA, navigate the maze within the retirement planning process and steer through the financial markets may be of substantial value to you, and average-priced advisors may not provide that same level and quality of service. Likewise, you may have chosen to drive a higher-priced BMW or Mercedes, which might be comparable to selecting a service provider who offers you an exclusive relationship manager and open architecture investment access. You will likely pay more to have a dedicated manager who takes ownership of the service and support you receive, makes on-site visits, initiates solutions, and provides proactive support. A lower-cost plan might only offer you a call center by comparison or have a limited investment menu and only provide reactive service. Clearly, you will pay more for a quality automobile as compared to average- or below-average-price models, but your driving experience is bound to be superior, the service experience is expected to be better, and the life span and resale value of the car is likely to be enhanced to a point above the resale value of average cars. If that is important to you and you believe it's a value to the plan overall, there is nothing that says you cannot enjoy higher quality services.

When I get my car serviced, I have my own service manager who gets me in and out quickly by appointment and always has my rental or loaner car ready and waiting. I don't have to ask for it nor do I get charged. It's included in the service experience. To me, that is an important benefit that saves me time and hassles. In the end, I know I pay for this service, but I don't get nickel-and-dimed for it. I call my guy, tell him what I need and when I want to come in and it's done. They have a car ready and waiting for me and I'm on my way. When I pick up my car, it is washed, waxed and in tip-top shape. They do it right and they do it consistently, expeditiously and professionally. I know I pay more overall, but I prefer that kind of experience.

An exceptional 401(k) provider, administrator, and advisor is going to provide a different kind of experience than an average team provides. You should not expect to get a great customer service experience and a superior investment menu along with excellent plan management and an expert consultant at a below-average cost. Indeed, you are not likely to even get that experience at an average price. You should expect the fees to be aligned to the experience. Of course, if superior service and professional expertise is not important or of value, you should not be paying above-average fees. If your plan fees are higher than average and cannot be justified, you need to either negotiate fees or change providers. On the other hand, if you like outstanding service and support, you must be prepared to pay more to get it. Know what you need, what you want, and what is reasonable relative to your needs and desires. We may like driving a fancy luxury car, but we can't expect to own one at the same price as an economy car.

The problem in the industry today as I see it is that plan sponsors are so focused on fees that the market is now compressing costs to the point that such quality distinctions may not even be available in the future. You simply cannot get the same quality of materials, engineering, and service from a car priced at $33,560 as you can from a $60,000 car. Likewise, you cannot enjoy the benefits that will help you lead your employees toward retirement success if you expect to pay economy fees. A one-size-fits-all plan may be cheap in price, but it will also likely be very low in quality. The attention is so focused fees that quality is being overlooked. It would be a shame to lose the option of having a superior plan with excellent service and support simply because the market demand diminishes enough to make it no longer attractive for such service providers to offer such an experience. Porsche would sooner go out of business than cut their prices and quality to low-budget levels. I believe the regulatory environment has tightened so much that fiduciaries are missing the point of fee disclosure, and plan sponsors remain quite confused as to how to fulfill their duties in the spirit of the law.

IN SUMMARY

When it comes to fees, what you don't know can hurt you. Regulations have tightened because of abuse, negligence, lack of transparency, and excessive fees. I fully support regulations and fee disclosures and feel it is a shame that such abuse took place. However, being an advocate of education, I believe that had plan sponsors been properly educated about pricing structures in the first place, less abuse and negligence would have occurred. In general, I find plan sponsors care about their employees' welfare and do not want to impede retirement success. They just don't know what they need to know to run a successful plan.

Not having sufficient staff, time, knowledge, or resources to follow a regimented diligence process is not going to relieve you of the liability and obligation you have. We know that 401(k) plans are not free. It is important to remember that your participants bear the brunt of the expenses associated with your plan. Consequently, you are required to ensure that fees paid to service providers and other expenses of the plan are reasonable in light of the level and quality of the services provided. In doing this evaluation, you may do the work yourself or hire an advisor or third-party firm to perform the work for you. Regardless of whether you tackle the task in-house or outsource the job, the responsibility for the due diligence process falls on you to ensure the evaluation is being done correctly, timely, and according to the law. It is your duty to be sure all fees paid are reviewed and compared on a regular basis, and it is important to know you cannot abdicate that duty to anyone else. Take the time to demonstrate the same care with monitoring plan costs as you would with managing your own money and not only will you fulfill your duties as a fiduciary but also, and most importantly, you will help enable your employees to pursue retirement success.

Over the past decade, the industry focus has failed to center on education. Although it is changing as financial wellness interest grows, I still see many plan sponsors looking at fees in a vacuum. In fact, I think the 401(k) industry as a whole is a bit challenged when it comes to how to deliver the right service at the right price. For sure, the value of services means that good and fair pricing lies somewhere in between the excessive fees of the 1990s and the scramble to the bottom today. The pendulum has swung the other direction, from excessive fees to plan sponsors seeking such low costs that it is difficult for consultants such as me to provide the needed support. Plan sponsors need strong support to run a successful plan, and this will not happen if all we focus on is lowering fees. It should never be just about cost; it should also be about value. At the end of the day, employees need a secure retirement, and that means investing in participant services. Your employees need good education and lots of support if they are to have a chance at being retirement ready.

CHAPTER 8
EMPLOYEE EDUCATION: BUILDING RETIREMENT READINESS

Jeromy is a sharp salesperson. He's making good money and participating in your 401(k). With the recent market rally, Jeromy's been paying closer attention to the daily prices of his funds. He's also moving more of his retirement savings into aggressive funds. In December, he comes to your office very upset because the Empire Small Cap Fund offered in your 401(k) just dropped $2 a share, despite the fact that the market was up that particular day. Jeromy tells you he just moved his all money out of the fund, but he suggests you find out what's going on because it looks suspicious. How can a fund drop $2 in value in one day when the market is up? How do you respond to Jeromy?

PLAN HEALTH MEASURES: HOW DO YOU SPELL SUCCESS?

How do you measure the success of your 401(k)? Is it measured by participation rates? Do you feel like you've done a great job if you have 90 percent participation in your plan? I certainly would feel good if I knew 90 percent of my employees were saving for their retirement, but what if eight out of every ten of those employees were not saving sufficiently to meet their retirement income needs? Is that success? Probably not.

When companies set out to measure the health of their 401(k) plan, they don't generally base it on how comfortably their retired workers are supporting themselves or how many employees are on track for a seamless income transition into retirement. Instead, employers evaluate how many use the plan and whether the benefits offered are competitive. Although this is important, the purpose of the 401(k) is to provide retirement income benefits. Therefore, no matter how you choose to measure your plan success, your plan's ability to get your employees to a secure retirement should be the top priority. Indeed, a low participant rate is bound to lead to an even lower level of retirement readiness, so the first step is to seek to get participation in the plan. But the end goal is to get your employees to retirement. To give you an idea of what drives plan success, look at the list in figure 8.1, which highlights core plan health measures. At my firm, we like to measure the current plan statistics and set goals in three-year increments.

In this example, the plan has 65 percent of the eligible employees participating. The goal is to get at least 85 percent participation, so we will use the auto-enroll feature to help accomplish this. Next, we want to focus on increasing the contributions. The current salary deferral rate is 4 percent, but the goal is to encourage employees to stretch to a 7 percent deferral rate. In an effort to accomplish this, we will implement the auto-increase feature. The average investment rate of return is a bit below market, so the next goal is to attempt to improve investment performance. To pursue this objective, we will institute a re-enrollment followed with a three-part investment education series. Incidentally, we also like to monitor loan utilization and diversification to be sure the plan is used correctly. That helps tailor our education as well. Finally, we will review the retirement readiness index, which is the estimated percentage of participants forecasted to be retirement ready by age sixty-five. Retirement readiness is the cornerstone of a plan's overall success, so I believe this index is the most important measurement for plan health. Unfortunately, we still have a lot of work to do to change the national savings rates and retirement readiness index. Too many people are behind in their savings, but this plan has a good start with a readiness index rate of 37 percent and a goal set by the investment committee to hit 50 percent. Though it is ambitious, I am confident that with diligence, hard work, and a solid education plan, we can meet these objectives. What are your plan goals?

While success means different things to different people, retirement plan health measurements are designed to provide a standard baseline for plan effectiveness. With the numerous challenges we face today, it's no surprise that many workers feel discouraged about their retirement. Across all age ranges, 58 percent of workers today say they expect to have to work past age sixty-five, if they are able to retire at all. Sadly, a growing number of employees feel incapable of ever obtaining financial independence. Studies show workers in their sixties or older are the least optimistic about enjoying retirement, but even among twenty-something-year-old workers, 43 percent don't anticipate being able to retire before age sixty-five.

Topic	Current	Goal	Action
Participation Rate	65%	85%	Auto Enroll
Deferral Rate	4%	7%	Auto Increase
Rate of Return	5.6%	6.5%	Re-Enrollment
Income Replacement Ratio	33%	47%	Education
Loan Utilization Rate	18%	10%	Education
Diversification Rate	60%	80%	Re-Enrollment
Retirement Readiness Index	37%	50%	Education, Individual consultations, Retirement Projections

Figure 8.1.

American workers are dismayed. They don't have any confidence in the future of Social Security, and they feel too financially squeezed to be able to save adequately. Unfortunately, most don't even know how to determine if they are on track. To exacerbate this problem, plan sponsors are at a loss as to how to go about making a difference. But brushing aside the need for financial literacy is only compounding the problem. That is why we use the benchmarking in figure 8.1. We want to measure a plan's health and goals in a way that is SMART:

> **S**pecific
> **M**easurable
> **A**ctionable
> **R**ealistic
> **T**imely

When a committee can easily define where their 401(k) plan is today and where it needs to be, everyone can work together to promote favorable results. There is much employers can do to help employees take the steps necessary toward ensuring a secure retirement.

The basic concept for retirement readiness starts with an income replacement ratio. No one wants to take a substantial cut in income when they retire. Experts suggest a 70–80 percent income replacement is necessary to make a seamless transition into retirement. This means if today you have a household pretax annual income of $100,000, you will need $70,000 to $80,000 to enjoy the same lifestyle in retirement. Of course, some expenses will be eliminated, such as payroll taxes and 401(k) savings; others will likely be reduced, such as transportation expenses and clothing and food costs; and some may increase, such as health care and leisure activities. Plus, there's the impact of inflation to consider since retirees don't get pay raises. As a result, retirement may be more of a shift in living expenses rather than a substantial reduction. Consequently, if we account for social security, the average worker will need to replace about 45 percent to 50 percent of his or her income with personal savings. That means you will want to benchmark your plan for retirement readiness or plan health based on your participants' ability to track for at least a 45 percent income replacement ratio. We measure this based on current account balance, salary deferrals, employer matching, investment returns, and so on.

It may not appear that such factors are within the plan sponsor's control; however, with diligent planning, a dedicated team, and a desire for success, you may be pleasantly surprised to learn how much can be accomplished. By extrapolating information from your plan data and company census, you can use reporting tools to project each employee's tracking ratio and arrive at a retirement readiness index for the overall plan. Do you know what percent of your employees are on track for an adequate retirement income? You may be disappointed by the answer. Very few companies have more employees tracking for retirement preparedness than not, but with a little effort and time, statistics can be changed. Monitoring you plan health can enable you and your committee to identify your specific plan needs, recognize progress being made, and get more connected with your participants' actions. Plan success is a process that requires attention, time, and planning. Your plan health index sheds light on important information that is critical to your employees' financial wellness.

If your current team has not offered to do this health analysis for you, it might be time to consider looking for an advisory team who takes the time to support you in optimizing your plan's potential. Plan health studies will identify the strength of your employees' retirement readiness. A strong health index is a win for both you and your employees. Of course, you can't build a successful plan that gets employees on track toward a secure retirement unless you have a financially literate workforce, so let's talk about your education program.

EDUCATION PROGRAM

> *An investment in knowledge pays the best interest.*
> —Benjamin Franklin

What does your 401(k) education program look like? Can it be summed up in the action of passing out enrollment booklets—*booklets that get left at home on the kitchen table and never read?* Is it an occasional but sporadic live enrollment meeting—*meetings that are humdrum and that fewer than half your employees attend?* Does your provider email random notices to promote your plan—*emails that end up in the spam folder or buried beneath the hundreds of other emails?* What is the goal of your education program? Do you even have goal? Do you have a formalized education program? If not, why not? And if so, how do you measure education success?

I surveyed over one hundred different plan sponsors and asked them these questions. Most had no education program in effect, and when I asked why not, the typical response they gave was "because it has never done much." The truth is, most 401(k) education programs don't work because they are inconsistent and ineffective. They fail to incorporate adult learning techniques. Financial literacy today is so low that almost anything helps, but as a good steward of your plan, you should aspire to do more than just have a random, occasional enrollment meeting to promote participation. One of the reasons retirement education isn't working well is because educators don't motivate or create an interest to want to learn more. I'm afraid to say, most content tends to be either boring and elementary or excessively technical and complicated. I realize financial planning is not exciting to most, but it really is possible to deliver education that is energizing, stimulating, and fun.

Research shows that adult learning needs to be task-oriented. Very few employees want to sit and listen to a lecture. They want to be engaged, be involved, and participate. The subject of finance is complex, but studies show workers are interested in learning about the essential aspects of finance because it has an immediate relevance to and impact on their lives. But educators need to connect the distant goal of retirement to today's needs and realities, and they need to do it in a way that addresses your employees' uniqueness and diversity. A successful education program must acknowledge that workers respond differently to different learning methods. Some are visual learners and love graphs, diagrams, and illustrations. They enjoy learning by being shown. Others are auditory learners; "tell me" is their maxim. And then there are tactile or kinesthetic learners whose motto is "let me do it."

The single most important objective of education programs is to motivate employees to take action, and to do that requires a dedicated, trained team of educators who understand the challenges of adult learning. Whether it is enrolling in the plan, understanding retirement tools, learning about investment choices, or discussing the comprehensive topic of financial wellness, you need an advisory team who can effectively teach and help your employees. Furthermore, education programs should not be arbitrary or inconsistent. It's difficult, if not impossible, to motivate employees and maintain their focus if your meetings are not routine and persistent. Financial empowerment involves building on layers of knowledge and practiced applications. It's a process. You can't hold one meeting and be assured every one of your employees will have that aha moment. Therefore, employee education requires your diligence and ongoing support.

To illustrate this, let me tell you about one of the plans I worked with had a very low participation rate. The company was not ready to adopt auto-enrollment, so it was our job to motivate the employees to participate in the plan. That was quite a challenge because, at the time, the plan did not offer any matching contributions. However, we prepared an education program and set goals. The strategy was to segment the employees into groups based on age bands. The company had over three hundred employees. We connected with those in their twenties to early thirties by providing education on the power of time while also focusing on student loan payoff techniques and home-buying approaches. We drew those in their late thirties to mid-forties in with education on college funding for children and stock investment strategies. To attract those in their late forties to late fifties we educated on taxes and retirement readiness tools. And for those sixty and over we provided education on Social Security, health-care costs, and retirement income strategies. We spent five years building a diligent education program where we conducted interactive live sessions, collaborating webinars, and conference calls on various related topics. This, coupled with individual consultations that allowed employees to seek guidance on personal matters, enabled us to reach the employees in many different ways. Now, my educators are not only retirement planning specialists, they are certified in adult training so they have schooled knowledge in the basic theory for adult learning in the workplace. My educators know how to connect with adult audiences, so our education program may be rather unique. Nonetheless, our participant-focused, diverse education program enabled us to increase the plan participation rate by over 50 percent. And we increased the plan's retirement readiness index by over 70 percent. Of course, not all situations will have the same outcome, but it does highlight the potential impact of a sound education program.

Of course, building a successful retirement plan requires time. Employees who ignore the need to save and plan for retirement need direction. Those who are trying need encouragement, and steps need to be taken to help some "unlearn" common investment mistakes and illusions. Education is a process that can take years to affect a plan's health, so it certainly requires dedication, patience and determination. It is a constant progression that requires adjustments to account for natural employee attrition, changing market conditions, and the evolving changes in the financial industry. A firm will never complete or master its education program because, at the very least, there will always be new employees who need education and support.

Furthermore, under 404a-5 regulations, there is an implied responsibility for plan sponsors to promote financial learning and educate participants on how they may save and invest through their 401(k) plan. Therefore, it is believed plan sponsors who support financial education can reduce their risk as well as enjoy increased employee productivity. If you don't have a comprehensive education program in place today, you should consider the potential benefits of implementing one.

BASIC INVESTMENT STRATEGIES

Several of the basic yet often overlooked investment strategies are discussed below for the purpose of highlighting the value and importance of implementing a comprehensive financial education program. Most employees simply do not understand basic investment approaches that are very effective in building retirement savings within a 401(k), such as dollar cost averaging and dividend reinvestment. Investors don't generally understand how to manage risk, nor do they understand the investment options within their plan. It really is essential that plan sponsors develop an education program that highlights the urgency of preparing for retirement and the benefits of sound investing. Through a great education program, you can provide the knowledge and tools your employees need to retire ready.

DOLLAR COST AVERAGING

In a 401(k), participants have the opportunity to follow a simple but effective strategy called Dollar Cost Averaging (DCA). Since no one can predict the short-term direction of the market, and because market timing strategies have been proven to be all but impossible, dollar cost averaging is an approach that may ease the discomfort of market fluctuations and manage downside risk. The objective is to remain steadfast with a regular investment plan, even during market upsets. This is more easily accomplished by focusing on accumulating shares rather than watching the daily price movement of the fund. Since more shares can be acquired for the same amount of investment capital when prices fall, the emphasis is on celebrating the ability to accumulate more shares during market upsets, rather than fretting about the current price declines.

Because the 401(k) is a systematic savings program, DCA can be effective in building shares and helps you take advantage of compounding. Your participants need to understand that the number of shares matters when it comes to retirement accumulations. Most employees get upset when they see their accounts fall in value, yet this is part of the natural process of investing. Unlike a bank account, 401(k) share values fluctuate, and at times they absolutely will go down. If they didn't, investors would not have the opportunity for significant positive returns. After all, it is the unpredictability of the daily prices that enables us to participate in market *opportunities*. Of course, most employees don't think about this before they invest. Instead, they think avoiding market losses is necessary to accumulating wealth. However, since it is more or less impossible to avoid losses, the workers with this mind-set set themselves up for failure (or at least major disappointments) by having unreasonable expectations and unobtainable goals.

With dollar cost averaging, the goal is to pay more attention to *average* share price and less attention to the *current* share price. Participants buy more shares when prices fall, which follows the logical "buy low" approach. In fact, when employees follow this strategy, they recognize the *opportunity* when prices drop, rather than fear market declines. We want to discourage employees from selling out at inopportune times. Dollar cost averaging not only keeps employees focused on the bigger picture but also helps manage risk. Have you ever seen a women's shoe sale at Nordstrom's? Don't get in a shopper's way, because she will knock you down to get her hands on as many of her favorite shoes as she can to buy at a deep discount. When items go on sale at the grocery store, people buy extra. Ours is the only industry where people literally run away when prices are discounted! But with DCA, your employees learn to appreciate the potential value of discounted shares.

Let's look at what happens when dollar cost averaging is applied. You can see in figure 8.2 that employee A invested $9,600 in January in your stock fund, anticipating the market was going to go up for the year. He paid $100 a share for the stock fund, acquiring 96 shares. Unfortunately, it was not a great year. The fund ended the year at $75 a share, so his account value fell to $7,200. Employee B had a different outcome for the same amount of investment. Instead of trying to time the market, he purchased shares monthly in the amount of $800. As the price dropped, he was able to buy more shares; therefore, the average price per share he paid ended up being $82.75, which means that for the same amount of investment, employee B accumulated 116.01 shares. More specifically, whereas the account value of the market timer was −25% for the year, the DCA strategy was −9.3% by comparison. While dollar cost averaging doesn't avoid losses, a participant can manage his market risk and focus on building investment shares over time, instead of worrying about where the market is going in the short term. It's an effective strategy, particularly during periods of market uncertainty.

		Employee A		
Month	Price Per Share	Contribution	Shares Acquired	Market Value
January	$100	$9600	96	$9600
February	$89	0	--	$8544
March	$94	0	--	$9024
April	$85	0	--	$8160
May	$87	0	--	$8352
June	$82	0	--	$7872
July	$79	0	--	$7584
August	$73	0	--	$7008
September	$81	0	--	$7776
October	$85	0	--	$8160
November	$72	0	--	$6912
December	$75	0	--	$7200
Total	Average Price Paid $100	$9600	96	$7200

Employee B				
Month	Price Per Share	Contribution	Shares Acquired	Market Value
January	$100	$800	8	$800
February	$89	$800	8.99	$1512
March	$94	$800	8.51	$2397
April	$85	$800	9.41	$2967
May	$87	$800	9.20	$3838
June	$82	$800	9.75	$4417
July	$79	$800	10.12	$5054
August	$73	$800	10.96	$5471
September	$81	$800	9.88	$6870
October	$85	$800	9.41	$8010
November	$72	$800	11.11	$7584
December	$75	$800	10.67	$8701
Total	Average Price Paid $82.75	$9600	116.01	$8701

Figure 8.2. This hypothetical illustration does not include deductions for plan fees and expenses. Actual results may vary. Market value rounded to the nearest dollar. Dollar cost averaging involves continuous investment in securities regardless of fluctuation in price levels of such securities. An investor should consider their ability to continue purchasing through fluctuating price levels. Such a plan does not assure a profit and does not protect against loss in declining markets.

Of course, there is a trade-off. During strong markets, this approach is less likely to maximize the upside in a given year. However, it still follows a bit of the "buy low, sell high" approach in that fewer shares are purchased when prices are higher. Ultimately, dollar cost averaging can be an easy automatic approach for 401(k) participants who remain steadfast with their investment strategy and make systematic contributions to their plans. I'm sure many of your participants follow this strategy unknowingly today.

Because there are two forms of contributions identified in the investment allocations (current dollars and future dollars), when current dollars remain invested, those dollars can pursue the long-term upside potential of the markets while the future monthly contributions can participate in dollar cost averaging. As already noted, this may be especially valuable during periods of market upset or volatility. Although dollar cost averaging does not guarantee a profit, it is a strategy that serves to manage market risk and effectively build the number of shares over time. Perhaps of greatest importance is the fact that it encourages employees to focus on the value of *accumulating shares* rather than on today's *current price*. The more participants adhere to these sound investment principles, the better apt they will be to retire ready.

DIVIDENDS

While not all mutual funds or subaccounts held in your 401(k) pay dividends, many do. And the value of dividends should not be underestimated. Dividends are another way to boost the accumulation of shares. Over time, dividend compounding can be quite meaningful. Like dollar cost averaging, dividend reinvestment is a way to participate in an effective strategy to help build retirement savings. The term *dividend* is derived from the Latin term that means "thing to be divided." With dividends, companies divide their profits among shareholders. Companies have been paying dividends for over four hundred years. In the early 1600s, the Dutch East India Company was the first company on record to ever pay a dividend. Do dividends matter? You bet! Since 1929, dividends have accounted for over 40 percent of the S&P 500's total return.

Most participants, however, don't understand the value of dividends or how they impact shares. If a mutual fund pays a dividend, that dividend is normally paid out monthly or quarterly. Of course, because of the diversification in a mutual fund, dividends are the result of the collective dividends received by the stocks held in the portfolio. Dividends can also be the result of interest earned on bonds. Within a 401(k), dividends are automatically reinvested, so participants who invest in funds that pay dividends automatically build up their retirement accounts through increased shares. However, to truly benefit from dividend compounding, long holding periods are required.

A dividend distribution is paid based on the number of shares held at the time the dividend is declared. In other words, how much you get depends upon how many shares you hold. For example, suppose XYZ fund declares a 0.20 dividend this quarter. This means for every share you own of XYZ fund, you will receive twenty cents. If you own one thousand shares, you would get a $200 dividend. If you own ten thousand shares, you would get a $2,000 dividend. The more shares you have, the more dividends you receive. Over time, dividends really can make a difference. Keep in mind that even if the price per share fluctuates, dividends typically continue to pay. Thus, with dividend-paying funds, there is the potential for return even in down markets. In fact, over time the dividend reward may increase with reinvestment. For instance, if you start with one thousand shares of a fund paying a quarterly dividend of $0.35 per share (1.4%), in thirty years you will have a dividend yield of 6.97%, assuming the dividend stays the same. This is because as your shares increase with every reinvestment, so does the dividend payment. That is the potential power of dividend compounding over a long period of time.

In 2014, Warren Buffett's Berkshire Hathaway fund indicated it owned four hundred million shares of Coca-Cola stock at a cost of $1.299 billion. Today, each share of Coca-Cola pays $1.56 annual dividends which suggests Berkshire Hathaway would get $624 million in dividend payment from Coca-Cola. Note: that translates as an annual yield of 48%. Buffett acquired shares of Coca-Cola in 1988, and at the time he wrote, "We expect to hold these securities for a long time. In fact, when we own portions of outstanding businesses with outstanding management, our favorite holding period is forever." Although past performance does not assure future results, Warren Buffett understands the value of dividend compounding. Furthermore, dividends don't discriminate. If you purchased Coca-Cola at the same time as Berkshire Hathaway and reinvested your dividends all these years, your dividend yield would also be 48%, even if the dollar amount would be different. Imagine that!

Some stocks are what are called "growth stocks," others are

"income stocks," and some are both "growth" and "income." Income stocks aim to pay out higher dividends, whereas growth stocks seek to grow shareholder value through price appreciation. In other words, there are trade-offs. Dividend stocks tend to have more price stability, but of course, all stocks are still subject to market risk. For instance, Coca-Cola shares fell from $29 to $18 during the 2008 financial crisis, although the company did continue to pay *rising* quarterly dividends throughout the crisis. In fact, many investors did not know that during the 2008 financial crisis, most companies continued to pay dividends. In 2008, despite the financial crisis, 236 out of the 500 companies in the S&P 500 index actually *raised* their dividends, and in 2009, 151 companies increased their dividends. In fact, only 11 companies in the S&P 500 decreased their dividend during this period. Surprised? For sure, the media would have had you believe all companies were forced to halt dividends during the financial crisis, not increase them. If participants focused on dividend trends, they might not be so inclined to panic during market drops. Many flagship large-cap companies have not only paid dividends consistently for many decades but also have consistently *increased* dividend payouts.

Because the dividend payment is independent of the price, it isn't the price that matters but the number of shares. As already noted, accumulating more shares translates into greater compounding potential. Dividends are not guaranteed, but companies who pay them are typically determined to continue paying them because they understand their importance to shareholders. In many cases, such companies not only try to pay steady dividends but also seek to increase the dividend payout. Since it is in the best interest of a company to retain its shareholders, maintaining a steady dividend is a strong focus of many blue-chip companies.

Dividends are an important part of investing; therefore, it's important that participants understand how they are paid within the 401(k). First, a dividend is declared (called the *declaration date*), and at that time the company will set a *record date*, which is the date all shareholders of record at close of business will be eligible to receive the dividend payment. On the *ex-dividend date*, the dividend is deducted from the fund's net asset value on a per share basis and paid to shareholders on the *payment date*. This may sound confusing, but it impacts share prices temporarily, so participants should be aware of how this works. Let me offer an example. Suppose the board of directors declares a dividend on November 8 for shareholders of record as of close of day on February 16 to receive the dividend, which will be paid on March 9. As illustrated in figure 8.3, this means anyone who buys the shares on or before February 14 will be entitled to the dividend. (Due to the fact that settlement is the trade date plus two business days [T + 2], the ownership is not actually until two days after the trade date.) If you aren't familiar with trade date, consider that most security purchases take a day or two to settle. Think of escrow on a house purchase; it normally takes about thirty to forty-five days to change title of the property. Within the securities markets, it typically takes two days to record the shares under the new owner. In this example, then, investors must plan ahead and place the trade to purchase shares on or before February 14 to participate in the upcoming dividend.

On February 15 the stock trades ex-dividend, meaning the price per share is adjusted downward by the dividend. Anyone who buys shares this day will pay less per share because they will not get the dividend payment. On March 9, eligible shareholders will get the dividend payment (even if they sell the shares after February 16).

Example of Dividend with Trade + 2 Settlement

| Dividend Declared November 8 | Shareholders must purchase shares by February 14 (T+2) to receive dividend | Ex-Dividend Date February 15 (Shareholders who purchase on this date will not get dividend) | Record Date February 16 | No Dividend Eligible February 17 | Payment Date March 9 |

Figure 8.3.

The ex-dividend date often confuses investors because they see their share price drop. Suppose you own 1,000 shares of XYZ fund, currently priced at $10.42. Your market value at the end of the day is $10,420, but tomorrow, the fund is trading ex-dividend because it will be paying out a 0.12 quarterly dividend. This means the share price will be adjusted by the distribution, down to $10.30. On the payment date you will see a cash dividend posted to your account in the amount of $120. In your 401(k), this dividend will automatically reinvest and buy additional shares. In the above example, all else being equal, 11.65 shares will be added to your account. By the end of the day, you now have 1,011.65 shares priced at $10.30 per share, for a market value of $10,420. *But wait,* you say, *in the end my account value is unchanged!* Indeed, it is. *But you have more shares.* With that said, let's look out a little longer. In the next quarter, the dividend is paid again at a rate of 0.12, but this time you have 1,011.65 shares, so your dividend paid for this quarter is $121.40. All things being equal, you will get 11.78 additional shares. As this continues, your dividend increases with every quarterly payment, and as the dividend continues to increase, the number of shares increases, compounding the dividends.

Furthermore, the dividend payout is absorbed through the share price because the price of a stock is presumably equal to the value of the assets of a company divided by the number of shareholders. Of course, there is more that influences share prices, such as management, market sentiment, outlook, innovation, and debt, among other variable factors. However, in most cases it does take between a few days to a few weeks for the stock price to recover from a dividend payout, and it could certainly take longer if the company or market fundamentals deteriorate. In 2011, for example, the market overall was rather lackluster, and on average it took about eight days for Coca-Cola's share price to recover from the dividend payout. In 2017, the market rallied strong, and it took only about four trading days on average for Coca-Cola's price to recover from the dividend payout.

Dividends play an important role in a retirement plan, whether in the form of compounding or eventual income payments. It is important for participants to understand how dividends work, why they are important, and how to utilize dividends as a part of a retirement investment and income strategy.

CAPITAL GAIN DISTRIBUTIONS

In additional to dividends, most mutual funds also pay out periodic capital gain distributions. A capital gain distribution, which is generally paid out at the end of the year, is the result of gains realized over the course of the year within the *managed* portfolio. With active trading, net gains must be paid out to shareholders each year. Mutual funds are not tax-exempt, so they are required to pay out capital gains to shareholders for tax purposes. However, within a 401(k), earnings are not taxed, so capital gain distributions simply increase shares, similar to a dividend distribution. To make matters more confusing, capital gain distributions can be small and insignificant one year, can be very substantial the next, and may not be paid at all the next. They vary by year based on net gains realized within the fund. Additionally, some funds can have price appreciation for the year and pay no capital gains, while others can depreciate in price and still pay a capital gain. Confused? It can be especially confusing when a participant sees the price per share drop substantially in a given day for no apparent reason.

Let me give an example to better illustrate. Suppose your XYZ fund is priced at $10 a share and the fund declares a capital gain distribution of $2.50. If you own 1,000 shares, you will receive a $2,500 distribution. In your 401(k), this distribution is automatically reinvested just like dividends. And, like dividends, the share price on the ex-dividend date would drop by the amount of the distribution ($2.50), so the price would fall from $10 to $7.50. This sharp drop may alarm participants if they watch the prices daily. However, just like with dividends, your account value would be the same because you would have more shares, equal to the $2,500 distribution in this example. This is yet another reason why focusing on shares makes a difference. Suppose you start the year with 1,000 shares and end up with 1,333.334 shares with capital gain distribution paid in December (assuming you didn't add to the fund throughout the year). Any dividends or future capital gain distributions will be higher because, as already noted, they are paid out based on the number of shares. So, in the end, capital gain distributions are another form of share compounding. They are a return of profits paid to shareholders, and with dividend reinvestment and dollar cost averaging, shares have the potential to compound more and more.

It is important to know that not all 401(k) investments pay dividend or capital gain distributions. Bond funds typically pay dividends but rarely have capital gains. By contrast, most stock funds pay capital gain distributions (even growth funds) at year end but, again, only if they have net realized gains, while not all stock funds pay dividends. Exchange Traded Funds (ETFs) may pay dividends but do not typically have capital gain distributions. Collective Investment Trusts (CIT) do not pay dividends or capital gains distributions. Instead, dividends and capital gains are accumulated in the trust's net asset value. If you have ETFs or CITs in your 401(k) or are considering adding them, I recommend you read more about these investments in chapter 6. If you find this overly complex, that's because it is. And that is all the more reason why I encourage you hire a professional investment expert to help guide you.

Dividends and capital gain distributions are a way to increase shares, and while price will fluctuate up and down, number of shares never go down unless you sell them. Therefore, increasing shares is a way to control what happens within your investment account. You can increase your shares with dollar cost averaging, dividends reinvestment, and capital gain distributions. These all serve to support the potential for compounding. If your participants can learn to focus on accumulating shares and stop watching the daily share prices, they may be more apt to stay invested and be in a better position to be retirement ready.

THE POWER OF TIME

Besides following the strategies mentioned above, one of the best ways to pursue profits in stock funds is to expand your holding period. Some people compare investing in stocks to gambling, but I would argue that investing is exactly the opposite of gambling, for many reasons, but perhaps one of the most significant reasons is the holding period. In Vegas, the longer you sit in the casino, the greater the odds are that the house will win. That is why if you are lucky enough to hit big, the casino will give you a complimentary room, offer you tickets to a show, or provide a free meal—anything to keep you in the casino so they can win back the money. On Wall Street, however, the longer you hold a diversified portfolio of quality stocks, the odds for positive returns have historically been better, although of course past performance cannot predict future results. And unlike in Vegas where there is a winner and a loser with every bet, with stocks, bonds, and mutual funds there can be a winner on both sides of the trade. Unlike gambling, winning with stocks, bonds, and mutual funds isn't at the expense of someone losing.

Manage Risk with Increasing Holding Periods

Source: S&P 500 Index with dividends included. 1928-2017 probabilities of positive returns.

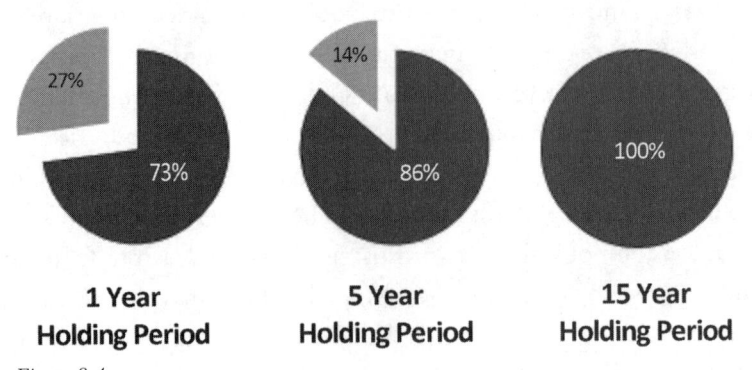

1 Year Holding Period	5 Year Holding Period	15 Year Holding Period
73% positive, 27% negative	86% positive, 14% negative	100% positive

Figure 8.4.

Based on history, we have learned that the possibility of gains in the stock market increased over longer holding periods. For example, going back to 1928 the S&P 500 had a positive return 73 percent of the time over the span of a one-year period. It's fair to say the chances of a positive return in any given year are pretty good, but there's historically been about a 1 in 3 chance of a loss. However, over five years, the S&P 500 has had a positive return 86 percent of the time. That certainly looks even better, however, over 15 years the S&P 500 index has had positive returns 100 percent of the time going back to every single rolling 15-year period since 1928. Economist Paul Samuelson said, "Investing should be more like watching paint dry or watching grass grow." If you don't have at least five years before you intend on cashing out your investment, it makes little sense to invest in stocks. On the other hand, when it comes to retirement, most of us are investors for life, which means stocks for the long term make sense. Of course, past performance is no guarantee of future results. Nonetheless, history is a good guide. Keep in mind, you cannot invest directly in the S&P 500 Index, and index performance is not indicative of the performance of any investment. Furthermore, unmanaged index returns do not reflect fees, expenses, or sales charges which could impact results. There is no guarantee that a diversified portfolio will enhance overall returns and diversification does not protect against market risk. Nonetheless, if you have a diversified portfolio, time has proven to be an effective way to manage risk and still pursue the opportunity for higher investment returns.

STOCK MARKET VOLATILITY

While there is no guarantee that future results will be the same as the past, we do have a rather long history filled with calamities, and yet the market has historically trended up over time. When I started in the business thirty years ago, for instance, the Dow Jones Industrial Average was at 2,000. Today it's pushing 26,000. If you extend your holding period long enough, the market has always eventually come back. Of course, this is based on a diversified portfolio of quality companies. If you make wild bets on high-flying stocks, your portfolio may very well be like an egg. What happens when you drop an egg? *It breaks!* Owning a diversified portfolio of profitable companies, however, is more like a ball. Prices may fall, but they have a better chance of bouncing back.

Unfortunately, the media blasts headlines of doom and gloom every time the market falls, which certainly doesn't help to instill confidence. When participants hear or read about the "mayhem on Wall Street," they fear the market will go into a free fall, down into a bottomless pit, permanently sweeping away their money. This is largely because the average worker simply doesn't understand what he owns. Many participants have only a vague understanding of what they are investing in, and for some, it might as well be akin to sending their money out into a different galaxy in our universe. When they see their accounts going up, it's as if the cosmos is randomly showering gifts upon them and they are elated, but when the market falls, they fear their assets will get sucked into a black pit of doom, like a vacuum.

The market to some is like the wizarding world of Harry Potter, where magic and mystery are engulfed in a hidden realm, where portfolio managers are sworn to secrecy in a domain of dark arts and manipulation. And this idea isn't exclusive to inexperienced investors. Many ultra-affluent investors unrealistically expect their portfolio managers to have the ability to avert the curse of the normal market correction by waving their enchanted wands, casting a few spells, and turning their portfolios into pots of gold. Setting unreasonable expectations is how very intelligent and successful people fell victim to Bernie Madoff's Ponzi scheme.

Practically speaking, it makes sense to seek to avoid losses. After all, everything we do in life is about managing risks. We buy a car and immediately buy auto insurance to protect ourselves from losses. We buy a home and purchase fire insurance. We secure our children in safety belts and helmets and cover them with sunblock. We have burglar alarms and smoke detectors. We build fences to protect our property. We get wellness checkups. It's normal to feel that the right thing to do during a market upset is to get out. When there is anxiety and uncertainty in the world, it seems logical to retreat to cash and wait until things clear up. Unfortunately, this has been proven to be very ineffective. There are ways to manage risk, but abandoning a sound investment strategy is not the action that will drive results for retirement success. History has taught us that the absolute best way to success is to remain steadfast and resolute with what you own. Warren Buffett says when stock prices fall, they return to their rightful owners. He also said, "I never attempt to make money on the stock market. I buy on the assumption that they could close the market the next day and not reopen it for five years." If employees are going to have a chance at success, they need to learn more about how our capital markets work; they must distinguish facts from fiction and understand what they own.

Indeed, it takes a tremendous amount of courage and emotional discipline to act sensibly during market turmoil, and ultimately, very few have this courage and discipline. Emotional intelligence is perhaps the greatest value gained by hiring a personal financial advisor. Just like professional athletes use coaches to (among many other things) build mental strength, great financial advisors use their leadership and knowledge to build emotional strength so investors can pursue peak performance. If investors just learned to focus on their shares, they would discover the number of shares they own doesn't change, even during the worst of times. Of course, if the companies they own go bankrupt, that's a different story. However, with mutual funds, such likelihood is nearly improbable. If every one of the leading companies in the world, or in the United States for that matter, go bankrupt simultaneously, we will have far bigger problems than the market value of our 401(k). Our grocery stores will be gone, as will our gas stations, utility companies, and so on. Let's face it, if Armageddon hits, the last thing we are likely to do is go online and check our 401(k) account balances.

Whatever you choose to call them—market dips, crashes, corrections, or even recessions—they are a normal part of investing. They occur regularly, usually without warning, and typically in the wake of a potential looming crisis. Of course, more often than not the crisis never actually materializes, or at least not to the degree investors anticipate. If there is one lesson I teach repeatedly it is to never underestimate the power and resiliency of our economy. As Sir John Templeton said, "The four most dangerous words in investing are: 'this time it's different.'"

Since 1926, we have seen lots of economic and world chaos: numerous wars, political upheavals, and crises. The S&P 500 has experienced numerous double-digit drops, with the typical decline of 24.3% lasting for 232 days. But every single time, the market has returned to its prior high and then, eventually, hit a new one. I have seen over 550 market highs in my 30-year career.

Participants must always be prepared for a sharp drop, and they must be prepared for it to last seven months or more. This is what we've learned from history. To expect the market to behave any differently than it has in the past would be unreasonable and unrealistic. By the same token, it is rare to see the market down for more than two consecutive years in a row. Eventually, the markets have rebounded, and it usually does so rather sharply and unexpectedly. Total recovery, depending upon your actions, may take a few more years beyond that, which is why you should always have sufficient liquidity so you don't have to sell your investments at an inopportune time. To be successful, investors need to be prepared, as Buffett advised, and let their investments sit for at least five years.

Perhaps as investors, we can learn a thing or two from farmers. For instance, take the Hass avocado. It is the most popular avocado in the world, and sales have been exploding over the past decade. The Hass avocado is high in nutrition and has a rich, nutty taste that many people love, me included. If you go to the store, you will discover the Hass is not a cheap avocado. And when I want to make guacamole, I usually have to plan ahead because it's hard to find a ripe avocado.

I learned that this is because the fruit doesn't actually ripen on the tree. However, it does take twelve to fourteen months to harvest the avocado, which explains the high price. From a seedling, the Hass avocado tree takes five to thirteen years to bear fruit, and even then, it may only do so every other year. *Now that's called patience.* Maybe we need to start thinking of our stock portfolios as an avocado tree and accept that it will take five to thirteen years for them to bear fruit. But with patience comes the potential for reward, as both farmers and successful investors have learned. *Isn't that what we teach our children?* It's time we practice what we preach!

Based on the Dow Jones Industrial Average going back to 1900, we have learned that 5% drops occur typically about three times a year. Yet, every time the market falls, the media reacts with such dramatic headlines that investors are left to believe it's a shocking, abnormal occurrence. Hold on to your stomachs, because on average, the Dow falls 10% or more about once a year! Today, that means you should expect the market to fall roughly twenty-five hundred points *every year.* That's quite a roller-coaster ride. Indeed, as of this writing, the Dow is in correction mode, and the headlines just the other day were "The Market Is Right in the Eye of the Storm!" For sure, the media exploits these periods because they draw attention and the media make money from disasters. We know the media exploits stories, and we largely dismiss most of the hyperbole, but we pay attention to the stock market because it directly impacts us. We see the implications in our own nest eggs, and it's difficult to ignore the commotion.

Figure 8.5 shows the historical declines in the Dow Jones Industrial Average since 1900. Based on history, we know a typical 10% correction should be expected every year and that it tends to last about four months. This means on average the market is down at least one trimester out of an entire year. That's a lot of volatility. Why are we so surprised when the market gyrates? To me, it's ironic that investors are so impatient. It makes you wonder. Why do investors get so shaken up over market drops when these drops are so *normal*? I hope to live long enough to someday see investors learn to accept market fluctuations and become desensitized to the media's rhetoric. Your participants unquestionably need to learn how to withstand market dips so they can be retirement ready.

A HISTORY OF DECLINES
DOW JONES INDUSTRIAL AVERAGE
1900–2017

Decline	Average frequency	Average length
–5% or more	About three times a year	47 days
–10% or more	About once a year	115 days
–15% or more	About once every 2 years	216 days
–20% or more	About once every 3.5 years	338 days

Figure 8.5.

Let's take a journey back in time and look at the average returns up to December 31, 2017, in figure 8.5. Look at the period closest to the time you were born. What has been average on the S&P 500? If you are eighty years old, you've seen the S&P 500 average about 11% per year since you were born. If you are sixty-five years old, the S&P 500 has averaged 10.75% a year over your lifetime. If you are fifty years old, the market has averaged 10.06% annually. If you are thirty-five years old, the market has enjoyed an 11.45% average annual return. And if you are twenty years old, you've seen 7.16% average annual returns since you were born. Although the average has varied, notice the range of variation tends to diminish with longer holding periods. This is no coincidence. Regardless, I think you would agree these are attractive returns and support the case for long-term investing.

\multicolumn{4}{c}{S&P 500 Index with Dividends Reinvested}
Time period	Average annual return	Time period	Average annual return
Dec. 2007 – Dec. 2017	8.31%	Dec. 1967 – Dec. 2017	10.06%
Dec. 2002 – Dec. 2017	9.66%	Dec. 1962 – Dec. 2017	10.25%
Dec. 1997 – Dec. 2017	7.16%	Dec. 1957 – Dec. 2017	10.47%
Dec. 1992 – Dec. 2017	9.61%	Dec. 1952 – Dec. 2017	10.75%

S&P 500 Index with Dividends Reinvested			
Time period	Average annual return	Time period	Average annual return
Dec. 1987 – Dec. 2017	10.70%	Dec. 1947 – Dec. 2017	11.31%
Dec. 1982 – Dec. 2017	11.45%	Dec. 1942 – Dec. 2017	11.55%
Dec. 1977 – Dec. 2017	11.77%	Dec. 1937 – Dec. 2017	11.02%
Dec. 1972 – Dec. 2017	10.30%	Dec. 1932 – Dec. 2017	11.25%

Figure 8.6. *S&P 500 Index with dividends reinvested. Source: Dow Jones Industrial Average. Assumes 50 percent recovery of lost value. Measures market high to market low. Past results are not predictive of results in future periods. The S&P 500 is an unmanaged index that cannot be invested into directly.*

Of course, it's not the average market returns that are problematic for investors. Indeed, I'm quite certain we would also love to enjoy any of these returns listed here. Although these are actual results of the market, fluctuation, volatility, and uncertainty is what spooks investors and causes them to sell out, leading them ultimately to miss out on these potential returns. Retrospectively, over and over again the facts are indisputable.

Although I don't recommend limiting a portfolio to just large-cap stocks, look at the holdings in the S&P 500 Index. You can look up all the S&P 500 components online. Apple, Microsoft, Amazon, Facebook, Berkshire Hathaway, JP Morgan Chase, Johnson & Johnson, Exxon Mobil, Google, Bank of America, Intel, Chevron, Visa, UnitedHealthcare, Wells Fargo, Cisco, Home Depot, Pfizer, Verizon, AT&T, Boeing, Proctor & Gamble, Citigroup, MasterCard, Coca-Cola, McDonald's, Walmart, GE, Merck, Disney, DuPont, 3M, Amgen, Union Pacific, and 465 other major companies make up this index. Surely you recognize every single one of these companies. You probably buy products or services from nearly all of them. The market capital of all the companies held in the S&P 500 Index is $17 trillion, and these firms generate over $10 trillion in revenue by selling goods and services all over the world. They also provide jobs for over 24 million people. The power is in the diversification of this index, or the diversification of the funds held in a 401(k). As Peter Lynch with Fidelity said, "Know what you own, and know why you own it." Take a look at your annual reports because they list the individual holdings in every fund you own. When I share these reports with participants, they are dumbfounded by how many different companies they have an ownership in.

INVESTING FOR RETIREMENT

Investing for retirement is a lifelong journey. It isn't about getting to an end goal, such as accumulating one million dollars by age sixty-five. Retirement has no terminus, or at least no known terminus, since we don't know when we are going to die. Most of us go through life with set dates in our minds. We get to drive at age sixteen, and we go to college at eighteen. In our mid-twenties we get our first real job, maybe move to our own apartment. We expect to get married by our early thirties, buy a home and have children before we're forty, and retire at sixty-five. It's all mapped out consciously or unconsciously, and we compartmentalize life a bit like a game of hopscotch. We jump from one square to the other as we progress through life, with each square representing a step toward the last box—retirement—as if that is the final step to personal happiness and satisfaction. Of course, the pursuit of financial security, a happy marriage, and good health doesn't stop just because we stop working. Even in retirement, we must still work at taking care of our physical and mental health, our marriage, and our spiritual selves and finding our sense of purpose. And we must continue to work to protect our finances. Retirement is by no means the end. It is not the final box we jump into and suddenly reach eutopia. Retirement is merely of a new phase of our everyday lives and, as you will discover, will likely be filled with happiness, rewards, frustrations and challenges.

Retirement may be a time when our paycheck stops, but our income is still dependent upon our own choices and actions. We still must demonstrate discipline with our spending and diligence with our investing and overcome our fears of economic upsets. If that sounds pretty much the same as what you are you doing now, you can see that retirement isn't all that different. Throughout our retirement years we can expect interest rates to go up and down, the economy to go through booms and busts, investment values to gyrate, new presidents to enter office, and political challenges to arise. Taxes will go up, government policies will change, the federal debt will rise, and there will be wars and global upsets. In other words, life will continue just as it has your entire life.

Perhaps of greatest significance is the fact that the rising costs of goods and services will continue to squeeze our budget. We will also wrestle with companies over billing disputes, stand in long lines, be left on hold, and sit in traffic, and we will surely feel dismay over the changes in the world. Our kids will bring us joy, worry, and annoyance, as always. Our grandchildren will make us laugh and smile. Bills will keep coming in the mail. We will count our blessings most days and languish in our woes other days. We will have painful losses, and we will have joyful gains. Indeed, life in retirement life will continue largely unchanged.

This means when you retire, you need to realize your investment strategy must continue to address your needs for growth just as much as your income does. If you focus only on keeping *the number of dollars* you have, the value of your retirement capital will depreciate with the rising cost of living. Unless you want to risk spending down your savings, you will want to focus on growing the value of your assets in order to grow your income. These days, we need a *rising income* in retirement. Most of us simply can't afford to just "preserve our wealth." We need to grow the value of our portfolios even in retirement.

Here's why. Suppose you have one million dollars the day you retire at the age of sixty-five. I remember when one million dollars was a lot of money. Still, in about twenty years, assuming a hypothetical inflation rate of 3 percent, inflation will cut the value of your million dollars nearly in half, to have the *buying power* of about $500,000. Now, the real value of your retirement savings is the income it can generate. So, one million dollars might sustain an income of about $45,000 to $50,000 a year. If your yearly income distribution from your 401(k) the day you retire is $50,000 and you focus on only keeping your principal, your income distribution after twenty years will presumably remain the same. Unfortunately, however, in this example that $50,000 isn't going to be buying as much as it did when you retired. You may begin to notice that the cost of health care is consuming more of your income. Prescription drugs, home maintenance, car repairs, utility bills, and even eating out is getting more expensive. That means your $50,000 income is buying less and less. After twenty years, it may be only buying about $25,000 worth of goods and services. Let's look at the impact of inflation on a retired portfolio, assuming a retiree fails to account for inflation, which unfortunately happens all too often. When a retiree invests only for income today, the effects of longevity risks become very predominant.

Age	Retirement Savings	Inflation-Adjusted Savings	Income	Inflation Adjusted Income
65	$1,000,000	$970,481	$50,000	$48,524
66	$1,000,000	$941,835	$50,000	$47,091
67	$1,000,000	$914,033	$50,000	$45,701
68	$1,000,000	$887,053	$50,000	$44,352
69	$1,000,000	$860,869	$50,000	$43,043
70	$1,000,000	$835,457	$50,000	$41,772
71	$1,000,000	$810,796	$50,000	$40,539
72	$1,000,000	$786,863	$50,000	$39,343
73	$1,000,000	$763,636	$50,000	$38,181
74	$1,000,000	$741,095	$50,000	$37,054
75	$1,000,000	$719,219	$50,000	$35,960
76	$1,000,000	$697,989	$50,000	$34,889
77	$1,000,000	$677,386	$50,000	$33,869
78	$1,000,000	$657,391	$50,000	$32,869
79	$1,000,000	$637,986	$50,000	$31,899
80	$1,000,000	$619,154	$50,000	$30,957
81	$1,000,000	$600,877	$50,000	$30,043
82	$1,000,000	$583,141	$50,000	$29,157
83	$1,000,000	$565,927	$50,000	$28,296
84	$1,000,000	$549,222	$50,000	$27,461
85	$1,000,000	$533,010	$50,000	$26,650

Age	Retirement Savings	Inflation-Adjusted Savings	Income	Inflation Adjusted Income
86	$1,000,000	$517,277	$50,000	$25,863
87	$1,000,000	$502,008	$50,000	$25,100
88	$1,000,000	$487,189	$50,000	$24,359
89	$1,000,000	$472,808	$50,000	$23,640
90	$1,000,000	$458,852	$50,000	$22,942
91	$1,000,000	$445,307	$50,000	$22,265
92	$1,000,000	$432,163	$50,000	$21,608
93	$1,000,000	$419,406	$50,000	$20,970
94	$1,000,000	$407,026	$50,000	$20,351
95	$1,000,000	$395,011	$50,000	$19,750
96	$1,000,000	$383,351	$50,000	$19,167
97	$1,000,000	$372,036	$50,000	$18,601
98	$1,000,000	$361,054	$50,000	$18,052
99	$1,000,000	$350,396	$50,000	$17,519
100	$1,000,000	$340,053	$50,000	$17,002

Figure 8.7. Hypothetical example of 3% inflation rate eroding the value of a million-dollar retirement savings generating a $50,000 annual income. Assumes 5% earnings rate. Actual inflation rate and/or earnings may be more or less than illustrated.

In figure 8.7, you can see the erosion of the value of both savings and capital for a retiree who lives to age one hundred based on a 3 percent inflation rate. You can see that one million dollars has the buying power of approximately $340,000 at age one hundred and that the income buys about the same as $17,000 buys today. Our grandparents may not have had to worry much about inflation risk, but with longevity comes two added costs: inflation and health-care expenses. If we only focus on keeping the dollars we have today, we will probably feel a steady squeeze and may come to realize our income doesn't last to the end of the month anymore.

Now take a look at figure 8.8, where the retiree withdraws more money from his savings to keep up with the rising cost of living. Instead of accepting a gradual decline in his standard of living, the retiree withdraws more from savings. The risk in doing this is the accelerated depletion of capital. Let's look at what happens to the account value in that scenario.

Age	Retirement Balance	Earnings from Savings @ 5%	Withdrawal with COLA
65	$1,000,000	$50,000	$50,000
66	$999,873	$49,993	$51,520
67	$996,780	$49,839	$53,087
68	$991,917	$49,595	$54,702
69	$985,146	$49,257	$56,366
70	$973,324	$48,666	$58,080
71	$965,293	$48,264	$59,847
72	$951,891	$47,594	$61,667
73	$935,942	$46,797	$63,543
74	$917,263	$45,863	$65,476
75	$895,659	$44,782	$67,467
76	$870,923	$43,546	$69,519
77	$842,836	$42,141	$71,634
78	$811,164	$40,558	$73,813
79	$775,695	$38,784	$76,027
80	$736,171	$36,808	$78,308
81	$692,323	$34,616	$80,657
82	$644,387	$32,219	$83,077
83	$591,037	$29,551	$85,569
84	$532,453	$26,622	$88,136
85	$468,295	$23,414	$90,780
86	$398,206	$19,910	$93,504
87	$321,808	$16,090	$96,309
88	$238,700	$11,935	$99,198
89	$148,461	$7,423	$102,174
90	$50,645	$2,532	$105,239
91	$0	$0	$108,396
92	$0	$0	$111,648
93	$0	$0	$114,998
94	$0	$0	$118,448
95	$0	$0	$122,001
96	$0	$0	$125,661
97	$0	$0	$129,431
98	$0	$0	$133,304
99	$0	$0	$137,313
100	$0	$0	$141,433

Figure 8.8. Hypothetical example of inflation eroding the value of a million-dollar retirement savings generating a 5% return with income adjusted for inflation. Actual inflation rate and/or earnings may be more or less than illustrated.

As you can see, the earnings decline because the capital declines; thus this retiree would run out of money at the end of age ninety. While that may be sufficient for those who don't have longevity, the risks of outliving income are rising for most all of us, particularly if we are married. A sixty-five-year-old couple has a 45 percent chance that one of them will live at least to age ninety, according to the Society of Actuaries Retirement Participant 2000 Table. As life expectancies increase, this risk increases exponentially. Do you want to risk running out of money?

Unfortunately, this doesn't account for the inflation impact on other income we may have, including pension and Social Security, which also will be eroded by inflation. Lacking sufficient cost of living adjustments, our personal savings will have to do double work—generate enough income to offset inflation on our savings and potentially offset other income like Social Security. (Social Security does offer cost-of-living adjustments; however, such increases have been inconsistent and are generally offset by Medicare premium increases.)

So how do we overcome inflation risks? We must think like investors for life. We must think long term. I realize at age seventy-five, people want to stop worrying about the stock market. We are trained to think we ought to be reducing our risk as we get older. Common sense certainly suggests this is reasonable and logical thinking. I wish we had the luxury of being able to afford to accept lower rates of return as we age, but inflation doesn't stop just because we get older. While we may not have the luxury of time on our side, we all face the *certainty* that the rising cost of living will erode the value of our savings. As we get older, we still need to recognize the risks of spending down our money. There is no perfect situation for most people. It's merely a matter of trade-offs: accept short-term volatility or long-term devaluation.

So, what is your trade-off? Would you rather tolerate more risk in your portfolio during retirement or accept the risk of inflation eroding your savings? I personally think tolerating more volatility is a more logical solution. However, to do this means we must understand risk.

We also must manage risk in ways we can control. We cannot control interest rates, taxes, the stock market, or the economy. But we can control our asset allocation, how we react to market upsets, how much we withdraw from our portfolios, and how we spend our money.

Back in the days of the pension, employees didn't have the liberty to withdraw money from their pension accounts. They had a fixed check that arrived in the mailbox every month like clockwork alongside their Social Security check. It was pretty simple; if you couldn't get by on the income, you had to find another way to make ends meet. Granted, most people didn't live long enough to have a great threat of inflation, so it worked out okay for most retirees. (It typically takes about ten years to begin to feel the effects of inflation.)

Think about how you view inflation. If you are in your thirties, you may have heard about it, but you are not very likely to have felt it. By the time you get into your forties, you begin to have some comparisons. *I remember when dinner out cost $50.* And by the time you hit your fifties, you begin to notice how car prices are skyrocketing. You will likely remember what you paid for your first brand-new car compared to today's prices. For instance, when I was nineteen years old I bought my first brand-new car for $14,000. Today, a comparable car would be about $35,000. That's inflation. I paid $205,000 for my first house in 1996, and today that same house is worth about $600,000. That's called inflation. I remember when gasoline hit a dollar a gallon in Los Angeles in 1987. My roommate and I paid $600 monthly rent for our first apartment. Today, comparable apartments are renting for over $1800 a month. And when I was a kid, I remember going to the dime store and getting an ice cream cone—5¢ for one scoop, 10¢ for two scoops, and 15¢ for three scoops. When we're working and enjoying pay raises, these reminiscences are just fun "remember when" stories. When we're retired and living on a fixed income, it's not so fun when we can't afford our rent, mortgage or car insurance and we have to borrow money from our children to get by, or we have to make concessions on the quality of our health care or prescription drugs because we can't afford the costs.

With the 401(k), of course, there is no fixed income. It's not a pension check but a bucket of money that retirees must manage. You can withdraw whatever amount you choose. Of course, if you choose wisely, you leave a legacy for your family or charity. But if you choose poorly, you run out of money and end up broke. That's a substantial price to pay for the wrong choice. Since most people aren't saving enough to afford retirement in the first place, the spend-down or withdrawal rate required to support retirement is probably higher than it should be, even without inflation. Most people don't want to confine their active retirement years to a rocking chair watching soap operas, so they spend more than they should, even at the expense of their later retirement years.

So how much can you afford to withdraw from your 401(k) in retirement? It depends upon how you allocate your investments. Of course, whatever factor you use as your rate of return, you should prepare to deduct at least 3 percent for inflation. For example, if you estimate a 5% earnings rate, you can withdraw no more than 2 percent if you want an inflation-adjusted retirement income (5 percent − 3 percent inflation = 2 percent withdrawal rate). *But wait! That doesn't support much retirement. One million dollars will only provide $20,000 a year income!* Yes, that's correct. *What if it's not enough?* Well, another option is to invest to seek a higher return. Let's suppose, instead, you decide to seek 7% average return. This will give you an income of 4 percent (7 percent − 3 percent inflation = 4 percent withdrawal rate), which means you can enjoy about $40,000 annual income from one million dollars in savings. But that means you must accept market risk, which, in short, means you must weather volatility. If you don't handle it and you panic and sell during a calamity, you will compromise everything. Even in retirement, you have to be able to buckle your seat belt and tolerate the volatility of our markets. *That doesn't sound like a great set of options!*

The alternative is to risk spending down your retirement savings and potentially run out of money. Is it more or less painful to be broke at eighty-five or ninety years of age compared to living a frugal retirement? Or is it more reasonable just to work longer, perhaps until the Social Security full-retirement age of sixty-seven or, better yet, continue working to get the maximum Social Security benefits at age seventy? You see, it's about choices. Investing for retirement requires a tremendous number of considerations, both before and during retirement. Workers not educated about the trade-offs don't understand their options. Would you rather work longer or accept more risk? Do you want to enjoy a little less today so you can save more, or would you prefer to risk running out of money in retirement? The sooner your employees understand their options, the more likely they are to make sound decisions that will help them be retirement ready.

RATE-OF-RETURN TARGETS

I think it's fair to say that the reason most of us invest in stocks is not because we like risk or even because we are greedy. Most of us invest in stocks because we need to get higher returns on our money. Period. If the risk-free investment (measured by ninety-day US Treasury securities) is 1.63%, as is the case today, logically we can deduce that any level of return desired above this will come with an additional level of risk. Clearly, we cannot build wealth, or even protect it, if we only earn 1.63 percent Inflation alone will erode the value of our money. In fact, most of us need to earn between 6 percent and 8 percent to secure our retirement considering longevity risks, inflation, and taxes.

Indeed, most of us could certainly benefit from the potential to earn even more. Too many workers are behind in their savings to have their money sitting idle. Our money needs to work as hard as we do. We can't have it sitting lazily around earning 1.63%. I'm not talking just about preretirement savings but also about savings during retirement. The risk of spending down our nest egg while we still have a lot of life left is simply too great. Therefore, we must consider the need to invest at least some of our retirement assets in stocks. This is true for most of us over our entire lifetimes, not just until we get to retirement. This is because stocks are historically one of the only investments that has been able to beat inflation. Consider the long-term historical average returns of the different investments:

Time Period	S&P 500 Index	3 Month T-Bill	10 Year T-Bond
1928-2017	9.65%	3.39%	4.88%

Figure 8.9. Data for Treasury bond and Treasury bill returns is obtained from the Federal Reserve database (FRED) in Saint Louis. The return on S&P 500 includes both price appreciation and dividends. The Treasury bill rate is a three-month rate, and the Treasury bond is the constant-maturity ten-year bond, including coupon and price appreciation. It will not match the Treasury bond rate each period. . Returns do not reflect fees, expenses, or sales charges and are not indicative of the performance of any investment. Past performance is no guarantee of future results.

Based on long-term history, the risk-free historical rate has been 3.39%, while the US stock market has provided investors with a 9.65% average return. Of course, the volatility of the stock market has also caused tremendous losses for those unable to hold on through the sharp drops. It is for this reason that we seek to reduce or manage risk by building a *balanced* portfolio.

If you were to target a 6% return, for example, you must incorporate stocks. You can do the math based on historical performance to dial in projected return targets quite effectively. Of course, over the past decade interest rates have been far below the historical norm, which has only driven investors to take more risk to get a decent return. This is a situation that is unlikely to unwind in the foreseeable future given the size of our federal debt. However, if we use long-term averages, we can see that a fifty-fifty portfolio (50 percent S&P 500, 50 percent ten-year Treasury securities) would have generated an average return of 7.27%. Today, such a portfolio would be more likely to generate 5–6% based on our environment of unusually low interest rates. Suppose your retirement projections suggest you need to earn an 8% return preretirement. Is that possible? Well, naturally, nothing is guaranteed, but to seek to achieve that return, we can calculate that a portfolio made up of 80 percent stocks and 20 percent T-bills would have achieved an 8.39% historical average return.

What if you aren't comfortable with 80 percent of your portfolio subject to stock market risk? In that case, the simple answer is that you must accept a lower rate of return. The trade-off will be either (a) work longer, (b) save more, or (c) have less income at retirement. So, you see, there is no shortcut. While everyone is trying to earn high returns with less risk, such a strategy will doom more people to failure. It just doesn't work. The mistake many employees make is that they say they are okay with market risk when the market is booming, but as soon as there's upset or chaos, they abandon their strategy. When the participant changes her allocations in reaction to markets, the chance of achieving a 6%, 7%, or 8% average return is significantly reduced.

Just look at the impact of the 2008 financial crisis on 401(k) accounts. Many employees moved their funds out of stocks and went to cash. In fact, some even stopped 401(k) contributions altogether. I heard people declare, "I'm just putting good money after bad if I put money into my plan!" That's because they were focusing on the current market value, not the number of shares they were accumulating! The participant who sold out in the midst of the 2008 crisis likely did so with a decline of at least 35%. And most who did this sat in cash all through 2009 when the market gained 27.2% and again in 2010 when the market gained another 10.9%. They probably didn't buy back in 2011 either, because the euro was going to collapse and the S&P was −1.8%. And they also likely missed 2012 with a gain of 15.6%. In fact, most even missed out on 2013 when the S&P 500 gained 32.4%, because the economy was still unstable. I know many people didn't participate. I've met many who didn't get back in the stock market until well after 2013, when they felt good about the future again.

Let's look at what would have happened to a hypothetical fifty-year-old employee with a $120,000 401(k) balance before the 2008 crisis. In this example, we will assume employee A retreated to cash at the end of 2008. While she continued making contributions ($7,000 a year), she allocated her current and future funds to a cash account earning 1% until she felt that the economic outlook improved and the market stabilized. Finally, in January 2014, the participant decided to get back into the stock market with 100 percent allocation in S&P 500 Index from 2014 to 2017. What happened to her account balance?

		Employee A		Employee B	
Year	S&P 500	Account balance	Average annual return	Account balance	Annual average return
2008	−37%	$88,334	−37%	$88,334	−37%
2009	26.50%	$96,253	−17.49%	$122,721	−4.65%
2010	15.10%	$104,252	−10.95%	$150,095	2.25%
2011	2.10%	$112,331	−7.68%	$160,346	2.21%
2012	16%	$120,492	−5.74%	$195,506	5.21%
2013	32.40%	$128,735	−4.45%	$277,295	10.13%
2014	13.70%	$154,979	−1.46%	$325,219	10.69%
2015	1.40%	$164,207	−1.04%	$336,847	9.40%
2016	12%	$192,431	0.67%	$386,965	9.72%
2017	20.70%	$243,974	3.03%	$482,825	10.94%

Figure 8.10. Hypothetical. The S&P 500 is an unmanaged index which cannot be invested into directly. Unmanaged index returns do not reflect fees, expenses, or sales charges. Index performance is not indicative of the performance of any investment. Past performance is no guarantee of future results.

She fully recovered, as you can see in figure 8.10, but it took her until 2016 to have a positive average return. By comparison, employee B had the same account balance of $120,000 before the crisis and contributed the same amount over the same period ($7,000 a year), but this participant stayed the course and remained invested in 100 percent stocks as represented by the S&P 500 Index through the entire debacle. Compare the average returns of the two employees. Employee A suffered negative average annual returns for eight years, whereas employee B only had two years with negative average annual returns. And by 2013, within just five years, the participant who stayed the course was back on track with positive returns.

Of course, hindsight is 20/20. However, we can go back in history and analyze a host of calamities and see the outcome doesn't change much. Granted, the assumption here is "all or nothing," meaning all stocks or all cash, and of course, there are many other options within a 401(k) investment menu, so this is an overly simplistic view. A balanced portfolio surely would have ended up somewhere in between these two outcomes. But the point is to highlight the result of abandoning a sound investment plan. Now a decade later, at sixty years of age, which employee is more likely to have a secure retirement? I understand the fear and uncertainty during the 2008 crisis caused many to worry they would not have anything left for their retirement, thus many employees justified abandoning sound strategies to protect their savings. However, the history of the market has taught us invaluable lessons that *this time it is not different.*

IN SUMMARY

Your employees are utilizing your 401(k) to work toward retirement security, which goes far beyond accumulating money in an account. That may be the first step in the process, and a very important one, but retirement success is much more than that. Life is no longer a simple game of hopscotch. We must be actively involved in our finances and understand how every decision impacts our future. It's often the little things that make a big difference.

I often hear pundits say, "If it doesn't feel comfortable, don't invest." That's akin to teaching our children "When life gets hard, it's okay to quit." Long gone are the days when our employers and the government took care of us. We have to take responsibility for ourselves financially, and this represents a paradigm shift. Your employees have yet to fully understand the scope of this responsibility, let alone how to translate it into retirement security, which is why employee education is critical. Your employees need help. They don't know what it takes to build retirement readiness. You have the power to provide an invaluable benefit—knowledge. Workers in America have demonstrated an extreme lack of financial literacy, and this is highlighted by our national retirement crisis. Most participants simply do not understand the basic financial principles required to successfully negotiate the investment markets, manage risks effectively, and avoid financial pitfalls. They don't think in percentages, averages or financial equations.

You may be surprised to know that research has shown that while the level of financial literacy varies according to education and income level, even highly educated participants with high incomes can be just as ill-informed about critical financial issues as anyone else. We are all busy running our lives, raising our families, and trying to create a work–life balance. It doesn't help that financial decision-making is getting more onerous for everyone. Employees are shouldering more financial decisions than ever before in history, especially with retirement planning. Past generations depended on pension plans to fund the bulk of their retirement lives, and the obligation for funding and managing pension funds was on the company. Workers were not involved in any of the decision-making, but today, employees bear the sole burden and responsibility of making major financial decisions that directly impact their futures. Investment decisions, funding decisions, taxes, risk management, inflation, health-care costs, longevity risks, and much more must be considered.

Clearly, these options are more complex and sophisticated than in the past. Undeniably, we are asking employees to make decisions they are not adequately prepared to make. To make matters worse, banks, credit unions, brokerage firms, insurance firms, credit card companies, mortgage companies, financial planners, and other financial service companies are all vying for their assets, creating even more confusion for employees and retirees alike. To further challenge the worker, the financial landscape is constantly in flux and quickly changing. It's more dynamic today than ever with globalization and technological advances. There are more participants in the capital markets and many more factors that influence them, which means the markets move swifter than ever before.

There is no shortfall of opinions, either. Conflicting views make it difficult to follow a plan or adhere to a strategy. Participants start off with one strategy they think is right and then change direction because they are being persuaded by different thoughts and opinions.

Lacking financial knowledge of their own, they find themselves simply overwhelmed and frustrated.

Financial literacy is crucial to helping your employees save enough to secure their retirement. Studies have proven that those with lower financial education levels tend to overuse credit and lack sufficient savings. Even more worrisome is the fact is that these same employees often believe they are more financially capable than they really are, causing a false sense of confidence.

While retirement planning may seem like an individual challenge, it is broader in nature and more influential on the entire economy than most employers realize. The financial crisis of 2008 highlighted the magnitude of the impact resulting from a lack of understanding of financial products such as home loans. Even many affluent and highly educated individuals found themselves caught in overleveraging real estate. A financially unskilled workforce has broad implications for our future economic health, including the impact on your own business. Providing financial security for all employees and especially those who are aging serves to offer sustainability for the business and stability for the overall economy. Our national retirement crisis is *our* problem, not a government problem or an individual problem.

I firmly believe any improvement employers can make in financial education will have a profound impact on our future. Your employees are being asked to decipher more-complex products and options. Supporting a comprehensive financial education program may be the best course to take in building retirement readiness and financial wellness. The sooner you start your program, the sooner you will give your employees the boost they need for their financial well-being.

CHAPTER 9
BEHAVIORAL FINANCE: HOW EMOTION AND PSYCHOLOGY IMPACTS SUCCESS

Larry is one of your star employees. He is sharp and level-headed and is a very dedicated worker. He is also sixty years old and quite enthusiastic about your 401(k). He has been "playing" in the market by moving his 401(k) monies in and out of various funds within your investment menu. He frequently stops by your office to share his latest success and give you a few tips. Today he swings by to tell you he has put all of his 401(k) into the most aggressive fund in your menu. He is confident this is going to be a smart move and set his retirement in five years. You point out that the market is quite high, but he waves off your remark, countering that the economy is doing great and he is going to make a lot of money while the "going is good." Do you shrug your shoulders and leave Larry to his own devices, hoping for the best, even though you know of others who lost dearly by taking undue risks in the past, or should you do something to stop Larry from making a potentially irreparable mistake?

THE PSYCHOLOGY THAT IMPACTS YOUR EMPLOYEES

A man purchased a new refrigerator and didn't want the hassle of selling his old fridge or hauling it away, so he put a sign on it saying FREE to Good Home and left it on the curb. It sat there for days. No one wanted it. So, he replaced the sign with Fridge for Sale, $50. It was stolen within a day.

A wine bar wanted to boost its wine sales. The average glass sold for $9, but the owner wanted his customers to experience the finer wines on the list. He decided to change the way his wines were listed. Instead of listing the lowest-priced wines first, he listed the highest-price wines at the top. Profits doubled.

In 2005 Amazon launched an experiment called Prime. For $79 a year, customers could enjoy free two-day shipping on over one million different items. Amazon made it simple—make the decision once, and then for the rest of the year, you don't have to think about it. Nearly anything they want, need, or desire from the millions of products, members get their orders quick and easy with "free" expedited shipping. Today four out of every five original Prime customers are still members, myself included. Amazon is the fastest-growing company in the United States and one of the first companies to hit a trillion dollars. Jeff Bezos understands the consumer.

Are we rational human beings? Do we follow a logical process? Do we make decisions based on facts? The truth is that while we understand logic, it is largely emotion and intuitive guidance that leads most of the thousands of decisions we make every day. It's called psychology. As humans, we are emotionally engaged in every decision we make, from how we spend our money to whom we decide to marry and whether we save for retirement. It's not just the busy lives that we lead today that are stopping us from tending to our financial wellness. It's probably as much human nature as it is modern lifestyle. Behavioral finance is the process of scientifically recording and studying human behavior as it relates to finances, and what we learn from this study is that our natural tendencies are contributing as much to the retirement problem as anything. The study of behavioral economics includes how financial decisions are made and the mechanisms that drive these choices. For instance, were Americans saving more or less for their future back when there was only one breadwinner in the home? Were our financial houses in better order fifty years ago when we weren't spread so thin with our time? Do single people without children save more as a percentage of their income than those with family obligations? We've discovered that while common sense might suggest more freedom with time would translate into the ability to make better financial decisions, or that fewer financial obligations would enable a higher savings rate, this has not been the case. The question then becomes why not, which is what behavioral finance seeks to address.

Companies use behavioral finance with marketing by trying to attract your dollars as a consumer. We are being manipulated with advertisements daily. Every time we walk into a store, go online, or watch television, advertisers are vying for our attention. A hundred years ago it might have been a trader sweet-talking you into buying a lame horse, but today it's a website asking for your credit card number so the company can provide a "free" trial promotion, which it knows you'll forget to cancel before you're charged. Point-of-sale merchandise is another example that works really well to get you to buy those last-minute items you don't need and don't want but that are seriously tempting you while you're standing in line at the register.

These subtle but aggressive tactics are constant and play into our natural inclinations. How many times have you bought something impulsively off a shelf while standing in line at the store? Would you have bought that magazine or pack of gum had it not been staring you in your face for the few minutes you were waiting to check out? Businesses know the longer you stand there, the more likely you are to purchase one more item. Compulsive buying, or what is known as "seeing is buying," is a strategic tactic used by most retailers. Sometimes it's hard to resist. This is especially true for children. When my daughter was a toddler, she may have been too young to understand marketing, but when she waited in line at the grocery store and saw candy or toys, suddenly she *had to* have something. The urge was very strong, and since children are very impulsive, it became almost an obsession. Immediately she started asking for the toy or candy, which quickly turned into begging and whining. A few minutes earlier she had no idea she wanted it. She was merrily walking beside me as we picked up some groceries. But as soon she saw *it*, she absolutely had to have it. You may remember your own children crying, screaming, or fussing about something they saw and simply needed to have when you were shopping. Every store you visit these days will have point-of-sale products displayed at the register. The products are there because they boost sales. In other words, the tactic works! Items are sold that may never otherwise be bought. After all, how many upside-down writing pens, microwave bacon cookers, or Clapper wall sockets do you need? Undeniably, human nature involves compulsive behaviors.

Your employees are falling victim to natural behaviors that also adversely impact their financial wellness. It may be more subtle than the impulse of a child, but it is ever present. This is called behavioral finance. Understanding these behaviors, and more importantly how to help your employees recognize these natural tendencies, can be very important to successfully cultivating a financially savvy workforce. As Benjamin Graham, Warren Buffett's mentor, said, "Wall Street has a few prudent principles; the trouble is they are forgotten when they are needed the most." Below are details about some of the key psychological behaviors that can cause financial setbacks for employees as they prepare for their retirement years. The more you and your committee understand these behaviors, the better equipped you will be to help your employees overcome their self-imposed limitations.

OVERCONFIDENCE BIAS

I'm putting all of my money in real estate because real estate always goes up!

Overconfidence bias is an example of a miscalculation of probabilities. Not to be confused with optimism, which is an attitude, overconfidence bias is an error in calculating statistical probabilities. The problem with overconfidence bias is that it often leads to failure. It tends

"Are you sure you want to put your entire nest egg on #4 'Lags Behind?'"

to promote unreasonable and sometimes downright self-destructive behaviors. For example, if you go to Vegas, put a quarter in a slot machine, pull the handle, and hit 777, are you going to take your winnings and stop, or are you going to put in another quarter and see if you can hit it again? Common sense (and the logical, left side of the brain) says you would walk away, but when presented with the situation, what do most people *really* do? The emotional side kicks in, of course. We succumb to what is called "overconfidence bias," where we think we are on a streak and are likely to win again. Every time we pull the handle, the left side of our brains is telling us that our winnings are going down, while the right side of our brains is telling us that we are very close to hitting again. Las Vegas banks on the temptations that tug from the right side of the brain—the emotional side.

Although investing is not the same as gambling, when investors use the right side of their brains, they can quickly turn investing into gambling. For instance, when an investor gets lucky and rides up a stock, he suddenly thinks he is really smart and more competent as an investor. He mistakes luck as skill.

Studies show that 80 percent of drivers rate themselves above average. Think about it. I bet you are probably one of them, as, of course, am I. But naturally, the math doesn't add up. Studies show that roughly one out of every three drivers suffers from overconfidence bias. On a scale of one to ten in looks, you probably rate yourself as a seven. And you're not alone. We all think very highly of ourselves, yet would you rate the average person on the street a seven? Most of us also overestimate our IQs. Ninety-four percent of professors rated themselves "above average" in intelligence relative to their peers. It makes one wonder who their peers might be. And in another study, one-third of all employees thought they performed better on the job than 95 percent of their colleagues. Is it bad to feel really good about yourself? I'm no psychologist, but I would much rather have an employee who is overconfident than one who is insecure if given the choice.

However, the *overconfidence effect* is a well-established bias in which a person's subjective confidence in his judgment is reliably greater than his objective *accuracy*. This is most problematic when confidence is relatively high. After taking a quiz, for example, it was documented that people rated their answers as "99 percent certain," but they were actually wrong 40 percent of the time. Overconfidence has been called the most "pervasive and potentially catastrophic" of all the cognitive biases to which human beings fall victim. It has been blamed for lawsuits, strikes, wars, and stock market bubbles and crashes.

How does it affect retirement success? Overconfident investors tend to believe they are better than everyone else in choosing the best stocks, the best mutual funds, and so on. They think they are even better at determining when to enter and exit the market. This bias usually appears when an investor enjoys a few easy successes. Such a person doesn't attribute the success to luck but, instead, starts believing he has the capacity to select winning investments. When it comes to the 401(k), we find that these types of employees tend to disregard risk, trade too frequently, and are quick to assign blame when investment decisions turn bad. It is critical that these individuals become aware of their limitations, because not only do they pose a risk to themselves, but also they tend to be a greater liability to fiduciaries.

To help your employees guard themselves against making mistakes arising from overconfidence, you can limit the amount of allocation allowed to your aggressive investments or company stock option. By restricting no more than, say, 10 percent of your allocation to the emerging market fund or your aggressive tech fund, you can attempt to avert a major financial setback that could compromise the employee's retirement. You can also restrict trading activity for those who abuse the trading privileges within your plan. At the very least, your 401(k) team should carefully monitor participant behavior to identify risks and determine, at the committee level, any appropriate action needed to seek to preserve the integrity of your retirement plan. It may be that a simple education meeting will remedy the problem, or perhaps a re-enrollment can reduce the portfolio risk.

Reprinted with permission from Dan Waserman

LOSS AVERSION

*I never invest in the stock market.
My grandfather lost everything in the 1929 crash!*

Nobel Prize–winning economists Daniel Kahneman and Amos Tversky learned that people care more about losing a dollar than they do about gaining a dollar. In the thirty years that I've been managing money, it has never ceased to amaze me that although I may have made clients several hundreds of thousands of dollars, they are inclined to obsess over one small investment where there were losses. It could be a $2,000 loss compared to $200,000 in gains, yet that one tiny investment becomes a point of contention. This is a classic example of *loss aversion*.

The other extreme is when some investors cannot accept defeat and instead hang on to losers for an indefinite amount of time. Philip Fisher wrote in his book *Common Stocks and Uncommon Profits*, "More money has probably been lost by investors holding a stock until they could 'at least come out even' than from any single reason." Some investors held onto devalued tech stocks five to ten years after the dot-com bubble burst. Why do we do this type of thing? Because human nature is such that we tend to feel the pain of loss more acutely than we feel the pleasure of gain. In other words, we may like to win, but we *hate* to lose. For some, promptly eliminating losers enables them to move on, even at the risk of a potential recovery, whereas for others, they can't part with a loser and hang on to the bitter end, awaiting a recovery that may never happen.

Kahneman offers an illustration by making a proposal to his students. He says, "I'm going to toss a coin, and if it's tails, you lose $10. How much would you have to gain [if it lands on heads] in order for this bet to be acceptable to you?" According to Kahneman, students wanted more than $20 before the bet was acceptable. The same was true for wealthy people. When asked the same question (except the loss was $10,000 instead of $10), they said they wanted to receive $20,000 if they won before they'd take the bet. Although there is a 50 percent chance of winning, people wanted double the payout to accept a chance of loss.

Kahneman illustrates another interesting observation of loss aversion. He discovered people will drive across town to save $5 on a $15 calculator but not drive the same distance to save $5 on a $125 coat. My favorite was an experiment with monkeys that showed the tendency toward loss aversion. Two monkeys were playing happily together when one monkey was given an apple. The monkey contentedly started eating his apple. The other monkey was given two apples, but then one was taken away. Instead of eating the remaining apple, the monkey threw a fit, jumping about and screaming. I dare you to try this with candy on your kids. You'll learn the meaning of loss aversion very quickly!

I see the same situation with investors. The stock market goes up and down. It's called volatility. Indeed, history has proven that we should expect this, and I carefully educate my clients to anticipate such volatility. However, there have been plenty of times when a client focuses on the loss. A few years back I was meeting with a client, Edward, to review his portfolio. Earlier in the year he was up $1 million from his initial $5 million investment. However, the market dipped, and at the time of our meeting the market value of his gains was $800,000. Edward was very upset because he "lost $200,000," while I insisted he had made $800,000. We went back and forth on this. I went so far as to put a glass of water between us and note, "You see this glass as half empty, and I see it as half full." Which one of us is correct? His loss aversion bias did not allow him to comprehend the significant gains in his portfolio. Now, mind you, this was a very successful business owner who had a substantial net worth. But not everyone is wired to understand finance.

Many years ago, I made a $20,000 investment for Marge, a wealthy client who wanted to speculate with a small portion of her money. The stock she purchased stagnated for many years, but during the tech boom it ultimately grew to be worth $370,000. When I called Marge and told her it was time to sell, she rejected my recommendation on the basis that she didn't want to pay taxes. I insisted she sell. We spent weeks debating this trade. With every call she grew more emphatic. "Terri, I don't want to pay taxes!" Her loss aversion was about sending a check to the IRS for $140,000 (her share of capital gains tax on the sell). Despite my diligence, including pointing out that she was still going to enjoy a $200,000 plus profit on this small investment, Marge would not heed my advice. Ultimately, within just a matter of months the bubble burst. In the end, I told her the good news was that she didn't have to write a check to the IRS. The bad news was that instead of a $350,000 gain, she had a loss, as her shares were only worth $10,000.

Have you ever wondered why clothing stores offer you those handy shopping bags for gathering all your potential purchases? Retailers know that once you hold an item in your hand, you're psychologically tied to it and don't want to give it up. The longer you have it in your possession, the stronger that connection and the more unwilling you are to part with your new stuff. People feel the pain of loss more than the joy of gains.

The psychology behind this is the same as that of the punch of an insult. Suppose you receive ten compliments on your tie and then one person declares it the ugliest tie they've ever seen. Every time you pull out that tie, you remember that someone said it was ugly, which has a greater influence on whether you wear it again than the ten compliments you received. The problem with loss aversion as it relates to retirement planning is that it causes people to be unable to weather market volatility in order to seek to achieve above-average long-term returns. Investors don't handle the "punch" of a market drop any better than the blow of an insult. Consequently, they are shortsighted with their investments and compromise their long-term averages.

When it comes to financial incentives, loss aversion also works against the employer. Studies show that if you are going to give out financial incentives, you must keep giving them. For instance, have you ever offered employee bonuses? Maybe you had a great year and gave your employees a nice fat bonus check. At the time it was wonderful, and everyone was elated. But what happened the next year when you didn't give out the bonuses or the checks were much smaller? Employees were surely disappointed and may have even felt slighted. You may have even heard some offhanded comments about it. Financial rewards, such as bonuses, tend to have limited effective life spans.

The loss aversion effect may also result in highly unlikely events or low probability risks being given more weight than is justified. People naturally overestimate the probability that these events will occur, such as major stock market crashes like the Great Depression. Many people missed out on the recent market recovery because they remained in cash for fear of a depression. Most investors continue to fear an impending repeat of the financial crisis or market calamity, so they have avoided the stock market. At the very least, evidence shows they are now hypersensitive to volatility. That is how powerful loss aversion is. The paradox of loss aversion is that our worst fear becomes realized in our attempt to avoid a loss.

The best way to help your employees protect themselves from loss aversion is to educate them. They need to understand the history of the markets, past performance, and performance during economic disasters. Perhaps it would be even better to provide them with a clear understanding of what they own. Unfortunately, in today's high-tech world, employees see a trading symbol of a mutual fund that may as well be as random as the symbols €¿&í^. Sure, they may understand their money is invested in the markets, but without sufficient knowledge, they may see €¿&í^ as being as insubstantial as the piece of paper it's written on. Your employees need to see €¿&í^ as a tangible asset. After all, behind that cluster of letters is a diversified portfolio of securities. Therefore, when they understand what the portfolio of securities in €¿&í^ actually consists of and understand the companies they own, along with the diversity, the management, and so on, they are more likely to have a greater sense of confidence in what they own and will be more likely to withstand the market, economic risks, and the uncertainties of the future.

CONFIRMATION BIAS

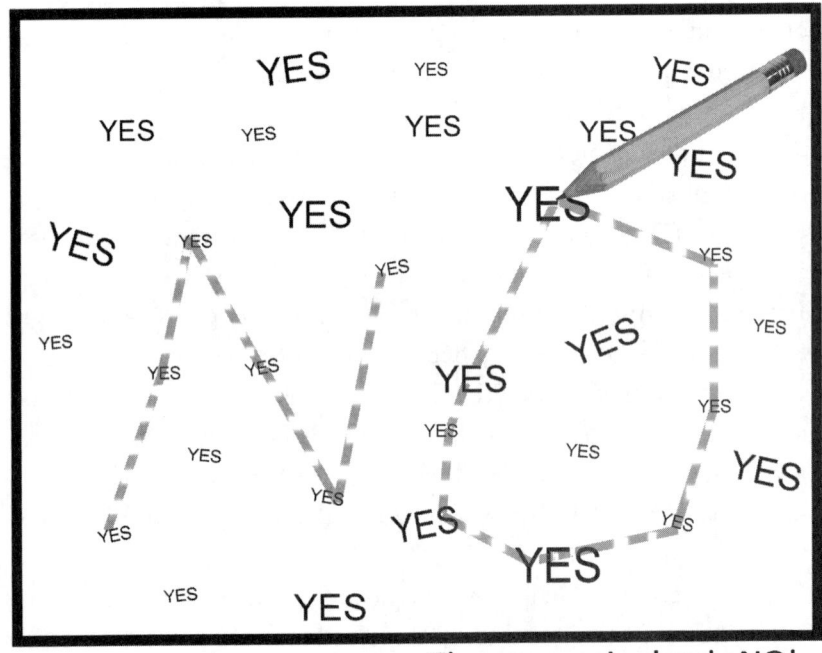

The answer is clearly NO!

Confirmation bias, also called *my side bias*, is when people make decisions based on *selective information* otherwise known as their bias. We are often drawn to information or ideas that serve to validate our existing beliefs and opinions, and when we ignore or *devalue* the relevance of what contradicts our beliefs, we have fallen in to the trap of *confirmation bias*.

Have you ever noticed that when you are considering buying a particular color or model car, you suddenly see it on the road everywhere? Or you're expecting a child and you think there must be a baby boom because you notice pregnant women and babies all over? If you've ever had a serious argument with your spouse, you might have ignored all the good things he or she does for you and, instead, obsessed over all the shortcomings. Or perhaps you have fallen for someone before because you were so enamored with his or her positive qualities, but you later realized, perhaps with regret, that you completely ignored some serious problems. Confirmation bias is seeing the world through a filter.

Suppose you heard the story that your great-grandfather lost everything in the stock market during the Great Depression. Everything you read seems to validate the instability of the stock market. When the market falls, the media reminds us of the dark days of the Great Depression. Of course, because of your bias, those headlines stand out to you. Confirmation bias draws you to stories that reinforce your fear of investing, whereas you unconsciously completely ignore or discount the stories of success. Even though the market has outperformed over the long term, unfortunately this bias prevents you from trusting the potential for gains in the equity markets. Instead, you focus on the losses and use periods of decline as a way to validate your bias.

People do this often when it comes to finances, politics, or religion. For instance, an employee is in denial about his life expectancy risks. He's fifty years old, he is inadequately prepared for retirement, and he rationalizes his overspending by declaring he isn't going to live long enough to worry about it. When he reads the news, he sees stories of celebrities, musicians, artists, and icons who happen to grab the headlines because they died prematurely. Headlines like *Cancer! Heart attack! Stroke!* pop out. At the same time, he completely ignores those celebrities and personalities who are still alive and well, making films well into their eighties, or those who enjoyed life well beyond their life expectancy.

An investor may have a belief about market conditions and gravitate toward information sources that confirm that belief. It happens frequently when an investor favors an investment. Take for example real estate. With confirmation bias, the person seems only to find stories and forecasts to further support and validate the prosperity and success that comes with the owning of real estate. Many employees who acquire company stock through a stock purchase plan develop a confirmation bias toward that stock. They fail to understand the risk of owning a concentrated position because of their overconfidence in the performance of the stock. It may very well be the only stock they have ever owned and is likely the only stock they have diligently tracked and monitored, but they have a higher degree of confidence in it because of their bias. Enron employees fell victim to confirmation bias.

When it comes to investing, confirmation bias can impact those on the opportunist side or those on the risk-averse side. Either way, this bias causes undue risk and tends to drive an employee farther from retirement success. Oftentimes, confirmation bias is greatest when we attach an emotional emphasis to the outcomes we desire. For example, if you have an employee who is behind in retirement savings and is now seeking to catch up by chasing performance, taking more risk than appropriate, given the recent success in the stock market, this employee might have overconfidence in the economy and selectively read articles or forecasts that further support economic growth.

Confirmation bias can also hurt the employee who hides in cash after he has experienced severe losses. Stories forecasting doom and gloom garner his attention, while he discounts those headlines that predict economic strength and improvements. Employees with confirmation bias suffer greater volatility because their feelings prevent them from being objective. They fail to adhere to sound investment principles because of their emotions. Instead, they see the investment world in a vacuum.

Hopefully, you are beginning to see what happens with these psychological handicaps. While most people start out enthusiastically with their retirement plans, many natural human tendencies often unwittingly get in the way and cause serious financial setbacks. It's not the market that fails people, it's people's inability to see things objectively. When we suffer losses, instead of approaching investing in a logical manner (e.g., "I lost a lot of money last time, so I need to get educated and better understand what went wrong in order to avoid repeating those mistakes"), it is in our human nature to blame others. We blame the markets, Wall Street, government, or greedy corporations. Rarely, if ever, do we blame ourselves. Instead, "The stock market is dangerous"; "Our politicians caused this"; "The system is rigged against the little guy"; "My broker did me wrong." In most cases, an objective review will reveal investors should have asked a lot more questions before they invested.

In addition to providing education, an employer can help employees overcome confirmation bias by having a professional advisor who provides timely market and economic updates to help employees put the current market condition in perspective. Employees need objective guidance aligned with a retirement focus, not a day-trading mentality. Your employees also need to understand basic economics and how the business cycle functions. The media might headline a recession as being a surprise or shock to the markets, but recessions are a normal part of the business cycle. Investors must understand the natural economic and market rhythm. Of course, not all recessions are as deep and widespread as the Great Recession, nor are economic declines as dark as the Great Depression, but the media posts black-and-white pictures of the soup lines as they announce "Recession!" and people panic. They call it "Market Crash!" instead of what it really is—a market decline. The media is now using a new word, *convulsing!* Apparently, the stock market plummets, crashes, and convulses! *Who wants to own something that does all of that?* You can help combat the dramatization by the media that provokes emotions with sound education and important investment principles to help your employees use logic in their decision-making. In incorporating a logical approach, they will be more likely to achieve retirement success.

CONTROL BIAS

ILLUSION OF CONTROL AND SELF-CONTROL BIAS

My advisor should have seen this coming!

Illusion of control is the tendency of human beings to believe they or someone else can control or at least influence outcomes, when in fact they have no influence. For instance, after a major plane crash some people refuse to fly, declaring they "feel more in control when driving." Many are resolute in this, despite decades of research showing that air travel is statistically much safer. According to recent data, there is one death for every 23.9 million commercial flights, as compared to one car fatality every 15 minutes, in the United States.

"I told you I didn't want to lose ANY money!"

A similar thought process applies to investment decisions. The illusion of control begins with the word *should*, as in, 'Someone should have seen this coming.' People who have this belief have trouble coming to terms with the irrationality of this supposition and fail to see the impossibility of their expectation. "The portfolio manager within my 401(k) should have the expertise to know when to get out of the market." Self-control bias can be described as a conflict between people's wishes and their inability to think rationally about the pursuit of those desires. Plenty of people sabotage their own goals, such as failing to shed unwanted pounds, because they can't resist the temptation of a triple-fudge sundae, yet they tell themselves they'll work it off at the gym tomorrow. Or how about the college student failing to achieve a higher GPA because he can't say no to a frat party and still tells himself he'll study for that test in the morning?

Control bias makes us fool ourselves. It also prevents us from learning from our mistakes or even taking responsibility for our mistakes. Day traders often think they can get out of the market before an upset and thereby avoid losses. Indeed, some investors unrealistically expect their financial advisors to be able to avoid losses. Illusion of control causes investors to have unrealistic expectations, to underdiversify, and to trade too often.

I have found the only way to overcome control bias is with good education. Your education program should offer your employees a balanced perspective and not be biased or slanted toward any particular investment, strategy, or (one-sided) opinion. Offering a historical perspective on the capital markets in terms of performance, booms, and busts, and sharing some hindsight, can help mitigate the risks of control bias. However, sometimes the best approach is automatic re-enrollment. It may be more efficient to reset the allocations for everyone. That, along with an education meeting to prepare your employees for a change in the business cycle or a market correction, can go a long way toward ensuring everyone has realistic expectations.

RECENCY BIAS

Stock market returns are going to be low for a very long time!

When gas prices rise, sales of large sport utility vehicles and trucks tend to decline. It's not difficult to see the connection: consumers believe what's happened recently will continue to happen. Even though a family of six might very well need a SUV, they fear gas prices will skyrocket and therefore refrain from buying one. In reality, gas prices may have peaked and actually be on the verge of falling. The phenomenon also exists with investing. It's no secret that investors tend to chase past investment performance, often piling into an asset class just as it is peaking. Recency bias is the irrational state of mind where recent activity suggests permanence. *'Because the investment has enjoyed great recent performance, such will remain the case going forward'* or *'Because the market has "crashed," it's going to fall again very soon.'* High probabilities are overestimated, while at the same time, low likelihoods are grossly underestimated. Unfortunately, research has shown that it's essentially impossible to predict which asset class, sector, or geographic region will be the top performer in any given year. But recency bias can be a strong driver leading people to chase past performance because few people want to feel left behind.

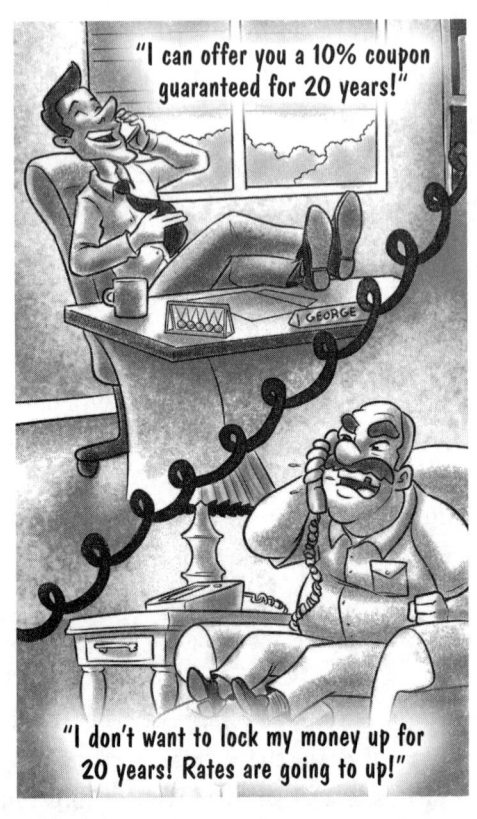

After the 2008 crisis, unemployed workers fell victim to recency bias. "I'm never going to get a job!" So, what did they do? They stopped looking! Which, of course, only served to highly increase the probability that they would not find work. Managers can be victim to recency bias with employees, focusing on what has happened lately when conducting an employee performance review. Some managers may inadvertently weigh what the employee appears to have done (or not to have done) in the past few weeks rather than evaluating the employee's performance over the entire year.

When I started in the business, interest rates were double-digit. Today, if I could offer clients a 10% bond guaranteed and backed by the US Treasury for twenty years, they would likely want to invest nearly everything they could into it. But back in 1988, I couldn't give those deals away. No one wanted to "lock up" their money for twenty years. Why not? Well, they were accustomed to double-digit interest rates—heck, FDIC-insured certificates of deposits (CDs) were paying as much as 15%. *Why would I want to tie up my money for twenty years at 10% when I know interest rates will remain high or even go up?!* Many people were victims of recency bias back then. Today, many are quite complacent with these exceptionally low interest rates, neglecting to lock in fixed rates.

After the financial crisis, many pundits declared investors and consumers alike would be "irrevocably transformed" by the impact of the Great Recession, and they forecasted stock market performance would be subpar for a "very long time." We were also told consumers and businesses would likely never extend themselves with debt again because we would be facing a new era of "deleveraging" that would last for decades. Ironically, the facts show a very different outcome within a rather short period of time.

HINDSIGHT BIAS

I knew that would happen!

Who hasn't said or heard that before? Really? How did you *know* that would happen? The truth is, we tend to overestimate the accuracy of our predictions. A person with hindsight bias doesn't necessarily have any insightful information to share when it matters, but he certainly portends to be knowledgeable and aware *after the fact*.

Hindsight bias is a psychological phenomenon where past outcomes seem to be more prominent than they appeared while they were occurring. *I knew the market would crash! I knew real estate prices would rebound!* The problem with hindsight bias is that it can lead an individual to believe that an event was more predictable than it actually was, and this can result in an oversimplification of cause and effect. The "knew it all along" effect is the inclination *after* an event has occurred to see it as having been predictable, despite there being little or no objective basis for such a prediction.

Hindsight bias has been seen with elections ("I knew Trump would win!"), with sports ("I knew the Eagles would win their fifth Super Bowl!"), and with investments ("I knew it was a good time to buy my house!"). What's wrong with hindsight bias? We all shrug our shoulders when thinking of "shoulda, woulda, coulda," don't we? That is, we recognize hindsight for what it is. However, when it is a bias, people tend to distort or "misremember" their earlier prediction or behavior, which is often different from the outcome. This is the investor who says, "I'm really worried about the stock market because I *know* Hillary is going to win!" But when the world was surprised and taken aback by a Trump win and the stock market went up, the same person declared, "I knew he was going to win!" But now she's upset at her advisor because she played it too safe and missed the market rally after the election.

The tendency to believe we knew the answer all along, when in fact there was a total contradiction or no evidence substantiating this, can be quite problematic. I can't tell you how many investors have told me they "knew" all the things that have happened over the past thirty years *after the fact*. "I knew Y2K was a hoax!" said Bob. Only Bob forgot he was the one who sat in my office for an hour talking about ways he could try to protect himself from the inevitable computer crash.

The real estate boom of the 2000s and the eventual credit collapse took nearly everyone by surprise. Yet there are those who say in hindsight, "I saw it coming!" The truth is, if the formation of a bubble had been obvious at the time, the real estate market (or the stock market, or the energy sector, or the technology sector, or any other asset) probably wouldn't have escalated in the first place. Investors would have recognized the overvaluations and avoided the investment; thus, there never would have been a bubble and, therefore, there would never have been a burst.

People with hindsight bias tend to view events as inevitable, assuming they were bound to happen. Worse yet, they pin blame on others for not seeing a negative event as such. Say a woman receives a false-negative mammogram, shortly thereafter is diagnosed with breast cancer, and then blames the doctor for being incompetent. Or take the person who buy an off-brand item at a discount store and then complains about the quality: "I knew it would be junk!" Then there is the person who buys a fixer-upper, gets angry about the financial costs to restore the home—"I knew this was going to be a money pit!"— and then blames the realtor. Say the market crashes and an investor blames the financial advisor. Clearly to assume one can foresee events when there is no rationale evidence supporting this can certainly cause distorted or unrealistic expectations.

Hindsight bias can fool an investor into believing the onset of some past event was predictable and completely obvious, whereas in fact the event could not have been reasonably predicted at all. When it comes to retirement planning, hindsight bias can lead to one of the most potentially dangerous mind-sets that an investor can have: overconfidence.

INERTIA

> *Nothing happens until something moves.*
> —Albert Einstein

Inertia is a tendency to "keep on doing what you're doing," even if it's not in your best interest. It is a powerful force in preventing change, even if illogical. People have a general preference for the status quo, even if change may be a better alternative. We don't want to suffer the regret that comes with making a wrong decision. We would rather keep our situation the same, unchanged. Inertia is the tendency to keep doing the same thing but somehow expecting different results. Some say this is also the definition of insanity.

"Inertia son, is the resistance of an object to change its speed, direction..."

People fall victim to inertia when experiencing marital problems or discord. Instead of working on finding solutions, couples keep going along, avoiding the matter. Of course, this doesn't fix the problem, and as many will argue, it makes matters worse. Those who succumb to inertia are more afraid of a change than they are of maintaining the status quo. We fear the change may be less rewarding than our current choice, even if our current choice is not yielding us the results we want or need. We can fall victim to inertia with jobs, living with a sense of discontent about our careers because we don't want to act to change the situation. After all, there is always the risk we might not like a new job or different career. The consequence of inertia is that our resistance to change prevents us from potentially enjoying a better outcome.

Participants who fall victim to inertia rely on familiar assumptions and exhibit a reluctance or inability to revise those assumptions, even when the indications supporting such assumptions no longer exists or when other evidence calls them into question. For example, an employee neglects to participate in the 401(k) and is reluctant to do so even when he acknowledges the need to save for retirement. He feels he needs to "research the 401(k) investment options" or "read up on the plan" first. Yet he never makes time to do this, so inertia kicks in. Months or years pass without any action toward retirement planning. Or an employee stays with the same salary deferral options even when she knows it's probably insufficient. Or an employee remains in cash for fear of making bad investment timing decisions. Even an employee who leaves money behind at a former employer can be subject to inertia. Instead of rolling over the account, she, afraid of making a mistake, keeps her money as is. Soon, there are three different old 401(k) accounts and no one is monitoring them, and she may not even update her address with her ex-employers. You probably know how difficult it is to track down ex-employees with account balances.

An individual subject to inertia may weigh the potential losses arising from switching from the status quo more heavily than the potential gains. "If I roll over my 401(k), I might not like the new plan!" The fear of making a mistake gives the individual a reason to do nothing right now, and then procrastination kicks in. In no time, the person grows comfortable with the status quo. We tend to oppose change for fear of making a mistake, even if that change may bring about marital bliss, financial security, or a more rewarding job.

HERD MENTALITY

Everyone is getting out of the market! You'd better get out now!

People are social animals. No one wants to be left out of a trend or a movement. Marketers know this, and they have become rather adept at creating social proof: since other buyers like their products, so should you. Following the crowd is reassuring. "Over 247 Billion Served" works! Studies have demonstrated that when we don't have a strong opinion about the choices presented to us, we simply mimic others around us. Rather than asking questions or spending time learning about products, people defer to the "social default."

When it comes to investing, this is absolutely true. Just because the larger herd is stampeding into or out of the market doesn't mean that's the right move for an individual investor based on his or her own objectives, but there is a comfort in following the crowd. Imagine you are in a building and suddenly a mass of people start running toward you yelling, "*Fire!*" Are you going to (a) ignore them, pushing through the crowd and carrying on with your business, (b) stop people and start asking carefully calculated questions to ascertain the situation, or (c) start running out of the building with the crowd? My guess is you are going to start running with the crowd and ask questions after you get to what you deem to be a safe place.

Investors who don't understand what they own, why they own it, or how the investment works tend to do exactly that—follow the crowd—when the market falls. The media tells them the market is "plummeting," they hear "everyone" is selling—their peers, friends, and family—and they see their account values falling quickly, so they hit "sell" and figure they will seek safe ground and ask questions later. Individually, most people would not necessarily make the same choice, but the social pressure to conform can be a powerful force no matter what the subject. "Everyone is buying property; therefore, so should we!" "Everyone is taking on more debt; we're all in the same boat!" "Everyone is struggling, so it's normal to be falling behind with retirement savings." The herd mentality is the tendency for individuals to follow the actions, whether rational or irrational, of a larger group. And we do this even if it is not in our best interests.

Within an organization, colleagues are often influenced by others to follow investment trends. In social circles, we adopt certain behaviors based on the trends followed by our peers, be it our choice of cocktail, our vacation spot, or our investment portfolio. Most people have a natural desire to be accepted by a group rather than be branded as an outcast. "If everyone is buying stocks, so should we!" "If everyone is driving a Tesla, so should we!" The second reason the herd mentality is powerful is the common rationale that it's unlikely that such a large group could be wrong. After all, even if you are convinced that a particular course of action is irrational or incorrect, you might still follow the herd because *they must know something that you don't*. This is especially prevalent in areas in which an individual has very little experience.

"The market is falling, and investors are getting out quickly! They must know something I don't! I'd better get out fast!" The media plays right into this, too. They track the "smart money" as if there is such a thing.

IN SUMMARY

Where your employees tend to need the biggest nudge, if not a push, is in making financial decisions. Unfortunately, the effect of emotions on investment decisions is usually negative. *The market is too high! The market is too low! There's too much euphoria! There's too little confidence. It's too hot! It's too cold. I have too much debt! I'm too old! I'm too young! I don't have enough money.* It's never the right time to start 401(k) contributions. It's never the perfect time to increase deferral rates. It's never the right time to invest in stocks. To your employees' disadvantage, much of economic and financial theory is based on the notion that individuals act rationally and consider all available information in the investment decision-making process. But we know this is seldom the case.

Instead, we are victims of irrational behavior and repeated errors in judgment. Today, it is almost impossible to turn on the television, open a newspaper, or go online without seeing some mention of a looming crisis or predictions of a market crash. Increasing numbers of employees are fearful of a poverty-stricken retirement and crippling national debt. The negativity is prevalent, and this only serves to confuse investors or influence them to be negative as well. There is also evidence of widespread misunderstanding among consumers about financial services products. There is no shortfall of opinions, commentary, or favoritisms in today's information age. As a result, employees are frequently misdirected, paralyzed, or ill-informed. Ironically, getting sound financial guidance when information today is overly abundant is perhaps the greatest challenge of all.

Employees need help. There is no question about that. They also need to have confidence in the source of their financial guidance.

They need strategies aligned to their retirement goals. What they don't need is someone to opine on today's market or the hottest investments of the day or give them stock tips. And although some financial wellness programs provide access to great online tools for budgeting, calculating retirement needs, and meeting other financial goals, fewer than 20 percent of employees take the time to access these tools and utilize them. This is because employees are still confused, are overwhelmed, or lack the knowledge needed to translate this information into a plan of action. They need guidance.

The stock market has enabled us to advance and enjoy a much greater quality of life over the past hundred years. Yet, the average person simply doesn't understand how Charles Dow and Edward Jones (the founders of the Dow Jones Industrial Average) helped changed the world for our enjoyment. Investors provide the capital by investing in our markets, and that, in turn, helps finance innovations and provide jobs. Ultimately the capital markets enhance the quality of all our lives. Yet, the average person just dives into investments without proper training or education.

Investing successfully for retirement is a great responsibility. I believe it will be the greatest expense we must finance. The cost of retirement today will likely far surpass the cost of our home or that of our children's college education. But the average American gets no schooling in finance. Instead, they are handed a 401(k) enrollment form and a list of investment options and are told to make investment decisions. They may go online and answer a few risk questions to help them allocate their dollars, but how does that help them make sense of retirement? It's no wonder we have a retirement crisis.

I my opinion, the best approach to helping your employees overcome their emotional instincts and their tendency to procrastinate and to promote financial competency is to provide ongoing education and make a commitment to engaging professional experts to address the constant challenges we all face as we prepare for our retirement. It takes decades to reach our goals, and we all face numerous challenges along the way, be they personal, economic, or financial. We need to be prepared, know how to use our heads in making smart decisions, and have confidence in our planning. Using the automatic options within your 401(k) can also help your employees overcome their own limitations, such as inertia. Retirement planning is a process. There is no sidestepping this. With diligent effort, you can help drive retirement success and empower your employees with the knowledge they need to circumvent amateur mistakes that could otherwise cause major financial setbacks for millions of hardworking Americans.

It is time for plan sponsors take a proactive approach. It's not just about offering employees access to a plan; it's about helping them overcome their self-imposed limitations, combat the misguided direction from the media, and practice sound investment principles that will stand the test of time. One of your first steps can be to think carefully about your plan design and determine whether it is influencing the right type of behavior. Another step is to develop a sound education program designed to help employees understand their natural tendencies and teach them how to avoid succumbing to the normal temptation of these biases. A comprehensive financial wellness program may not solve all the problems, but it can help your employees better understand the natural impediments to success, learn sensible ways to overcome them, and gain a sense of clarity when it comes to their financial needs and goals. The goal of the 401(k) is to get workers to a secure retirement, and the success of the plan can only be measured by the success of your participants.

CHAPTER 10
THE 401(K) FINANCIAL ADVISOR

You understand there is a financial advisor assigned to your 401(k). You see his name on your plan statement, and he occasionally calls to have a conversation with the owner of your company, but you have no idea what he does for your plan. Whenever you need help, as the HR manager, you always call the recordkeeper or TPA. On the rare occasion when you've suggested an employee call the advisor to get an answer to a question, the employee generally later complains that they did not receive the help they needed, so you either did the research for them or had them call the recordkeeper. One day your employee, Jennifer, questions the advisory fees being charged against her account. She explains that because her husband is a CPA and handles her investment decisions, she doesn't feel she needs advisory help. She wants to understand why these fees are being assessed. How do you answer?

Fiduciary duties under the Employee Retirement Income Security Act (ERISA) "are the highest known to law" (Donovan v. Bierworth, 680 F.2d 263, 271 [2d Cir.1982], cert. denied, 459 U.S. 1069).

Among the most common mistakes plan sponsors make is not understanding the role and value of the financial advisor specific to their 401(k)'s. A qualified advisor can be your key consultant and advocate in the plan design, operation, and maintenance, and in the overall success of your plan. In addition, an ERISA 3(21) investment advisor can serve as a co-fiduciary, thus helping you mitigate risk. Or a 3(38) investment manager can serve as a plan investment manager and save you time and possibly also save you money. No matter which you choose, a qualified advisor can help you assess gaps in your fiduciary practice management, assist with structuring your risk management, provide fiduciary training for your committee, help you document your standards of care, recommend and assist in monitoring vendor relationships and plan expenses, and provide valuable retirement education and counseling to your employees. A good advisor is not a sales representative but, rather, an independent trusted advisor who specializes in the support of 401(k) and other qualified retirement plans.

"Where a trustee does not possess the education, experience and skill required to make a decision concerning the investment of a plan's assets, he has an affirmative duty to seek independent counsel in making the decision" (Katsaros v. Cody, 744 F.2d 279 [2d Cir. 1984]). Indeed, it may be imprudent for plan sponsors not to engage experts in the operation of their company-sponsored retirement plans.

If you needed a root canal, would you go to your family medical doctor? Would you want your psychiatrist to perform your colonoscopy? How valuable is your optometrist going to be in helping you with Achilles tendonitis? The key is to find the right specialist for the services needed. Hiring the right financial advisor is arguably the most important choice in the entire 401(k) process.

A 401(k) advisor has a very important job, but it is a very different job from that of a wealth advisor, financial planner, insurance broker, or securities representative. Even though these professionals may be licensed to do the job, if they do not have expertise in this area, they will not be in the best position to serve you. Choosing an advisor who is not a 401(k) specialist is among the most common mistakes made by plan sponsors, leading to a less than favorable experience. If you determine you have not hired a 401(k) specialist on your company-sponsored retirement plan, you will likely find yourself and your participants dissatisfied and perhaps downright frustrated with the advisor's inability to properly support your plan and drive retirement readiness.

A specialist, however, can help reduce your risks, promote ERISA compliance, provide valuable guidance on plan design, offer provider support, perform investment monitoring, and provide enhanced employee education in an effort to give your participants the best chance for retirement success. While some of these functions might appear to overlap with those of your plan provider, the depth and level of support an advisor can provide is a big distinction from all other parties involved in running your 401(k). That's because a good financial advisor is an objective consultant. Like your lead counsel is your go-to for legal protection or your CPA is your authority for sound tax decisions, a qualified 401(k) advisor should be the lead expert you rely on to help you successfully manage your 401(k). Your TPA might help you design your plan and can be a valuable consultant for that service, and your recordkeeper should be able to provide some insight on plan features and benefits that align to your goals, but it is the financial advisor who pulls it all together in one cohesive plan. The advisor is the quarterback who can define, qualify, and articulate the options, terms, and benefits to you and your employees.

Unfortunately, because there is a lack of understanding of this role, plan sponsors tend to focus more attention on fees and not enough on the quality of the services. Consequently, plan sponsors often miss the opportunity to benefit from engaging a great advisor who specializes in 401(k). Of course, as with hiring any service provider, decisions should be based on how the services fit with your plan's goals and your needs as well as those of your participants. Decisions should not be based on hiring the lowest-cost advisor or the one who manages your personal portfolio, even if you trust and like him or her. In fact, more problems have arisen by hiring a relative, personal broker, or nonqualified advisor because of conflicts of interest. The Department of Labor (DOL) and the courts expect you, as a plan sponsor, to follow a prudent hiring process when selecting your advisor, just as with any other service provider. While this may end up being your personal advisor or nephew, your process of scrutiny and due diligence should not be different because of your relationship.

When advisor fees are paid by the participants through the plan, your hiring decisions are considered *fiduciary decisions*. Most companies do not pay for the advisor but rather bill the services to the plan. Of course, if you choose to pay the advisor out of company funds, you may be able to avert these due diligence issues. However, it would behoove you to review this with an ERISA attorney.

Selecting a financial advisor or reviewing your relationship with a financial advisor is a good opportunity for you, as a plan sponsor, to decide which functions should be done in-house and which should be outsourced. Fiduciary services are one of many categories of services that an advisor may provide. And although hiring a qualified advisor is a great opportunity for you to mitigate risk, it is prudent to start with a clear idea of the functions you want your advisor to perform. Some advisory services to consider include the following:

- Formulation of an Investment Policy Statement
- Devising and structuring an investment committee
- Investment committee fiduciary education
- Investment monitoring and due diligence
- Discretionary investment management
- Plan compliance review
- Fee analysis and benchmarking
- Fiduciary services
- Service provider monitoring and support
- Plan retirement readiness monitoring and review
- Participant education and consulting
- Plan design consulting
- ERISA compliance best practices
- Capital market assumptions and economic outlook
- Additional consulting as needed

You may not yet be able to identify the difference between a general financial advisor or wealth advisor and a 401(k) advisor because industry titles do not necessarily distinguish these areas of expertise.

However, the nature of the advisory business is changing, and increasingly plan sponsors are questioning the qualifications, services, and skill sets needed from their plan advisors. There are many advantages to hiring a dedicated 401(k) advisor instead of a generalist to oversee your plan, but first you may ask the question, why do we need an advisor at all?

A 401(k) expert can serve as a co-fiduciary for your plan. As an investment expert, your advisor can also help you understand and fulfill your fiduciary obligations with investment monitoring. The right 401(k) advisor is also qualified to help you properly manage your plan and meet your fiduciary requirements. A great advisor, however, will do more than that. He or she will help you build a successful retirement plan. Plan success, remember, is defined as getting your employees to retirement. However, it's important to understand that the key role of the advisor is to serve as a consultant. The fees charged are not for a product but, rather, for knowledge and expertise. Just as you engage a CPA or legal counsel for their consultative expertise, you engage a qualified financial advisor because such a person understands far more than just the issues as they relate to investments and capital markets. Your financial advisor should be an expert in ERISA requirements, IRS rules, fiduciary standards, 401(k) plan metrics, and plan designs. He or she knows the market, including recordkeepers, administrators, and CPA auditors, and their individual strengths and weaknesses. In addition, a great advisor will have expertise and credentials in personal retirement planning and financial wellness and will be able to work with and assist your employees. You may want to engage a Certified Financial Planner® (CFP®). The CFP certification is recognized as one of the highest standards in personal financial planning. It is a comprehensive program that sets strict requirements for education, experience, and ethics. A lighter version of this certification is the Chartered Retirement Plan Counselor® (CRPC®). While it does not demand the same rigorous comprehensive studies, it does provide specialized education in retirement planning. The Accredited Investment Fiduciary® (AIF®) designation supports investment professionals who serve as fiduciaries and provides them with the knowledge and tools they need to support employees' best interests and help plan sponsors adhere to the global fiduciary precepts. Although certifications do not guarantee satisfaction, an advisor should have credentials designating specific skills, aptitudes, and competencies specific to the expertise you seek.

Additionally, if you want your advisor to engage with your employees through educational meetings or individual consultations, you want to be sure he or she has a system for providing such education and individual support, including adequate staffing, a methodology, and engaging presentation skills. You'll want to understand the scope of the presentations, including the breadth and depth of covered educational topics, material, and method of engagement, to ensure the right quality content for what you are seeking. You might have an advisor who works great with your committee, but if he or she uses technical language and lingo with your employees, they are likely to be turned off and it may end up being a frustrating experience for them. Likewise, if the content is too basic, simplistic, or repetitive, your employees are likely to get bored and lose interest after a few meetings. If the frequency of the education program is inconsistent and sporadic, your participants are unlikely to gain financial competency.

Think of your advisor as your sounding board. A good advisor is going to help you and your committee share ideas and best practices, test opinions and thoughts, and help you measure the effectiveness of your plan and assess how you are managing the plan under the rules of ERISA. A good financial advisor should be someone you turn to for advice and guidance on matters that relate to your plan, the plan administrator, design, investments, and employee support. A diligent advisor will *proactively* initiate and lead a dialogue with you and your committee and should also be able to support your employees and drive financial wellness. As you can imagine, these roles can be quite involved and may require an entire team rather just one advisor, depending upon the size of your firm.

Once you decide you need to hire an expert, be sure to hire an advisor who can provide objective advice. If there is any conflict of interest, it needs to be disclosed and carefully considered. For instance, if the advisor is an employee of the provider or the TPA or of your firm, he or she may not be able to act as an objective advisor if there are any compensation incentives tied to your other vendors. A transparent fee-based arrangement will ensure you avert such conflicts, such as commissions or revenue sharing paid by the recordkeeper or TPA. You will want to identify any influences that prevent the advisor from remaining objective. If the advisor gets paid a commission by recommending a certain provider or has a financial incentive that can create a bias, such conflicts should be disclosed by the advisor and carefully considered by plan fiduciaries. If the advisor has personal relationships with senior management, this conflict should be acknowledged and carefully scrutinized by the committee to ensure the advice and services are supporting the plan and not favoring the relationship.

This issue is called "revenue neutral," and in its simplest form it means investment fiduciaries must not have the potential to benefit from their own choices or recommendations, such as through variable levels of compensation or revenue sharing for recommending investments or financial products. If the advisor is paid a commission from the recordkeeper and also collects a fee as a financial advisor for your plan, the compensation is likely to influence provider recommendations. Documentation of any conclusions should be maintained to demonstrate your due diligence process. The best defense is one that demonstrates a due diligence process. Of course, when in doubt, confer with an ERISA attorney.

Your plan advisor may recommend investments or insurance products and collect a fee to manage personal assets for employees; however, such arrangement must be disclosed, and both the plan sponsor and employees must consent to this arrangement on the basis that employees have a choice to hire any financial advisor they so choose so long as the advisor is providing objective advice and guidance. The process, called "disclosure and consent," is a formal process whereby potential conflicts are disclosed to the plan fiduciaries and are carefully considered by the committee. All parties must consent, preferably in writing, to the arrangement. This gives an opportunity for all parties to approve the potential conflict before the advisor is engaged. While not a problem in and of itself, if an undisclosed conflict exists, it can be problematic for fiduciaries. To ensure impartiality, your advisor should be engaged under a separate engagement contract. Ask your advisor is there are any compensation incentives with the provider, including additional service fees, commissions, or indirect compensation, because such arrangement needs to be considered very carefully since it is your duty to be sure your advisor can act objectively and independently.

At this point you may be wondering why the provider or administrator isn't sufficient. You may be getting some of the aforementioned services from your provider or plan administrator. Employee education, investment reviews, and perhaps even co-fiduciary support are not uncommon value-add services offered by recordkeepers. Although such services enhance the value of the provider agreement, the fact remains that plan providers or recordkeepers cannot offer objective advice or guidance. They have a self-serving interest. For example, investment reviews may be biased toward proprietary investments (investments offered by the provider) or those that pay higher revenue sharing fees. Employee education may be more focused on promoting the provider's services, website, and proprietary investments (including target date funds) rather than on promoting financial wellness. Even when such a situation is properly disclosed, the question is, do these favoritisms or biases really support objectivity for you and your participants? The answer is obvious: *probably not*. Can your employees reasonably expect to get the best support and service when those they look to for direction have conflicting interests? This is not to say representatives from your recordkeeper or TPA have ill intentions. To the contrary, I think most professionals in the industry share a sincere passion to help people and do the best job they can. Nonetheless, the fact remains that if your trusted advisor is unduly influenced, conflicts exist. Plan sponsors have a responsibility to take such conflicts as a very serious matter. There is no substitute for an objective financial advisor.

Another mistake may involve hiring "buddies" or relatives irrespective of credentials. You will want to avoid the appearance of undue influence. While it may be perfectly acceptable to hire a friend or relative, the matter needs to be carefully and objectively reviewed. If a documented due diligence process is followed and the advisor competes equally with other qualified candidates to win the contract based on his or her merits, not because of the relationship, then hiring a friend or relative on your plan is deemed to be acceptable in the free markets. Still, how does this appear to your employees? Remember, advisor fees are paid directly or indirectly by each and every participant in your plan. Would you want to pay fees for an advisor who happens to be your boss's golfing buddy? or your CFO's son? Even the illusion of a conflict of interest might cause your employees to be reluctant about sharing pertinent information that would otherwise be helpful to their retirement success.

For sure, you are not required to hire an advisor when you set up and manage a 401(k) plan, but it certainly makes good sense to do so in today's litigious world. Whether your company is a small manufacturer, a multibillion-dollar distributor, a service firm, or a machinery or trucking company, managing your retirement plan is a legal obligation and requires expertise. How much do you know about monitoring investments and determining if 401(k) fees are reasonable? Very few firms, if any, have this know-how. That is why they hire an advisor. It just makes good business sense. A good advisor will save you time so you can focus on running your business. A great advisor can help you create a successful 401(k) that becomes a valuable part of your compensation package, which helps you attract and retain valuable employees.

The good news is that advisory fees can be paid proportionately by your plan participants, so you can engage a co-fiduciary who need not be a cost to your firm. Of course, fiduciary breach, penalties, and legal fees are company expenses and may even be a personal liability for plan fiduciaries. Does it make better business sense to hire an advisor? I'll let you decide.

However, because this is a plan-operating cost, ERISA says you must exercise prudence when selecting an advisor. This is where many firms, especially smaller firms, are likely to run into problems. You see, when 401(k) plans first became popular, many companies set up the plans through someone they already worked with, such as their insurance broker, payroll company, or CPA, or perhaps even the advisor who handled the CEO's personal account. Some firms signed up with a big company with a recognizable name and a flashy sales presentation without ever going through a due diligence process. After all, these plans were often sold as "free" because there were no direct costs to the company. So why the need to be scrutinizing when it's "free"? Of course, by now you have learned these plans carry many layers of fees and expenses, and in some cases, 401(k) fees can be excessive. Even the fee disclosure documents can be convoluted since there is no standardized reporting. Consequently, hiring someone who is not a plan expert may fail to help you fulfill your duty. Managing a 401(k) is complex, and hiring someone lacking the expertise to do it properly can actually be a liability.

If you currently do not have a qualified advisor on your plan, or if you aren't truly satisfied with the care and attention your advisor offers, you should start the process of hiring an expert. For all the reasons explained in *Retire Ready*, it is important to have a dedicated expert help you run a successful plan that gets your employees to retirement. If you have an advisor but are not sure you have hired an expert, now is a good time to assess your advisor. Even if you are happy with your advisor, it is important to review and document the monitoring of all your service providers.

A plan sponsor is better protected from liability risk when it has utilized the expertise of an investment expert. A qualified advisor can decrease your fiduciary risk of acting imprudently. This is because an experienced advisor should know the correct procedures to follow for compliance, the right questions to ask for plan monitoring, and how to document the due diligence process. If you do not have the expertise to appropriately analyze your plan and its investments, know that DOL guidance (along with the courts' direction) implies that plan sponsors have the duty to seek investment expertise. Of course, the mere retention of an advisor is not enough. You cannot simply follow the advice given regardless of the advisor's qualifications. Plan fiduciaries must make their own decisions based on the advice and consider the recommendation carefully. Perhaps an even greater reason to engage a financial advisor is to help your participants make informed investment and financial decisions to support retirement readiness.

This is a highly specialized area, so be careful to hire not just any advisor but one who has the credentials and expertise to help you properly manage your company-sponsored retirement plan. A little due diligence and a few basic questions can help you determine a candidate's qualifications.

INVESTMENT ADVISOR VS. BROKER

What is the difference between an Investment Advisor (IA) and a broker? First of all, both call themselves "financial advisor," so there is no real distinction by title. In reality, so long as your advisor is a plan expert, acknowledges his or her position as a fiduciary by written contract, and charges a fee for service rather than collects a commission, how the person is registered is ultimately of little concern. Fundamentally, both investment advisors and brokers are licensed professionals who assist investors with their financial goals. These days, there's not a great deal of difference between an IA and a broker, and when they act in the capacity of a plan advisor, they are likely acting as an "Investment Advisor" regardless.

In the old days, brokers sold securities to qualified individuals and were paid commissions for the trade. You may remember the term *stockbroker*. When I started in the business, that's exactly what we were called. We may have sold stocks, bonds, or mutual funds, but we pitched investments to affluent investors for a commission. It was about that same time that the industry was beginning to transition to more of a planning-oriented focus, but to be honest, most investors simply weren't ready for it. I remember making many people uncomfortable when I asked them about their retirement plans or wanted to see their investment portfolios or income tax returns. Consumers were still very transaction-minded, and they guarded their privacy. They *wanted* to buy financial products. Your parents or grandparents may never have shared their incomes or net worth with you. That was a different generation—a different time—and people weren't accustomed to talking about their financial information with others.

But, of course, people needed far more than just a good stock or bond. They needed to address their families' life insurance needs, retirement needs, tax strategies, risk management, legacy planning, and so on. The concept was rather new back in 1988, but I understood the depth and breadth of financial planning needs and complexities, and I used my knowledge as a market distinguisher. My competitors were still pitching products while I focused on solving financial problems.

In the late 1990s, the internet introduced a new, much fiercer type of competitor: online trading. Anyone could go online, open a brokerage account, and buy and sell securities *without a broker!* The exchange of information with technological advancements changed the brokerage industry, and within the span of about a decade, clients started asking questions about tax implications of 401(k) rollovers and Required Minimum Distributions. People wanted to know why they needed living trusts and how to address their estate tax problems. Frankly, if a broker couldn't answer the questions, the client found someone who could. So, brokers learned that survival meant transforming their practices from a transaction-based product sales business to a planning-oriented advisory practice.

The expansion of the "Investment Advisor" role, who, by definition, is paid exclusively by fees (either a straight fee for time or a percentage of the assets under management), began to grow as a result, and today clients are embracing the fiduciary duty of an advisor versus the salesperson role of a broker. Investment advisors are legally prohibited from giving investment advice that may conflict with their clients' needs. Today, investment advisors can also be licensed and registered with a broker dealer, so they may collect commissions on certain products that are not structured for fee-based compensation, such as life insurance, retirement annuities, and 529 college plans, because clients need these solutions. Likewise, a broker can be registered as an investment advisor and charge according to a fee-based structure to fulfill the advisory needs. In other words, the lines are now blurred, and one of these professionals is not necessarily better than or superior to the other. Indeed, we are usually acting in both capacities, so ultimately the difference may be inconsequential so long as you have your advisor declared a fiduciary.

What you must know is if the advisor you hire is collecting a fee or a commission or both. All forms of compensation should be transparent, fair, and reasonable, relative to the services rendered. The advisor should state in a written contract that he or she is a plan fiduciary. If these terms are met, the real distinction between advisors is not their titles but rather their service and expertise. At the end of the day, you are hiring the individual based on his or her expertise, competency, communication skills, trust, and likability factor above all else.

3(21) FIDUCIARY OR 3(38) FIDUCIARY

What is the difference between a 3(21) and a 3(38) fiduciary? How do I know which I need, and which is better? It is important a plan sponsor understand the role of an investment advisor and investment manager is provided under the different statutes of ERISA. In other words, to what degree the investment provider is acting as a fiduciary is defined based on her role or in what capacity she is serving. The fiduciary standard itself, and the liability protection provided to you, depend upon the level of services you are utilizing.

A retirement plan advisor can serve as either an ERISA §3(21) investment advisor or an ERISA §3(38) investment manager, and in some cases both. Again, the needs and desires of the plan sponsor typically dictate the specific arrangement. If you want assistance with your fiduciary responsibilities but still want to maintain discretion and control of your plan, you will want to hire an advisor to serve as a 3(21) fiduciary, meaning the advisor is performing *advice-giving* functions. If hired under this arrangement, your advisor will engage in a "sharing" of fiduciary duties and be responsible in a co-liability manner. The advisor renders investment advice for a fee and is legally liable to render advice that is in the participants' best interest. However, the investment committee and/or plan sponsor ultimately retains the right to make the final decisions and has signing authority on the plan. Therefore, whether the advice of the advisor is followed is determined by the plan fiduciaries. The plan fiduciaries hold the duty to make final decisions pertaining to the management of the plan, including investment options or changes, plan design features, and employee communications. If you want to retain the right to make those decisions, you need to hire a 3(21) co-fiduciary. An advisor who serves in this capacity is considered an ERISA §3(21) investment advisor. The scope of his or her services is to act in an advisory role only.

Technically, anyone can be a 3(21) fiduciary if the person chooses to accept such liability. The individual need not be an investment expert. Such fiduciaries are known as "investment advisors" because these professionals are responsible for providing investment advice and/or aiding in investment decisions. Professionals who have the qualifications to do this generally include wealth managers, financial advisors, trust officers, financial consultants, investment consultants, financial planners, and fiduciary advisors. Again, I am of the strong opinion that you should hire someone who is not just an investment advisor but is also an expert of 401(k) plans. You can find plenty of experts willing to serve as a 3(21) fiduciary. Such an advisor is legally obligated to render advice that is in your plan participants' and beneficiaries' best interest. He or she will be responsible for documenting conversations, making recommendations, and keeping track of all meetings and supporting documentation used to render such advice for his or her own protection, just as you do for your plan sponsor decisions. But it is important to understand that a 3(21) fiduciary is not responsible for your decisions, only for the advice.

A 3(38) investment manager, on the other hand, is responsible for making *decisions* and, given this fact, does not render *advice*. Consequently, you cannot engage just anyone to be an ERISA §3(38) investment manager. This role is limited to a specific class of entities who may be appointed to control the investments of a plan, that is, registered investment advisors, banks, and insurance companies. Investment Managers are professionals who have the *discretion* to make investment decisions and manage plan assets. A 3(38) fiduciary is contracted specifically to transfer full discretionary authority of plan investments and make plan investment decisions.

This arrangement goes back to the days of the pension plan when private money managers were hired to manage retirement plan assets. With the 401(k), most plan sponsors offer a menu of investment options, but the plan assets are self-directed by the participant. Therefore, very few plans actually need a 3(38) investment manager. However, if you want to defer your plan's investment menu selection and management decisions to an expert, this may be a better arrangement for you. When we are engaged to act as a 3(38) fiduciary, we retain full discretion over the selection of the investment menu and have full responsibility and authority to add and remove investment options to and from the policy as written in the firm's Investment Policy Statement. We do not involve the plan sponsor in the decision-making. If you prefer to defer investment decisions to experts, you will want to hire a 3(38) advisor. Keep in mind, however, that when it comes to other plan decisions, such as determining matching formulas, creating vesting schedules, and deciding whether to include the Roth option, your advisor will likely render advice on these matters rather than make plan decisions singularly. The question is whether you demand a seat at the table and a voice in the retirement investment decisions made for your employees or whether you want to defer those decisions to someone else. If you seek to share in the decision-making process, know that you will also share in the legal consequences if anything goes wrong.

You may also find that you want to hire an investment manager to offer a custom-managed investment alternative in your investment menu. Perhaps you want to offer a better alternative to the target date funds and you have an advisor who is presenting the ability to manage asset allocation models utilizing lower-cost or more-diversified mutual funds or ETFs. Such an advisor would be making discretionary decisions regarding the allocation and rebalancing of investment models, adding and removing funds, etc. In other words, your advisor would be acting as an investment manager, and in that case, you need a 3(38) fiduciary to maximize liability protection. The key distinction lies in whether you need to hire an advisor who has discretionary decision-making authority or one who provides the plan sponsor and/or committee with advice only.

If you seek an advisor, a 3(38) fiduciary is irrelevant because he or she will be performing functions as an investment *advisor*. However, if you want an investment *manager* with discretionary authority, be sure that you hire a 3(38) fiduciary and clearly understand the agreement. Should you inadvertently hire a 3(21) fiduciary to perform *manager* functions, you will not have the liability protection needed to mitigate the risk and liability for those discretionary decisions. Most plans choose to retain control of the decision-making process and, thus, seek a 3(21) advisor; however, you have options, depending upon what may be the best fit for you. Finally, while a 3(38) arrangement represents the highest level of investment liability transfer possible under ERISA, that doesn't mean a plan sponsor is absolved of all investment-related fiduciary duties. Engaging a 3(38) lessens your investment-related responsibilities and risk; however, the process of selecting and engaging a 3(38) itself is a fiduciary responsibility.

THE SEARCH PROCESS: TO RFP OR NOT

If you feel it is time to start the advisory search process, I suggest you ask for a list of qualified advisors from your ERISA attorney, recordkeeper, CPA, TPA, HR association, or other business professional. You may find the use of a formal advisor search through a request for proposal (RFP) process helpful to efficiently narrow the field of respondents, although an RFP is not always necessary. In fact, it's challenging to get the RFP in front of the right audience. And if I may speak candidly, I don't think the RFP process is effective when initially conducting a 401(k) advisor search. It's time-consuming for you to create an RFP and then sift through the responses. It is equally time-consuming for the advisor to prepare and respond to RFPs when they don't have any opportunity to identify your needs or build any rapport. In the end, it's about whether you like the person and if he or she fits in with your organization. If you have a list of qualified candidates already, you can save a lot of time by setting up preliminary meetings with a few of them.

Did you use an RFP to hire your CPA? How about your corporate attorney? risk management advisor? employment law attorney? business consultant? sales coach? You probably found your most trusted consultants through word-of-mouth or referral, not an old-fashioned and arduous process called the request for proposal. While it's tempting to try to see every potential candidate's proposal and try to transform the search into a beauty contest or a bidding war, hiring a financial advisor based on a swanky proposal is like hiring a dentist based on a fancy brochure or like hiring a CPA who charges the lowest price. Finding a good advisor is no different from hiring a CPA, an attorney, or any other professional consultant. That is why I believe the best process is to line up two or three potential candidates based on referrals and set up meetings. Get to the heart of the matter and save everyone involved some time. I recommend you prepare a list of standard questions to ask, such as those that follow. Also, you will need to be prepared to provide specific details of your plan.

1. How are you going to provide value to us as a plan sponsor?
2. What is your education background?
3. Do you have any advanced education or specialized professional credentials?
4. What licenses do you hold?
5. How long have you been a 401(k) investment advisor?
6. Do you have any customer complaints or disclosures on your record that you care to tell us about?
7. Are there any potential conflicts of interest we need to consider should we choose to engage you?
8. Do you consider yourself a fiduciary under ERISA?
9. If hired, will you acknowledge in writing that you have a fiduciary obligation as an investment advisor?
10. What kind of liability protection and/or limits do you have per client/incident?
11. What percent of your clients are 401(k) plan sponsors?
12. What does your ideal client look like?
13. How do you measure plan success?
14. What kind of tools do you use to help plan sponsors monitor their retirement plan, and are these tools provided by an independent firm or are they developed by your company?
15. What are you most passionate about as an advisor, and how do you translate that into your service model?
16. Do you provide participant-level services, and if so, what is the scope of those services?
17. Do you provide investment education? What is your education policy?
18. What kind of comprehensive retirement planning services do you offer our participants?
19. What is your approach to financial wellness?
20. How many on your team are available to help our participants?

The meeting is also a great opportunity for you to assess how well prepared the advisor is. It should be as much a discovery process for the candidate as it is for you. Much can be gleaned by what is *not* said or *not* asked. Did the candidate ask questions about your goals and objectives? Did the candidate seek to identify potential problems within your plan? How are his or her listening and communication skills? Did he or she explain the engagement process and review the service model with you? These are things that cannot be articulated in an RFP. Ultimately you may eliminate or identify true candidates quicker through a preliminary meeting rather than spending an hour reading a thirty-page proposal. Granted, a proposal should be expected *after* the meeting, and only after having an opportunity to perform a comprehensive review of your plan, but I do not recommend that you lead with the RFP. What you can't see through a colorful proposal is the personality of the advisor. Your own sense is often a better judgment than you can make by reviewing a fancy proposal. Just like interviewing a job candidate, meeting with potential advisors in person allows qualifications, personalities, and capabilities to stand out more than they ever could in a proposal.

The RFP, by comparison, is a conventional pitch. It is a rather impersonal process that tends to completely ignore the essence of the relationship. Advisory services are not transactional. Just as you are not likely to find a great attorney by sending out letters or queries, you are not likely to find the best advisor with an RFP. Remember, anyone can invest some time in creating pretty proposals filled with photos, graphs, and charts. However, that does not ensure competency, delivery, or dependability. I believe you will yield a better pool of qualified potential candidates if you seek recommendations from other professionals and do a little research on your own.

The RFP itself can be convoluted and muddled, typically because the person making the request is frequently unclear about their needs and the different professional roles within the 401(k). It is a waste of time for advisors to respond to a formal request when the parties involved are imprecise about the nature of their request. Plus, you may eliminate great potential candidates by approaching this process so impersonally. Additionally, just as you want to hear the advisor's views on creativity, innovation, inspiration, insight, and intuition, the advisor needs to understand your views of plan goals, motivation, and insight into your duty as a fiduciary. In other words, a successful engagement is a two-way street, and the RFP is a one-way road.

Regardless of how you decide to approach this, you should be willing to provide as much detail about your plan as possible. This includes a plan asset statement, an employee census (obviously omitting employees' personal information), an active versus eligible participant count, participation rates, nondiscrimination testing results, loan utilizations, plan assets, the current investment menu, plan fees and expenses, your different office locations, and information about any other employer-sponsored retirement plan offered, such as deferred compensation or pension. Don't be afraid to disclose information, because the more transparent you are with your potential candidates, the more complete and accurate information you will receive regarding services, support, and fees. I recall a plan sponsor once asking for a proposal but refusing to provide plan details, as if the details would unduly influence my recommendations. To the contrary, I can't help you without full transparency. You wouldn't expect your doctor to offer you treatment without a diagnosis. Don't expect to get a quality advisor without transparency. The more serious you take this process, the better the pool of potential candidates you are likely to have. Needless to say, I passed up the opportunity, to the chagrin of their CPA. Qualified advisors are likely to ignore or dismiss a plan sponsor who is unwilling to share information. Additionally, experts recognize the ineptness of an inexperienced plan sponsor, and an ineffective RFP may be disregarded or rejected.

When you hire an advisor, you are seeking consultative services, which include problem solving and proactive solutions to drive superior results. Holding back information will only prevent you from enlisting the best consultative advisors. What would a prospective doctor do if you told him or her you weren't willing to share your medical information? The doctor would refuse to accept you as a patient. It's a waste of everyone's time to do this halfheartedly.

THE FINALIST PRESENTATION

Upon identifying those who are clearly qualified to serve as your plan advisor, the next step is to invite the finalists to make an in-person formal presentation to your committee. In most cases, qualifications, deliverables, and pricing structure is very competitive among the finalists, so the goal is to identify the best person to hire for the job. There is no set number required to be a part of the finalists' presentations. Larger companies tend to favor three or four finalists, while smaller companies may have only one or two. Regardless, before you get to the final's presentation, you should follow a fundamental due diligence process. This includes a review of the compensation agreement and service contracts. The committee should review the findings after the final presentation to document the process and discuss the pertinent issues. Also, it is important to retain written records of the entire search and review process in the event of an investigation or DOL audit.

Naturally, final candidates should be given sufficient time to assemble their teams and prepare their presentations. The final presentation is an opportunity for the committee to gain a better understanding of the service model, process, methodology, and value of the proposition offered, so it is important to have your committee members attend. The goal is to determine the best fit based on your plan's needs and goals and the personalities of your team members. When hiring an advisor, remember that you are engaging the person responsible for providing advice and guidance, so be sure to assess the candidate's abilities more than the company behind him or her. The final decision should be based on the committee's best judgment of the candidate's fit for the firm and the plan's participants. There should be an alignment of goals and a satisfactory level of comprehensive services provided at a reasonable fee.

For example, you may have a highly qualified candidate who offers a great service contract but who during the final presentation uses technical jargon and speaks over the heads of the investment committee. How is the committee to make decisions about the plan if this advisor doesn't provide information in layperson's terms? It might appear that the candidate is well versed, but there may be a disconnect that could become problematic in the future. Is this individual going to be effective if put in front of your employees? What about the advisor who disparages the competition? Competing advisors should be addressing their merits for the job. Your fiduciary duties demand professionalism and objectivity. What about the presentation? Is the message precise and pithy? Is it well organized? Was the advisor prepared and able to address the particular issues that were important to you, or did he or she fail to tackle the tough questions? Was the presentation jumbled or disorderly? Did the candidate answer questions clearly and completely? Listening skills are as important as presentation skills. Was the method of the plan management process articulated to the committee and easily understood, or was the process overly complicated and difficult to follow? Perhaps there was no process explained (in which case there is cause for other concerns). Are there specific services offered by a candidate that you favor, and how do those differ from others? The final presentation, obviously, is an opportunity to make distinctions between candidates and ultimately to help you make the best hiring decision possible. Be sure to retain documentation of your due diligence process for a period of no less than six years.

HOW ARE ADVISORS PAID?

If you don't know how your financial advisor is getting paid, now is the time to get very clear on the compensation. After all, it is your duty. Most advisors get paid in one of two forms: commissions or fees. Fees can either be flat-dollar or asset-based or a combination of both. Most advisors prefer asset-based because they have a direct incentive to grow the plan assets. Some advisors, especially with smaller plans, receive payment from commissions or revenue sharing arrangements (12b-1 fees), but this can be ambiguous compensation. If you do not have a separate advisory engagement contract with your financial advisor, now is a good time to consider changing the compensation structure. One of the first questions to ask your advisor is "Are you a fiduciary?" If the answer is yes, this should be noted in a contract and the fees should be paid separately in the form of a flat dollar or percentage of assets.

Most advisors negotiate fees based on services rendered, so how much is considered fair and reasonable is a matter of contract. If you want your advisor to provide participant-level services including education and consultations, expect the fees to be potentially twice as much as those charged by advisors who only provide plan sponsor support. While the fees may be higher, your employees may benefit the most from this kind of service. Since your job as a fiduciary is to manage the plan in the best interest of your participants, you can easily argue the value of a strong employee education program.

The advisor fees can be paid by your organization, and if so, monitoring and benchmarking does not have to be done in the same fashion. While it makes good business sense to still do so, remember that ERISA is concerned with your role as a fiduciary (caring for your employees' money). The fiduciary standards-of-care requirements only apply if your participants are paying the fee. Of course, I suspect if you were paying such fees, you would carefully monitor the advisor since it makes good business sense to do so. However, most 401(k) plans charge the advisor fees to the plan assets. If you follow suit, it is equally important to know how your advisor is getting paid. You have a legal duty to assess and monitor advisor fees, just as you do with all other fees assessed against your plan.

The rationale for charging fees to the plan is simple. The advisor provides services required to properly maintain the plan for the benefit of the employees. Every plan needs an investment expert at the very least. Consequently, each participant is paying a proportionate share of the fees. If you choose not to provide participant education in your advisor service agreement, your advisor can help monitor the investments and support other key drivers within your plan that directly impact participant retirement success. However, as already noted, employee education can be a big value-added benefit for everyone involved. If you are unclear about the ERISA rules regarding your fee structure with your advisor, it is recommended that you review the arrangement with an ERISA attorney.

THE ONBOARDING PROCESS

Once the selection is made, the advisor will formally accept the offer, and then an engagement contract or agreement is put in place. At that time, the onboarding process begins. In most cases, the first step is to

On Boarding Process

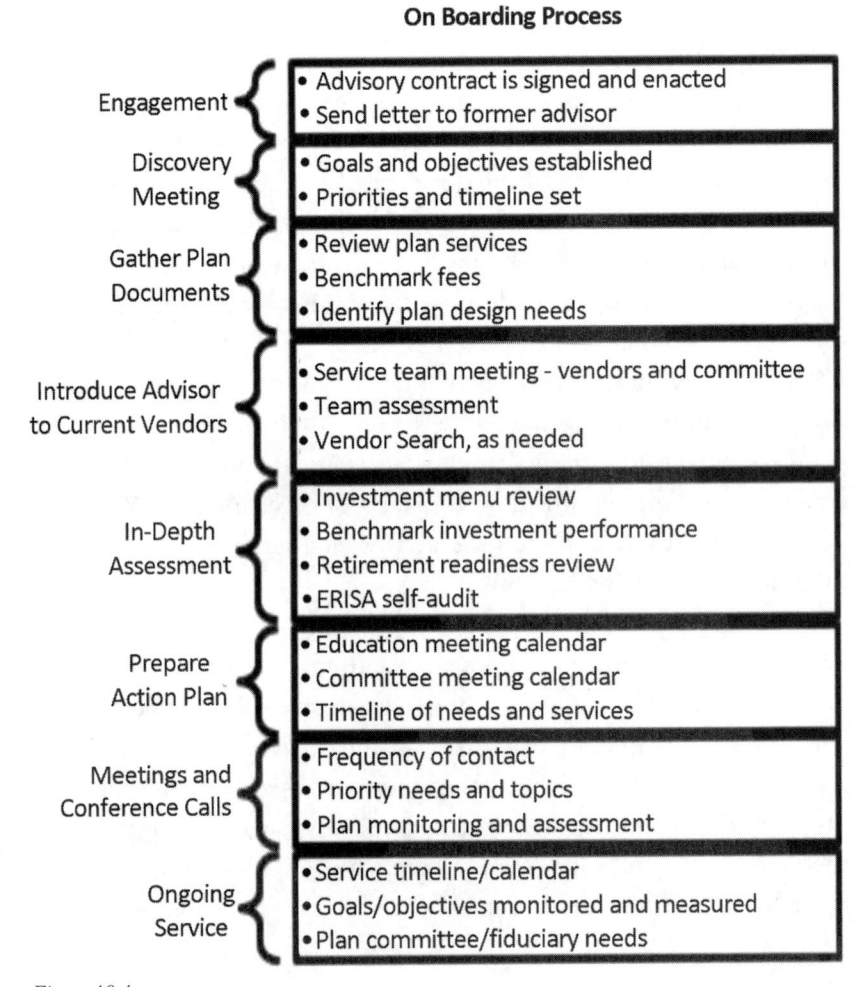

Engagement	• Advisory contract is signed and enacted • Send letter to former advisor
Discovery Meeting	• Goals and objectives established • Priorities and timeline set
Gather Plan Documents	• Review plan services • Benchmark fees • Identify plan design needs
Introduce Advisor to Current Vendors	• Service team meeting - vendors and committee • Team assessment • Vendor Search, as needed
In-Depth Assessment	• Investment menu review • Benchmark investment performance • Retirement readiness review • ERISA self-audit
Prepare Action Plan	• Education meeting calendar • Committee meeting calendar • Timeline of needs and services
Meetings and Conference Calls	• Frequency of contact • Priority needs and topics • Plan monitoring and assessment
Ongoing Service	• Service timeline/calendar • Goals/objectives monitored and measured • Plan committee/fiduciary needs

Figure 10.1

clean up the plan and get it aligned to the goals and objectives, which may involve modifications to plan design or investment menu lineup. Conference calls or in-person meetings typically take place, perhaps as often as weekly, with all parties to discuss the progress, duties, and responsibilities. No one person within your firm should shoulder all the responsibilities, which is why the retirement committee is critical in this process. If you don't have a formal committee, you should be sure your advisor is capable and willing to help you formally establish one. The services provided will be included in the advisor contract and will likely include providing fiduciary education to everyone involved. Figure 10.1 highlights an example of our onboarding process which, as you can see, is a comprehensive process that looks out over the next twelve months, however most of the work is done in the first three months. The onboarding process ends when the plan sponsor is satisfied that all necessary policies and procedures are in place and are documented properly and that the plan is set to operate accordingly.

Although the onboarding process may have ended, the monitoring and maintenance process will continue indefinitely. This should include annual self-audit support, employee education and support, and plan committee reviews. An education calendar should be established if participant-level services are included in the engagement, as should a committee calendar. Typically, the first twelve to twenty-four months of onboarding a new advisor will involve a monthly activity of some sort to get the plan up to speed, whether it is conference calls, meetings, or specific reviews such as an ERISA self-audit assessment. Be prepared to invest some time in the process as this will determine the success of the advisory relationship and the quality of the work to make your retirement benefit the best it can be for your participants.

ADVISOR EVALUATION

For a quick evaluation of the services and effectiveness of your current plan financial advisor, complete the following assessment questions. It is recommended the evaluation and results are reviewed with your plan committee.

		Clearly	To Some Extent	Not at All	Unsure
Regulatory					
1.	The advisor has provided written verification of his 3(21) or 3(38) fiduciary status.	☐	☐	☐	☐
2.	The advisor has a high degree of knowledge of and experience with the fiduciary and regulatory requirements of plan oversight and has demonstrated competency in fulfilling his duties.	☐	☐	☐	☐
3.	I am confident there are no unidentified conflicts of interest with respect to commissions or incentives that may unduly influence our advisor's recommendations.	☐	☐	☐	☐
4.	Our fees and 408(b)(2) statement have been reviewed and compared to the market to ensure our fees are fair and reasonable.	☐	☐	☐	☐
5.	The advisor has advanced education and credentials specific to the qualified plan market.	☐	☐	☐	☐
6.	The advisor conducts annual self-audit ERISA compliance reviews to ensure our plan is in order.	☐	☐	☐	☐
7.	The advisor has read and reviewed our Investment Policy Statement within the past year.	☐	☐	☐	☐
8.	We have a formalized plan committee that meets regularly for plan management or oversight and our advisor is fully engaged in these meetings.	☐	☐	☐	☐
9.	Our advisor reviews our fidelity bond and fiduciary insurance policy regularly to ensure we understand and have adequate coverage.	☐	☐	☐	☐
10.	Our advisor helps us with our meeting minutes and supporting documentation to demonstrate our due diligence process.	☐	☐	☐	☐
11.	A provider search has been conducted within the past three years.	☐	☐	☐	☐

ADVISOR EVALUATION

For a quick evaluation of the services and effectiveness of your current plan financial advisor, complete the following assessment questions. It is recommended the evaluation and results are reviewed with your plan committee.

		Clearly	To Some Extent	Not at All	Unsure
12.	Our plan passes annual testing and our HCE's are able to adequately contribute to the 401(k).	☐	☐	☐	☐
13.	I am confident that our fiduciary responsibilities are being fulfilled.	☐	☐	☐	☐
14.	I am confident our internal controls and documentation will pass a DOL investigation.	☐	☐	☐	☐

Investments and Plan Design

		Clearly	To Some Extent	Not at All	Unsure
1.	Our advisor has a high degree of knowledge of and experience with qualified plan investment management.	☐	☐	☐	☐
2.	We follow the policies defined in our Investment Policy Statement.	☐	☐	☐	☐
3.	We regularly add or remove funds to conform with our Investment Policy Statement.	☐	☐	☐	☐
4.	Our investment menu is monitored and benchmarked at least annually.	☐	☐	☐	☐
5.	We are using the lowest cost share class available by our recordkeeper.	☐	☐	☐	☐
6.	If applicable, the committee understands our target date funds glide path, risk and expenses.	☐	☐	☐	☐
7.	I am confident our QDIA meets ERISA requirements and that we exercise the limited safe harbor relief as defined under 404(c).	☐	☐	☐	☐
8.	Our investment menu offers competitive pricing, performance and risk relative to our peers and covers a diverse range of asset classes as defined in our IPS.	☐	☐	☐	☐
9.	Our advisor provides recommendations that support improving participation, contributions and investment outcome potential.	☐	☐	☐	☐
10.	Our advisor keeps us current with plan design options, benefits, features and best practices to optimize our plan performance.	☐	☐	☐	☐

ADVISOR EVALUATION					
For a quick evaluation of the services and effectiveness of your current plan financial advisor, complete the following assessment questions. It is recommended the evaluation and results are reviewed with your plan committee.					
		Clearly	To Some Extent	Not at All	Unsure
Participant Level					
1.	Our advisor regularly conducts effective participant education meetings.	☐	☐	☐	☐
2.	The education meetings are engaging, productive and cover a broad range of financial wellness topics.	☐	☐	☐	☐
3.	The results from our education program are measured and feedback is gathered from employees.	☐	☐	☐	☐
4.	Individual discussions are available, so employees can address personal needs and concerns with a retirement specialist.	☐	☐	☐	☐
5.	Alternative educational presentations are available such as webinars, conference calls, podcasts, etc. as needed to reach our diverse employee base.	☐	☐	☐	☐
6.	Our advisor helps boost participation, increase salary deferrals and promotes retirement readiness within our organization.	☐	☐	☐	☐
7.	Our employees are gaining financial literacy with the help of our advisor.	☐	☐	☐	☐
8.	We are comfortable with the number of employees who are currently on track for retirement readiness.	☐	☐	☐	☐

Figure 10.2.

HOW DO I KNOW IF MY ADVISOR MEASURES UP?

As already mentioned, there are a limited number of advisors who are retirement plan specialists. Still, there is no standard for service and support, so you need to make sure your advisor measures up to your firm's needs and continues to meet expectations. If you haven't seen or heard from your advisor in six months or more, it's a good indication you need to do an assessment and perhaps begin a new search.

I've provided an advisor assessment in figure 10.2 to help. As you will see, there are many questions that should be considered when hiring and overseeing a professional advisor. Use the scorecard and see how your advisor measures up. This is a review of thirty-three different types of support provided by a great advisor. If you can answer confidently that you are mostly clear on these assessment questions, consider yourself quite fortunate to have a competent advisor who has clearly made your 401(k) a priority for service and support. Of course, you still need to monitor your advisor and document your due diligence as a part of your fiduciary requirements (including fee comparisons). But, naturally, don't expect to get outstanding support at average or below-average costs. That formula generally won't work. Your employees' retirement readiness may be at stake, because great advisors will simply move on to work with clients who value and are willing to pay for their dedication. There is only so much time in a day, and an advisor cannot support an infinite number of clients.

On the other hand, if your advisor is scoring below average, with most of your responses being "unsure" or "not at all," it may be time to conduct an advisor search. There is no good justification to have an advisor collecting fees for services not rendered. In fact, it is your duty as a fiduciary to act in the best interest of your participants and their beneficiaries, which includes ensuring your participants are not paying excessive fees. Certainly, a poor advisor collecting any fee could be classified as unfair and unreasonable. Remember, it's not just the recordkeeper or administrative fees that must be monitored, but also the advisor fees.

Since it is your duty to monitor fees, your advisor should be reviewing your fee disclosure 408(b)(2) and benchmarking these fees for you periodically. Revenue sharing arrangements, proprietary funds, and other potential "hidden fees" or conflicts of interest should be identified in order to permit an objective review. Remember, the 408(b)(2) is subject to ambiguous information, so your advisor should be able to help you scrutinize the fees more thoroughly. This process should be reviewed and documented by the committee in an objective discussion. If your advisor hasn't recommended a fee benchmark within the last three years, it's time to ask questions. Likewise, your committee should not be passively engaged but actively asking to be involved in the oversight of your plan.

In order to assess the quality of the service from the recordkeeper, a light search should be conducted every few years. Your advisor can initiate this if it is included in your service contract. In addition, your 5500 form should be reviewed by your advisor periodically to ensure your TPA did not overlook something, such as 404(c) safe harbor relief. The Department of Labor periodically review 5500 filings to seek out potential audit flags. You certainly don't want to raise audit flags for either the DOL or the IRS. Plan provisions should be followed, vesting schedules and loans should be reviewed, and you should ensure there are no prohibited transactions. Annual compliance self-assessments should be completed to check your due diligence with your plan. Your fidelity bond coverage and fiduciary insurance should be reviewed. A fiduciary check should be completed at least once a year, including a review of the fiduciary audit file. You can see these services go far beyond the scope of investment monitoring. If your advisor is a generalist, he or she may be unqualified to offer this level of full-service support.

Of course, investment monitoring should be a part of the process as well. This goes beyond investment benchmarking and includes reviewing your Investment Policy Statement, your investment menu, selected asset classes and their suitability in the current economic environment, share classes of your funds and a careful consideration of alternative options if any. The process involves scrutinizing your QDIA, investment performance, risk, peer group comparisons, benchmark comparisons, participant self-directed asset allocation choices, assess overall risk for participants, and be sure to have a firm understanding of the glide path for your selected Target Date Funds, if applicable. Not only does this help ensure you are offering the most competitive and attractive investment menu, but also it will help determine your participants' education requirements.

Speaking of employee education, not all advisors include comprehensive education programs in their contracts. However, since this is a critical component to help drive retirement success, you may want to reevaluate the service contract and reassess the need and desire for this service. Group education meetings are very helpful not only to promote enrollment but also, and more importantly, to develop your workforce's financial competency. If your advisor only does enrollment meetings, it might be a good time to discuss and/or review alternative educational programs that go beyond enrollment. In fact, today plan sponsors are seeking to incorporate financial wellness into their employee education programs. This covers more comprehensive issues like budgeting and debt management, insurance needs, college savings, and other important financial topics that may seem to extend beyond retirement but that can directly impact one's retirement savings. One-on-one meetings are also very helpful in enhancing the retirement success potential for your employees. The ability to offer your employees sit-down meetings with a qualified advisor to ask personal financial questions can go far in driving retirement readiness. But, of course, this is only offered with a comprehensive service model. Expect there to be additional fees for this type of support.

Retirement readiness tracks the percentage of your employees who are on track to meet their retirement needs based on set criteria. It's a good idea to have an advisor who measures this progress regularly with the committee and sets education goals to drive that number higher. After all, what is the purpose of the 401(k) if not to help your employees get to a secure retirement?

IN SUMMARY

The retirement industry continues to evolve, and so does the role of the financial advisor. While once upon a time an advisor simply sold plans, the new specialist's role is evolving as liabilities are increasing. Differentiating the roles of different financial advisors and recognizing those who have expertise is more important than ever. An advisor can educate you, guide you through your options in the fiduciary maze, and help you smoothly run a plan. Of course, to ensure impartiality, your advisor should not have any compensation incentives with the provider, including commissions.

If your advisor is not fulfilling his or her duties proactively and without conflicts of interest, it may be time to shop for a new advisor. A great advisor can make the difference between an okay plan and a great one. It can make the difference for you as a plan sponsor between a tedious process filled with headaches and confusion and one that is smooth and easy. To ensure a great experience for you, your committee, and your employees, engage a plan expert who can help you run the best plan possible—a plan that is positioned for retirement success for your employees. Your employees need the best help they can get, and your advisor may play the most important and most direct role in helping them retire ready!

CHAPTER 11
DEPARTMENT OF LABOR INVESTIGATIONS AND PLAN AUDITS

Dear Sir or Madam:

The Employee Benefits Security Administration of the US Department of Labor has responsibility for the administration and enforcement of Title I of the Employee Retirement Income Security Act of 1974 ("ERISA"). Title I established standards governing the operation of employee benefits plans such as the [your company name here] Welfare Plan (the "Plan").

The office has scheduled a review of the above-mentioned plan to determine compliance with the provisions of ERISA ...

The last thing you want is to get such a letter from the Department of Labor (DOL). An audit, or investigation, by the DOL or the IRS can be an employer nightmare. If you were to get such a letter, it would surely cause anxiety, especially if your plan files were not in order. The purpose of a DOL investigation is to look at specific documents and processes you have established with a focus on ensuring the assets within the plan are being managed in favor of your participants. Consequently, it is important that you have documents in order and that your oversight process is defined, understood, and followed diligently.

A Department of Labor or IRS audit is different from an annual

401(k) CPA audit. The federal law requires an annual CPA audit for all 401(k) plans with 100 participants, but the audit may be delayed until there are 125 participants. (Refer to chapter 2 for details.) The purpose is to protect the best interest of participants and ensure your plan is operating in compliance with the federal regulations set by the IRS and DOL. These regulations ensure compliance of written plan documents as well as certify that all plan financial information is accurately reported. An annual CPA audit is required for "large plans."

In addition, every year the IRS and Department of Labor conduct thousands of their own audits or investigations. While IRS audits focus on the compliance of your 401(k) with the Internal Revenue Code, DOL investigations focus on violations of the Employee Retirement Income Security Act of 1974 (ERISA). It is important to keep in mind that the IRS and the DOL enforce different laws, so the scope of the audit will vary based on the agency conducting investigation. The IRS has primary jurisdiction over the tax-qualified status of retirement plans, which includes examining plans and processing requests for determination letters to ensure the plan meets the requirements for the tax status. As a result, IRS audits generally focus on compliance with the Internal Revenue Code. By comparison, the Department of Labor enforces ERISA and has the authority to conduct civil and criminal investigations of employee benefit plans. Consequently, DOL audits generally focus on violations of ERISA, including fiduciary issues, prohibited transactions, and reporting/disclosure problems. Over the last several years, auditors at both agencies appeared to be increasingly focusing on the internal controls that plan sponsors maintain for their employee benefit plans. At the same time, heightened compliance requirements make it very evident that employers need help prioritizing their efforts at managing their internal controls.

If you aren't mindful of audit risks, you should be. In March of 2010, the DOL announced a joint initiative with the IRS to improve enforcement of workplace laws, and the results have been astonishing. In 2015, over twenty-four hundred DOL investigations were closed, resulting in fines for 67 percent of those entities investigated. The reported number of plans audited and the fines assessed are both rising, with average fines today reportedly assessed at $600,000. The Department of Labor has an expanded $183 million budget for enforcement. Given our retirement crisis, it's no surprise that audits are on the rise. Even firms with just two employees are at risk. Additionally, the DOL's audit force is being expanded with the addition of over one thousand investigators a year. The risks of a DOL audit are increasing for plan sponsors of all sizes. With this in mind, it might be helpful for you to understand the compliance issues that are the most often cited by the IRS and DOL.

Keep in mind, audits may not be just for the one year. In fact, the DOL can go back a minimum of three years and will often go back up to six years if a substantial error is identified. The agency may be willing to sign a tolling agreement with a plan sponsor, which can stop time from running on the statute of limitations. This allows the auditor to complete the audit and resolve any concerns and also minimizes the risk that a plan sponsor will get stuck with penalties that could have been avoided. As you can imagine, engaging an ERISA attorney during an audit is generally a wise business decision.

Audits can be quite involved, costly, and very tedious. Therefore, you may want to review some of the reasons your plan could be identified for an audit, such as:

- A participant complained about a possible violation under ERISA, COBRA, HIPAA, or ACA law.
- The IRS referred your case to the DOL.
- The DOL used its database to identify red flags based on your 5500 filing (while screening for plans, they had reason to believe yours was out of compliance).

Audits are usually precipitated by information contained on Form 5500 or by phone calls to the Department of Labor from discontented plan participants. Approximately $400 million in benefits is restored annually just through participant complaints alone. However, some audits are simply random. Former DOL auditors have confided that they will sometimes identify a potentially problematic retirement plan for audit and then randomly pick other retirement plans in the same geographical region to audit in order to maximize their time and resources. Of course, a DOL or IRS official will never tell you exactly why your plan was selected for an audit, but after reviewing your plan records and reports, an ERISA professional may be able to pinpoint the issue. There is usually at least one issue the regulators have isolated. IRS and DOL auditors are highly trained to identify areas of noncompliance. Suffice it to say, they know the laws, rules, and requirements, and they probably know them better than you do.

Although audits by the IRS and DOL cover many similar areas, each agency will have a different audit focus. The Internal Revenue Service will want to review a plan's historical operations and the documentation supporting your plan's processes, such as your plan's definition of compensation, allocation of deferrals, and employer matching contributions; nondiscrimination testing (ADP and ACP); hardship distributions; and the timing of your payroll deposits into the plan. The IRS is looking at your plan for lapses in IRS compliance. The DOL will primarily examine areas of potential participant discrimination, prohibited transactions, evaluate your prudent investment oversight, ensure you are following the proper engagement of service providers, processing plan distributions correctly, sending out required employee notices, processing beneficiary designations and consents, and review your plan documents. An audit conducted by the US Department of Labor will examine different aspects of your plan to make sure that your operations are fully compliant with ERISA. The main purpose of the DOL in conducting these audits is to examine and/or correct a specific issue raised by either a complaint or a discrepancy that generated a red flag. The main purpose of the IRS audit is to verify that you manage your plan according to its written terms and meet operational requirements. Regardless of what triggers the audit, the intention behind either of these audits is to ensure that the assets within your company's benefit plan are managed for the sole benefit of your employees.

Since your plan is at risk for an audit at any time, the question is, how well would you fare if your plan and internal controls were scrutinized by the IRS or DOL today? If you aren't confident that you have taken the right steps to safeguard yourself as a plan fiduciary, protect your company from costly fines, penalties, or litigation, and secure your participants' interest by following the correct procedures and ensuring adequate internal controls are being followed, now is certainly the time to make sure you aren't exposed to undue risk. To do this, it's best to take certain steps, not just today but on an ongoing basis. The objective is to know if (or perhaps, more accurately, when) an audit is conducted, you can support your case. Ideally, you are prepared for an audit *before* being contacted by the IRS or DOL. I recommend plan sponsors conduct regular plan compliance reviews, otherwise known as annual self-audits, with their 401(k) advisory teams. These reviews give you the opportunity to establish or modify internal procedures and controls and keep current on your responsibilities. Your entire fiduciary committee should be involved, at least to review the overview of the self-audit procedure and findings, since each fiduciary is at risk for any violation or fiduciary breach.

Another benefit of a documented self-audit is that it may demonstrate good faith to a government agency should there be the need. It is good management practice to periodically review all plan documents, participant disclosures, and administrative forms to ensure accuracy and compliance with regulatory requirements. Your 401(k) advisor may help facilitate this. You may also want to coordinate with an ERISA attorney to get a legal perspective on your internal controls. A self-assessment goes beyond a CPA audit and evaluates how well you are meeting the fiduciary standards of care. There are approximately eighty different areas that are reviewed by my firm when we do a self-assessment for a client, including a review of administrative practices and procedures, specifically with finance and payroll staff; a review of fee agreements; and an evaluation of the responsibilities of outside vendors. If you are not conducting an annual assessment, it may be time to reconsider your need for checks and balances for your plan.

The DOL is concerned with proper processes and procedures. They look for internal monitoring, documentation, reporting, and operational practices so this is where your due diligence will be critical. The IRS looks for internal controls, and many parts of the investigation from IRS and DOL overlap. Some of the more commonly overlooked items you will want to check on are as follows:

Plan Documents – Having out-of-date plan documents could be the first misstep that leads to penalties being assessed. Incomplete or sloppy documents will most certainly work against you. Plan documents need to be regularly updated to comply with tax law changes, and there are different time frames for different types of amendments. For instance, "discretionary" amendments generally include amendments that a plan sponsor makes by choice, such as adding a new loan feature or a new matching benefit formula, and these amendments must be adopted in writing by the end of the plan year in which they are effective. "Interim" amendments are made to comply with a change in tax law requirements, and such amendments typically have specific required dates. The IRS requires that plan documents be updated and resubmitted for review and approval, called a plan restatement, approximately every six years. Also, make sure your plan documents are signed. While this seems like an obvious step, you would be surprised to learn how often it is overlooked. The lack of signatures could lead to unnecessary complications.

Employer Match Contributions – If you offer an employer match, you need to make sure that all participating employees received their matching contributions as per the agreement on time. Be sure you understand how compensation is defined and which form of compensation is entitled to matching, especially if you have employees who are paid bonuses or commissions. This also applies if you have a Profit-Sharing Plan.

Loan Documentation – Audit failures due to plan loans are one of the top five problem areas identified in IRS audits, and it is also a top issue with the DOL. One of the simplest things that many employers fail to keep track of is their plan loan procedures. If your 401(k) allows participants to take loans, you need to make sure that documents and loan payments are up to date, including loan applications, terms, and repayment schedules. Your documents must specify the procedures for applying for a loan and the repayment terms for the loan. Repayment of the loan (outside of home purchase loans) must occur within five years, and payments must be made in substantially equal payments, including principal and interest. Payments must be paid at least *quarterly*. Defaulted loans need to be treated as a taxable distribution and adhered to as written by the plan documents in terms of timing.

In-Service Distribution Rules – The IRS looks for errors in payments made to plan participants while they are still employed, such as hardship withdrawals or in-service withdrawals. Hardship withdrawal procedures must be followed carefully, including a six-month suspension of contributions. Many plan sponsors neglect to follow the established procedures for proof and documentation of a qualified hardship.

It is your job to ensure hardship withdrawal procedures are not being abused by participants.

Individuals' Roles – Oftentimes, there is more than one person within an organization involved with administering a retirement plan. If this is the case for you, you will want to make sure you know who does what within your office and also make sure those employees understand and follow your internal controls. These individuals should also be prepared and available to answer any questions by investigators when the plan undergoes an audit.

Definition of Compensation According to Your Plan Documents – The plan's definition of compensation is used for a variety of important purposes including the calculation of an employee's allocation, adherence to limitations on allowable compensation under Code §415, performing nondiscrimination testing, and determining whether a plan is top-heavy under §416. The plan's definition of compensation may be the same for each purpose, or it may differ. Make sure you know how compensation is defined within your plan, how it applies to different components of your plan, and that there is consistency in following the definition for all plan calculations.

Target Date Funds (TDFs) or "Life-Cycle Funds" – These funds are currently a focus for the DOL. A target date fund is a fund designed to provide a blend of different types of investments (such as stocks, bonds, and cash) all wrapped up in a single fund and aligned to the retirement date of the participant. Although the principal value of a TDF isn't guaranteed at any time, the fund's allocation and risk is designed to change over time so that as a participant gets older, the investment mix moves toward more conservative investments. The DOL has released detailed guidance on what plan fiduciaries should understand about their plan's target date funds, which clearly states plan fiduciaries must obtain information adequate to evaluate their TDFs. Fiduciaries must understand the differences between various TDFs and must document how and why they selected the specific TDFs in their plan. Plan sponsors should fully understand how their plan's TDF operates (i.e., with a "through" or "to" glide path) and make sure they are complying with DOL monitoring requirements.

Revenue Sharing and 12b-1 Fees – The DOL has indicated that it will increase its focus on a plan's use of revenue sharing and 12b-1 fees. The DOL recently released an advisory opinion in which it made clear that plan fiduciaries must understand the formula, methodology, and assumptions used to determine any revenue generated from plan investments and ensure the arrangement for revenue allocation is handled correctly, meaning applied as expected. The revenue sharing fees paid to providers must be fair and reasonable, the plan must ensure it is being credited with the correct amounts, and the payments must be applied as agreed in the plan documents.

Float – The DOL is also focusing more on a plan's use of "float." *Float* means the earnings that a service provider, trustee, or Third-Party Administrator accrues as a result of holding funds in an account for a short-term period. Recent case law has raised questions about whether these earnings belong to the plan and, hence, the plan participants, or whether they belong to the plan's service provider. The DOL takes the position that float should be regarded as part of the service provider's compensation for services related to a plan, and they will ask about float compensation during plan audits, including the assessment of fair and reasonable fees. If you aren't familiar with how your provider uses float, now is a good time to have that conversation.

Consultants and Investment Manager Monitoring – Another issue for the DOL is how plan fiduciaries select and monitor consultants and investment managers. Plan fiduciaries should adhere to DOL recommendations regarding hiring plan consultants or investment managers and identify whether the consultant or advisor has any conflicts of interest. For example, does the advisor get a bonus based on business placed with a particular recordkeeper or investment firm? Does the advisor receive additional compensation from "preferred vendors"? What is the policy on receiving gifts from vendors the advisor does business with? Another thing to do is to confirm whether the consultant or advisor is a fiduciary. If so, have the advisor put this in writing via your engagement contract. Also, it is good to know if your advisor maintains adequate E&O (errors and omissions) insurance coverage and to have the details of the amount of protection they carry. Finally, are the advisor's fees reasonable? Document your process for proper assessment.

Late Payroll Deposits – One of the most common DOL audit issues continues to be the timing of when participant contributions can reasonably be segregated from payroll and then turned over to the plan trustee. The DOL will examine your payroll process to be sure you are depositing contributions within a reasonable period of time. In recent years, the DOL has implied it believes three days should be the maximum period of time it takes to allocate participants' contributions to the plan, although it maintains a seven-day safe harbor for small plans (with fewer than one hundred participants). Of course, depending on the payroll information, the DOL may conclude that a specific plan's maximum may even be fewer than three days.

ERISA Fidelity Bonds – Another common plan failure noted by the DOL is a plan's inadequate maintenance of an ERISA fidelity bond. ERISA §412 generally requires that every fiduciary of an employee benefit plan and every person who handles funds or other property of such a plan be bonded. ERISA's bonding requirements are intended to protect employee benefit plans from risk of loss due to fraud or dishonesty on the part of fiduciaries. A fiduciary bond must be for at least 10 percent of the amount of plan assets, subject to $500,000 maximum ($1 million maximum for plans that hold employer stock). Errors that arise include failure to maintain the required amount, bonds that require a deductible, failure to name the plan as the insured, and failure to cover all individuals who handle plan assets. Plan fiduciaries should obtain a copy of their ERISA fidelity bond and review it periodically to ensure compliance with ERISA requirements. (Note that this is different from fiduciary insurance, discussed later in this chapter.)

Blackout Notices – The DOL consistently requests copies of any blackout notices during audits. Therefore, plan sponsors should know the blackout rules and make sure that the blackout notices are properly distributed and contain the right information when required. Employers also should make sure they keep a copy of the blackout notice in their plan records, along with all the appropriate distribution dates, since they will be required to demonstrate to the DOL that the notice was provided if the plan gets audited. Refer to chapter 4 for more details regarding Blackout Notices.

Investment Policy/Guidelines – The DOL will want to review a plan's Investment Policy Statement (IPS) to ensure that the plan adheres to the policy or guidelines it has adopted. Plan fiduciaries should know and understand their plan's IPS, which means the policy should be reviewed regularly with your plan investment committee members. Plan committee members should always refer to their Investment Policy Statement when discussing any changes to plan investments since this document provides written guidelines for investment management and monitoring. It is also recommended to note the IPS reference in your meeting minutes. Although an IPS is not required, it can help prove that guidelines have been defined and are being followed. Of course, you want to make sure your IPS fits your plan goals and is written so that the policies can reasonably be followed by your committee. Your advisor or ERISA attorney can help you review, write, or rewrite your Investment Policy Statement.

Plan Committee Meetings – There is no defined rule pertaining to the frequency of committee meetings. Because ERISA does not specifically state how often designated fiduciaries must meet to perform their duties, best practices are used as a general guideline. Most plan committees meet quarterly, but there is no defined ERISA rule. However, a minimum of semiannual meetings may prove prudent. The DOL will always ask for copies of all plan committee minutes, sometimes spanning several years. The inference is clear—committee meetings are expected, so take that duty seriously. Minutes of the meeting should be taken during the actual committee meeting, not after the fact, when one's memory may be sketchy. Include any written materials presented at the meeting as attachment and maintain all records in a safe place and in an orderly manner. Without minutes, it will be difficult to demonstrate the process followed by plan fiduciaries no matter how prudent it may have been. It makes sense to review the meeting notes before they are filed to ensure the minutes say enough about what went on at the meeting to be a helpful reminder of what happened but that they do not contain incomplete notes, which can be ambiguous, raise unanswered questions, or appear to present unaddressed conflicts of interest. Remember, the minutes demonstrate your due diligence and will serve as your defense if your plan is ever challenged through investigation or litigation. You don't want your minutes to note that the committee reviewed XYZ investment because the performance of the fund was below the benchmark but then fail to mention what was to be done about the problem, as that will raise more questions than provide answers about your procedures. In fact, it's a good practice to review prior meeting minutes briefly with the plan committee at the beginning of each meeting to identify any tasks or items that may need to be addressed, such as funds that may have been placed "on watch" or a discussion that was initiated on implementing a plan change. Proper meeting minutes are essential to keeping your plan in good standing and maintaining your personal liability shield.

Changing Recordkeepers – When you are changing plan recordkeepers, the underlying documents and information must be transferred from the old recordkeeper to the new recordkeeper. All required plan information needs to be available in case of a DOL plan review. The DOL often requests information related to previous years, and there is no acceptable excuse for missing records, such as "the records were destroyed." Documentation should support the rationale for the recordkeeper change, the due diligence, the review and approval process including fee comparisons, the service model review, and any additional supporting information that led to the selection of the new recordkeeper, along with account data and reconciliation of account balances, loans, vesting schedules, etc.

While the above are all very important steps to take in the day-to-day management of your plan, another step you need to take is to make sure that you have up-to-date information on your plan participants, including terminated employees. You need to demonstrate that you are able to locate and communicate with them on a regular basis. Staying on top of all this will ensure that if a question is raised in an audit, you will be able to provide all the documentation necessary to prove that you are handling your responsibilities appropriately and in compliance with law, guidelines, and best practices.

Clearly, there are numerous steps employers should be taking to make sure they, as plan sponsors, remain in compliance with IRS and DOL requirements. As you read through the foregoing list, you may conclude that your internal controls need a little more attention. The objective is to avoid costly fines and fees and to do a good job running your plan for the benefit of your employees. Upon reviewing your procedures and comparing them to these guidelines, you may conclude it is time to engage experts to assist you to mitigate these risks. If you are not prepared, a DOL audit can result in a tremendous amount of stress, time, and money.

The following list itemizes common documents the DOL will ask to review during an audit. As you can see, the list is extensive. There are hundreds of different plan details reviewed and addressed. This list can serve as a standard guide for your internal controls and self-assessed annual audits. Of course, the requested items may extend beyond this list, so you should be prepared to provide additional information as required, particularly if your plan holds any unusual investments or has additional complexities.

1. Plan documents
   a. Adoption agreement
   b. Amendment(s)
   c. IRS determination letter
   d. Trust agreement(s) and amendments
2. Most recent Summary Plan Description (SPD)
3. Summary Annual Reports (SARs).
4. Summaries of Material Modifications (SMMs), if applicable
5. Forms 5500 (signed copies), together with all attachments, including accountant's opinion, financial statements, and notes on the financial statement
6. Most current ERISA bond

7. Fiduciary liability insurance policy, if any
8. Year-end trust statements
9. Minutes of any meetings related to the plan and any attachments or supporting documentation
10. Blackout Notices, if applicable.
11. A sample quarterly individual benefit statement provided to Plan participants from the most recent quarter
12. Service provider agreements, including all fee schedules and description of services
13. Summary pages of payroll reports showing employee contributions and loan repayments, if applicable
14. Contribution history report for the Plan, including the date and amount of each deposit to the Plan broken down by employee contributions, employer contributions, and loan repayments
15. Company information
    a. A list of the company owners and shareholders, with names of officers and members of the board of directors
    b. List of all companies and affiliates
    c. Copy of participation agreements signed by any participating employers, if applicable
    d. Articles of incorporation and bylaws for the company
16. A list of custodians where all assets are on deposit, by name, address, and account
    a. Individuals or trustees who have authority to:
        1. Make deposits
        2. Transfer plan assets or make distributions
        3. Make investment changes
        4. Change the administration of the Plan
17. Parties and Entities
    a. A list of "parties-in -interest" as defined by ERISA Section 3(14)
    b. Documents sufficient to show the Plan's and the company's accountants/auditors, attorneys, appraisers, independent

fiduciaries, investment managers, investment advisers, insurance representatives, and investment:
1. the names of the individuals, company or firm, address and telephone number; and the year(s) served as an official of the plan
18. Plan's Investment Policy Statement, if any
19. Forfeited account balance statement showing the forfeitures are segregated from the employees' accounts
20. Documents describing any investments not held by the Plan custodian
21. Plan expenses (including fees and commissions); copies of all invoices or documents upon which plan expenses are paid; and a description of the basis upon which plan expenses are charged
    a. A copy of the recent plan sponsor fee disclosure
    b. A copy of the recent plan participant fee disclosure
22. Reports or correspondence from independent fiduciaries, pension consultants, and investment advisors regarding the Plan–
23. Documents describing:
    a. SEC 12(b)(1) fees rebated to the Plan, company, or any parties-in-interest
    b. Finder's fees rebated to the Plan, company, or any parties-in-interest
    c. Sub-Transfer Account (Sub-TA) fees rebated to the Plan, company, or any parties-in-interest
    d. Any other fees and revenue sharing rebated to the Plan, company, or any parties-in-interest
24. Documents describing any compensation paid to the Plan, Plan fiduciaries, independent fiduciary, company directors, or company employees, including any revenue sharing, "soft dollars," and any type of revenue enhancement
25. All 408(b)(2) disclosures from the Plan's service providers, concerning Plan-related and investment-related information

26. A sample 404a-5 participant disclosure, describing investment-related and Plan-related information, including administrative and individual fees, if available
27. Forced distribution accounting or statements for funds rolled over to an IRA or removed from the Plan in some other manner because the Plan participant is unlocatable. Proof the Plan participant notices have been returned as undeliverable. Documents describing any uncashed checks
    a. If the Plan has a mandatory distribution policy or IRA rollover policy for terminated employees for account balances under a certain limit, details regarding the policy and procedures
28. Employee Census
29. Documents describing service provider changes, including any documents comparing all contenders for the Plan's services, if applicable
30. Participant loan policy, including documents describing who is responsible for setting the Plan's interest rate. Include a sample loan application form. Provide a detailed list of any outstanding loan balances, date of the loan, and interest rate
31. Documents describing how employer contributions are remitted to the Plan

An investigation is an extensive process and can result in headaches for plan sponsors who are not prepared and well organized. The most common 401(k) error found by the Department of Labor is said to be the failure of the trustee to timely remit 401(k) contributions and loan repayments to the plan. The most common error found during IRS audits is the failure of plan sponsors to have the proper plan documents. Serious violations can cause a 401(k) or pension plan to lose its tax-qualified status, which means the money in the plan then becomes taxable to the employees. The DOL collects about $1.7 billion in fines from plan sponsors each year.

Other overlooked errors are as follows:

- **Excluding certain compensation.** By far, a frequent error plan sponsors make is excluding certain types of compensation when determining employee deferrals and employer matches for a certain pay period. The most typical payments that are improperly excluded are bonuses, overtime, and vacation pay.

- **Excluding benefits described in the plan.** Your plan document describes who is covered under your plan and what contributions or benefits will be provided to those covered employees. Your employees' rights to contributions and benefits are derived from the plan document. Therefore, you must operate your plan strictly in accordance with the terms of your plan document; that is, you must cover the employees that your plan document describes as being covered *when* the plan document says they should be covered, and you must provide them the contributions or benefits set out in the plan document. (Even if the terms of your plan do not reflect your intent, you must follow what is written in your plan.) For example, if you intended on new employee eligibility to be after thirty days but your plan document says twelve months, you cannot enroll new employees until they satisfy one year of service. This is why reading your plan documents and reviewing them with your administrative staff periodically is good practice. Of course, the terms of your plan may be amended. Nonetheless, you are required to follow them as written. A DOL investigation will likely challenge any discrepancies.

- **Prohibited transactions.** The DOL is always looking for conflict of interest or misuse of plan assets and often finds "prohibited transactions" when it takes a closer look at a company's 401(k). Know the rules about prohibited transactions to avoid severe penalties.

- **Make sure that no plan amendment reduces a participant's benefit accrued before the amendment.** Section 411(d)(6) prohibits the reduction of any participant's accrued benefit by an amendment of the plan. This means that no employee's account can be reduced because of a plan amendment, such as a change in vesting schedules. Suppose you currently have immediate vesting but you change to a six-year vesting schedule. You will need to track two separate vesting schedules—the current schedule for those currently participating and the new schedule for new participants. Be careful with the timing and handling of *reduction* in benefits. If you were to amend your plan from, say, a six-year vesting to an immediate vesting, this would not be a reduction in benefits.

- **Employee eligibility.** The IRS will look for examples of an employer's failure to follow the plan's eligibility or enrollment rules. This includes the improper exclusion of part-time employees or a merged-in group of employees, a misclassification of independent contractors, failure to adhere to hours-of-service counting rules, or rehire enrollment errors. If your plan has automatic enrollment, be sure to automatically enroll all eligible employees on a timely basis. And for new hires, be sure you have a system in place to provide and maintain complete enrollment package materials.

WHAT TO DO IF YOU GET A DOL AUDIT LETTER

When a plan sponsor receives a notice from the DOL's Employee Benefits Security Administration (EBSA) saying that its plan has been selected for an investigation, chances are the DOL is looking for something specific. It may be acting on a complaint from a plan participant, on a government referral, or on a referral from a service provider, or its computer programs may have red-flagged certain items. Regardless, receiving a letter from the Department of Labor that says you are being audited can make any plan sponsor's heart palpitate. Not only can the process of investigation be overwhelming, but also the fines that result from errors or noncompliance can be substantial.

If you receive such a letter, you will also get a list of documents the DOL wants to review. While initially you will likely be notified through the mail, the auditor will establish a time to meet with you and any plan personnel in order to conduct interviews and obtain or review additional documentation. Naturally, it is important that you are all prepared for this interview and that you carefully review plan documents prior to the meeting. Everyone should be aware of the procedures and policies, and it's a good idea to refresh plan fiduciaries' recollection of all policies before meeting with the auditor. Once on-site, the auditor will continue to review plan documents and likely develop an additional list of documents to examine. As the auditor continues to review the plan documents and interview plan personnel, issues and errors that require correction will be identified. Such issues may or may not result in excise taxes, penalties, or fines.

SHOULD YOU HIRE AN ERISA ATTORNEY?

You may want to contact an ERISA attorney and consider legal representation if you receive an audit notice. Although an attorney is not required, retirement plans use legal documents that have legal consequences; therefore, a minor investigation can inadvertently lead to larger problems. If you want to err on the side of caution, you should hire an ERISA attorney immediately upon receipt of the letter. After all, the cost of an attorney may pale in comparison to the cost of fines or penalties. On the other hand, research indicates one in four audits lead to no costs or problems, and many are handled without an attorney. There is no standard practice. The choice is yours.

Keep in mind that because an ERISA attorney understands ERISA compliance (which is typically the impetus for an investigation), if you do decide to engage an ERISA attorney, he or she will typically answer IRS and/or DOL questions directly on your behalf. Because of their expertise, attorneys know to avoid volunteering information that could lead to further investigation. Consequently, legal representation may help ensure greater problems don't ensue. Of course, if you choose to enlist the services of an ERISA attorney, the decision should be made with care and prudence. A hasty hire of someone may not give you the outcome you expect. In other words, penalties and/or fines may not be avoided even with legal representation.

Another option is to work with the Department of Labor in the investigation before hiring legal representation and only seek out an attorney to negotiate a reasonable outcome with the regulators if problems are found. If you decide to work with the DOL directly, keep in mind that it is absolutely essential to give them the information requested and to do so in a timely manner. But it is also advisable to avoid providing extra or supplementary information that is not requested. You don't want to create unnecessary problems. It's also important to keep close track of what's being turned over to the DOL and for what purpose. Retain photocopies and notes of dates and details for your protection. And particularly if you feel the need to engage legal representation in the future, you will want to furnish copies for your attorney to also review. Generally speaking, documents requested by the auditor must be provided within ten days. Once you provide the requested list of documents, it then becomes a process of waiting. It could take weeks, months, or even in the most extreme cases years to complete the audit.

Because audits are on the rise, here are a few things to keep in mind if you ever face one:

1. Respond immediately.
As mentioned, an initial letter by the Department of Labor is accompanied by a laundry list of requested documents. That means as soon as you receive the initial letter, you should talk to your advisor, service provider, and/or legal counsel about organizing the plan documents and complying with the request.

Logic suggests that the more organized the information you provide the DOL, the less likely the agency is to intensely scrutinize the plan. When employers fail to respond to the initial letter sent by the DOL, drastic steps may be taken by the agency to get the information they need. This can include requesting a deposition of the company's fiduciaries or even issuing subpoenas. Therefore, it is not wise to cause delays.

2. Work with the Department of Labor.
A DOL investigator is unlikely to let you know exactly why your plan is under investigation; however, if you have an idea of what they are looking for, it's better to be proactive in furnishing that information rather than having them pry it from you. Not only could rebelling against the audit make the investigation more stressful, but also fighting the feds is not generally going to be good for you in the long run.

3. Do not make up answers.
If you are not sure, do not be afraid to answer honestly. Making up answers can often create more complications and raise additional questions. Provide reasonable assistance and try to maintain a cordial relationship with the auditor. The more help you provide, the sooner the auditor can finish and depart. Of course, ignorance is not an adequate defense, and an "I don't know" answer is not likely to dismiss you from potential fines or penalties.

4. Gather the requested documents and make them available.
Act quickly once you receive the letter. It is not a good idea to sit on an audit notice. You will need

ample time to collect the documents, notify your legal counsel and independent auditors or advisors, and enable the team to plan with plenty of advanced notice. Your 401(k) team can provide invaluable assistance throughout the process. It may be advisable to have them present during the audit if they are willing to be.

5. Designate a point person.
It makes sense to appoint one person to be responsible for coordinating with the agency on the timing of the audit, assembling and reviewing documentation, coordinating meetings with personnel, and reporting to internal management. This will make the process easier to manage. The point person should be the only one to answer questions and provide information, unless the point person and plan counsel agree otherwise. Consequently, the point person should be duly prepared, competent, and able to work directly with the DOL.

6. Identify all plan fiduciaries and trustees.
The DOL will likely make on-site visits and interview plan trustees and other fiduciaries as a part of the investigation. All plan fiduciaries and trustees should be available to meet with the DOL should they request an on-site visit. If your company has concerns about this visit, talk to your legal team and ask if they should be present as well.

7. Coordinate with your vendors.
If you outsource administration of your retirement plan, your vendors will likely play a role in the audit process. Engage your vendors, because they can be very helpful. However, they are not the ones being

audited, so it is ultimately your responsibility to work with the investigators and help facilitate the audit. Do not expect your vendors to work with the DOL on your behalf.

ERISA-REQUESTED DOCUMENTS

For obvious reasons, you will want to review all the documents and supporting evidence before submitting it for the investigation. You also ought to organize your records in advance. This groundwork will prepare you for the EBSA's questions and may provide insight into what they are investigating specifically with regard to the plan. Don't expect the DOL interviewer to disclose the purpose of the audit, but he or she may informally disclose what the DOL is *not* targeting.

As part of the audit process, the EBSA representative will interview the employer and other plan fiduciaries. Everyone involved in the administration and oversight of your plan should be prepared to answer questions about the plan and its operations. As with any proceedings, it's wise not to volunteer additional information or provide explanation beyond a straightforward answer to the questions.

The following are DOL audit targets and current "hot" investigation issues:

- Timeliness of deposits of participant deferrals
- Employer stock issues
- Payment of plan-related expenses
- Funding policy
- Procedures for allocating plan administrative responsibilities
- Investment process
- Prohibited transactions
- Accuracy of financial data reported on Form 5500
- Fidelity bond
- Reporting and disclosure

DOL VIOLATIONS

If an audit uncovers an apparent violation, which is the case in an estimated 75 percent of all audits, the EBSA will issue a voluntary compliance request letter. The letter informs the employer of the results of the investigation, cites pension law provisions that the DOL considers having been violated, and asks for correction of the violation(s) through full compliance. Depending on the violation, correction may include restoring losses of plan assets and lost investment earnings.

The Employee Benefits Security Administration (EBSA) oversees about 681,000 retirement plans, in addition to 2.4 million health plans and a similar number of welfare plans. These plans cover about 143 million workers plus their dependents. In 2017, the DOL closed 1,707 investigations, a figure higher than in years past which is consistent with the DOL's strategic plan that calls for increased civil enforcement. Out of those investigations, over 1,100 resulted in $1.1 billion in direct recovery payments to plan, participants and beneficiaries. Out of those investigated, 134 cases were referred for litigation. Additionally, EBSA closed 307 criminal investigations which led to the indictment of 113 individuals – including plan officials, corporate officers, and service providers – for offenses related to employee benefit plans.

PROACTIVE APPROACH

As DOL audits continue to increase, consider taking a proactive approach to protect yourself and your plan. Annual self-audits are a recommended best practice. If you happen to receive notice of an IRS or DOL investigation, know you are not alone and you are not necessarily being singled out. However, if you receive such a notice, be cooperative, consult with your qualified advisors, and begin immediately preparing for the audit. Certainly, the better prepared you are beforehand, the easier such an investigation will be should it ever arise.

IF YOU DISCOVER AN ERROR THROUGH INTERNAL SELF-AUDIT

Because 401(k) plans have numerous moving parts, mistakes can and do happen. If you discover an error, correct it proactively and quickly. Both the Internal Revenue Service (IRS) and Department of Labor (DOL) have voluntary compliance programs to allow plan sponsors methods to correct errors with minimal penalties. About 1,643 applications were filed last year to disclose and self-correct violations. Do not fear self-reporting; it does not flag you for an audit. But if you don't fix a plan error, the penalties will be more severe if the error is uncovered through an audit or litigation.

Some of the common errors you may discover include the following:

- **Missing Reinstatements**
  Every five to seven years, plans need to be amended to conform to a new law and/or regulation. While this is typically initiated by your plan administrator, you may find that sometimes a document hasn't been drafted. Reinstatements have deadlines for signing off, and if these deadlines are missed, your plan may be disqualified as a qualified plan. This means previous tax deductions for employer contributions will be disallowed and your participants will have to declare their retirement accounts as current taxable income. Such action could be quite devastating to your participants. Because you can't backdate plan documents, you must have all the missed amendments drafted and signed to correct the plan, and then you will have to submit the plan and the amendments to the IRS through the Voluntary Compliance Program (VCP) of the Employee Plans Compliance Resolution System (EPCRS). There will be a set penalty that will be assessed based on the number of participants involved and, the cost for overall correction may be thousands of dollars, but it's far less costly than having this error discovered on audit.

- **Not Operating the Plan According to Its Terms**
  Every plan is required to operate according to the terms of the plan document. For instance, if your plan document states employees can become participants after completing a year of service, you can't let them become participants after only six months of employment. If you discover that there has been a mismatch between your plan document and your procedures, depending on the error, you may be able to self-correct without having to submit to the IRS through the Employee Plans Compliance Resolution System (EPCRS). However, if the error is substantial in nature and/or the error was spread across a several years, it should be submitted to the EPCRS, and you may have to pay a set penalty based on the number of participants impacted. Speak with your plan administrator or other counsel to determine the correct course of action.

- **Late Deposit of Salary Deferrals**
  When it comes to depositing salary deferrals into a 401(k) plan, for many years plan sponsors relied on the regulations stating that there would be no issue if the plan sponsor segregated the deferrals from payroll and deposited funds in the plan before the fifteenth day of the following month. A few years ago, however, the DOL reinterpreted the rule to mean that the fifteenth is the *maximum* deadline. The DOL has a seven-business-day safe harbor rule for plans with fewer than one hundred participants, and larger plans have even less time. Consequently, many plans have had late deposits of deferrals. If yours is one of these, this problem should be corrected immediately. Late deposits must be noted on Form 5500, and the regulators will know if this is reported properly. Late deposits can be self-corrected by paying interest as per IRS set underpayment rates to impacted participant accounts, but if the number of late deferrals is considerable or the deferrals ran for a period of years, it may be best to file with the Department

of Labor's Voluntary Fiduciary Compliance Program (VFCP). By reporting your late deposits to the DOL, you may be able to circumvent a DOL-triggered audit. Again, speak with your advisors to determine the best approach if you believe you have violations with late deposits.

- **Missing Enrollment Dates**

    If your employees have met the eligibility requirements but the Plan has mistakenly not made enrollment available to those eligible participants, you must make a fully vested, qualified nonelective contribution to the plan for the affected employees to compensate them for the missed deferral opportunity. The amount of this contribution is equal to 50 percent of the missed deferral, as determined by the ADP (actual deferral percentage) for the employees' group. Your plan administrator can help with this calculation. Any matching or employer contributions missed should be paid as well. This error can be corrected through the self-correction or VFCP program.

- **Loans Out of Compliance**

    A loan to a participant must meet a number of rules under Code §72(p) to prevent the law from treating it as a taxable distribution to the participant. The plan must base the loan on a legally enforceable agreement, and the amount of the loan cannot exceed the lesser of 50 percent of the participant's vested account balance or $50,000. Terms of the loan should require the participant to make level amortized repayments with interest at least quarterly. The participant must fully repay the loan within five years unless the loan was taken to purchase a primary residence. If your plan documents didn't allow loans yet such loans were made, any impacted participant's illegal loan would be treated as a taxable distribution. If the loan exceeded the maximum limits, the participant must repay the loan or re-amortize the remaining balance. An application to the IRS VFCP program would also be required since this is an exception to the prohibited transaction rules.

You should know that if you happen to discover an error through an in-house audit, both the DOL and the IRS have voluntary correction programs you can use to correct the problem without worrying about harsh penalties. However, you may want to consult with an ERISA attorney or specialist to ensure proper handling of the self-correction. The best course of action is to be proactive to correct any problems that are discovered.

FIDUCIARY INSURANCE

Although you may have the best of intentions when you offer your employees access to a retirement plan, by sponsoring a 401(k) or Profit-Sharing Plan, you are subject to liability and risk. The risks of errors in plan administration and the potential breach of duty under ERISA may mean you need to consider fiduciary insurance. Employers are increasingly being held accountable for the benefits they offer employees. Under ERISA, not only can your company be held liable, but plan fiduciaries can too. The law says fiduciaries can be held personally liable for losses to a plan even if the alleged error or breach was unintentional. When you manage a company-sponsored retirement plan, you face risks from plan participants (including ex-employees), the IRS, the Department of Labor, and the Pension Benefit Guarantee Corporation. So, how do you ensure that your retirement plan is handled responsibly and that the plan trustees and fiduciaries are protected against giving improper advice, making administrative errors, having conflicts of interest, making impudent investment decisions, and/or making funding errors? One option is to purchase fiduciary insurance.

As you have already learned, the fiduciary laws are complex and ever evolving. Unfortunately, so too are insurance policies. If you have fiduciary insurance but haven't reviewed your policy in the last year or two, now is a good time to review your benefits and better understand what is covered and what isn't. There may be unknown gaps in your coverage. If you have not considered adding fiduciary insurance as a part of your liability insurance package, it would be wise to discuss your options with your insurance broker. In general, fiduciary insurance is designed to pay the legal liability costs arising from claims, including fines and penalties; to pay for legal defense; and to protect the personal assets of executives and committee members. Of course, fiduciary insurance does not negate the need for following a prudent fiduciary process. It is prudent to avoid claims in the first place, but fiduciary insurance can add a valuable layer of protection against the financial risks.

As to be expected, however, not all insurance policies are alike, and fiduciary insurance is no different. Coverage, limitations, and policy benefits can vary substantially from one carrier to the next. To make it more complicated, not all decisions directly involved in managing a plan (even when conducted by a fiduciary) fall under the fiduciary role as defined by ERISA. Some plan management decisions are business judgment-type decisions and are called "settlor" functions, which means a fiduciary insurance policy may not cover these types of functions even though there are still liability risks. Some decisions, such as plan options, are viewed as business decisions (in insurance terms, also "settlor" functions) that may not be covered in a standard fiduciary policy. It is important to review optional benefits available to ensure adequate coverage for you and your plan fiduciaries.

Furthermore, a standard fiduciary policy, or rider, may not cover everything you need or expect to be covered, such as defense costs for regulatory investigations. Therefore, you may want to add extended coverage to provide more protection and fill in any gaps. A standard policy may not cover trustee and administrative functions such as plan amendments and plan design and features. As already mentioned, endorsements may be desired to protect against settlor functions. Also, a comprehensive review of policy language is important. For instance, the definition of *wrongful act* can vary by insurer, with some policies offering a broader definition than others. Some plans may cover the costs of voluntary compliance program expenditure, whereas other policies do not. To the extent that there may be coverage included, the limits can vary substantially from one policy to the next. Are attorney and accountant fees covered? What about fees, penalties, and sanctions paid under the voluntary compliance program? A good fiduciary insurance policy will provide comprehensive coverage that includes wrongful employment practices, professional services, investigatory expenses, negligence, and fiduciary breach. Does your fiduciary policy cover all your liability needs? Now is a good time to review with your insurance broker and 401(k) advisor.

CYBER RISK

Have you considered cyber risk? Unfortunately, falling victim to a cybersecurity attack is becoming increasingly common. Because your 401(k) depends on technology, you may face data breach and cyberloss risks including threats from hackers, who can even be employees. The most popular type of attack in the past year has been ransomware, whereby hackers get unwitting users to install software on their computers that gives the hackers the ability to encrypt the entire hard drive. Another attack is known as "phishing," of which you are probably aware. An email is sent to a company or person with an enticing message that appears to be from someone they know. The goal is to get the unsuspecting victim to give information that can be used to gain access to the accounts.

In other situations, a cyberattacker will pose as a high-level executive and ask an employee to transfer some of their funds to a specific account. This kind of attack can be especially effective with retirement plan participants, including office administrators, because often the person on the receiving end trusts the "high-level executive" and will do what is asked. Another form of hacking is with malware, which is harmful software written with the intent to damage or take over a targeted network, giving cybercriminals access to personal and detailed financial records.

Cyberexposure is real, and retirement plans are notorious targets for these attacks because they involve a high volume of sensitive information—the kind of information that is invaluable to criminals with malicious intent. Plan participant and financial information is generally shared with many different parties, making it more vulnerable. Whether you need a separate cyberliability policy to cover your plan is something you may care to discuss with your insurance broker.

FIDELITY BOND INSURANCE

Fidelity bonds are required by law (ERISA bonding). This insurance protects participants against fraud or dishonesty. When dishonest administrators or trustees have financially harmed an employee benefit plan, a fiduciary bond will protect the benefits of the plan and the plan's beneficiaries. This bonding insurance, however, will not protect the trustees themselves from liability claims and is thus distinctly different from fiduciary liability insurance.

The fidelity bond requirement for your 401(k) is 10 percent of your plan assets, up to a maximum of $500,000 ($1 million maximum if your plan includes company stock). Because this is a mandatory ERISA bonding requirement, the Department of Labor does review plan 5500 filings for adequate coverage. You may be surprised to discover how many filings have a misstated or incorrect amount of bond coverage. Whether it is because the plan sponsor has not followed the rules or, perhaps more likely, because the TPA has not reviewed the information for accuracy, you should always confirm that your bond coverage is current, up to date, and reported correctly before you sign off on your 5500, as this can be an audit trigger.

EMPLOYEE BENEFIT LIABILITY INSURANCE

Another related type of coverage is employee benefit liability (EBL) insurance. EBL insurance policies cover many claims arising out of errors or omissions in the administration of a benefit plan, including the failure to enroll an employee in the plan and the administration of improper advice as to benefits. But EBL insurance does not cover all situations of fiduciary responsibility, especially those involving imprudent investment of funds. Likewise, fiduciary liability insurance coverage may or may not encompass EBL insurance coverage. It depends upon the insurer involved, the purchasing entity, and the specific type of fiduciary liability coverage. Your insurance broker will be able to help you ultimately determine what scope of coverage is provided or available and suitable based on your needs. However, the point is to be aware of the limits in coverage, be sure you understand what benefits you have, and be sure you understand what you may be on the hook for.

OTHER BUSINESS LIABILITY INSURANCE

You may be able to add a fiduciary endorsement to your directors and officers (D&O) liability, commercial general liability (CGL), or trust E&O (errors and omissions) / professional liability policies provided your policy has attached an endorsement specifically tailored to cover fiduciary liabilities. These are not standard benefits covered under a liability policy, and you ought to be aware most D&O policies exclude ERISA claims. A fiduciary insurance policy or endorsement may protect the plan itself, as well as the corporate sponsor and individual nonofficer fiduciaries, but again an addition to a general liability policy may or may not provide all the coverage you want or need, so be sure to read your policy carefully and consult with a professional insurance expert to be sure you are aware of any gaps or policy limits. You may have substantial expenses to cover out of pocket if you lack sufficient insurance. It is best not to be faced with this type of surprise in a time of need.

INSURANCE OPTIONS—CONCLUSION

Any organization offering employee benefits can potentially be mismanaged, whether by way of negligence or intent; consequently, it is recommended you have fiduciary liability insurance. Organizations that do not have this protection in place may be exposed to a host of issues, especially with regard to retirement benefits. Normally, an employee benefit liability insurance policy will cover mistakes, but many fiduciary activities fall into the realm of professional liability. Whether or not your company (and plan fiduciaries) is found to be at fault for a loss, the costs involved in your legal defense can be significant. With fiduciary insurance, however, most of these costs can be covered. While the cost of a basic plan will depend on the size of your retirement plan, including the assets and the number of participants, along with other factors, fiduciary liability insurance can be an affordable protection. Keep in mind, fiduciary insurance generally provides a pretty good amount of protection relative to the cost, but it's still important to shop around for the best rates. Contact your local insurance broker to discuss your options.

IN SUMMARY

The Department of Labor and the Internal Revenue Service are developing new and innovative ways to regulate employee benefit plans. For sure, the days of leniency are over. The national retirement crisis is a growing concern, and its impact on our economy and national welfare is substantial. Consequently, budgets have expanded and the DOL is making a concerted effort to focus its resources on compliance. As audit risks continue to increase, consider taking a proactive approach to protecting yourself. Many plan sponsors have found it helpful to conduct their own plan audit periodically or hire a consulting firm to do it for them.

If you receive notice of an IRS or DOL audit, remember that you are not alone and you are not necessarily being singled out, but you do need to get yourself prepared. Consult with qualified advisors who have been through the IRS and DOL audit process previously, and promptly prepare for the audit. A 401(k) audit is not pleasant, but if every plan sponsor is prepared and all plan fiduciaries are educated as to their responsibilities, liabilities, and requirements, then everyone will be better off in the end. The more you do now, the better off you will be. There is no denying that federal audits of company-sponsored retirement plans are picking up and that all plan sponsors of all size plans are at an increasing risk of an investigation.

Audits can be random, can be triggered because of a red flag on your 5500 filing, or can result from a complaint by a plan participant. Therefore, taking some steps in advance to be sure you avoid potential conflicts is wise. For instance, before you submit IRS documents such as your Form 5500, you need to review the filing carefully with your 401(k) team to avoid any errors or potential red flags that might be inconsistent with ERISA rules or requirements. Of course, great employee communication and a strong education program will go a long way toward helping keep everyone on track for success and will help avoid any participant misunderstandings that could trigger a DOL call or complaint. It might be a good policy to help provide transition education for terminated employees to avoid any potential discrepancies. However, even with your diligent efforts and dedication to your employee welfare, your plan could still be chosen at random for a DOL or IRS review. Employers often dismiss the risks of an audit or litigation because they underestimate the actions of their participants. In 2017, 617 new investigations were opened as a result of complaint calls. Employees will act if they feel slighted, feel disgruntled, or have serious concerns about the plan. You may not even be aware of their concerns, but if they make a phone call that seems to be of interest to the Department of Labor, you just may find yourself embroiled in a headache. That is why I recommend your best practices include conducting annual self-audits. The best defense is a good offense, and that means preparing your fiduciary team for an audit long before one occurs.

The problems that have resulted from today's risks are likely due to the fact that too many plan sponsors have neglected the rules and requirements. It can be difficult to keep up with the regulatory knowledge necessary to keep a plan compliant. That is yet another reason why having a competent and qualified advisor can be of value. The truth is many of the legal problems plan sponsors face today would wane if sponsors just spent the time to ensure they are managing their plan for the sole benefit of the employees and their beneficiaries. As complex as this appears, it's actually quite simple. Employees who are happy with their benefits are going to be happier workers. And happy workers are the cornerstone of a successful firm.

If you make your plan and its success a priority, the chances are that you will inherently take the steps necessary to mitigate your audit risks. When you act as a champion of your 401(k), you will intuitively embrace the care and prudent standards required by law. Fiduciary standards, remember, are the *minimum* requirements needed to run a successful plan. Following the rules does not ensure or guarantee retirement security for your employees, but it does help ensure you are setting them up for the best chance of success. To overcome our national retirement crisis, your employees need your advocacy.

CHAPTER 12
HUMAN CAPITAL MANAGEMENT: EXPANDING OPPORTUNITIES

> *Would you rather have $10,000 paid to you every day for the next thirty days or collect a penny that doubles every day for thirty days?*

If you had to make a quick decision—$10,000 a day for thirty days *or* a penny that doubles every day for thirty days—what would you choose? Most people's initial reaction would be to choose $10,000 a day because simple math suggests that surely $300,000 is worth more than a mere penny doubling for only thirty days. But in choosing this, you would pass up the opportunity to get $5,368,709.12! When you help your employees understand the importance of this decision and, more importantly, how to comprehend the power of compounding, you provide them with information that many other companies are not offering. Knowledge is power. The ability to deliver education and provide experiences to help your employees gain the wisdom they need to make better financial decisions, secure their retirement, and protect their families goes far in helping to build the right culture within your firm. The old-school bureaucratic management system no longer drives employee satisfaction, just as offering a 401(k) is no longer enough to demonstrate your regard for your employees' retirement. Anyone can offer attractive salaries and benefits, but the company that can offer perks that go beyond the job and directly touch the heart of the employee's personal well-being is going to earn a loyalty and respect that surpasses a paycheck. In short, financial wellness can give you a low-cost option for driving a truly employee-centric company.

How do you attract and retain talent? Offering high wages might attract applicants initially, but what is going to retain them is a competitive salary combined with benefits *and* perks. Perks may not cost much, but they can go a long way toward building loyalty. After all, if it were just about salary, it would be easy for a competitor to woo your employees away with a higher wage. What is going to stop workers from leaving your company for a competitor is your total benefits package and how employees feel about working at your company. Wages and salary may get employees in the door, but benefits will attract the talent, and a good, strong culture will keep those who have it.

As the economy improves and unemployment rates drop, employees are gaining bargaining power. Social websites such as LinkedIn and Glassdoor are making it more challenging for companies without a strong employment brand to attract great talent. Information is now public thanks to technology, so if your company isn't a great place to work, candidates will find out fast. Deloitte research shows that culture, engagement, and employee retention are now some of the top challenges facing business leaders. In fact, many businesses today have serious retention problems. As you know, turnover is very costly to a business, especially for smaller companies. Companies with strong positive cultures are now the most in-demand, as the most sought-after workers are seeking culture-driven firms who explicitly put their people first.

Some define it as "what happens when nobody is looking." Others refer to it as "how a company treats its employees," and still others define culture as the way a company is internally managed. Culture evolves quietly but steadily as it creeps into a company, and it is one of the most important components that drives a company's long-term success. Culture is the result of company-wide value systems that trickle down from management. It is the sum of everything from how management communicates to the employees, to how employees work with and relate to one another, to the work environment itself and the attitude of the people who make up the company, particularly the leaders. No one wants to work for a company that treats it employees poorly. But culture is also defined by dress code policies, business hours, office setup, hiring decisions, treatment of clients and client satisfaction, and the sum of all facets of operations and management. That is why it's important to respect the power of culture.

Workers are sensitive to how they feel on the job. Managers and HR teams must think about the total employee experience in order to be competitive today. This includes everything from the break room and office space, to the type of people you hire, to the general attitude of management. Do you offer your employees burnt coffee in a dirty coffeepot, or do you have an espresso machine with an assortment of specialty drinks? Do you charge your employees for drinks and snacks, or do you provide them for free? Is your lunchroom a comfortable lounge where employees want to hang out, build friendships, and share ideas, or is it dark, grungy, and uninviting? Stand back and look at your environment. Are the office doors closed or open? Is leadership engaged or is there a lack of leadership presence? Does your management lead with arrogance or engage in demoralizing or critical behaviors, or do they smile easily and use positive reinforcement? Do you conduct inconsistent performance evaluations? When was the last time you had an employee appreciation event? Do you celebrate your employees' birthdays, work anniversaries, and personal accomplishments? Do you promote community work and volunteerism for charities? While these may sound like unimportant details, all of them play a role into the total sum of job benefits perceived by employees.

Of course, the more typical benefits such as basic health-care coverage, a 401(k) plan, and vacation time are essential to attract good talent, but by adding complimentary benefits, you can make a difference in employee retention, and by understanding culture you can make a big difference. The good news is that employers can offer several different benefit options that are very important to employees but that are low cost, such as a floating holiday, an employee-of-the-month parking space, company-paid lunch breaks, and casual Fridays. This type of regard for the employee fosters a strong sense of allegiance. Flexible work hours are important to employees according to several different surveys. Another low-cost benefit option is financial wellness and retirement support. When you demonstrate that you understand, as an employer, the magnitude of the complexity of retirement planning facing your workers, and when you support financial health and wellness, your actions will go a long way in setting your company apart from others.

Empowering your employees with the tools and resources they need to secure their futures and prepare for when the day comes that they transition into retirement can help nurture a much-needed employee-centric culture, something more and more businesses today are seeking. Firms need an edge when it comes to recruitment, and financial wellness is certainly one of the more attractive benefits that is helping great companies develop that competitive advantage. Being sensitive to the individual needs of your diverse workforce is a way to improve company culture. Most employees regardless of age, gender, or income are concerned about their retirement, and with good reason. But there are specific challenges that are unique to certain groups of your employees, and conveying your regard for their unique needs can play a big role in promoting a positive culture. How you lead your company by your behavior, values, and reward systems impacts virtually every aspect of your organization. Supporting financial wellness and retirement success can go a long way in inspiring and motivating employees and driving employee retention and productivity. In this chapter, I highlight the distinct challenges specific groups of employees may face when they are addressing financial wellness. As an employer, if you deliver specific, relevant, and timely information to your employees that focuses on their unique predicaments, you will make a strong statement that you are concerned about and are understanding and supportive of their individual needs. It will also help find smart solutions to enable your workers to move past hurdles and begin the journey toward retirement readiness.

RETIREMENT FOR WOMEN

Women face unique challenges when it comes to retirement planning. Divorce, longer life expectancies, and a host of other issues confront women and create greater financial challenges for this segment of the workforce. A recent study by the US Government Accountability Office indicates that despite the increase in women's workforce participation, the poverty rate for women sixty-five and older is still nearly *twice* the rate for men. The risks of poverty are especially increased for widows. Women also have a tougher time saving for retirement, in part because they take time out from the workforce to care for family members. And for those who continue working, they still tend to have lower earnings than men, with average wages about 70 percent those of men. For these reasons, women tend to have less for retirement than they need. Women who are between the ages of fifty and sixty-nine are said to have about 20 percent less in retirement savings than men in that same age group, and only 35 percent of female Baby Boomers have $200,000 or more of retirement savings, compared to 50 percent for male Boomers.

Worse still, nearly a third of women between ages forty and sixty-nine have no idea how much money they can reasonably withdraw annually from their retirement accounts. Unquestionably, men are confused about this as well, but nearly one-third of women in their forties and fifties naively think they can withdraw between 11 percent and 30 percent of their savings annually. These unrealistically high annual withdrawal rates will certainly leave these women vulnerable to spending down their savings and running out of money. While both men and women are underfunding their retirement, women tend save less than men of the same age. Because women live about five years longer than their male counterparts, they need more capital. But when asked how much they are aiming for in retirement savings, women tend to aim lower, with a median goal of about half that of the goal stated by male workers.

The problem is magnified because women tend to change jobs more frequently than men, and they often leave the workforce to take care of young children. Still others take a leave of absence later in their careers to care for aging parents. According to the National Alliance for Caregiving and AARP, 66 percent of caregivers are women. Caregiving includes taking care of spouses, parents, parents-in-law, friends, and even neighbors. In fact, the average caregiver is a forty-nine-year-old woman who provides twenty hours per week of unpaid care to her mother. While many women work full time in addition to caring for someone, some exit the workforce altogether, subsequently compromising their retirement savings. Regardless, the stress and demands impact women, affecting either their own health risks or their finances. MetLife estimates that the negative impact on a caregiver's retirement fund is approximately $40,000 more for women than it is for men.

When we stop working to care for children, parents, or others, even if only for a few years, this results in lower Social Security retirement benefits as well as reduced 401(k) savings. According to Social Security statistics, the average female worker receives about 25 percent less in Social Security retirement benefits than the average male worker. Leaving the job market is also clearly disruptive for 401(k) growth. Women also tend to job hop more than men, and that, too, can be costly to retirement. According to the Bureau of Labor Statistics (BLS), women born between 1957 and 1964 held an average of 11.5 jobs from ages 18 to 48. With approximately 70 percent of waiting periods for 401(k) participation formerly averaging six months to one year, job hopping for these women meant they may have lost eight years of potential participation in a company-sponsored retirement plan. This does not include the impact on retirement savings, such as the loss of contributions during furloughs, the cost of procrastination, and the loss of employer matching dollars.

Job hopping is not necessarily a unique challenge for women. However, the cost of missing opportunities can be especially costly for women when compounded by the sum of other implications. Of course, many women change jobs for pay increases and career advancement, which can boost retirement savings. But research indicates more women are likely to change jobs at a reduced income to seek less stress, to escape an incompetent or negative boss, or to find a work–life balance. While I don't suggest anyone stay at a job where they are truly unhappy, I will say that men tend to deal with job dissatisfaction for the sake of income more so than women.

All workers these days are vulnerable to job layoffs due to recessions, company reorganization or relocation, and issues beyond their control. Sadly, job losses are added risks we all face, and the risk serves to further adversely impact our retirement success. But women need to be especially careful to avoid mistakes that can send them into poverty. A surprisingly large percentage of women are duly worried about becoming homeless. The term "bag lady" is not lost on most women, as many have a genuine concern they will end up homeless in their elderly years, perhaps carrying around their possessions in shopping bags. Fortunately, this is not the reality for most women in the United States, but longevity and long-term care risks make retirement planning especially important for them.

The good news is that women tend to be better at managing investments than men according to numerous studies. Since women require extra capital because of their longer life spans, following prudent investment principles is vital. However, since women tend to be more conservative by nature, some fail to reach the growth requirements needed to support longevity. Fortunately, studies show that women who do get on the right track with their investment strategies tend to stick with the plan better than men and, therefore, are better able to reap the rewards that come with patience and discipline. Based on my own experience working with women, I have found women to be very shrewd and sensible investors. But I believe the success is largely dependent upon the breadth and depth of education and professional support women receive.

Twenty-five years ago, I hosted my first financial education class specifically for women. I was pleasantly shocked to see the room filled with over seventy guests. Each had a notebook and pen in hand, ready to learn—something I must admit I hadn't seen with any prior audience. I learned very quickly that women want to be taken seriously as investors and that when given the opportunity, they embrace the ability to learn, listen attentively, and ask great questions. As a financial advisor, you can't ask for better attributes in an audience.

In general, women tend to feel less confident in their investment abilities, but eventually most will be responsible for their own financial well-being. The US Bureau of Labor Statistics indicates that 90 percent of women will have to manage their finances on their own at some point in their lives. This means it is especially important that employers help women understand what it requires to be retirement ready and how their needs may be different from those of men. Studies show women are often hesitant to talk to professionals about planning and investing, citing they are intimidated by the investment world. Those who have limited knowledge of finances are reluctant to seek help for fear of being taken advantage of, not being listened to, being unable to comprehend or follow along with the jargon, or being pressured to make decisions. While most women confidently handle their day-to-day finances, for generations women have largely shied away from the investment world, often deferring those decisions to their spouses. Of course, a financial professional can be a valuable resource for all your employees, but this is especially true with your female employees. They need help developing a plan specific to their unique needs to get on the right track for retirement. The fact is that women are generally great savers. They just need a little help getting pointed in the right direction, especially with investment strategies.

When women are properly educated, they make great investors. In fact, they are more apt to reach success because they stick with the plan and have proven to be exceptional students, following advice and making disciplined decisions. But women need an advisor with good listening skills, one who communicates clearly, demonstrates a sensitivity to their need for knowledge, and will not rush them into making decisions. An advisor who uses technical words or fails to explain things carefully is likely to be quickly dismissed by your female employees. Moreover, when women are given the opportunity to learn about the world of investing, they typically embrace the process and enjoy it far more than their male counterparts. As investors, women have demonstrated more patience, greater discipline, and a stronger willingness to learn. Consequently, an education program is likely to be especially valued by female employees. An advisory team who is sensitive to the needs unique to women will be an important alignment to help drive retirement success within your firm.

RETIREMENT PLANNING FOR OLDER EMPLOYEES

Workers in their late fifties or sixties face a unique set of challenges when it comes to retirement planning. There are generally two types of older employees: those who have prepared for their retirement, and everyone else. If they have prepared properly and are looking to transition into retirement, they face several important planning decisions, such as when and how to claim their Social Security benefits and how to draw an income from their 401(k)'s. On the other hand, if they have not prepared properly, they are likely to feel tremendous anxiety about being behind in their savings. They know they don't have enough to support their retirement, but they don't know how to deal with it, and the financial stress can be quite consuming. In fact, the reality of their situation can cause real fear because they know if they lose their job or face health problems, they will be forced into an early retirement and have a severely reduced standard of living. Many fear having to work in their elderly years to make ends meet, and they know finding respectable work as they age may be difficult. The joke of becoming a Walmart greeter in retirement is not so funny when you are faced with the reality of this situation. While those who are prepared financially are often overwhelmed by the decisions required to transition into retirement, those who have failed to plan and save properly are burdened with the stress of facing the reality of their negligence.

Time has a way of catching up to all of us. It is this age group who feels the impact of time more than any other. For those who are diligently saving and preparing, they need to know they are making the right choices as their working years wind down. Whether it is determining appropriate investment strategies for their age, protecting their retirement accumulations, addressing taxes, Social Security claiming strategies, Medicare, and health insurance coverage, or dealing with the host of other financial concerns that retirees face, as the clock ticks closer to retirement, these questions and concerns become more of a priority. For those who have insufficient savings, avoiding the issue is no longer an option. They need to learn how to confidently take steps now to protect and control what they can. There is plenty older workers can still do to shore up their retirement if they act sooner rather than later. The problem is, many of these employees feel helpless and discouraged, so they are prone to continue to do nothing or to let inertia prevail. Doing the same thing that only served to create the problem in the first place will not get these folks closer to financial wellness. Most employers have several employees like this, and although they want to help them, they just don't know how.

Hopefully, you have employees in their fifties and sixties who are on track for retirement. If so, still they may need help identifying and prioritizing their needs. They need to determine which planning decisions will have the most impact on their retirement and tackle those decisions carefully. You might think that finding the very best investments or minimizing taxes are the most important things to this age group, but studies show that the most important decisions for older, middle-income workers is deciding when to leave the workforce. They don't know whether to transition slowly into retirement by working fewer hours or making a hard stop and going right into retirement. It's not just about the financial decisions, of course. In fact, for those who are financially prepared, the timing and process of retirement is a very personal decision. Not everyone is emotionally or mentally ready to step out of the workforce completely, even if they can afford to do so. Consequently, they need to understand their employment options within your company and elsewhere. For instance, if they want to jump into retirement and collect Social Security benefits early but then decide they aren't ready to stop working completely and decide to take on part-time employment, or perhaps contract work with your firm, they first want to know how that might impact their Social Security benefits. Others are concerned about whether retirement timing needs to be synchronized with collecting Social Security benefits, and they want to understand claiming strategies to help them protect their 401(k)'s and personal savings. There are many basic questions that weigh heavy on the minds of these employees. Retirement is never just about the money. Still, everyone wants to make the best financial decisions.

Those who are not properly prepared need help learning how to live comfortably with reduced expenses both now, so they can save more, and in retirement. They need help finding resources to be able to save more today, invest wisely, and be realistic about evaluating their retirement income abilities. For instance, moving and deploying home equity to help finance retirement may be an option, but people considering this need help weighing various strategies such as a reverse mortgage, downsizing, or even low-income housing options. Social Security claiming strategies are also important to understand for these workers. While it may be too late for these older, ill-prepared employees to spend their golden years living in a gated community on a golf course, traveling the world, and enjoying a life of luxury, they certainly can find a way to create a lifestyle that is sustainable, realistic, and secure in their old age. We want everyone to transition to retirement with dignity. In order to make this happen, those who are unprepared need help addressing their situation today. There is a growing sense of urgency for these workers. They could really benefit from the expertise of a financial planner who can address the host of options and resources available and help build the confidence these workers need to reduce their stress and anxiety about their finances.

With a little extra work, older employees can be empowered with a plan and still be able to pursue a secure retirement. You, too, will benefit from improved productivity and the benefits that come from employees who have a reduced level of financial stress.

As we approach retirement age, it's natural for us to have reservations about when and how to go about making this transition. There's a great deal of financial uncertainty, regardless of how well you planned for retirement. Planning around so many unknown variables in today's complex world, such as future investment returns, sustainable withdrawal rates, health-care costs, the future of Social Security benefits, inflation, taxes, and life expectancy, can be quite daunting. And this doesn't include the concerns many have about how to keep themselves occupied and content without a job. Work gives people a sense of purpose, helps them maintain a sense of importance and value, and fulfills their desire to be needed and appreciated. While on the surface, retirement may be seen as exciting and enticing, there are a multitude of emotional and mental challenges some have when faced with the reality of retirement. The financial concerns are quite overwhelming in and of themselves, and while not everyone hesitates to consider how they will enjoy the freedom of their time and life in retirement, some workers have real angst over exiting the workforce.

When you retire, there's no place to call into when you're sick. Those yearly performance reviews, raises, or promotions come to an end when you stop working; as a result, no one pats you on the back anymore to say "thank you for the hard work" or praises you for doing a great job. The mental rewards of solving problems, leading or being part of a team and bringing expertise to a company can be priceless to some individuals. Disengaging or departing from something that is bigger than oneself is not easy for those who love their jobs. Even if older workers are physically tired and want to enjoy their own time, exiting the workforce is a lifestyle change that not all of them are eager to face. Therefore, identifying those sensitive issues and being able to offer planning support as needed for those employees who hesitate to dive into a retirement discussion is helpful to ensure a smooth transition, whenever that transition may occur.

Helping older workers understand that the depth of a retirement decision extends beyond just the affordability will assist them in making a graceful transition into retirement. Employees need to feel confident in their planning decisions, and when the day comes for them to decide to exit the workforce for good, they need to know their decision has been well thought out and is ultimately well executed. A professional expert who can lead the way toward retirement success is clearly an asset for all employees, but such expert guidance can be especially helpful to those who are within a handful of years of retirement. Some of your employees may already have professional guidance from outside sources, and if so, they will be in a better position to make this move confidently. However, for those who do not have a professional resource readily available to assist, the anxiety and risks of making a mistake can result in costly errors or may cause distress. While proper planning cannot guarantee a sustainable, enjoyable, and secure retirement, it can help ensure a less stressful and more assured transition. These employees need to be equipped with the knowledge needed to make important financial decisions that could have lasting implications.

RETIREMENT PLANNING FOR MARRIED COUPLES

While you may not have many (or any) couples both employed at your company, you most likely have employees who are married. When it comes to money and retirement, married couples have differences that can interfere with retirement readiness. You may not be responsible for your employees' spouses, but your employees are likely to be influenced by their spouses, and sometimes in ways that adversely affect retirement planning. For example, often within a marriage there is a spender and a saver. These differing financial habits and attitudes about money can result in excessive debt racked up by the spender. This can, in turn, impede savings and create financial stress for both.

Often, a couple's vision is not aligned; therefore, planning can be quite difficult. In fact, many don't know their spouse's ideals and dreams for retirement, much less whether they are saving enough to be able to fund those dreams. Communication, or lack thereof, is often the root of the problem. According to a Fidelity study, one in three couples don't have the same expectations for their quality of life in retirement, nor do they agree on the age at which they will retire. In other words, as many as one-third of your married employees may run into major roadblocks before they even begin to take their first steps toward planning for their retirement. If the majority of your employees are married, this could impact a large percentage of your workforce.

How much responsibility does an employer have to help married employees find smart solutions to overcome their money issues? You might feel that it is not your responsibility at all. However, financial stress can hinder job performance and increase operating costs. We've already addressed the fact that aging employees who can't afford to retire can be extremely costly to a company with wages, health care, and workers' compensation. Over 30 percent of workers admit their money concerns prevent them from doing their best on the job, and nearly 40 percent of employees do not feel they will ever be able to afford to retire. Therefore, any action you can take to support retirement planning will help alleviate financial stress for the employee and also relieve potential liabilities to your business. Couples who are jointly involved in financial decision-making are generally better prepared in retirement and more optimistic about their lifestyles once in retirement than those who make financial decisions separately.

Nearly 75 percent of couples agree they use their workplace retirement plan as a primary retirement income source, so one of the easy solutions is to have your 401(k) team create a special educational series designed for your married employees and allow them to invite their spouses to participate. Perhaps an early morning or late afternoon meeting might accommodate working spouses, or they may prefer to participate over a lunch break or even join remotely through a video conference or webinar. Often, we do live meetings that include spouses when we work on-site or remotely with companies. According to Fidelity, more than one-third (37 percent) of couples they surveyed disagreed on lifestyle expectations in retirement. An educational meeting or even individual consultations can help a couple determine what they both want from retirement and construct a plan. Will they retire at the same time, or will one continue to work? One in three couples differ on their expected retirement ages. What if one employee dreams of traveling the world while his spouse has no interest in traveling? Such disconnect can stymie a plan. Another point of contention between some couples is where they will live in retirement. When they can't agree on major issues like that, it's very difficult to calculate retirement needs. A married couple needs to work together to seek to achieve their retirement objectives. A professional advisor can expertly walk the couple through some decisions to at least get a plan in place and work toward a common goal.

One in four couples admit they have not factored health-care costs into their retirement savings strategy, yet a married couple is estimated to require over a quarter of a million dollars just for health care during retirement. Additionally, the majority of couples don't agree on the frequency with which their retirement portfolio reviews should take place. You can easily see how this discord can impact retirement readiness. Some couples think in terms of "my money" and "your money." One spouse may invest her retirement money quite conservatively while her spouse takes a more aggressive approach. A husband may contribute the maximum amount to his 401(k), while his spouse contributes only a small amount. Lacking a harmonious plan, a couple's retirement security can be compromised.

In many marriages, it is normal to have one spouse who is the primary decision maker. The other spouse may not be comfortable making major money decisions or may not have the knowledge or skills to evaluate investment options. How will the less proficient spouse handle things if he or she loses the partner? As a team, your married employees can work toward a better outcome by planning together. Supporting planning for your married employees will go a long way in driving retirement preparedness, relieving financial stress, and improving financial wellness. Hopefully you see your role as an employer being more than just giving your employees a paycheck. Because your employees are an important asset, anything you can do to help support healthy living and financial security will unquestionably be returned you with loyalty, productivity, and tenure. Money is the number one cause of stress in a marriage and the third leading cause of divorce. It may be wise to consider enlisting the help of a third party who can help married couples get on track for retirement wellness.

RETIREMENT PLANNING FOR SINGLE WORKERS

With high divorce rates, risks of premature death of a spouse, and more people forgoing marriage altogether, solo retirement is increasingly a reality for many people. According to US Census Bureau statistics, nearly one-third of employees ages forty-five to fifty-four are single, and there are currently approximately seventeen million single retirees living in the United States. As you can imagine, single adults have different challenges when preparing for retirement than married couples. For example, singles tend to have less money saved by the time they get to retirement. According to a study by the National Bureau of Economic Research, the average married household has nearly ten times more saved by the time they retire than a single person. Furthermore, the cost of living in retirement for singles is estimated to be nearly 50 percent higher than for married couples. This is because single people typically pay more in taxes and health care than married couples on a per person basis, and they tend to do more traveling, eat out more, and spend more money on extracurricular hobbies.

Single adults also spend less time planning for retirement than their married counterparts do. This may be because singles generally have less discretionary income to put toward savings. There is a greater risk to and impact on the finances when there is only one income in a household. Without a spouse's income to lean on, singles must work carefully to build their needed financial security. There are some distinct financial considerations single people need to consider. While the fundamental aspects of retirement planning hold true regardless of marital status, there are different nuances for single retirees that are worth noting.

For instance, although all workers need an emergency fund in the event of a crisis, single workers ought to keep 50 percent to 100 percent more on hand than those in a dual-income household. This is because they must rely on their own savings to support them. Having adequate disability insurance is especially important for a single worker. The odds of having an accident or illness are higher than the risks of death, and the financial implications of a disability can be especially difficult for single people since they don't have a second income to rely upon. Moreover, there is an added element of concern of declining health risks due to old age or medical issues. Married people can expect that a spouse will provide caregiving support, but singles need to plan to take care of themselves, not just mentally but also physically, as they age.

According to the Social Security Administration, 71 percent of unmarried persons receive 50 percent or more of their income from Social Security, and about 43 percent of single retirees rely on Social Security for 90 percent or more of their income. Clearly, Social Security retirement benefits amount to a substantial sum of retirement security for single people. Therefore, understanding Social Security claiming strategies and options is especially important for these workers. The difference between cashing in too early and optimizing Social Security benefits can amount to hundreds of thousands of dollars of lost income over one's retirement lifetime. It is important for these employees to be able to rely on sound financial input from professionals who understand their needs and have their best interest at heart. Lacking a spouse or trusted partner with a vested interest in their financial well-being, single individuals are less likely to have a sounding board for their financial decisions. They need direction and support from someone with whom they feel comfortable discussing money concerns, vetting ideas, and checking plans. A professional advisor can be especially valuable for your employees who are responsible for their own financial welfare and who generally make their own decisions, often in a vacuum.

Finally, single individuals often overlook the need for estate planning; however, they should pay extra attention to this. Even when working, unmarried individuals should have the right powers of attorney in place and have current health-care and financial directives should they become incapacitated. An accident or illness can leave a single individual quite vulnerable with respect to determining who is authorized to make important health-care decisions, pay their bills, and manage their finances when they are unable to do so. Whereas a spouse is usually the default beneficiary, is typically the authorized individual for health-care directives, and usually has signing authority on bank accounts and the like, single people are less likely to have appointed individuals and, thus, are at risk of leaving their families and friends mired in conflict and legal battles if they have not tended to their estate planning. In the absence of these documents, anyone who wishes to undertake these tasks would have to go to court and be officially appointed as the person's guardian, which can take time and cost money, not to mention the potential risk that the most desirable person may not be the one appointed by the court to make such personal decisions. Wishes ought to be clearly and legally documented, and this goes beyond just updating beneficiary information on 401(k) accounts. Single individuals should also consider the benefit of drafting a will, a living trust, and other estate documents

Single retirees are solely dependent upon their own decisions and resources. Therefore, it is important they are adequately prepared for the costs of retirement and also have their affairs in order in case of an emergency. As an employer, delivering the education and tools your single employees need to seek to secure their retirement will go far in building respect, trust, and appreciation. Taking the time to demonstrate your regard for these workers will set you apart from your competition and build allegiance. Protecting your most valuable asset—your employees—goes beyond just encouraging enrollment in your 401(k). It's no surprise employees are lacking confidence in the future and their retirement. There are many challenges to consider. We need to help them retire ready.

RETIREMENT FOR WIDOWS OR WIDOWERS

When most married couples think of retirement, they imagine growing old together, sharing dreams and experiences, maybe traveling or living in their desired retirement community, and enjoying life free from demands and stress. They don't typically imagine their retirement years being spent alone or without their spouse. However, the sad reality is that for those age sixty-five and over, 34 percent of women are widows and 19 percent of men are widowers. Surviving your spouse can be an overwhelming experience at any time, but it can be especially difficult if this occurs as you approach retirement. The loss of a spouse can crush a person's retirement dreams.

Unfortunately, this happens to very bright, capable, and yet rather ordinary people every day. The statistics are rather shocking: every hour in this country more than fifty people between the ages of forty-five and sixty-four die. The causes range from heart diseases, cancer, and other illnesses to accidents, suicides, and overdoses. These are employees, mothers, fathers, wives, and husbands. When one spouse takes care of all the financial issues, the surviving spouse is at risk of having to take on that role during his or her time of grief. Your employees may not be able to prepare emotionally for the loss of a spouse, but they can be prepared financially. The goal of financial wellness is to develop a plan that promotes long-term financial security no matter what the future may bring.

Widows or widowers have different considerations for Social Security. They need to understand how the Social Security rules impact them, both now and when they reach retirement age. They need to understand survivor benefits. If the children are over the age of sixteen and the surviving spouse is under the age of sixty-two, there may be a blackout period with Social Security benefits they need to understand. If they eventually think they might get remarried in the future, they need to understand how their Social Security retirement benefits might be impacted before they make marital decisions. If the deceased spouse had pension benefits or a 401(k), the rules for distributions, withdrawals, and rollovers are different for beneficiaries, and specifically for spouses. It is important the surviving spouse understands the options and how to secure his or her own retirement in light of the change in marital status as well as current and future income needs. Adjusting to a single income when the household may have had a dual income can put a lot of financial strain on the surviving spouse. Life insurance, if there was any, can be spent down quicker than anticipated unless there is proper income planning.

Widows or widowers tend to think differently about the future. While they may have leaned on their spouse for help in providing shared financial assistance, the sudden adjustment to life without the income and financial stability of a partner can be difficult. Taking on an active role in managing finances for those who relied on their spouses to take care of their finances can be a daunting task during a time of loss. But they still need to take steps to get organized and understand what they have, how to manage their investments, and ensure continued income. If they have to adjust their standard of living because of financial loss resulting from the premature death of their spouse, they need to understand how to go about taking the necessary steps, such as downsizing, paying off credit card and other debts, and planning for life as a single individual.

Widows and widowers also need an adequate emergency reserve to cover funeral expenses and living expenses while the estate is being settled. Eventually, they will want to be sure they have a current will, living trust, or estate plan modified to include the change to their marital status. They should understand powers of attorney and be sure to carefully consider individuals they can rely on for help should they need it. Beneficiary designations need to be updated on their retirement accounts and insurance policies to be sure they are consistent with the estate planning goals. The loss of a spouse is extremely difficult. Your widowed employees don't need money worries on top of the tremendous emotional hardship they will be experiencing.

I'm sure as a part of your benefit package you offer your employees the option of purchasing additional term life insurance. Unfortunately, most employees have no idea how much life insurance they really need to protect their families in the event of their premature death. And still others are confused about what coverage their spouse may or may not have available through their work. It's certainly not the most pleasant thing to think about, but planning for one's family's future can help keep a worker financially secure if his or her spouse is not there to take care of him or her.

When a spouse loses a mate, everything in life changes, including retirement plans. Your employees who are left vulnerable need to learn how to secure their future and address their financial needs. Although their plans may have changed, their longevity risks have not. Long-term-care risks, health-care costs, living expenses, and lifestyle needs continue with or without the spouse. In fact, some of these risks and needs increase after the loss of a spouse. Retirement may not look or feel the same for a widow or widower, but we all have the same basic financial needs, and it is especially important your employees who have lost a spouse understand how to take steps toward securing their future and ensuring retirement security. A financial wellness program that follows a holistic approach and helps those employees in need will likely reduce financial stress, absenteeism, and workers' compensation costs for the firm. Perhaps most important, it's just the right thing to do. It is with good reason that employers are now adding a financial wellness program to their menus of employee benefits.

MILLENNIALS AND THE FUTURE OF RETIREMENT

Millennials have some distinct advantages over their parents and prior generations when it comes to retirement planning. In fact, retirement just may be far superior for this generation. Millennials are those born from the early 1980s to the early 2000s. They have become as popular of a generation as the Baby Boomers, albeit less due to the size of their group but more for their attitude. Baby boomers (those born between 1946 and 1964) represent the largest segment of births in US history. This generation of roughly eighty million has influenced everything in this country from Gerber baby food to rock-and-roll music and blue jeans. But as they age, this segment of the working population is diminishing and transitioning out of the workforce. Millennials, by comparison, are growing in size as young immigrants expand their ranks. They are surpassing the size of Baby Boomers, which means they will likely dominate everything for years to come.

Millennials are coming of age, entering the workforce, and taking on leadership positions. This generation represents our upcoming politicians, soon to become lawmakers, teachers, doctors, attorneys and business leaders. Many are already extremely successful entrepreneurs. When you think of the stereotypical "lazy" Millennial, do you think of Evan Spiegel, the twenty-seven-year-old cofounder of Snapchat presently worth $3.1 billion? Or when you think of this "entitled" generation, does Joe Gebbia, the thirty-six-year-old who founded Airbnb and who is worth $3.8 billion, come to mind? Probably not. Of course, there is Lukas Walton, the thirty-one-year-old Millennial who inherited Walmart and is worth $13.2 billion, but does Mark Zuckerberg, the thirty-three-year-old founder of Facebook and major philanthropist who gave away eighteen million shares of Facebook really represent a member of the "me generation"? These Millennials are in good company with many others. In fact, Los Angeles is home to over twenty-five thousand young Millennial millionaires, and New York has another twenty thousand (and these figures don't include the Silicon Valley). This is a unique generation who may not have the most respect from older generations, but they are certainly making a strong footprint.

Millennials have grown up in the digital age and have been fundamentally rewired because of it. Although this generation has been described as lazy, narcissistic, and entitled, we must take a step back and understand how this generation evolved, because insomuch as every generation is criticized for its progressive attitude and reformist mind-set, there is plenty to respect and value in this group of individuals. At the very least, we need understand how to be effective in helping these employees with financial wellness.

This is a very powerful group that has a connectivity to the world like no other. They know how to use the power of large numbers and put it to work in ways the rest of us, well, simply don't. While most of us grew up protecting our privacy and were unlikely to have shared much personal information with anyone except our best of friends, the Millennials have learned there is power in sharing and have discovered the benefits of transparency. Whereas prior generations saw the world as a big and perilous place, Millennials embrace the world because they have grown up communicating globally. Technology and immigration has shrunk earth. Because of this, Millennials share with everyone, and they crave feedback from anyone. While this might earn them the title of "self-centered," they have learned to be extremely efficient with collaboration because they grew up with computers and electronic games. From Nintendo to Wii, computing power, software, and electronic devices have shaped everything about this generation.

Once upon a time, in the 1920s, mothers measured the length of their daughters' skirts with scorn and objected to them dancing the Charleston. My own mother (of Bob Hope's generation) vehemently opposed my older sister wearing blue jeans and having straight "stringy" hair (the standard of the 1970s). It's natural to resist changes introduced by newer generations, and certainly it's easy to see how parents see some of those changes as a degradation of society. The flapper broke away from the Victorian image of womanhood with her playful, sassy, and rebellious nature. This generation of young women dropped the corset, chopped their hair, eliminated layers of clothing (which increased ease of movement), wore makeup, created the concept of dating, and became sex figures. Indeed, flappers led the movement toward what many consider to be the "new" or "modern" woman, and most of all us have certainly benefited from this progression. But, at the time, these rebellious young women were largely looked down upon with disdain from older generations.

To understand the Millennials, we must understand how they grew up. They came of age at the same time parents were growing wary of the "unsafe" outdoors. Instead of playing freely outside with the neighborhood kids, these kids were taught that riding bicycles unsupervised was dangerous. Therefore, kids had to find ways to entertain themselves. Fortunately, Nintendo, Sony, and Sega were ready to meet the demand. What started out as a simple digital gaming console grew to full-color graphics, multiple controllers, and digital sound. The games became more complex, more intuitive, and more challenging. It wasn't long before the internet and superprocessors allowed kids to play games with friends, family, and others online. When I was a kid, Monopoly never told me "Way to go!" or "Better luck next time!" But Millennials grew up playing tech games that provided feedback on their skills, strategies, and results, and this experience has impacted how Millennials approach work, teams, and communication. Gaming offers constant feedback loops, opportunities to make a difference by saving the world, and global collaboration as the kids play games alongside peers located halfway around the world. These concepts of teaming and collaboration are now expectations Millennials are pulling into the workplace.

This is the first generation in history for whom digital technology platforms are the essential mediators of social life and information acquisition. Millennials leverage social media to consume, collaborate, and contribute. Facebook, Twitter, and other social media platforms not only connect people but also have defined a way of life for this generation. From selfies to tweets, growing up with access to the internet has empowered Millennials to contribute and have a voice. They also require feedback because that's what they are used to. They don't know a life without social attention. They crowdsource major life decisions. They have learned to network in ways that honestly leave me dumbfounded. But this vast networking substructure has become a source of support, confidence, and assurance for their major decisions. Millennials ask their network about where to live, what to eat, what to buy, and where to apply for a job. They are heavily persuaded by their peers and constantly turn to their networks for new opportunities, to stay in touch, to connect with a brand, and to acquire news.

Speaking of employment, Millennials value lifestyle and relationships over work. It's not unusual for a Millennial to choose a city before securing a job. And when they do seek employment, Millennials turn to Glassdoor.com to get the inside scoop on companies and read employee reviews to learn about salaries, benefits, and more. They seek complete transparency in the job market today, they know what companies can offer, and they want to ensure a better fit and salary. Of course, if this doesn't give them enough of a picture, they turn to Facebook friends and YouTube videos to get insight into what it's like to work at other companies, and they use platforms like LinkedIn to connect with anyone they can at that company. As you surely already know, today's connected and transparent culture is holding companies accountable to deliver exceptional employee experiences in order to retain top talent.

This generation has learned to use Google since childhood, and they know how to leverage the internet. The world's information has been at their fingertips practically from birth. Whereas I had libraries, teachers, and encyclopedias, this generation hasn't considered their parents or teachers as the authority but rather the internet. They treat the internet as their external brain and approach problems in a whole new way from previous generations (admittedly, in ways that I simply cannot comprehend). You may recall the first time you decided to give your son or daughter a cell phone. If you were like most parents of the early 2000s, you did so for two primary reasons: safety and logistics. But your Millennial child saw the cell phone as freedom, and he or she probably quickly discovered texting and likely ran your phone bill sky-high by sending thousands of texts back in the days when text messaging cost ten cents apiece.

Undoubtedly, the Millennials will continue to usher unparalleled and unavoidable changes into every industry and workplace. This is a group that is very tech-savvy and has a tech advantage over other generations. Millennials are a new breed of employee because they had an upbringing like no other in history. Because future generations are likely to be more like Millennials, employers must use this new understanding of the Millennial journey and evolution to influence how they lead, connect, and communicate with the next generation workforce.

Therefore, when it comes to retirement planning, the good news is that 58 percent of Millennials are actively saving for retirement, which is a tremendous improvement over other generations at the same age. Thirty-eight percent of millennials know how much money they'll need to retire, which is more than any other age group. This generation has the benefit of knowledge and time, both of which are very powerful when it comes to retirement success. Clearly, Millennials are off to a great start. Unlike prior generations, this generation has started their careers with some level of 401(k) education and awareness. They may not know what a pension is, but they do know a 401(k).

Millennials also have grandparents who are living or have lived into their nineties, so they are intuitively aware of longevity, granting them a better sense of their own retirement needs. They don't believe they can count on Social Security or the government to take care of them, and they accept that it is not in their future. They want quality of life both now and in retirement, so they recognize the need to start saving early. Because of social media, they talk to their friends and embrace investing. They use online tools and software with ease to determine how much they need for retirement. They don't hesitate to use apps to monitor their spending habits and track their financial situation. While other generations are mystified, frustrated or perplexed by these tech programs, Millennials embrace them. They seek efficiency. Mobile apps are their way of life. Older generations continue to seek to protect their privacy and question the security of the internet, opting not to use mobile banking services or apps that share personal financial information, even if it is for their benefit and will help them better track their retirement progress. Millennials, however, depend on these apps and seek the reinforcement and feedback of being on track for their goals. They need programs that will give them directions including how much more they need to save, and they like knowing how much they need to earn on their savings to reach their goals and how to monitor their progress. They don't want to have to contemplate the complexity of finances, but they do embrace a point-and-click method of instructions. And if given the right tools, they will adhere to the plan and do what they are directed to do to seek to achieve their goals.

Many studies show that Millennials openly admit to a desire to save even more for their retirement. This is quite a contrast to their predecessors, who didn't give much consideration at all to retirement savings at such a young age. Auto-enroll features are surely aiding in getting younger workers actively participating in their 401(k)'s, but the reason also lies with a heightened awareness. They saw the impact the Great Recession had on their parents. Consequently, this generation has an inclination toward saving.

Because Millennials are wired differently, they are responding more favorably to efforts to drive retirement readiness. The use of technology makes it easy for them to take an active role in the progress of their retirement plan. Having access to apps that will give them the ease to track and monitor their retirement is essential for this generation. Millennials are multitasking pros because of their lifelong use of computers, cell phones, handheld devices, and gaming consoles. They have honed skills that allow them to juggle many responsibilities at once. This is a true asset for employers and a plus for them to easily comprehend the multipronged approach of financial wellness.

Millennials are also open-minded and eager to learn from others. Their collaborative nature instinctively draws them to embrace financial educational meetings, particularly when they are round-table, peer-type discussions. They value learning from one another and want to understand others' experiences. Financial education centered on focus groups or that involve interactive games are far more effective for this generation. The majority of companies still only communicate via monotonous statements, ineffective postcards, or lackluster slide presentations. These traditional or passive methods are ineffective with most employees, and this is especially true for Millennials. In general, hands-on education is far more effective in reaching this group.

Finally, Millennials may seem carefree or lackadaisical about their time, but they are serious when it comes to seeking results. Therefore, tracking and benchmarking their progress is valued and important. It's also a great motivator. A 401(k) advisor or team who can offer a more interactive experience for your younger employees will go far in driving retirement success. Fewer than 10 percent of firms offer education through mobile technology or have tried games designed to motivate employees, yet these approaches have proved especially useful among young workers.

MOTIVATING EMPLOYEES

When it comes to retirement planning, you can't simply order your employees to contribute to your 401(k) and expect them to do what you want. In fact, it's hard to "order" employees to do anything since most people don't like to be told what to do. It takes a bit more finesse to motivate employees to take the right steps toward retirement success, even if it is for their own benefit. There are two main ways to get your employees' cooperation when it comes to retirement planning: motivate and inspire. Although those two words are used interchangeably, they mean two different things.

Motivation is about moving people to act in a way that achieves a specific and immediate goal. Making sure your employees know you believe they need to contribute at least as much to the 401(k) as required to get to their retirement goal is an important call to action. When you have group meetings or webinars on your 401(k), do you participate? Having the owner, CEO, or senior leadership present is very important because it sends a message to your employees that leadership believes in the 401(k) and supports their involvement.

Fear is also an effective motivator. "If you don't save diligently, you may never be able to afford retirement." Obviously, fear overused can serve to demotivate workers or desensitize them to the reality of their situations. *"Yeah, I know. I'm never going to be able to retire. Blah, blah, blah."* Certainly, most people prefer to be motivated by positive reinforcement like excitement, pride, a sense of belonging, and the thrill of achievement. That is why your employees need to hear from you, the firm leadership. They need to know you care about their retirement and support their financial wellness, not just by having a meeting but also by showing up. Even making a short speech to tell them why you care enough to offer a 401(k) and support the financial wellness program will go a long way to engage and motivate your employees. Of course, you can also demonstrate your concern by offering an employer matching option.

Inspiration, however, is more effective than motivation and can have a greater impact on employees' long-term success. Inspiring people involves changing the way they think and feel about themselves so that they *want* to take positive actions. It taps into people's values and desires. Inspiration appeals to the best aspirations of people, and its underlying, often unspoken message is *You can do this!* For example, employees who are debt-ridden, struggling to make ends meet, and living paycheck to paycheck need inspiration. For them, it is hard to imagine a life free from financial burdens. Indeed, they may never have that sort of life if they aren't inspired to change their values about money and reprioritize personal desires. Ironically, those who are the least able to save today are the ones who will most likely never be able to save *even if you double their pay.* This is because for most in that situation, it is not the income that is the problem but rather their attitude and values.

Above all else, your reputation, character, and behavior will inspire your employees. The only way to call the best out of others is to expect the best from yourself. That is why your engagement is so important to the success of your plan. When you inspire others, you're not telling them exactly what to do or giving them precise directions. Instead, you're empowering them to be their best, trusting that they will then do the right thing. When this is done sincerely, your employees will be inspired by the sacrifice needed to succeed with their retirement plans and will likely surpass what they themselves thought possible.

Motivation and inspiration are tools used to bring out the best in people. It's just a matter of knowing the right time and the right situation. When there's an immediate short-term specific goal that you want your people to achieve, you need to motivate them. But when you want to shape people's long-term aspirations, you need to inspire them. Your 401(k) team and, ideally, your advisor can set the stage, while you and your leadership team can boost the effect by showing you care. Telling your employees why you offer the 401(k) is a great start, but remember, retirement readiness is a process that requires years to achieve. To keep your employees going, you need to give them inspiration.

Consider this: It may take an employee saving $150 each paycheck (paid bimonthly with a small employer match) twelve years to accumulate the first $100,000 in his 401(k) (assuming a hypothetical 7% average rate of return). That's twelve years of saving, paycheck after paycheck, month after month, year after year. After twelve long years, the employee only has $100,000, which doesn't go very far for retirement these days. It's hard to be inspired when, after all that sacrifice, such little progress is made. But once you get the first $100,000, the next gets easier. It will only take about six years to get the next $100,000, continuing with the same contributions and rate of return. *That's half the time!* This is because of the magic of compounding. It takes only a little over four years to get the next $100,000 and a little over three years for the next $100,000. *Now that's inspiration.* Unfortunately, though, it takes about twenty years to start to really see the effect. That's a lot of time to wait and stay motivated, which is all the more reason why your leadership and your 401(k) team need to guide the way and keep the enthusiasm going until your employees see the fruits of their labor. How many of your employees have small 401(k) balances left behind at former jobs? Why are they left behind? Typically because the employees are uninspired to consolidate them. Yet, if they pooled their funds, they just might see the compounding effect.

IN SUMMARY

The practice of human capital management involves recruiting, managing, developing, and optimizing the human resources of an organization. Investing in human capital management means you recognize the value of your employees and see them as an asset to the organization. HR plays a supporting role in the development of human capital management by supporting the theory that your team is an asset that can create significant value for your company. Employees view the sum of their jobs by measuring salary and compensation, benefits, perks, and incentives, along with considering the culture and environment within the firm. In light of this, financial and retirement wellness touches the heart of human capital management and the core of your firm's success.

The cost of aging employees financially unable to retire can be substantial to an organization, in terms of both raw dollars and implications to firm culture. Individuals who don't want to work but have to are not typically supportive in fostering positive morale. By comparison, senior employees who choose to work because they love the job are perhaps the greatest asset to a business, despite the higher costs. How can a firm cultivate the right kind of employees? By supporting financial wellness.

Financial wellness doesn't just benefit the employee, of course. It is a considerable advantage for employers as well. Investing in your employees' personal development transcends job training in today's competitive market. Take the steps necessary to embrace your retirement benefits package and invest in a comprehensive financial wellness program that addresses the diverse needs of your workforce. Your employees need it. Ideally, your business will thrive as a result, the economy will prosper, and America's national retirement infrastructure will strengthen. We need to work together to move our national retirement from a C grade to an A. Join the millions of companies across the country who are welcoming a new approach to retirement benefits, and strive to develop innovative human resources management. After all, the future belongs to those who prepare for it.

For more information, please visit www.retirerightseries.com.

For more information, timely updates, and links to valuable reference materials, please visit www.retirerightseries.com.

RESOURCES

"401(k) Plan Fix-It Guide - The plan was top-heavy and required minimum contributions weren't made to the plan". irs.gov. 2015-10-23. Retrieved 2016-04-01.

"401(k) Resource Guide – Plan Participants – Limitation on Elective Deferrals". Internal Revenue Service.

AARP. *Enhancing 401(k) value and participation: Taking the automatic approach.* A report for AARP prepared by Towers Perrin. Washington, DC: American Association of Retired Persons (June).

Age and Retirement Benchmarks: Key Analytics that Drive Human Capital Management. The ADP Research Institute.

Amato, P. R. The Consequences of Divorce for Adults and Children. Journal of Marriage and the Family.

American Psychological Association. *Stress in the Workplace Survey Summary* Harris Interactive.

Andeason, A.R. Attitudes and Consumer Behavior: A Decision Model in New Research in Marketing (Preston).

Bannon, S., Ford, K., & Meltzer, L. Understanding Millennials in the Workplace. CPA Journal, 81(11), 61-65.

Barr, Paul, *How Baby Boomer Will Affect the Health Care Industry in the U.S.* Geriatrics Interest Group. AMSA.org, "The Boomer Challenge," H&HN.com.

Beshears, John, James J. Choi, David Laibson, and Brigitte C. Madrian. 2010. "The Impact of 401(k) Loans on Saving." NBER

Retirement Research Center Paper, no. NB 09-05 (September). Cambridge, MA: National Bureau of Economic Research.

Blanchett, David *Estimating the True Cost of Retirement* Morningstar Investment Management 22 W Washington, Chicago, IL.

Blitzer, David. S&P U.S. Indices Methodology Update, McGraw Hill Financial.

Board of Trustees of the Federal Old-Age and Survivors Insurance and Disability Insurance Trust Funds. 2017. Washington, DC: Government Printing Office.

Bovens, Luc (2009). *Preference Change*. Theory and Decision Library. Springer, Dordrecht.

Brady, Peter. 2012. The Tax Benefits and Revenue Costs of Tax Deferral. Washington, DC: Investment Company Institute (September).

Bricker, Jesse, Brian Bucks, Arthur Kennickell, Traci Mach, and Kevin Moore. 2011. "Surveying the Aftermath of the Storm: Changes in Family Finances from 2007 to 2009." FEDS Working Paper, no. 2011-17. Washington, DC: Federal Reserve Board.

Bricker, Jesse, Lisa J. Dettling, Alice Henriques, Joanne W. Hsu, Lindsay Jacobs, Kevin B. Moore, Sarah Pack, John Sabelhaus, Jeffrey Thompson, and Richard A. Windle. 2017. "Changes in US Family Finances from 2013 to 2016: Evidence from the Survey of Consumer Finances." Federal Reserve Bulletin.

BrightScope and Investment Company Institute. 2016. The BrightScope/ICI Defined Contribution Plan Profile: A Close Look at ERISA 403(b) Plans.

BrightScope and Investment Company Institute. 2018. The BrightScope/ICI Defined Contribution Plan Profile: A Close Look at 401(k) Plans.

Buck Consultants, "401(k) Plans: Survey Report on Plan Design."

Bureau of Labor Statistics. 2017. National compensation survey: Employee benefits in the United States, March 2017 Bulletin 2715. Washington, DC: Bureau of Labor Statistics Federal Reserve Board Finance and Economics Discussion Series Working

Paper No. 2005-17. Washington, DC: Federal Reserve Board of Governors.

Bureau of Labor statistics. 2018. Published by Debt.com, LLC.

Burson, Katherine; Larrick, Richard; Klayman, Joshua. "Skilled or Unskilled, but Still Unaware of It: How Perceptions of Difficulty Drive Miscalibration in Relative Comparisons". Journal of Personality and Social Psychology. 90 (1): 60–77.

Butler, S., Pension Dynamics Corporation, "Statement before the U.S.Department of Labor, Pension and Welfare Benefits Administration Public Hearing on 401(k) Plan Fees."

Butrica, Barbara A and Karamcheva, Nadia S. "The Relationship Between Automatic Enrollment and DC Plan Contributions." July 2015 Center for Retirement Research at Boston College.

Buttonwood, "Divvying up returns," The Economist, September 2, 2010.

Cass Sunstein, R. (2016-08-24). *The Ethics of Influence: Government in the Age of Behavioral Science.* Cambridge University Press.

Center on Federal Financial Institutions. Pension reform: Summary of final 2006 bill. Washington, DC.

Center for Retirement Research at Boston College (February). The state of private pensions: Current 5500 data. Issue in Brief No. 42. Chestnut Hill, MA: Center for Retirement Research at Boston College (February).

Center for Retirement Research at Boston College, *The financial crisis and private sector defined benefit plans.* Issue in Brief No. 8-18. Chestnut Hill, MA.

Cerulli Associates, The Cerulli Report: Retirement Industry Update: Trends in 401(k) and IRA Markets.

Ciccotello, C.S. and Grant, C.T., "Information Pricing: The Evidence from Equity Mutual Funds," The Financial Review.

Coalition of Collective Trust Funds, *Collective Investment Trusts* (2015).

Collins, Sean, Sarah Holden, James Duvall, and Elena Barone Chism. 2017. "The Economics of Providing 401(k) Plans: Services, Fees, and Expenses, 2016." ICI Research Perspective 23, no. 4.

Colvin, Randall ; Block, Jack; Funder, David "Overly Positive Self-Evaluations and Personality: Negative Implications for Mental Health". *Journal of Personality and Social Psychology*. American Psychological Association.

Committee on the Global Financial System. The shift from defined benefit to defined contribution pension plans. Global Retirement Perspective. New York, NY: Mercer Human Resource Consulting.

Congressional Research Service summary of H.R. 3763, P.L. 107−204 (Sarbanes-Oxley Act of 2002).

"Default Investment Alternatives Under Participant Directed Individual Account Plans; Final Rule" Department of Labor.

Deloitte Consulting LLP Defined Contribution Benchmarking Survey—*From Oversight to Participant Experience: Plan Sponsors Are Taking Their Fiduciary Role Up a Notch*. New York: Deloitte Consulting LLP., the International Foundation of Employee Benefit Plans, and the International Society of Certified Employee Benefit Specialists. 2015.

Defined Contribution Benchmarking Survey: 2017 Edition. New York: Deloitte Consulting LLP.

Devlin-Foltz, Sebastian, Alice M. Henriques, and John Sabelhaus. 2015. "The Evolution of Retirement Wealth." Finance and Economics Discussion Series, no. 2015-009. Washington, DC: Board of Governors of the Federal Reserve System.

Donhardt, Tracy. "Too many cashing out of 401(k)s." Indianapolis Business Journal.

Duarte, Fernando & Tenreiro Machado, José & Monteiro Duarte, Gonçalo. (2010). Dynamics of the Dow Jones and the NASDAQ stock indexes.

Dychtwald, K, Erickson, T and Morison, T. "It's Time to Retire Retirement." Harvard Business Review.

Employee Benefit Research Institute, Databook on Employee Benefits, 7th Edition. EBRI.

Employee Benefit Research Institute *An evolving pension system: Trends in defined benefit and defined contribution plans*. EBRI Issue Brief No. 249. Washington, DC.

Employee Benefit Research Institute, *EBRI Issue Brief* No. 289. Washington, DC: EBRI.

Employee Benefit Research Institute, EBRI, Retirement Confidence Survey. April, 2018.

Employee Benefit Research Institute. Retirement Income Adequacy after PPA and FAS 158: Part one. *EBRI Issue Brief* No. 307. Washington, DC.

Employee Benefit Research Institute. Washington Bulletin; "Toward a More Complete 401(k) History", EBRI Notes, vol. 24, no. 12.

Federal Reserve Bank of New York, Quarterly Report on Household Debt and Credit.

Federal Reserve Board. Demand Institute Housing & Community Survey; 2013 Survey of Consumer Finances.

Fetini, Alyssa (16 October 2008). "A Brief History Of: The 401(k)."

Fidelity Investments, "How to plan for rising health care costs." 2018.

First Trust Advisors L.P., Morningstar. History of U.S. Bear & Bull Markets Since 1926.

Gallagher, Emily. *Trends and Experience in 401k Plans,* Hewitt Associates.

Government Accountability Office. [GAO] GAO-08-817. Washington, DC: Government Accountability Office. *401(k) Plans: Greater Protections Needed for Forced Transfers and Inactive Accounts.* GAO-15-73. Washington, D.C.

Government Accountability Office. *401(K) Plans: Increased Educational Outreach and Broader Oversight May Help Reduce Plan Fees.* GAO-12-325. Washington, D.C.

Government Accountability Office. House of Representatives Report to the Ranking Member, Subcommittee on Tax Policy, Committee on Ways and Means, House of Representatives October 2016 GAO-17-69.

Government Accountability Office. *Private Pensions: Changes Needed to Provide 401(k) Plan Participants and the Department of Labor Better Information on Fees.* GAO-07-21. Washington, D.C.

Government Accountability Office. *Private Pensions: Low Defined Contribution Plan Savings May Pose Challenges to Retirement Security, Especially for Many Low-Income Workers.* GAO-08-8. Washington, D.C.

Government Accountability Office. *Private Pensions: Pension Tax Incentives Update.* GAO-14-334R. Washington, D.C.: March 20, 2014.

Government Accountability Office. *Private Pensions: Some Key Features Lead to an Uneven Distribution of Benefits.* GAO-11-333. Washington, D.C.

Government Accountability Office. *Retirement Security: Federal Action Could Help State Efforts to Expand Private Sector Coverage.* GAO-15-556. Washington, D.C.: September 10, 2015.

Government Accountability Office. *Retirement Security: Most Households Approaching Retirement Have Low Savings.* GAO-15-419. Washington, D.C.: May 12, 2015.

Government Accountability Office. *Retirement Security: Women Still Face Challenges.* GAO-12-699. Washington, D.C.: July 19, 2012.

Hayes, Timothy, Ned Davis Research, Inc. *Returns of S&P 500 Stocks by Dividend Policy,* Stock Market Focus.

Helman, Ruth. Greenwald & Associates; and Adams, Nevid, Copeland, Craig VanDerhei, Jack. "Confidence Rebounds—for Those with Retirement Plans."

Holden, Sarah, and Schrass, Daniel. 2018. *Defined Contribution Plan Participants' Activities, First Three Quarters of 2017.* ICI Research Report.

Holden, Sarah, Schrass, Daniel and Bogdan, Michael. 2017. *Ownership of Mutual Funds, Shareholder Sentiment, and Use of the Internet, 2017.* ICI Research Perspective 23, no. 7.

Holden, Sarah, and VanDerhei, Jack. *Contribution Behavior of 401(k) Plan Participants*. Investment Company Institute Perspective 7, no. 4.

Holman, J. and MacDonald, C. U.S. Population Mortality Observations Updated with 2016 Experience, Society of Actuaries.

Howard, Thomas PhD, "The Power of Dividends" January 25, 2011, Advisors Perspective.

Hustead, E. "Retirement Income Plan Administrative Expenses," Pension Research Council.

Investment Company Institute 2017 *Investment Company Fact Book: A Review of Trends and Activities in the Investment Company Industry*. Washington, DC.

Institute of Management and Administration, "Managing 401(k) Plans: Plan Cost & Bundled Service Provider Survey."

Investment Company Institute. *The US Retirement Market, Fourth Quarter 2017* (March).

Kagel, John H.; Battalio, Raymond C.; Green, Leonard (1995). *Economic Choice Theory: An Experimental Analysis of Animal Behavior*. Cambridge University Press.

Kahn, V.M., "Policing 401(k) Performance."

Kelley,D. Corbett, Andrew, Kim, Phillip and Majbouri M., 2017 GEM Report Babson College, Boston MA.

Levenson, A. *Millennials and the world of work: an economist's perspective. Journal of Business & Psychology,* 25(2), 257-264.

Levin, Michael and Lowitz, Joshua, Amazon Prime research, Consumer Intelligence Research Partners, LLC (CIRP).

Lu, Timothy (Jun), Olivia S. Mitchell, Stephen P. Utkus, and Jean A. Young. 2015. "Borrowing from the Future: 401(k) Plan Loans and Loan Defaults." NBER Working Paper, no. 21102. Cambridge, MA.

Mitchell, Olivia, Stephen P. Utkus, and Tongxuan Yang. 2007. "Turning Workers into Savers? Incentives, Liquidity, and Choice in 401(k) Plan Design." National Tax Journal 60: 469–489.

Munnell, Alicia Haydock; Sunden, Annika E. *Coming up short: The challenge of 401(k) plans*. Washington, DC: Brookings Institution Press.

National Tax Journal 59(2): 211–234. Urban Institute Retirement Policy Discussion Paper, 9-03. Washington DC.

Hayes, Timothy, Ned Davis Research, Inc. *Returns of S&P 500 Stocks by Dividend Policy,* Stock Market Focus.

Oliver Richard L. "A Cognitive Model of the Antecedents and Consequences of Satisfaction Decisions," Journal of Marketing Research.

Orenstein, Michell A. In *Pensions, Social Security and the privatization of risk,*, ed., 72–85. New York, NY: Columbia University Press and Social Science Research Council.

Organdonor.gov.; U.S. Government Information on Organ Donation and Transplantation.

Plan Sponsor Council of America. 2018. 60th Annual Survey of Profit Sharing and 401(k) Plans: Reflecting 2016 Plan Experience. Chicago: Plan Sponsor Council of America.

Plan Sponsor Council of America. 2016. US Department of Labor, Employee Benefits Security Administration. 2012. Private Pension Plan Bulletin, Abstract of 2005 Form 5500 Annual Reports (Version 1.1). Washington, DC: US Department of Labor, Employee Benefits Security Administration.

Reid, Brian. *Trends in the Expenses and Fees of Funds*, 2016. ICI Research Perspective 23, no. 3.

"Retirement Topics 401k and Profit Sharing Plan Contribution Limits | Internal Revenue Service". www.irs.gov. Retrieved 2018-04-15.

S&P Dow Indices, a Division of S&P Global. S&P Dow Jones Indices: Index Methodology, July 2018.

Schrass, Daniel, Seligman, Jason and Bogdan, Michael. 2018. *American Views on Defined Contribution Plan Saving,* 2017. ICI Research Report (February).

Schmitt, Ray. *The future of pensions in the United States,*, ed., 114–125. Pension Research Council. Philadelphia, PA: University of Pennsylvania Press.

Schoenborn CA. Marital Status and Health: United States, Hyattsville, MD: National Center for Health Statistics.

Siegel, Jeremy. *Stocks for the long run:* New York, NY: McGraw-Hill Companies.

Smith, Allen. "IRS: Self-Certification Permitted for Hardship Withdrawals from Retirement Accounts". *Society for Human Resource Professionals.* April 3, 2017.

"Supreme Court Permits Cause of Action for Putting 401(k) Investments in Retail as Opposed to Institutional Shares". Archived from the original on 2016-03-05. Retrieved 2015-08-06.

Teresa Ghilarducci, Tony James, Americans Haven't Saved Enough for Retirement. What Are We Going to Do About It? Harvard Business Review. 2018.

UNOS, Transplant Living. *Talking About Transplantation.* 700 North 4th Street, Richmond, VA 23219.

Urban Institute. *Modeling Income in the Near Term: Revised projections of retirement income through 2020 for the 1931–1960 birth cohorts.* Final Report, SSA. Washington, DC.

US Department of Labor, Employee Benefits Security Administration. 2012 Private Pension Plan Bulletin, Abstract of 2006 Form 5500 Annual Reports (Version 1.1). Washington, DC.

US Department of Labor, Employee Benefits Security Administration. 2018. Private Pension Plan Bulletin Historical Tables and Graphs (2015 Data Release Version 1.0). Washington, DC.

US Department of Labor, Employee Benefits Security Administration. *Selecting and Monitoring Pension Consultants—Tips for Plan Fiduciaries.*

U.S. Department of Labor Employee Benefits Security Administration Office of the Chief Accountant May 2015.

Utkus, Stephen P., and Young, Steven. 2017. How America Saves 2017: Vanguard 2016 Defined Contribution Plan Data. Valley Forge,

PA: The Vanguard Group, Vanguard Center for Retirement Research.

Wiatrowski, William. Medical and retirement plan coverage: Exploring the decline in recent years. Monthly Labor Review.

Wharton School of the University of Pennsylvania. Pension Research Council Working Paper, Philadelphia, PA.

Wharton School of the University of Pennsylvania. *Why stock-price volatility should never be a surprise, even in the long run.* Interview with Knowledge@Wharton.

ACKNOWLEDGMENTS

I would like to thank the many people who made *Retire Ready* possible. First, I would like to acknowledge with my deepest gratitude, the support and love of my wonderful family - my "man who can" husband, Paul, for being my inspiration, best friend and soul mate and to my precious daughter, Jacki, for allowing me to work late even when it meant occasionally sacrificing "cuddle time." My family kept me going by extending their love, patience and encouragement.

There are hundreds of people who have been an inspiration for *Retire Ready*. I must extend a heartfelt thank you to Firoz Khan, my mentor who believed in me at the very young age of twenty-one and gave me a chance so many years ago to be a part of the financial services industry. He motivated and shaped me as an advisor.

I am thankful for the consideration and input from many others I solicited for advice and guidance. Jim Albrecht, Sharon Coleman, Spencer Garrett, Kinga Gwaron, Greg Greenstein, Calvin Hedman, Kris Krikorian, Evan Masyr, Bill Reed, Fernando Salguero, Gil Tobias, Rob Ward, and those closest to me during the editing and review of this manuscript. I am grateful for their time, attention and for showing confidence in my work.

I want to offer a special thank-you to the many plan sponsors who have engaged me to help them build retirement readiness within their organizations. It is such experiences which has enabled me to offer the perception and awareness shared in *Retire Ready*. I am blessed to have a job where I can also pursue my passion and build lasting friendships along the way.

I would like to thank my publisher, Archway Publishing, my illustrator, editor as well as Tina Nofzinger for helping me refine and polish this finished product. Their attention to detail and desire for perfection has enabled me to deliver *Retire Ready* it in a way that seeks to inspire and motivate a call to action for all readers, particularly those in leadership roles who can change lives and shape the future for America. Even if this only serves to motivate readers to review their own personal retirement plan, I am honored to have had such wonderful support and guidance to enable me to leave my footprint in the sand. I am beholden to all who have helped me tell my story.

My greatest debt is to my many wonderful clients who have stood beside me throughout the past thirty years, despite the market volatility and numerous economics challenges we have faced. I am so very thankful for their trust and belief in me to serve as their financial steward.

ABOUT THE AUTHOR

Terri McGray, CFP, AIF, is president and founder of Longevity Capital Management LLC, a company dedicated to supporting the needs of employers, employees, and retirees. She has spent over thirty years helping individuals and businesses with wealth management and retirement planning. She has trained and educated thousands of participants on financial wellness and conducts speaking engagements on finance and retirement planning nationally. Her expertise and focus on 401(k) and company-sponsored retirement plans compelled her to begin the Retire Right series.

Terri is steadfast in her pursuit to change the health of America's retirement infrastructure and to help lead the way to retirement readiness for employees. She works with companies across the country as an advisor and advocate. She is a proponent and champion of financial wellness. For speaking engagement inquiries, please visit www.retirerightseries.com.

Terri lives in Southern California with her husband and daughter. She enjoys food and wine, as well as art and music. She has had the good fortune to explore the world on nearly every continent, embracing unique and diverse cultures. From the Fijian Yavusa to the Tsonga in South Africa to the Paduang tribe in northern Thailand, Terri has expanded her curiosity about the world—its peoples' customs, laws, beliefs, and loves. Items on her bucket list include experiencing the spectacular aurora borealis from Iceland, exploring the abundant wildlife of the Galápagos Islands, and watching the sunset over Kata Tjuta rock in Australia.

Terri has been involved in her community and has served on the board of several nonprofits over the past twenty years. She is a devoted advocate against domestic violence and encourages "no more silence!" Terri is also a Girl Scout troop leader, supporting families and daughters. She has committed to the growth, development, and health of women. She served as a Big Sister through the Big Brothers/Big Sisters program, where she spent six years mentoring and ultimately becoming the foster parent for a young woman in crisis.